Perspectives
on Luke - Acts

Edited by
Charles H. Talbert

Association of Baptist
Professors of Religion
P. O. Box 2190
Danville
VA 24541
U. S. A.

T. & T. Clark Ltd.
36, George Street
Edinburgh EH2 2LQ
Scotland

Perspectives in Religious Studies 1978

To George W. MacRae, whose initiative brought the Luke-Acts Group (1973-78) into being.

Printed in the United States of America

For

Association of Baptist
Professors of Religion
P. O. Box 2190
Danville
VA 24541
U. S. A.

T. & T. Clark Ltd.
36 George Street
Edinburgh EH2 2 LQ
Scotland

ISBN 0-932180-04-3

Library of Congress No. 78-51610

Special Studies Series No. 5

Cover Logo by Joe Chris Robinson,

Mars Hill College

ISBN 0 567 02359 1

First printed 1978

Table of Contents

Editor's Preface

In 1974 the Association of Baptist Professors of Religion inaugurated the publication of *Perspectives in Religious Studies*, a scholarly journal containing articles and reviews of the widest interest for the professional scholar-teacher. This bold undertaking marked a significant departure for the Association. With only limited funds available it was truly a venture in faith. The journal has been well received and its contribution to the study of religion has been widely acclaimed. It appears three times yearly (Spring, Summer, and Fall).

Early in 1977 the Association began the second phase of its publishing program. This volume marks the fifth offering in the "Special Studies Series." We believe that, together with *Perspectives*, the Special Studies Series will make available the very best scholarly materials to the teacher of religion.

Watson E. Mills
Series Editor

Foreword

After consultations in 1972 and 1973, the Luke-Acts Group of the Society of Biblical Literature was formed in 1974 with a five year lifespan. This collection of essays is an attempt to bring together the results of some of the work that was undertaken between 1972 and 1978 by those related directly or indirectly to the Group. Some of these papers grew out of the annual programs of the Society of Biblical Literature; others have been produced specifically for this volume. It is hoped that this book will offer both assistance in and a stimulus to further study of the Third Gospel and Acts.

Appreciation must be expressed to the *Journal of Biblical Literature* for permission to use Paul J. Achtemeier's "The Lucan Perspective on the Miracles of Jesus: A Preliminary Sketch," *JBL*, XCIV (1975), 547-62, and to Scholars Press for permission to use Raymond E. Brown's, "Luke's Method in the Annuniciation Narrative of Chapter One," in *No Famine in the Land: Studies in Honor of John L. McKenzie,* edited by James W. Flanagan and Anita Weisbrod Robinson (Missoula: Scholars Press, 1975), 179-94.

Above all, thanks must be offered to the Department of Religion at Wake Forest University whose generous use of monies from its Robinson Fund has provided the main subsidy for this volume. The Graduate Council of Wake Forest University also contributed generously to the production of the collection and merits our gratitude.

Finally, to the editorial board of the Association of Baptist Professors of Religion and to the editor of *Perspectives in Religions Studies,* Watson E. Mills, we are indebted for their prompt approval and efficient publication of this book.

Charles H. Talbert

Chairman, Luke-Acts Group 1973-78

Contributors

Paul J. Achtemeier
Union Theological Seminary in Virginia
3401 Brook Road, Richmond, Virginia 23227

Raymond E. Brown
Union Theological Seminary (NYC),
3041 Broadway, New York, New York 10027

Schuyler Brown
11-13 Cavendish Square
London, England   W1M 0AN

F. Lamar Cribbs
The First United Methodist Church
Rt. 2, Box 391, Rocky Ford, Colorado 81067

Joseph A. Fitzmyer
Department of Biblical Studies,
Catholic University of America,
Washington, D.C. 20057

Fred L. Horton
Department of Religion, Wake Forest University
Winston-Salem, North Carolina 27109

Benjamin J. Hubbard
Department of Religious Studies,
St. Jerome's College
Waterloo, Ontario, Canada N2l3G3

Robert J. Karris
Catholic Theological Union,
5401 S. Cornell Avenue
Chicago, Illinois 60615

A. J. Mattill, Jr.
Private Scholar
Rt. 2, Box 49, Gordo, Alabama 35466

Donald R. Miesner
Department of Religion
Concordia College
Bronxville, New York 10708

Jerome D. Quinn
The Saint Paul Seminary
2260 Summit Avenue
St. Paul, Minnesota 55105

Vernon Robbins
Program in Religious Studies
University of Illinois at Urbana-Champaign
Urbana, Illinois 61801

Joseph B. Tyson
Department of Religious Studies
Southern Methodist University
Dallas, Texas 75275

Allison A. Trites
Acadia Divinity College
Wolfville, Nova Scotia, Canada BOP1XO

Fred Veltman
Department of Religion
Pacific Union College
Angwin, California 94508

Abbreviations

ANQ	*Andover Newton Quarterly*
ATR	*Anglican Theological Review*
Aug	*Angustinianum*
BLeb	*Bibel und Leben*
BibT	*Bible Today*
BVC	*Bible et Vie Chretienne*
Bib	*Biblica*
BR	*Biblical Research*
BZ	*Biblische Zeitschrift*
BBC	*Bulletin of the Bezan Club*
BJRL	*Bulletin of the John Rylands Library*
CBQ	*Catholic Biblical Quarterly*
CTSA	*Catholic Theological Society of America, Proceedings*
CT	*Christianity Today*
CQ	*Congregational Quarterly*
CurTM	*Currents in Theology and Mission*
DBSup	*Dictionnaire de la Bible, Supplement,* ed. Louis Pirot (Paris: Letouzey et Ane, 1926--).
EB	*Encyclopedia Biblica,* ed. T.K. Cheyne and J.S. Black (4 vols.; New York: Macmillan, 1912)
EvT	*Evangelische Theologie*
Exp	*The Expositor*
ExpTim	*Expository Times*
GIF	*Giornale Italiano di Filologia*
GL	*Geist und Leben*
HSCP	*Harvard Studies in Classical Philology*
HTR	*Harvard Theological Review*
HK	*Herder Korrespondenz* (Freiburg im Breisgau)
Int	*Interpretation*
IB	*Interpreter's Bible,* ed. G.A. Buttrick (New York: Abingdon-Cokesbury, 1951--)

Reflections on the
Semitisms of Luke-Acts[1]

Fred L. Horton, Jr.

Introduction

A history of the philological and linguistic advances of the 19th century would doubtless highlight the story of the great decipherments of that period. Prominent would be an account of Champollion's work on the Rosetta Stone and the publication of his Egyptian grammar (1836-1841) and dictionary (1843). Equal attention would be paid the efforts to decipher the cuneiform scripts, endeavors inspired by the remarkable transcriptions by Carsten Niebuhr of the inscriptions at Takht-i-Jamshid published in his *Voyage en Arabie* (Amsterdam, 1776-1780). Notice would be given the important work of O. G. Tychsen, F. C. C. Münter, G. F. Grotefend, R. C. Rask, and especially of Eugene Burnouf and Christian Lassen who put the study of Persian cuneiform on solid footing. Perhaps the greatest attention would be paid to the intellectually and physically daring exploits of Henry Creswicke Rawlinson, whose bravery led to the publication of the Behistun inscriptions and whose intellectual prowess led to the decipherments of Elamite and Babylonian, and, at a later time, of Sumerian.[2]

The journalist might take little note of important advances in the study of languages already known. To be realistic, the decipherment of an unknown script is far more exciting to the public than the illumination of a language already

---

[1]I am grateful to the Graduate School of Religion of Duke University for providing me library privileges and study space during the fall semester of 1977 to do research for this essay.

[2]An excellent journalistic account of the great decipherments is that of P. E. Cleator, *Lost Languages*.

known. Yet the same period in which the great decipherments occurred also witnessed a veritable revolution in the study of Greek which competes in significance, if not in glamor, with the decipherments of Egyptian, Akkadian, and Sumerian. During this time studies of non-literary papyri, ostraca, and inscriptions from the Mediterranian basin were providing New Testament scholars with the essential features of a Greek in some ways as unknown to them as Babylonian had been to the orientalist before the work of Rawlinson.

The reader may find it strange to speak of Greek as though it were an unknown language in a time when classical philology was making major advances. Certainly the New Testament scholar could pick up the Greek text and make a reliable translation from it, and in that sense the language of the Christian Bible was anything but unknown. Yet throughout most of the 19th century the philological basis for the study of the New Testament was Attic Greek, which by the end of the 5th century B. C. was the recognized language of Greek literary prose. From our perspective we can see how this worked as well as it did. By the 4th century B. C. the Attic dialect, modified in some respects by Ionic, was well on its way to becoming the standard Greek Koine, and through Alexander's conquests it became the language of an entire civilization. Further, by the end of the first century B. C. there were efforts to revive the pure Attic of the classical period as the language of elevated speech and literature. Both of these facts made the Greek of the New Testament intelligible enough from the standpoint of a classical Attic grammar as to discourage attempts to find a more contemporary model for the study of the language of the New Testament.

This is not to say that 19th-century scholars did not recognize that the language of the New Testament departed significantly from the speech of 5th-century Athens. The classical scholar would be apt to think in terms of an inferior Greek while his New Testament colleague would likely speak of a special Biblical Greek or Jewish Greek molded on the example of the Septuagint.[3] Whether the departures in the New Testament were to be regarded as vulgarisms or as Hebraisms, they were certainly to be regarded as departures from an ideal Attic Greek. The fact that the New Testament could be understood on the basis of Attic grammar made assimilation of the new evidence of the papyri, ostraca, and inscriptions difficult. These too could be read under the narrow beam of light provided by the Attic dialect simply as crude productions of an unlettered people. A. Deissmann rightly complains that the artificial Atticism of the Imperial period had its counterpart in the philology of the New Testament in the 19th century.[4]

That the key to Assyrian had been found was confirmed by the famous test conducted by Edwin Norris on behalf of the Royal Asiatic Society in which W. H. F. Talbot, J. Oppert, E. Hincks, and Henry Rawlinson independently submitted translations of clay prisms of Tiglath-pileser I to an adjudicating committee.[5] The claims of Greek scholars to have discovered the common language of the

---

[3]Adolf Deissmann, *Light from the Ancient East,* trans. Lionel R. M. Strachan, pp. 62-3.

[4]*Ibid.,* p. 69, n. 1. Deissmann is here quoting with approval a remark by J. Wellhausen that New Testament scholars need to be open to the evidence for the spoken Greek of the Imperial period and then goes on to say that Wellhausen's approach is colored by an inappropriate reverence for the Attic dialect.

[5]Cleator, *Lost Languages,* p. 100.

Hellenistic world could not be so simply handled. For the most part the evidence was, indeed, from relatively unlettered persons, and there was justice on the side of those who would argue that such evidence could hardly be used to illustrate anything other than popular misuse of the language. But the sheer weight of the evidence led finally to the admission that there was in existence in the Hellenistic world a robust, common Greek which demonstrated a remarkable unity and coherence in texts from Macedonia to Egypt.[6] Further, it could be shown that the language of the New Testament had more in common with this vernacular Greek than it did with the Greek of the classical period. The publication of A. Deissmann's *Bibelstudien* (Marburg, 1895) and *Neue Bibelstudien* (Marburg, 1895)[7] heralded a new period in New Testament studies in which the scholar would be obligated to appeal first to the common usage of words and phrases, as illustrated by the new evidence, before having resort to the older literature.

In a real sense a new language had been discovered, a discovery postponed and resisted by the illusion that it was already known. But this discovery has come to have a more profound effect on the day-to-day work of the New Testament scholar than the great decipherments have had on the work of the Old Testament specialist, for there is almost no sentence in the New Testament which does not change in aspect when viewed from the vantage point of the Koine instead of classical Greek. The stock items of the New Testament scholar's trade are mediators of the newfound dialect, from the grammars of Moulton and Blass-Debrunner to the vocabulary of Moulton-Milligan and the dictionary of Bauer.

It is understandable that as a result of the discovery of the Greek Koine of the Imperial period the estimation of the Hebraic contribution to the language of the New Testament had to be revised downward. For instance, parataxis, the setting side by side of independent clauses connected by *kai* (less often, *de*), had traditionally been thought of as a Hebraism,[8] since classical Greek style prefers subordination of clauses to coordination of clauses in a sentence. An example of such parataxis is to be found in Luke 2:8-9:

> And (*kai*) there were shepherds in the same country in the fields and (*kai*) they were keeping watch at night over their flock. And (*kai*) an angel of the Lord came upon them, and (*kai*) the glory of the Lord came upon them, and (*kai*) they were greatly afraid.

Judged from classical standards, this passage is atrocious, but in Hebrew the

---

[6]It is widely recognized that there were few differences in dialect demonstrated in the written Koine. Cf. J. H. Moulton, *A Grammar of New Testament Greek, Vol. 1: Prolegomena,* 3d ed. rev., pp. 32-4. An amusing choice of words on p. 19 gives, perhaps, unintended emphasis to Moulton's point that regional differences in the Koine were very slight. He says, "We may add that a highly educated speaker of standard English, recognisable by his intonation as hailing from London, Edinburgh, or New York, can no longer thus be recognised when his words are written down." An American, of course immediately sees that the author of this sentence is British by his spelling of "recognise."

[7]Both of these works are contained in the English translation by Alexander Grieve entitled *Bible Studies.*

[8]So, for example, E. von Dobschütz, "Johanneische Studien," ZNW, VIII (1907), 7, as cited by Deissmann, *Light,* pp. 131-2.

recurring "and" would be quite acceptable. Our knowledge of the Koine,[9] however, reminds us that parataxis is not at all unusual in non-literary texts, and this casts doubt upon the assertion that in Luke 2 it is a Hebraism.

The lack of significant differences in dialect among the remains of the Koine, even within a Jewish environment, highlights a new difficulty. Although a large number of alleged Semitisms could be explained along the lines provided by research into the Koine, not all of them could be so explained. Consider Luke 8:1:

> And it came to pass (*kai egeneto*) thereafter that (*kai*) he went through cities and towns preaching . . .

The formula *kai egeneto* (or *egeneto de*) followed by a resumptive *kai* is clearly not an attested formulation of the Koine. Indeed, it would have been most difficult for a speaker of Greek to have understood it. The formulation clearly reproduces the Hebrew *wyhy . . . w,* which was not even a feature of the colloquial Hebrew of the time but a classical form. It is not difficult to see that this unusual expression is based on the Septuagint's rendering of the classical Hebrew idiom. Yet the existing evidence for Jewish usage of the Koine shows us that the same writer who would use *kai egeneto . . . kai* in a religious writing would never resort to it in a contract or in a personal letter. So far as the written records show, there was no "Jewish Greek" in which Hebrew or Aramaic features were to be found with the single exception of religious texts.

Strangely enough, the isolation of the Koine as the dialect of the New Testament actually heightened scholarly awareness of the phenomenon commonly called Semitism. With only a classical model, a certain ambiguity attached itself to a departure from classical expression in that one might consider the departure either a simple error or a Semitism. With the discovery that many "errors" of this kind were, in fact, acceptable formulations in the Koine dialect, the formulations which could not be adequately paralleled from the Koine were given greater attention. For instance, Luke is especially fond of the formulation (*en*) *autē tē hōra* (2:38, 7:21(D), 10:21, 12:12, 13:31, 20:19, 24:33; Acts 16:18, 22:13). This expression is not completely unparalleled in the papyri,[10] but in the sense in which Luke uses it ("forthwith") it departs from its Koine meanings. There is, however, a perfectly good Aramaic idiom, *bh.š ᶜ t',* which corresponds in form and meaning to the idiom in Luke-Acts.[11] Knowledge of the Koine idiom showed that its meaning was unsuitable to the context in Luke-Acts and motivates the researcher to seek for a Semitic background.

The implications of seeking a Semitic expression seemed to be fairly obvious. At some point the material had been formulated in a Semitic language and, at a later time, had been translated into Greek. The only exception to this would be those occurances which could be shown to be imitations of expressions in the Septuagint. At the turn of the century, E. Nestle and J. Wellhausen both held for a

---

[9]We shall consider at a later point the question of overuse as pointing to a Semitic background. The point to be made here is that parataxis alone does not establish such a background.

[10]F. Blass and A. Debrunner, *A Greek Grammar of the New Testament,*trans., Robert W. Funk, § 288(2).

[11]*Ibid.* Cf. Matthew Black, *An Aramaic Approach to the Gospels and Acts,* 3d ed., pp. 110-2.

definite Aramaic substratum in the Synoptics, and F. Blass was contending that Acts 1-12 was a translation from an Aramaic original.[12] These views seemed to have a certain *a priori* claim to validity. If we begin with the assumption that Jesus and his disciples spoke Aramaic, then it must follow that our Greek accounts of the words and actions of Jesus must involve at some stage a translation of material from Aramaic into Greek. Hidden in this logical development, however, are certain assumptions which we find difficult to accept as self-evident: (1) Jesus taught only in Aramaic; (2) The language of the earliest Christians was Aramaic; and (3) There was an early Christian Aramaic literature since lost to us. G. Dalman in 1898 attacked the views on translation then current on the grounds that the supposed Aramaic constructions were often unattested in Palestinian Aramaic literature.[13] He held, rather, that one could assume an Aramaic original only for the words of Jesus.

The effect of Dalman's critique was to make investigators study their proposed reconstructions more closely in the light of attested Palestinian Aramaic, but Dalman's protests were not sufficient to put to rest other translation theories. Since the work of Dalman, both C. C. Torrey and C. F. Burney have claimed Aramaic originals for most of the Greek of the gospels and Acts. Burney's work, which concentrated on the Fourth Gospel and upon the poetry of Jesus,[14] will not concern us in this essay, but the claim of C. C. Torrey that all four gospels and Acts 1-15 were translated from Semitic languages will be of great concern.[15] In more recent times the theme of Aramaic backgrounds to the gospels and Acts has been raised more modestly by Matthew Black and Max Wilcox.[16] Both Black and Wilcox deal with the New Testament as a Greek document, not an Aramaic document in disguise, but both would allow for Aramaic background materials of various kinds, as will be made clearer below.

What is a Semitism?

It would be reasonable to suppose that there now exists something of a consensus as to what constitutes a Semitism. The disappointing fact is that no such consensus, in fact exists. C. C. Torrey gives us the most subjective definition of all by defining a Semitism as a difficult expression in Greek which an interpreter, well schooled in the Semitic languages, recognizes as being a Semitic expression.[17] J. H. Moulton and W. F. Howard defined a Semitism as "a deviation from genuine Greek idiom due to too literal rendering of the language of a Semitic original."[18] Max Wilcox understands a Semitism in terms of morphology

---

[12] "Die zweifache Textüberlieferung in der Apostelgeschichte," *Theologische Studien und Kritiken,* LXVII (1894), 87-90.

[13] Above all see his *The Words of Jesus,* trans. D. M. Kay.

[14] *The Aramaic Origin of the Fourth Gospel* and *The Poetry of Our Lord.*

[15] On Torrey see below.

[16] *Aramaic Approach to the Gospels;* Max Wilcox, *The Semitisms of Acts.*

[17] C. C. Torrey, "The Translations Made from the Original Aramaic Gospels," *Studies in the History of Religions Presented to Crawford Howell Toy,* ed. David Gordon Lyon, p. 284.

[18] James Hope Moulton and Wilbert Francis Howard, *A Grammar of New Testament Greek, Vol. II: Accidence and Word-Formation,* p. 14.

as "a word or phrase whose use or construction departs from normal idiomatic Greek usage in such a way as to conform with normal idiomatic Semitic usage."[19]

The three definitions given above are very different from one another. Wilcox thinks of Semitisms as unusual constructions in Greek without reference to possible translation. For Moulton and Howard, on the other hand, translation belongs to the definition of a Semitism. Torrey always assumes translation but is actually closer to Wilcox than to Moulton and Howard in that it is the structure of the Greek which determines a Semitism. Wilcox's definition is superior to Moulton's and Howard's in that he does not confuse cause with effect. For him, a Semitism is an unusual feature of Greek. The explanation for that feature may be translation or imitation of the Septuagint or something else. Yet Wilcox's definition is unsatisfactory in another way.

When we find an unusual expression or error in English, we do not normally call it a "Germanicism" if it happens to coincide with an allowable expression in German. It would probably not be an exaggeration to claim that almost any error in English could be paralleled with an allowable expression in some other language. We need some reason other than mere morphological identity to look for a Semitic backgroung to an expression.

Most scholars now recognize that it is insufficient to regard all Semitisms as direct translations. The wide-spread influence of the Septuagint in the first century could certainly account for at least some of the questionable Greek expressions deemed Semitisms without direct recourse to the theory of a Semitic source document. This would be especially true for constructions which represent archaic Hebraic forms. Two obvious examples would be the use of *kai egeneto . . . kai,* already discussed, and *apokritheis . . . eipen* (Luke 1:19, 35, 60; 3:11, etc.). The first corresponds to the classical Hebrew *wyhy . . . w,* and the second to the classical *wy^{c}n . . . l'mr.* Although Torrey seems to reject such a class of secondary Semitisms as somehow unworthy of Luke,[20] in fact almost no other reasonable explanation can be given in the light of the linguistic evidence. Such classical features were not even a regular part of the neo-classical Hebrew of Qumran.

Now in discussing "biblicisms" another question seems to go begging which has already been raised above. The Greek papyri from Egypt show us that such seeminly over-literal renditions as *kai egeneto . . . kai* do not appear in the writings of Egyptian Jews.[21] Such barbarisms are confined to religious works. On the whole, the process of linguistic influence seems to have moved from Greek to the local languages of the Hellenistic world and not the other way around.[22] We can rightly assume that the pronounced Semitic flavor of the Septuagint is intentional on the part of the translators and not a reflection of their inability to render Hebrew into idiomatic Greek. Thus some account of the unusual language of the Septuagint is necessary in the light of the papyri.

Appeals to translation or to "biblicism" raise more questions than they

---

[19]*Semitisms of Acts,* p. 17.

[20]"Translations Made from the Original Aramaic Gospels," p. 288.

[21]As N. Turner shows in his supplement to Moulton-Howard, *Grammar II,* pp. 414-5.

[22]Evidence for this, especially in vocabulary, abounds in Hebrew, Aramaic, and Coptic.

answer. We cannot point to a curious Greek construction, show its relationship to a Semitic idiom, explain the irregularity as stemming from translation, thinking in Semitic, or imitation, and consider that we have finished the task. Some historical and linguistic nexus must be postulated in which such explanations would make sense. Further, it should be obvious that with these outstanding ambiguities none of these explanations can belong to the definition of a Semitism.

I am inclined to follow Wilcox in his definition of a Semitism except to say that it defines only a possible Semitism. The next step in the inquiry would be to discover reasons for the departure from normal Greek usage and, if interference[23] from a Semitic language can be shown as a probable cause, then and only then will we be satisfied that we are dealing with a Semitism. No one explanation belongs to the definition, but some showing of interference from Semitic will be required beyond mere morphological similarities.

One more matter must be discussed before leaving this topic. The category of "overuse" of allowable Greek expressions which are similar to Semitic expressions is often claimed as a Semitic feature. Such things as hyperbaton, asyndeton, instrumental *en,* and the use of the dative in a possessive sense, are features of the Koine but are relatively more frequent in Jewish and Christian religious writings than in the papyri or in the literary Koine. No single instance of such a feature could be reasonably called a Semitism, but where overuse can be demonstrated statistically we may relate this to our definition where Semitic interference can be thought to exist.

The Investigation of Semitisms in Luke-Acts

In this brief essay it would be impossible to deal with the entire history of the investigation of Semitisms in Luke-Acts. The reader should also consult M. Black's *Aramaic Approach,* pp. 1-14 and Max Wilcox's *Semitisms of Acts,* pp. 1-19 for a more complete discussion of the history of research. Here we shall only be able to treat certain themes which are important for the approach of this study.

The study of Semitisms in Luke-Acts began with the study of certain variants in the text of Codex Bezae. Wilcox begins his historical survey with an account of W. W. Harvey's suggestion that the reading *ebarunate* (D, Iren) for the usual *ērnēsasthe* in Acts 3:14 reflected a misunderstanding of the Syriac *kpr* as *kbd*.[24] F. H. Chase held the view that this kind of variant demonstrated influence from the Old Syriac on the Bezan text of Acts,[25] but A. Resch held that the evidence pointed to two translations of an originally Hebrew Acts.[26] E. Nestle took the position that the Bezan variants at Acts 2:47 (*kosmon* for *laon*) and at Acts 3:14 (already discussed by Harvey) were clear evidence in favor of a Semitic

---

[23]The word "interference" is used here in the sense introduced by U. Weinreich in his *Languages in Contact,* p. 1: "The term interference implies the rearrangement of patterns that result from the introduction of foreign elements into the more highly structured domains of language . . ."

[24]*Semitisms of Acts,* pp. 1-2.

[25]See his work, *The Old Syriac Element in the Text of Codex Bezae.*

[26]*Aussercanonische Paralleltexte zu den Evangelien.*

original.[27] Following this, F. Blass, who was already on record in favor of a theory of two recensions of Luke,[28] now held that the language of Acts 1-12 justified a claim that this section was an overly literal translation of a Hebrew original which Luke had taken up with some corrections and made the first part of his longer account.[29]

Wilcox complains that the interest in the Bezan variants, which inaugurated the study of Semitisms in Acts, has not been characteristic of later studies of the subject.[30] Whatever account is to be of the Semitisms of Luke-Acts should include some attempt to resolve the enigma of Codex Bezae. A. J. Wensinck in his masterful study of the Semitisms of the Bezan text[31] shows that the number of Semitisms in the text is greater than those of the Alexandrian text even though in some instances D has actually removed a Semitic expression found in the Alexandrian witnesses. He points to an impressive number of possible Semitisms in D which, he holds, can have only resulted from translation of an underlying Aramaic text.[32] The important thing to note is that D, interpreted in this manner, can be taken to provide independent attestation of a Semitic original. If Wensinck is correct, the investigator does not have to depend solely upon conjectured reconstructions from the Nestle text as evidence for a Semitic original but may also point to the witness of D as possibly an independent Greek version of that original.

The opposition of G. Dalman to the investigations of Blass, Nestle, and Wellhausen opened a new chapter in the study and focused attention away from the peculiar problems of Codex Bezae. Dalman held that the earlier investigations had not taken account of the actual idiom of Jewish Aramaic and had not sufficiently taken into account the possibility of biblicisms. Further, some of the proposed Aramaisms made for bad Aramaic in any dialect.[33] M. Black has taken issue with some of the facile rejections which Dalman made of proposed Aramaisms,[34] but Dalman's criticism had a healthy effect on subsequent research. No longer could a scholar explain a possible Aramaism on the basis of an idiom in any dialect of Aramaic. The proposed construction would have to be possible in an Aramaic dialect which could have influenced the Greek writer.

We have already explained the effect which the isolation of the Koine dialect had upon the study of Semitisms in the New Testament. Deissmann did not go so far as to say that there were no Semitisms in the New Testament,[35] but his work certainly had the effect of minimizing resort to the explanation of Semitism for

---

[27]"Some Observations on the Codex Bezae," Exp 5th ser., II (1895), 235-6.

[28]"Die zweifache Textüberlieferung."

[29]*Philology of the Gospels*, p. 195.

[30]*Semitisms of Acts*, p. 3.

[31]"The Semitisms of Codex Bezae and their Relation to the non-Western Text of the Gospel of St. Luke," *BBC XII* (1937), 11-48.

[32]*Ibid.*, p. 48.

[33]*Words of Jesus.*

[34]*Aramaic Approach to the Gospels*, pp. 3-6.

[35]*Light*, pp. 69 n. 1 and 71 n. 3. For his comments on "Jewish Greek" see *Bible Studies*, pp. 67-8.

every difficulty encountered in the Greek text.

Yet, as we have seen, the discovery of the Koine made certain difficult expressions stand out in sharp relief. Luke 12:8 begins: *pas hos an homologēsē en emoi* ... and must be translated, "Whoever confesses me ..." The use of *en* here, following *homologēsē,* departs from normal Koine usage and, in fact, would be very difficult for a native Greek to understand. The use of *b* following *ydy* is attested in both Hebrew and Aramaic,[36] where *b* indicates the object of the verb "confess." In this case it would be difficult to say why such an outright eror would be made in writing Greek unless there were positive interference from a Semitic language. The phrase *homologēsē en emoi* is reminiscent of the overly literal reproduction of Hebrew prepositions in Aquila.

Since research into the Koine had made the existence of Semitisms even clearer then before, the stage was now set for the enormous work of C. C. Torrey of Yale, who in numerous publications[37] promoted the view that the whole of Luke and the first 15 chapters of Acts had been translated from Semitic. The hallmark of Torrey's work was his decisive mastery of Aramaic and his almost uncanny ability to relate difficult Greek expressions to Aramaic idioms. Although Torrey would admit that the discovery of the Koine demonstrated the relation of most of the New Testament to that dialect, he denied that this could be said of the gospels[38] and especially of Luke:

> Of all the four Gospels it (Luke) is the one which gives by far the plainest and most constant evidence of being a translation. His habit as a translator resembles that of Aquila.[39]

Certain constructions in Luke are not only incorrect in Torrey's view, they are inexcusable, such as *en de tō poreuesthai autous autos eiselthen eis kōmēn tina* (Luke 10:38a) and *sullabontes de auton ēgagon kai eisēgagon eis tēn oikian tou archiereōs* (Luke 22:54a).[40] These astounding construction can only be literal translations where the rendering in Greek is of no consequence so long as the Semitic original is faithfully reproduced, a translational characteristic he also finds in the Septuagint.[41]

It will not be possible for us to do justice to the full range of Torrey's work, and we shall have to be content with a few illustrations which show something of Torrey's method of reconstruction in the hope that the reader will consult Torrey's works directly.

In Luke 2:1 (see also Acts 11:28) the Greek text tells us that the Emperor decreed that the "entire world" (*pasan tēn oikoumenēn*) should be enrolled. This census in A. D. 6, however, was merely a preliminary step in the incorporation of

---

[36]Hifil in Hebrew and afel in Aramaic. Cf. M. Jastrow, *Dictionary of the Targumim, the Talmud Babli and Yerushalmi, and the Midrashic Literature,* p. 564.

[37]See the following works: *The Composition and Date of Acts; Documents of the Primitive Church; The Four Gospels;* and *Our Translated Gospels.*

[38]*Our Translated Gospels,* p. liv.

[39]*Ibid.,*p. lix.

[40]*Ibid.,* p. lviii.

[41]*Ibid.,* p. liv.

Judea into the system of Roman provinces,[42] and by no means included even the entire Roman world. Torrey contends that *pasan tēn oiloumenēn* reflects the Hebrew *kl h'rṣ* used in the restricted sense of "all the land (of Israel)." Luke did not understand this restricted sense of the Hebrew *'rṣ* and so rendered it wrongly as "world" instead of as "land."[43]

In Acts 4:25 Nestle reads *ho tou patros hēmōn dia pneumatos hagiou stomatos dauid paidos sou eipōn* which is practically untranslatable as it stands. Torrey contends that this is a mistranslation of an original Aramaic which reads *hy' dy 'bwn lpwm rwḥ' dy qwdš' dwyd ᶜbdk 'mr*. Evidently, *hy'*, which referred to the saying, was misread as *hw'* and led to the impossible translation attested in P[74] and the Alexandrian witnesses.[44]

A passage which as posed great problems for interpreters is Acts 8:10: *houtos estin hē dunamis tou theou hē kaloumenē megalē*. Did the people of Samaria really name Simon "the power of God which is called great?" Torrey does not believe so and gives the following reconstruction of the Aramaic : *dyn ḥyl' dy 'lh' dy mtgr' rb*. The last clause, *mtqr' rb*, modifies *'lh'*, not *ḥyl'*. The Samaritans reserved their highest praise for God, not Simon.[45]

Obviously Torrey does not confine himself to linguistic problems in his quest for Semitic sources. There is nothing wrong with the grammar of Acts 8:10 or Luke 2:1. In Acts 8:10 there is a theological problem for Torrey which he resolves with an Aramaic reconstruction. Likewise, it is history, not grammar, which impels Torrey to his hypothetical Hebrew for Luke 2:1. It would be unfair to claim that most of Torrey's reconstructions derive from historical and theological difficulties rather than linguistic difficulties, but some certainly do and are treated side-by-side with passages showing authentic problems of language.

Torrey's thesis provoked intense debate. Few scholars were prepared to challenge Torrey's constructions point by point, but what appeared as a glaring weakness in Torrey's case was perhaps said best by D. W. Riddle:

> The theory of translation Greek depends on a historical viewpoint which is more than doubtful. Proponents of the theory assume that there was a period in the history of Christianity when the Semitic language, whether Hebrew or Aramaic, was in use by Christians for the advancement of the Christian movement. It is assumed that writing in Hebrew or Aramaic was common in Judaism and Christianity. It is taken for granted that the characteristics of the supposed Semitic original may be inferred from the few bits of Semitic literature of approximately the same date which have survived. It is believed that even dialectical differences in the hypothetical originals may be detected.[46]

Most difficult to meet was Goodspeed's challenge that Semitic literature illustrating the hypothesis of a Semitic original be brought forward.[47] Here the critics knew themselves to be on solid footing, for nothing at all could be brought forward as an example of Christian Semitic literature from the first century, and in

---

[42]*Ibid.*, p. 84.

[43]*Ibid.*

[44]*Composition and Date of Acts*, pp. 16-8.

[45]*Ibid.*, pp. 18-20.

[46]"The Logic of the Theory of Translation Greek," *JBL*, LI (1932), 14.

[47]*New Solutions of New Testament Problems*, p. 71.

this era before the discovery of the Scrolls very little Jewish literature could be produced. If Christians had, indeed, published the faith abroad in Hebrew or Aramaic, it seemed reasonable to ask that at least a few shreds of hard evidence be displayed. The main evidence seemed to be only in the Semitisms which had been conjectured for Greek documents, and the circularity of this kind of argument was not lost upon the critics.

In Torrey's defense it must be said that he did make an effort to give evidence for the existence of Semitic originals for the gospels. Here he followed G. F. Moore[48] and R. T. Herford[49] in claiming that there was Rabbinic evidence that Aramaic gospels were known for a time in Palestinian synagogues and were studied there by Jews with some seriousness. Moore believes there is evidence that decisions by rabbis were sometimes based on "the Gospel" (^{C}wn gylywn).[50] The earliest evidence for rabbinic knowledge of the Christian gospels is to be found in *tos. Yad.* 2:13:

> hglywnym wspry hmynym 'ynn mtm'yn 't hydym. spry bn
> syr' wkl sprym šnktbs mk'n w'ylk 'ynn mtm'yn 't hydym.

Moore thinks this passage indicates that throughout the first century the gospels were read alongside sectarian books and Ben Sira in the synagogue, and it had to be made clear that these books were not inspired. Further, Moore relates this regulation to those regulations which prohibit saving heretical books, including gospels, from burning buildings on the Sabbath (*tos. Shab.* 13:5, cf. also *j. Shab.* 16:1 and *b. Sanh.* 38b).[51] He concludes that because of the Second Revolt in which Bar Koseba was regarded as messiah, the Christian menace to the synagogue was at an end.[52]

Torrey uses this kind of evidence to support statements like the following:

> The adherents of the Nazarene Messiah, as they became numerous, were tolerated as constituting a variety of Judaism, a sect within the Synagogue. The name then given to them, *Minim,* "sectaries" carried remonstrance, but (at first) no special approbrium. It was afterward applied to other heretics also, but continued to be prevailingly the designation of Jewish Christians.[53]

Torrey considers, then, that Jewish Christians were tolerated as sectarians within the synagogue well into the second century A. D., and their gospels (in Aramaic) were studied by other Jews. In the second century regulations had to be formulated to put an end to this association.

---

[48]"The Definition of the Hebrew Canon and the Repudiation of the Christian Scriptures," *Essays in Modern Theology and Related Subjects: A Testimonial to Charles A. Briggs,* pp. 99-125.

[49]"The Problem of the 'Minim' Further Considered," *Jewish Studies in Memory of A. Kohut,* ed. Salo W. Bacon and Alexander Marx, pp. 359-69.

[50]"The Definition of the Hebrew Canon," pp. 103-5.

[51]*Ibid.,* pp. 99-102.

[52]*Ibid.,* p. 122.

[53]*Documents,* p. 97. Also on the problem of the *minim* see Robert Gordis, "Homeric Books in Palestine," *JQR,* n.s. XXXVIII (1948), 356-68, and A. M. Honeyman, "A Tannaitic Term for the Christians," *JQR,* n. s. XXXVIII (1947), 151-5.

Although rabbinic evidence for Aramaic gospels is interesting, it is far from conclusive and no substitute at all for the original documents. We note that the rabbinic name for the gospels ('wn or ^cwn gylywn) is a parody on the Greek *euangellion,* and in all likelihood the reading of Greek documents in the synagogue was more widespread than Torrey would admit. Further, in the light of the *birkat ha-minim,* the separation of Christians from the synagogue seems to have come at the close of the first century, not in the second century. Finally, the discovery of the Scrolls possibly gives fuller meaning to the term *min* as used in the synagogue.

The reaction to, and, in some cases, qualified acceptance of Torrey's thesis mark the next significant period in the history of the discussion. It must be said that significant progress in the study of Semitisms depends upon there being scholars whose training in Hebrew and Aramaic allow them to speak with some authority. Devotion to Semitic studies and New Testament is enough of a rarity still to make the kind of brilliant thesis which Torrey brings forward something which happens once in a generation. This period of assimilation of Torrey's work, interesting as it is, will not detain us here in this paper.

One scholar whose work has probably not received sufficient study is A. J. Wensinck of Leyden, whose important study of the Semitisms of Codex Bezae has already been mentioned.[54] M. Black has included a summary of Wensinck's unpublished work on Aramaic backgrounds in his (Black's) *Aramaic Approach.*[55] Black credits Wensinck with being the first scholar to break with the tradition established by Dalman and Torrey of using the language of Onkelos and the Johnathan Targums as primary evidence for the Palestinian Aramaic of the first century in favor of Kahle's Palestinian Targum to the Pentateuch, Palestinian Syriac, and the Samaritan Targum.[56] In the article on Bezae, however, this shift is anything but obvious to anyone other than a specialist, and it has been, in fact, M. Black himself who has promoted this shift within New Testament scholarship.

The discovery of Aramaic documents at Qumran has certainly altered the linguistic picture, though not as much as one might expect. Scholars have had difficulty in assessing the relative position of the language of this material (primarily the Genesis Apocryphon) in the light of other later materials viewed as having a bearing on it. If one accepts Kahle's view that the language of the Palestinian Targums and Pseudo-Johnathan reflect a western dialect and Onkelos is relegated to the East,[57] then the affinities of the Apocryphon with Onkelos become a difficulty. E. Y. Kutscher has claimed that these affinities, especially those of vocabulary, favor the old suggestion by Nöldeke and Dalman that the Onkelos Targum had its origin in the West.[58] J. A. Fitzmyer complains that Kahle's view, followed by M. Black, is a stumbling-block to progress in the matter of understanding what sort of Aramaic was spoken in Palestine in the first century, and he challenges the students of Kahle to bring forward evidence in

---

[54]"The Semitisms of Codex Bezae."

[55]*Aramaic Approach to the Gospels,* pp. 296-304.

[56]*Ibid.,* pp. 296-7.

[57]P. Kahle, *The Cairo Geniza,* pp. 200ff.

[58]E. Y. Kutscher, "The Language of the 'Genesis Apocryphon'," *SH,* IV (1965), 10.

favor of an early date for the Palestinian Targum.[59] This debate continues without firm resolution. The Apocryphon is a first-century B. C. Aramaic work composed in Palestine with definite links in language both to Onkelos and to Christian Aramaic.[60] It is also a formal, literary piece which arose within what was probably a Hebrew-speaking environment. Even without the evidence of the Palestinian Targum it is unlikely that Qumran Aramaic could answer with certainty our questions about the common Aramaic of first-century Palestine.

M. Black's important study of the gospels and Acts concludes that we have evidence for an Aramaic tradition only in the sayings of Jesus and in the speeches of Peter and Stephen in the early chapters of Acts, although Black maintains that the evidence for the speeches is not as conclusive as for the sayings of Jesus.[61] Yet even the sayings of Jesus, in the form in which we have them in the gospels, are not simple replications of the sayings in Greek but represent Greek interpretations of those sayings. The gospel sayings are, indeed, "targums" on the sayings of Jesus.[62] In considering the problem of Codex Bezae, Black has not found it necessary to follow F. Blass in his two-edition theory; rather, he suggests that a period of fluidity in the texts of the gospels preceded the establishment of "Vulgate texts" which replaced local texts. Sinaiticus and Vaticanus, as well as Bezae, preserve such Vulgate texts, but Bezae, in his view, preserves "more of the characteristics of the pre-Vulgate 'fluid' textual period" than do Vaticanus and Sinaiticus.[63] Further remarks about the work of Black and his student Wilcox will be offered below.

The Reappearance of "Jewish Greek"

In 1951 Henry S. Gehman wrote an article in which he claimed that it was necessary to reintroduce the idea of a "Jewish Greek" into the study of the language of the Septuagint.[64] Gehman held that there was a demonstrable influence of Hebrew upon the language of the Septuagint which would have rendered that language difficult for one "not acquainted with the psychology of the Hebrew language.[65] For example, Gehman points to the whole new set of meanings which the conjunction *kai* acquires in the Septuagint:

1. "that" — Gen 4:8: "And it came to pass while they were in the field *that Cain rose up . . .*" (*kai anestē Kain*)

2. introducing a circumstantial clause — 2 Sam. 11:4: "And he lay with her, *while she was purified from her uncleanness.*" (*kai autē hagiazomenē apo akatharsias autēs*)

---

[59]*The Genesis Apocryphon of Qumran Cave I: A Commentary,* pp. 24-5. Fitzmyer provides a useful bibliography on p. 24 n. 61 for publication on the question of the Aramaic used in Palestine during the time of Jesus. For a simple and useful discussion of the question see Martin McNamara, *Targum and Testament,* pp. 54-62.

[60]Kutscher, "Language," pp. 9-11.

[61]*Aramaic Approach to the Gospels,* p. 272.

[62]*Ibid.,* p. 275.

[63]*Ibid.,* p. 280.

[64]"The Hebraic Character of LXX Greek," *VT,* I (1951), 81-90.

[65]*Ibid.,* p. 90.

3. introducing the apodosis — 1 Sam. 20:6: "If thy father miss me at all, then (*kai*) thou shalt say . . ."

4. "then" — Gen. 9:16: "When (*kai*) my bow will be in the cloud, then (*kai*) will I see to remember . . ."

5. "so", "therefore" — Gen. 3:22-23: "And now lest ever he stretch forth his hand and take of the tree of life and eat and live forever, so (*kai*) the Lord God dismissed him from the paradise of luxuriousness."[66]

Gehman says that the reader unacquainted with Hebrew would not merely "ramble along" mindlessly reading *kai* after *kai* without understanding but would, instead, develop a feeling for the parataxis which would lead to a proper understanding of the text.[67]   Consequently, even a Hellenistic Jew with no knowledge of the ancestral tongue might well come to understand the specialized vernacular of the Septuagint.[68]   Gehman resorts to the idea of bilingualism to explain the unusual language of the Septuagint, but a bilingualism in which the Hebraic side is diminishing. Hellenistic Jews did not speak a Jewish-Greek jargon, but at least for religious discourse there was a Jewish Greek which showed strongly the influence of Hebrew.[69]

Nigel Turner supported Gehman's contention with a study of the use of *ekeinos* and the position of *heneka* and *pas* in the Septuagint.[70] This study featured a careful statistical comparison with the New Testament and the papyri which supported his claim that the employment of all three terms in the Septuagint reflected a specialized usage which was quite different from that of the papyri.

It seems as though matters had come full circle. The discovery and publication of the papyri had challenged the older claim that the Greek Bible was composed in a kind of Jewish Greek spoken by Hellenistic Jews, but, as we have seen, this challenge brought into sharp focus those Semitisms which could not be accounted for on the basis of the Koine. Gehman and Turner cautiously reintroduced the notion of Jewish Greek in the light of the fact that the remaining Semitisms, especially those of syntax, would be difficult for a native speaker of Greek to understand.

It is difficult to accept Gehman's contention that the language of the Septuagint can be explained on the basis of a bilingual community when the papyri which come from that community do not contain the Hebraic features of the Septuagint. The existing evidence seems to support the theory that because Jewish Greek is confined entirely to religious texts, it is probably to be located in religious settings within the community.

Turner does not support his views about Biblical Greek by a theory of spoken Jewish Greek but by the influence of the Septuagint. In the second volume of Moulton's *Grammar*, Turner made the following observation: "But when once the

---

[66]*Ibid.*, pp. 81-2.

[67]*Ibid.*, p. 82.

[68]*Ibid.*

[69]*Ibid.*, p. 90.

[70]"The Unique Character of Biblical Greek," *VT*, V (1955), 208-13.

LXX had become a standard of sacred speech for Hellenistic Jews and proselytes, its idioms would easily find their way into free composition."[71] Thus, whatever linguistic situation might account for the curious language of the Septuagint, the existence of the Septuagint would change the linguistic situation for subsequent generations of Greek-speaking Jews. This greatly compounds the difficulty in identifying primary Semitisms, for once the Septuagint had achieved prominence among the Greek-speaking Jewish communities it might be imitated by persons who knew no Semitic language. Turner then goes on to claim that the only really convincing evidence for translation is mistranslation.[72] But the only sure evidence of this would be to have the original text and its translation at hand, and even here, as he shows, there can be several explanations for the mistranslation.[73] In the third volume of the *Grammar*, Turner says that "Biblical Greek is a unique language with a unity and character of its own."[74]

It is a positive step to follow Turner by not confusing the phenomenon to be studied (Biblical Greek) with possible explanations for that phenomenon (translation, imitation, thinking in Semitic, etc.). The Semitic cast of the language of the Septuagint and the New Testament is not merely a veneer but is a linguistic phenomenon which distinguishes Biblical Greek from other kinds of Greek. K. Beyer's important work on Semitic syntax in the New Testament[75] should, on completion, give us a much better understanding of Semitic Greek than we have previously had. Particularly interesting for this discussion is Beyer's definition of *Septuagintismen* as "Konstruktionen, die wegen falscher Verwendung hebräischer Sprachmittel nicht Hebraismen sein konnen.[76] In principle, we cannot tell the difference between imitation and direct Hebraic influence unless there is an error in the imitation:

> Richtige Imitationen hebräischer Ausdruckweise lassen sich dagegen von Hebraismen bzw. Semitismen nicht unterscheiden und werden deshalb dort eingeordnet.[77]

If we cannot tell translation from correct imitation of the Septuagint, then our ability to discern blocks of originally Hebraic material is diminished to extinction.

Against this tide of scholarship stands the impressive work of Raymond A. Martin who has attacked the problem of Semitic sources in a very different way from his predecessors.[78] Martin, who is a student of Gehman, believes that the presence of Semitic sources may be detected by an analysis of the relative frequency or infrequency of certain syntactical features of Greek in a text. These

---

[71] *Ibid.*, p. 478.

[72] *Ibid.*, pp. 478-9.

[73] *Ibid.*, p. 479.

[74] J. H. Moulton, W. F. Howard, and N. Turner, *A Grammar of New Testament Greek: Vol III: Syntax*, p. 4.

[75] *Semitische Syntax im Neuen Testament I/1.*

[76] *Ibid.*, p. 11.

[77] *Ibid.*

[78] "Syntactical Evidence of Aramaic Sources in Acts i-xv," *NTS*, XI (1964/65), 38-59, and *Syntactical Evidence of Semitic Sources in Greek Documents.*

features are not necessarily Semitisms and are all allowable in the Koine, but Martin shows that they occur in different frequency within texts translated from Semitic languages than within other Koine texts. Examples of such features would include the relatively higher frequence of *en* in relation to other prepositions in translated texts, the lower frequency of nouns separated from their articles, and the lower frequency of attribuitive adjectives preceding the nouns they modify.[79]   Martin provided a gold mine of information as to the linguistic peculiarities of Biblical Greek and is likely correct that these features derive from Semitic influence. We should have to question, however, whether this kind of study could determine the presence of Semitic originals. There seems to be no way for Martin to exclude the possibility of imitation of the Septuagint in those sections of Acts which demonstrate the syntactical features which he has isolated. Nevertheless, Martin's work deserves to accompany Beyer's as a first-rate resource for the peculiar features of Biblical Greek.

In the light of the above it is not difficult to understand why Wilcox, for instance, finds that what he calls "hard-core Semitisms" are not numerous in Acts and are confined to the first 15 chapters.[80]   Further, none of these Semitisms would support a theory that Luke is translating Semitic sources.[81]   One of Wilcox's important discoveries is that on occasion the scriptural references in Acts reflect a text different from the Septuagint, and in nine cases he found agreement with existing Targums.[82]   The divergences, however, do not consistently follow any one Targumic tradition, and Wilcox thinks that Luke already had the quotations before him in Greek translation.[83]   For Wilcox, the Semitisms which do appear as something other than imitation of the Septuagint represent vestiges of originally Semitic material in Luke's Greek which give a sense of antiquity and authenticity to them.[84]

Matthew Black has accepted the idea of a Jewish Greek along the lines laid out by Gehman and Turner which, he believes, may have its home in the spoken language of the synagogue.[85]   This peculiar variety of the Koine would be adapted to the special religious needs and interests of the synagogue and would provide the early church with a matrix from which the varieties of New Testament Greek are derived.[86]   This kind of speculation about spoken Jewish Greek is better founded than that of Gehman in that it is specifically limited to cultic language for which there is direct evidence. Turner quotes with approval H. J. Cadbury's analogy of modern extemporaneous prayer as illustrating the adaptation of Biblical language to religious speech.[87]   Some such context must

---

[79]*Syntactical Evidence*, pp. 5-16, 21-25, 30-1.

[80]*Semitisms of Acts*, p. 180.

[81]*Ibid.*, p. 181.

[82]*Ibid.*, pp. 20-55.

[83]*Ibid.*, pp. 54-5.

[84]*Ibid.*, p. 184.

[85]Matthew Black, "Second Thoughts IX: The Semitic Element in the New Testament," *ExpT*, LXXVII (1965), 20-3.

[86]*Ibid.*, p. 23.

[87]Moulton-Howard, *Grammar II*, p. 478.

be assumed if the language of the Septuagint is to be thought of as in any sense a spoken language. If the papyri suggest that ordinary Jewish discourse in Greek was largely unaffected by the Semitic languages, the Septuagint suggests just the opposite for religious discourse in Greek among Jews.

A Role for Mimēsis?

The classical scholar George Kennedy has suggested that greater consideration should be given to the phenomenon of *mimēsis* as a way of understanding how the process of translation would be influenced in style and diction by already existing exemplars of the same genre of literature.[88] Thus he suggested that if a translator of an Aramaic gospel had before him a gospel in Greek, that Greek gospel would be strongly influential in shaping the language of translation. In this regard the Greek translation of Josephus' writings demonstrate accomodation in form and language to already existing models of historical works in Greek.[89]

Mimēsis is a feature of the general movement called Atticism wherein the great literary examples of the Greek past are studied and imitated in an effort to resurrect the glories of the epics and oratory of Hellenic antiquity. The earliest statement of the theory of *mimēsis* was made in regards to oratory by Dionysius of Halicarnassus in a work, only partially preserved to us, entitled *On Imitation*, which was composed toward the end of the first century B. C. Atticism arose in opposition to the florid and undisciplined form of composition commonly called Asianism, exemplified above all in the writings of Hegesias of Magnesia (*fl. c.* 250 B. C.).[90] *Mimēsis* is not an attempt to parrot the great literary figures of antiquity but is, rather, a method, based on exhaustive criticism of the style and diction of the exemplars, of carrying on the literary and oratorical tradition of classical Greece.[91] It might be too much to speak of a passion for *mimēsis* in the first century, but there is no denying its influence on the literature of that century.

Do we have here a possible explanation for the imitation of the Septuagint to be found in Luke's work? Could one perhaps claim that the Septuagint would have provided Luke a "classical" exemplar which he attempted to imitate in the construction of his narrative? In terms of the historical reality called *mimēsis*, the answer would probably have to be a qualified "no." It would be wrong to attempt to apply whole cloth the theory of *memēsis* to the language of the New Testament since *mimēsis*, as a constituent of Atticism, is, properly speaking, a Greek movement and applies to translation only to the extent that there was an attempt on the part of Latin translators to imitate in Latin the language of the Greek

---

[88]"Classical and Christian Source Criticism," *The Relationships Among the Gospels*, ed. William O. Walker, Jr., pp. 125-55.

[89]*Ibid.*, pp. 145-6.

[90]J. W. H. Atkins, "Hegesias of Magnesia," *Oxford Classical Dictionary*, p. 408.

[91]Cf. W. Rhys Roberts, *Greek Rhetoric and Literary Criticism*, pp. 71-97. For an excellent discussion of the theory of *mimēsis* see J. Bompaire, *Lucien ecrivain: imitation et creation*, pp. 13-154. Also useful is B. P. Reardon, *Courants littéraires grecs des II*[e] *et III*[e] *siècles après J.- C.*, pp. 3-11.

classics they were translating.[92] Yet it would not be incorrect to imagine that the spirit of *mimēsis* would influence a writer such as Luke who was not without knowledge of proper Greek composition. Surely, though, *mimēsis* does not directly help us with an understanding of the historical reality of Jewish Greek. We must turn for help in an entirely different direction.

"Mixed Hebrew" and Synagogue Greek

It is well known that the Hebrew of the Dead Sea Scrolls, and, to some extent, the language of the Jewish liturgy in the first century, were modeled on the language of the Hebrew scripture. C. Rabin has distinguished three forms of Hebrew in the first centuries B. C. and A. D.: (1) Late Biblical Hebrew (Dead Sea Scrolls, Hebrew fragments of Jubilees and the Testament of the Twelve Patriarchs), (2) Mixed Style (liturgy, Story of King Yannai, Story of Simon the Just, Stories of the Sons of Levi), and (3) Mishnaic.[93] The Mixed Style is much more obviously influenced by Mishnaic grammar, syntax, and vocabulary than is Qumran Hebrew and is, Rabin thinks, a concession to the popular speech (Mishnaic) which for cultic purposes seeks to retain as much of the classical language as possible.[94] Rabin thinks the Pharisees adopted Mishnaic to the exclusion of the other forms to differentiate their teaching from the parties opposed to them.

If Rabin is correct that Mishnaic was the common spoken language (a position strengthened by the language of the Copper Scroll and the Mishnaic letters of the Second Revolt), then the Late Biblical and Mixed Style are conscious attempts to retain the ancient tongue for religious and literary purposes. Although the Hebrew of Qumran demonstrates a rich linguistic tradition,[95] it is probable that it was not spoken. The Mixed Style is a much better candidate for a religious vernacular since it seems to be more accomodated to secular speech than the Hebrew of Qumran.

There is a parallel to this situation in what has been noted about the composition of the Septuagint. The papyri, inscriptions, and ostraca suggest that Greek-speaking Jews employed the standard Koine for purposes of ordinary discourse. Only in religious writings have we found an attempt to carry over the sense and feeling of the Hebrew language into Greek. Here too we have a "mixed style" with the vernacular as the basis of the language enriched for religious discourse by Hebraic vocabulary and syntax. Just as the language of the liturgy in Hebrew is sometimes more, sometimes less Mishnaic, so too is the language of the Septuagint sometimes more, sometimes less Koine.

On this theory the language of the Septuagint is not a wooden replication of Hebraic idioms in an impossible Greek but is representative of the language of the synagogue. Hebraic forms are brought over directly into Greek, but not in an

---

[92]Kennedy, "Criticism." pp. 144-5.

[93]"Hebrew and Aramaic in the First Century," *The Jewish People in the First Century*, II, 1007-1039.

[94]*Ibid.*, pp. 1015-7.

[95]*Ibid.*

overly-literal way. The various compromises in the translations in the Septuagint between Hebraic expression and Koine idiom are best understood as reflecting the various balances between the two in the Greek-speaking synagogues of Egypt. Thus the Hellenistic Jew was not reading an unknown tongue in the Septuagint but one with which his religious training prepared him. This is not to say that the Septuagint exerted no influence on the cultic language of Hellenistic Jews. But it is to say that the Septuagint did not create that language.

Wilcox[96] has shown for Acts that direct imitation of the Septuagint is much less common and less regularly distributed than H. F. D. Sparks had suggested in the latter's attempt to explain the Hebraisms of Luke-Acts as being primarily "reminiscences of the translation-style of the Septuagint."[97] In his rebuttal of Sparks, Wilcox divides septuagintalisms into two classes: those which have an exact parallel in the Septuagint, and those which have only an appearance of being septuagintal in character.[98] Although Wilcox does not deny that such apparent septuagintalisms exist, his study is devoted only to the direct reproductions of expressions in the Septuagint on the theory that the second class invite subjectivism.[99] While accepting Wilcox's evidence, we would want to insist that the second class of "septuagintalisms" are vitally important as indicating the operation of the synagogue Greek. Direct imitation of the Septuagint may indeed be fairly limited in Luke-Acts, but the "septuagintal" character of the books is pervasive.

Black's suggestion of a synagogue Greek in the article previously quoted helps us to resolve the difficulty Wilcox has encountered. We are able to identify Hebraisms in Luke-Acts and identify them as such. Some of these will be direct replications of the language of the Septuagint and others will be unsuccessful attempts to imitate that language (as Dalman[100] showed). The remaining Hebraisms are open to various explanations, but the theory of a synagogue Greek would give an efficient explanation for most, if not all of them.

We may show this in reference to an important non-Septuagint Hebraism discussed by Wilcox in Acts 2:47: *epi to auto.* Wilcox agrees with Torrey that none of the Septuagint's uses of the phrase give us a suitable translation in this passage since in the Septuagint *epi to auto* normally translates *yḥd* or *yḥdw* "together".[101] M. Black has held that 1QS v. 7 contains an exact parallel to the Greek of this passage (*prosetithei . . . epi to auto*) in the phrase *bh'spm lyḥd*,[102] a suggestion which Wilcox accepts. The meaning "community" for *yḥd* allows Wilcox to render the passage: "And the Lord was day by day incorporating into

---

[96]*Semitisms of Acts*, pp. 56-68.

[97]The relevant publications of Sparks are "The Semitisms of St. Luke's Gospel," *JTS,* XLIV (1943), 129-38; "The Semitisms of Acts," *JTS*, n. s. I (1950), 16-28; and "Some Observations on the Semitic Background of the New Testament," *SNTS Bulletin*, II (1951), 33-42.

[98]*Semitisms of Acts*, p. 57.

[99]*Ibid.*, p. 58.

[100]*Words of Jesus*, p. 39.

[101]*Semitisms of Acts*, p. 93. Torrey, *Composition and Date of Acts*, p. 10.

[102]*Aramaic Approach to the Gospels*, p. 10 n. 4.

the fellowship those who were being saved."[103] Here is obviously a Hebraism which is not a septuagintalism even though the Greek phrase *epi to auto* is found in the Septuagint. The sectarian meaning of *yḥd* has evidently penetrated into the synagogue Greek and influenced the meaning of this prepositional phrase. This evidence for the contact of the synagogue Greek with the living Hebrew of Palestine. A parallel situation exists for the term *he hodos* = "Christianity" (Acts 9:2; 19:9, 23; 22:4, 24:14, 22).[104]

Synagogue Greek, not direct imitation of the Septuagint nor Hebrew sources, seems to me the best explanation of the Hebraisms of Luke-Acts and many of the general Semitisms. Obviously this style of Greek comes almost to a halt after Acts 15 as Luke now turns his attention to the spread of the Gospel into the wider Roman world. This shift is reminiscent of Dionysius of Halicarnassus in his remarks about Lysias (*Lysias* § 9) to wit that his speech was always appropriate to the subjects of his discourse in terms of age, race, and level of education. After Acts 15 the Gospel proceeds to the non-Jewish world to which the specialized language of the synagogue was not appropriate.

The Aramaisms of Luke-Acts

As mentioned above, Black finds most of the legitimate Aramaisms in Luke confined to the sayings of Jesus, and both Black and Wilcox find evidence of Aramaic in the speeches of Acts. If our discussion of the synagogue Greek has been on the right track, the prime linguistic interference on the Koine which produced the Greek of the synagogue was Hebrew, not Aramaic. The situation may have been somewhat different for Jewish-Christian communities. The Greek of the synagogue was not a mundane dialect of Koine but was a dialect directed toward the religious interests of the synagogue. The translation and transmission of Jesus' words within the church would have exerted some linguistic influence on the religious Greek of Christians.

M. Black holds[105] that the words of Jesus in the gospels are more like a Targum than a transcription of his sayings which contain residual Aramaisms that reflect the original language. He does not think the Evangelists are directly translating Aramaic sources. This implies that Aramaisms would then be entering into free composition alongside the established Hebraisms of the synagogue Greek but, for the most part, would be limited to the language of discourse. But this would not be an absolute rule. We have already mentioned the Aramaism (*en*) *autē tē hora*, and there are doubtless a few others which appear in narrative.

It would be incorrect, however, to try to distinguish a special Jewish-Christian Greek on the basis of the Aramaisms of the gospels even though it seems reasonable to suppose that Aramaic may have influenced Christians slightly more than Hellenistic Jews. N. Turner points to the saying in the Epistle to Diognetus 5:2 to the effect that the Christians "use no strange variety of

---

[103]*Semitisms of Acts,* p. 100.

[104]*Ibid.,* pp. 105-6.

[105]*Aramaic Approach to the Gospels,* p. 275.

dialect."[106] David Hill insists that the theological vocabulary of early Christianity was formed (at least for soteriological terms) on the vocabulary of the Septuagint;[107] and although we might want to hold for a greater influence of the synagogue Greek directly, we would agree that Aramaic has had no great effect. Further, some few Aramaisms may have crept into the synagogue Greek itself just as into the Mixed Hebrew. We note with interest that Wilcox treats with reserve several uses of the Greek verb sometimes held to be Aramaisms in narrative: (a) the participle as indicative and in periphrasis, (b) the redundant auxiliary verb, and (c) the impersonal plural.[108] He finds these representing Aramaisms most often in the discourses and not in the narrative proper.

To the extent that Aramaisms may have entered free composition we have the same difficulty as we have with Hebraisms in distinguishing translation from imitation. Only where the imitation is flawed might we detect a difference. Unfortunately, the dispute about the nature of first-century Palestinian Aramaic noted above makes the discovery of such flaws very difficult.

A Few Old Problems

This theory of synagogue Greek might help to suggest solutions to some of the problems surrounding variations in the text of Luke-Acts. Wensinck found that the text of D demonstrated considerably more Semitism than the Alexandrian text and held that this was evidence for an Aramaic original. But the transmission of Luke-Acts within a community which employed for religious purposes the synagogue Greek and which was influenced by the Greek translation of Jesus' Aramaic sayings might also produce the kind of Semitic variant which Wensinck notes. E. J. Epp[109] has reminded us that the anti-Jewish tendencies of Codex Bezae do not necessarily rule out a Jewish-Christian setting for the codex but may point us toward a group of Jewish-Christians in the midst of a controversy with other Jews.

Aramaic features which might be explained on this model would include such items as the proleptic pronoun (Acts 6:7[D], 7:52[D], 11:27[B, syh]),[110] and the ethic dative (Acts 14:2[D], 15:2[D]).[111] Not to be decided on the basis of Aramaic but Hebrew is the troublesome use of *polis* where proper Greek sense would require *chōra* (Luke 1:39, Acts 12:20 [E, 33]), and one example of the variant *chora* for *polis* (614).[112] Black notes that in Aramaic the determined form *mdynt'* means "city" whereas the undetermined form means "province."[113] No such difference between determined and undetermined states applies to Hebrew

[106]Moulton-Howard, *Grammar II*, p. 413.

[107]*Greek Words and Hebrew Meanings: Studies in the Semantics of Soteriological Terms.*

[108]*Semitisms of Acts*, pp. 121-8.

[109]*The Theological Tendencies of Codex Bezae Catabrigiensis in Acts.*

[110]*Semitisms of Acts*, pp. 128-30.

[111]*Ibid.*, pp. 130-2.

[112]Cf. C. C. Torrey, "Medina and *polis*, and Luke 1:39," *HTR*, XVII (1924), 83-90.

[113]*Aramaic Approach to the Gospels*, p. 12.

mdynh which can take on both meanings.[114] The ambiguity in Hebrew may have introduced a similar ambiguity in the synagogue's use of *polis* and *chōra.*

The interesting suggestion of E. Nestle (mentioned above) that the Bezan variant *kosmon* for *laon* (Acts 2:47) has resulted from reading ᶜ*m* as ᶜ*lm* should be mentioned. Against this conjecture is the fact that nowhere in the Septuagint is *kosmos* ever a translation of ᶜ*lm*. While Septuagint usage might not be an infalliable guide to the synagogue Greek, it is remarkable that the translation *kosmos* never occurs for ᶜ*lm,* and this suggests thst *kosmos* was deemed unsuitable to translate it. M. Black shows due caution in pointing out that the variant may simply derive from a scribe's desire to intensify the impression made by *laos.*[115]

While not a textual problem, we might look again at Torrey's difficulty with the word *oikoumenē* in Luke 2:1 and Acts 11:28.[116] Torrey suggested that the underlying Semitic was *'rṣ* (Hebrew) or *'r*ᶜ*'* (Aramaic) in the special sense "the land (of Israel)." Against this is the evidence of the Septuagint which, indeed, does translate *'rṣ* by *oikoumenē* in Ps. 71:8; Is. 10:23; 13:5, 9; 14:26 (Aℵ'), 27:17; 24:1; 37:16, 18. These translations, however, all occur in passages where *'rṣ* has the sense proper to the Greek word *oiloumene.* Wilcox rightly says that were Torrey correct about the original Semitic, the translation wold have been *gē.*[117]

One place where we might be led to posit an Aramaic original for the Greek text is in Luke 2:20 where for the Greek *ainountes* the Sinaitic Syriac reads *mmllyn* ("speaking"). M. Black accounts for this unusual reading by pointing out that in Palestinian Syriac the verb "to praise" is *hll* (pael), which in participial form would read *mhllyn.*[118] The difference is but a single letter. Black's accounting for the variant is quite convincing, but the change from *h* to *m* probably belongs to the history of the Sinaitic Syriac and offers no evidence for an Aramaic background to Luke 2:20.

No satisfactory explanation yet exists for the difficult variant *ebarunate* for *ernēsasthe* in D at Acts 3:14. Wilcox passes on Torrey's solution that an original *kdybtwn* was misread *kbydtwn.*[119] The main difficulty with this explanation is that *kbd* in the pael is not attested in Aramaic with the necessary meaning although it is so attested in the afel.[120] We note, however, that *kbd* in the pael does have the required sense in Syriac.[121] If we must seek for a solution to this variant from Semitics (and it is by no means sure that this is required), then we might suggest that the interchange of *d* and *b* is more likely in oral transmission than in writing, and the variant could be the result of oral midrash.

---

[114]Jastrow, *Dictionary,* p. 734 a.

[115]*Aramaic Approach to the Gospels,* p. 13.

[116]*Ibid.,* pp. 252-3.

[117]*Our Translated Gospels,* pp. 83-4; *Composition and Date of Acts,* p. 20.

[118]*Semitisms of Acts,* p. 146.

[119]*Ibid.,* p. 141.

[120]Jastrow, *Dictionary,* p. 607a.

[121]J. Payne Smity, *A Compendious Syriac Dictionary,* p. 203a.

Summary and Conclusion

The past century of research has seen us come from an understanding of the language of the Greek Bible as a "language of the Holy Spirit" through a study of it as the Hellenistic vernacular and now back to a judicious treatment of it as a special form of the Koine. In this essay I have attempted to give reasons for thinking that this latter stage in the investigation is on the right track. In particular, I have attempted to draw a parallel between the Mixed Hebrew of the Jewish liturgy and the development of the characteristic Jewish Greek attested in the Septuagint. The language of the Septuagint would be a "synagogue Greek" much like the "synagogue Hebrew" of Palestine.

I believe this emphasis may be helpful in correcting the tendency to identify all Hebraisms as septuagintalisms or as translations, for if they arise naturally from the religious vernacular of the synagogue, then an undue quest for sources or models is unwarrented. Talk about an oral synagogue Greek can, of course, only be theoretical since there is no way to verify or falsify our claims directly. Yet whatever theories are put forward about the Greek of Hellenistic Jews must be related to the written evidence which is at hand, and that evidence seems to me to suggest that Jews spoke no peculiar dialect of Greek in ordinary affairs but did resort to a specialized religious language for cultic purposes.

The time seems to be at hand when we shall be returning to the writing of a grammar of Biblical Greek, and the work of Turner, Beyer, and Martin are important first steps in this undertaking. I believe this kind of research will establish the author of Luke-Acts as being the great master of the Biblical dialect.

Source Criticism
of the Gospel of Luke

Joseph B. Tyson

Source criticism of the Gospel of Luke is inextricably related to the so-called synoptic problem. The similarities among the Gospels of Matthew, Mark, and Luke — similarities of content, order, and wording — have convinced most scholars that there is a literary relationship of some sort among these gospels. The synoptic problem is simply the problem of defining that relationship and thereby accounting for the similarities, as well as the differences, that exist among the synoptic gospels. Thus it will be necessary to refer to various solutions to the synoptic problem in order to understand source critical studies of Luke. But our purpose here is not to trace in an exhaustive fashion the history of research on this problem nor to sketch all of the various proposed solutions. Because of the limited nature of our topic, we shall deal only with certain representative solutions to the synoptic problem which have a bearing on the source criticism of Luke. The solutions that have been selected for discussion are those that are representative of the major viewpoints under current scholarly debate and also present distinctive approaches to the study of Luke. The reader may consult the notes for references to additional viewpoints.[1] After we have

---

[1]Cf. B. C. Butler, *The Originality of St. Matthew;* Pierson Parker, *The Gospel Before Mark;* Xavier Leon-Dufour, "The Synoptic Gospels," *Introduction to the New Testament*, ed. A. Robert and A. Feuillet, pp. 140-324; Antonio Gaboury, *La Structure des Evangiles Synoptique*; P. Benoit and M. -E. Boismard, *Synopse des Quatre Evangiles en Francais;* M. D. Goulder, *Midrash and Lection in Matthew.*

Butler makes Matthew the earliest gospel and Luke dependent on it and on "reminiscences of Mark." Parker believes that there was a document, K, which served as the source for Matthew and Mark. Luke, however, drew on Mark and Q, as in the two-document hypothesis. Leon-Dufour de-emphasizes the literary contact between the

presented the representative hypotheses, we shall turn to a discussion of some of the issues involved in current scholarly debate and research. A brief concluding section makes a suggestion about a new way to study the Gospel of Luke.

Options in the Source Criticism of Luke

The various proposed solutions to the synoptic problem may be approached mainly as proposals about the sources of Luke.

1. *The Two-Document Hypothesis.* The most widely accepted solution to the synoptic problem claims that Mark and Q were sources for the author of the Gospel of Luke. This hypothesis claims that Mark was the earliest of the synoptic gospels and that Matthew and Luke both used it as a source but did so independently of one another, i.e., Matthew and Luke are not directly related. The supposition of Markan priority and the independence of Matthew and Luke do not, however, explain all of the phenomena. There are some sections in Matthew and Luke which are not in Mark but which nevertheless appear to have a literary relationship. These sections are mainly devoted to the teachings of Jesus. In some pericopes there is a high degree of verbal agreement, but there is little agreement between Matthew and Luke on their placement or order. Since Mark is clearly not the source for these sections and since Luke did not get them from Matthew (or vice versa), it is concluded that they came from a source which is no longer extant. That source has been given the designation, Q. In the two-document hypothesis, therefore, Mark and Q are sources for Luke. Of course, there are many sections of Luke which are not accounted for by either of these sources. These are the narratives and sayings which are found only in the third gospel, and it is supposed that Luke obtained them either from (a) a single written source; (b) a group of written sources; (c) oral tradition; or (d) a combination of written and oral sources. The designation L or *Sondergut* (special material) is usually given to this material.

B. H. Streeter's *The Four Gospels*[2] is probably the best known presentation in English of this point of view. Streeter was not the first to propose the two-document hypothesis, but his work represents a kind of culmination and a setting forth of a consensus.[3] In *The Four Gospels*, he laid out the evidence which convinced him that Mark was the earliest gospel and was a source for Matthew and Luke. Because of its importance in the discussion of gospel relationships it is important to refer to this evidence. Streeter presented it in terms of five

---

synoptic gospels and emphasizes the influence of the oral tradition on each one. Gaboury maintains that the synoptic gospels were formed gradually and were dependent on hypothetical primitive sources. Benoit and Boismard use a multiple source theory to explain the origin of all four gospels. Luke, however, is dependent on a pre-canonical edition of Mark and on Proto-Luke. Goulder believes that Matthew wrote a midrash on Mark and that Luke used Mark and Matthew. In respect to Luke, Goulder is indebted to Farrer.

[2]References which follow are to the revised edition of 1930.

[3]A consensus about the two-document hypothesis was an accomplishment of German scholarship in the mid-nineteenth century. One of the most influential figures in that development was H. J. Holtzmann, *Die Synoptischen Evangelien, Ihr Ursprung und Geschichtlichen Charakter.*

arguments for the priority of Mark:

> (1) Matthew reproduces 90% of the subject matter of Mark in language very largely identical with that of Mark; Luke does the same for rather more than half of Mark; (2) In any average section, which occurs in the three Gospels, the majority of the actual words used by Mark are reproduced by Matthew and Luke, either alternately or both together. (3) The relative order of incidents and sections in Mark is in general supported by both Matthew and Luke; where either of them deserts Mark, the other is usually found supporting him . . . (4) The primitive character of Mark is further shown by (a) the use of phrases likely to cause offence, which are omitted or toned down in the other Gospels, (b) roughness of style and grammar, and the preservation of Aramaic words. (5) The way in which Marcan and non-Marcan material is distributed in Matthew and Luke respectively looks as if each had before him the Marcan material *in a single document*, and was faced with the problem of combining this with material from other sources.[4]

We shall have occasion later to comment on some of these arguments, but it is worth noting at this point that the way in which Streeter presented the evidence is, to some extent, prejudicial, i.e., the language presupposes that to which the evidence allegedly points. ("Matthew reproduces 90% of the subject matter of Mark," etc.)[5]

Streeter's fifth observation led him to embrace a further hypothesis which has direct bearing on the source criticism of Luke. In reference to the distribution of Markan and non-Markan material he says: "Matthew's method is to make Mark the framework into which non-Marcan matter is to be fitted, on the principle of joining like to like."[6] Luke's method, he said, is quite different. In general, Luke alternates between large blocks of Markan and non-Markan material. The general situation in Luke may be observed from the following table.

Non-Markan Material	*Markan Material*
Luke 1:1-4:30	
	Luke 4:31-6:19
Luke 6:20-8:3	
	Luke 8:4-9:50
Luke 9:51-18:14	
	Luke 18:15-43
Luke 19:1-27	
	Luke 19:28-22:13

From 22:14 to the end, Markan and non-Markan materials are interwoven. Streeter concludes:

---

[4]Streeter, *Four Gospels*, pp. 151-2.

[5]For a critique of Streeter's arguments, cf. David L. Dungan, "Mark — The Abridgement of Matthew and Luke," *Jesus and Man's Hope*, ed. D. G. Buttrick, I, 51-97.

[6]Streeter, *Four Gospels*, p. 166.

This alternation suggests the influence that the non-Marcan materials, though probably ultimately derived from more than one source, had already been combined into a single written document before they were used by the author of the Third Gospel.[7]

Streeter also states that *"this combined non-Marcan document* was regarded by Luke as his main source and supplied *the framework into which he fitted extracts of Mark."*[8] This is the theory of Proto-Luke. In other terms, Proto-Luke was a document which drew on Q and L as sources. Luke, therefore, combined Proto-Luke with Mark.[9]

2. *The Farrer Hypothesis.* A number of scholars who are convinced that Luke used Mark retain serious doubts about a document such as Q. Although most of those who have doubts still believe that Matthew and Luke are independent, Austin M. Farrer attacked that belief in 1955. In an article entitled, "On Dispensing with Q,"[10] he proposed that consideration be given to a hypothesis which, in some respects, was similar to that of Augustine of Hippo.[11] Farrer began by observing that the Q hypothesis "wholly depends on the incredibility of St. Luke's having read St. Matthew's book."[12] He said that we should start with the assumption that Luke had seen Matthew as well as Mark. If it can be argued that Matthew was in existence before Luke was written, that it had been in existence long enough to have become known, and that Luke could have had access to it, it is only natural to suppose that Luke was acquainted with the Gospel of Matthew. If it proves implausible for us to understand the situation this way, then we may resort to something like the Q hypothesis. But, says Farrer, there is no good reason for believing in the existence of a hypothetical source. For one thing, "there is no independent evidence for anything like Q."[13] Moreover, only if those sections common to Matthew and Luke are distinctive and "cry aloud to be strung together in one order"[14] and make up a complete book, should we then resort to a hypothetical source. But none of this applies. Clearly, the so-called Q material had no unalterable sequence, since Matthew and Luke are almost never in agreement about the location of these passages. Finally, says Farrer, it is inconceivable to have a document without a narrative about the death of Jesus, for the death was central to early Christian faith, and it constitutes the divine act in

---

[7]*Ibid.,* p. 167.

[8]*Ibid.,* pp. 167-8.

[9]The Proto-Luke Hypothesis was adopted also by Vincent Taylor, *Behind the Third Gospel; The First Draft of St. Luke's Gospel; The Gospels: A Short Introduction; The Passion Narrative of St. Luke,* ed. Owen E. Evans. Paul Winter came to a similar view. Cf. his article, "The Treatment of his Sources by the Third Evangelist in Luke 21-24," *ST,* VIII (1954), 138-172.

[10]In *Studies in the Gospels,* ed. D. E. Nineham, pp. 55-88.

[11]Augustine (*De Consensu Evangelistarum* I, 2-3) had said that Mark was the epitomizer of Matthew and that none of the evangelists worked in ignorance of his predecessor. Therefore, Matthew was first; Mark used Matthew; and Luke used both.

[12]Farrer, "Dispensing with Q," p. 56.

[13]*Ibid.,* p. 58.

[14]*Ibid.,* p. 57.

Christ, the event which explains the church's memory of Jesus. Farrer agrees that Luke's special material must be explained as coming from a hypothetical source, but this forms no significant part of his thesis.

As a counter to the Q hypothesis, Farrer claims that we can understand the relationship between Luke and Matthew as one of direct dependence. In his theory, Luke had access to both Matthew and Mark and faced the problem of combining them. He appreciated the distinctive qualities of each — the Markan stress on Jesus as a man of action and the Matthean emphasis on Jesus as teacher.

> He is struck by the special excellence of each and would be happy, if he could, to combine them. St. Mark has narrative vigor and rapidity of movement. St. Matthew has fullness of doctrine and exhortation.[15]

Farrer further claims that Matthew had arranged his material to conform to the Old Testament Hexateuch. Each of the Old Testament books appears in Matthew as a set-piece. Genesis is the genealogy of Jesus. Exodus is found in the baptism, temptation, and in the sermon on the mount, which remind the reader, respectively, of the crossing of the sea, the forty years in the wilderness, and the giving of Torah from Mt. Sinai. The set-piece of Leviticus is found in Matthew 10, the mission charge, and Numbers in chapter 13, which deals with the counting of the harvest and with the criteria for judgment. Matthew 18-19 represents Deuteronomy and deals with princely humility, divorce, and riches. Chapters 24-25 constitute "The Book of Jesus" (Joshua). Luke was, according to Farrer, clearly aware of Matthew's pattern, but he neither adopted it nor rejected it. "He allowed the general pattern to stand, but he redistributed the weight of the teaching, placing as much of it as he could in the Deuteronomic position."[16] The Deuteronomic position in Luke is 10:25-18:30. This is most of Luke's central section, which does indeed consist almost entirely of teaching material, some of which is also found in Matthew. But there is almost no agreement between Matthew and Luke on the sequence of the material. In regard to the other sections in Matthew's Hexateuchal pattern, Luke has not "entirely effaced them," but he has "rubbed them faint."[17]

---

[15]*Ibid.*, p. 67.

[16]*Ibid.*, p. 77. Cf. C. F. Evans, "The Central Section of St. Luke's Gospel," *Studies in the Gospels*, ed. D. E. Nineham, pp. 37-54; Bernard Orchard, *Matthew, Luke and Mark.*

[17]At the end of his essay, Farrer faces a serious objection to the hypothesis that Luke used Matthew. If we assume, as does Farrer, that Luke used both Matthew and Mark, he found some material in Matthew which was not in Mark but was in a certain Markan context. In most cases where Luke chose to use such material in his gospel, he transposed it from the Markan context in which he found it in Matthew. For example, in 8:16-17, Matthew has a narrative about healings at evening, which, according to Farrer, is drawn from Mark 1:32-34. It is followed, in Matthew 8:18-22, by sayings about following Jesus. Luke has these sayings in 9:57-62, in a context totally unrelated to the narrative about healings. This phenomenon occurs frequently enough to constitute a pattern. But Farrer has an explanation for it. He says that Luke followed Mark's arrangement of material up through Mark 9:40 (equivalent to Luke 9:50). In 1:1-9:50, Luke draws very little material solely from Matthew, and for what he uses he preserves the context he finds in Matthew. But when Luke deserts the Markan material at 9:50, he goes back over Matthew 3-18, "quarrying these chapters" for teaching material. When he does so, he has no trouble spotting Markan

3. *The Griesbach Hypothesis.* Farrer believed that Luke used both Matthew and Mark. But is it possible to understand Luke as dependent only on Matthew and the Lukan *Sondergut*? The Griesbach hypothesis, as interpreted by William R. Farmer, says yes. The theory, named for the eighteenth-century scholar Johann J. Griesbach, was reintroduced into scholarly debate in 1964 by Farmer.[18] The hypothesis as it is presently understood is a modification of the original. Griesbach himself understood Mark to be a conflation of Matthew and Luke, and he believed that Matthew was the earliest gospel, but he was uncertain about the relationship between Matthew and Luke. Farmer, however, combined the originial Griesbach theory with the claim that Luke was dependent on Matthew. Thus the Griesbach hypothesis now runs: Matthew was first; Luke used Matthew; Mark used both.

Farmer's book, *The Synoptic Problem*, was largely a review of the history of research on the synoptic problem and a critical appraisal of the achievement of a scholarly consensus on the two-document hypothesis. In the latter part of the book, however, he developed an argument for the Griesbach hypothesis and showed how one might understand the process by which Mark made use of Matthew and Luke.

Farmer's argument for the Griesbach theory begins with his exclusion of hypothetical sources which explain similarities between independent gospels. Farmer necessarily agrees that Luke had access to some material which came from a non-extant source, but this recognition has no real function in the Griesbach hypothesis. Farmer also recognizes that certain documents may once have been used and later disappeared, but he maintains that any theory that depends on the use of hypothetical documents to explain literary relationships between two documents is weaker than one that does not. In any event, says Farmer, first consideration should be given to those theories which do not depend on hypothetical sources. He then shows that there is a limited number of ways in which the relationships among any three documents may be conceived. Actually, only one kind of relationship is viable in the case of the synoptic gospels, one which understands that the first document was used by the second, and both the first and the second were used by the third. The reason is that "there are agreements between any two of the Synoptic Gospels against the third."[19] No conception of the relationships among the gospels is viable that does not explain these phenomena of agreement against. If, for example, Matthew and

---

material, for he has already used it. Thus, Luke "has no strict rule against Marcan material in his teaching section, but only against used material" ("Dispensing with Q," p. 83). Farrer claims that this is an adequate explanation of Luke's treatment of Matthew 3-18, but he admits that it will not explain his treatment of Matthew 19-25, since Luke had not yet skimmed off the Markan material in those chapters. Since Luke has incorporated some material from Matthew 19-25 in his central section, the problem must be faced. But, says Farrer, it is not a difficult problem, because Luke used only six sections from Matthew 19-25, and five of the six are "so whole and single, that they come away clean from their settings" (*Ibid.*, p. 84). In the sixth (Luke 17:22-37), "St. Luke must be credited with measuring the Marcan text against St. Matthew's augmented version of it, before he reaches the place" (*Ibid.*).

[18]William R. Farmer, *The Synoptic Problem.*

[19]*Ibid.*, p. 209.

Luke are independent of one another but dependent on Mark, we cannot account for the fact that they jointly agreed to omit a Markan expression and agreed on the expression to substitute for it. Thus, only that kind of relationship in which there is interdependence is adequate to explain the relationship of the synoptic gospels. If this is so, the crucial question is: Which was the third gospel to be written? Farmer claims that it is Mark, and he has two major reasons: (a) the character of agreement and disagreement in the sequence of material; and (b) the character of the agreements of Matthew and Luke against Mark. On the matter of sequence Farmer writes:

> With very few exceptions, which are no more difficult for one hypothesis than for any other, the order of material in Mark never departs from the order of material common to Matthew and Luke. Therefore, Matthew and Luke almost never agree in order against Mark. If Mark were third, this fact would be readily explained by the reasonable assumption that the Evangelist writing third had no chronological information apart from that which he found in Matthew and Luke, or that if he did, he preferred not to interrupt the order of events to which these two Gospels bore concurrent testimony.[20]

The character of the minor agreements of Matthew and Luke against Mark adds to the probability that Mark is third. These agreements, says Farmer, "tend to be minor in extent, inconsequential in substance, and sporadic in occurence."[21] They are just the kinds of agreements which any person writing third would tend to ignore. In this situation, it would not have been possible for Mark to have copied *all* agreements, and it is reasonable to expect that he would omit insignificant ones.

Farmer's position, therefore, is that if we are to give prior consideration to theories which do not require hypothetical sources to explain common material, the most viable solution is one that understands Mark to be a conflation of Matthew and Luke. Furthermore, if we are to discount the possibility of a non-extant source, it is necessary to say that there is a direct relationship between Matthew and Luke. In this case, says Farmer, both internal and external evidence indicate that it is more likely that Luke used Matthew than that Matthew used Luke. So we have Farmer's version of the Griesbach hypothesis: Matthew wrote first; Luke used Matthew; Mark used both Matthew and Luke.

4. *The Lindsey Hypothesis.* The view of Robert L. Lindsey places Luke first among the synoptic gospels and understands it as dependent upon two hypothetical documents, a primitive narrative (PN) and the document Q. The document to which Lindsey gives the designation PN is a Greek translation of a Hebrew or Aramaic original. It was, according to Lindsey, a basis for all three synoptics. His full theory, therefore, states that: (1) Luke combined PN and Q; (2) Mark combined PN and Luke; (3) Matthew used PN, Q, and Mark.

Lindsey first made his suggestions in 1969, in the introduction to his *Hebrew Translation of the Gospel of Mark.*[22] The heart of the theory is the priority of Luke

---

[20]*Ibid.*, p. 212.

[21]*Ibid.*, p. 216.

[22]Cf. *A New Approach to the Synoptic Gospels;* "A Modified Two-Document Theory of the Synoptic Dependence and Interdependence," *NovT*, VI (1963), 239-63.

to both Matthew and Mark. Lindsey was apparently led to the theory by his impression that Luke was more easily translatable into Hebrew than either of the others. He said that he had come to his initial discovery in the process of studying Mark 6:14-16 and parallels, the pericope about Herod Antipas' opinion of Jesus. Luke 9:7 says that Herod was perplexed, while Matt 14:2 says that he was sure that Jesus was John the Baptist returned from the dead. In Luke, Herod is confused; in Matthew, certain. But "Mark *combines* the story of Luke's *confused* Herod with a story of a Herod who is *certain!*"[23] Lindsey claims that, in this passage, it is not possible to conclude that Matthew and Luke independently used Mark, for there are some agreements of Matthew and Luke against Mark. He states:

> Either Mark had combined the texts of Matthew and Luke or he had combined the text of his proto-narrative with that of Luke. There were excellent reasons to reject the first alternative. The only possibility was the second. Mark had used Luke's text in writing his Gospel![24]

A confirmation of his theory of Lukan priority comes from what Lindsey calls the Markan cross-factor. This factor may be observed by examining the differences between material in all three gospels and that only in Matthew and Luke. In the former there is a high rate of agreement between Matthew and Luke on the sequence of parallel pericopes but a low rate of verbal agreement. In that material found only in Matthew and Luke, the opposite is the case: a high rate of verbal agreement and a low rate of agreement on sequence. Lindsey observes that this is a difficult fact to account for on the basis of the traditional two-documents hypothesis. It requires one to believe that Matthew and Luke independently came to the conclusion that Mark's sequence was good but not his wording and that the wording but not the sequence of Q was to be followed. To Lindsey, a more credible solution is to introduce the primitive narrative as one of the sources for all three gospels. On this assumption, it is then possible to say that all three synoptic gospels followed the sequence of the primitive narrative. Luke also followed the wording, but Mark intentionally attempted to find synonyms. Matthew, who had access to both the primitive narrative and Mark, had no trouble following the sequence, since both his sources agreed on that, but he had to make a decision about the wording, sometimes siding with Mark and sometimes with the primitive narrative. In their use of Q, Matthew and Luke faced the problem of fitting it into the framework they had previously used, so they differed in regard to sequence. But, following their usual habit, they differed very little on wording.

Although there are variations of each of the theories we have examined, these four represent distinctive approaches which affect the source criticism of Luke.[25]

---

[23]Lindsey, *Hebrew Translation,* p. 31.

[24]*Ibid.*

[25]Cf. e.g., Robert Morgenthaler, *Statistische Synopse.* Morgenthaler accepts the two-document hypothesis but believes that Luke became acquainted with the Gospel of Matthew in the last stages of his work. Theodore R. Rosché ("The Words of Jesus and the Future of the 'Q' Hypothesis," *JBL*, LXXIX [1960], 210-20) accepts the priority of Mark and its use by Matthew and Luke, but he concludes that there is no evidence for the existence of Q. Cf. also A. W. Argyle, "Evidence for the View that St. Luke Used St. Matthew's Gospel," *JBL*, LXXXIII (1964), 390-96; R. T. Simpson, "The Major Agreements of Matthew and Luke

It is clearly the case that the two-document hypothesis is the most widely accepted among scholars who attend to synoptic research. But the increasing attention that is paid to alternative solutions attests to the fact that there are significant problems relating to the relationships of the gospels and that these problems have no obvious solutions.

Issues in the Source Criticism of Luke

We turn now to a critical analysis of the hypotheses treated above.

The Lindsey hypothesis is the most radical of the four and probably has the least support among scholars. One of the most interesting features of his theory is the Markan cross-factor. Lindsey had observed that Matthew and Luke are in general agreement with one another and with Mark on the order of material which all three share (triple material), but they are rarely in agreement on the order of material which is found only in their gospels (double material). But in terms of verbal agreement, the opposite is the case. Matthew and Luke have a higher rate of agreement in the double material than in the triple.

Lindsey is surely correct in what he says about agreements. But his treatment of disagreements, both those of wording and those of order, is misleading. Take the matter of verbal agreement. If Matthew and Luke independently used Mark, it is possible that Matthew followed Mark's wording much more faithfully than Luke did. In that event, Matthew and Luke would disagree significantly in respect to wording. Or it is possible that both followed Mark's wording fairly faithfully but still disagreed with one another in the way in which they followed Mark. In a forthcoming study of verbal agreements, T. R. W. Longstaff and I are able to show that, in the material in all three gospels, Matthew agrees with Mark in about 55% of the words he has in the triple material and that Luke agrees with Mark in about 46% of the words.[26] In this material, Matthew and Luke agree with each other about 37% of the time.[27] These figures do not show that Matthew and Luke *agreed* that Mark's wording was bad. In fact, the reduced rate of agreement between Matthew and Luke is entirely what we would expect in this situation. Two writers who are using the same source will be found to agree more with the source than with each other.

On the matter of disagreements in order, much the same is true. If two documents follow a third and disagree on the order of materials, it is only necessary to say that *one* of the secondary documents was dissatisfied with the order of the source, *not both*. It is conceivable that Luke was faithful to the order of Q and that Matthew was not, and in that event the two gospels would be in disagreement with one another on the order of the materials in the double tradition.[28]

Against Mark," *NTS*, XII (1965/66), 273-84.

[26]*Synoptic Abstract,* to be published by Biblical Research Associates, Wooster, Ohio.

[27]Similar figures are given by A. M. Honoré, "A Statistical Study of the Synoptic Problem," *NovT*, X (1968), 95-147.

[28]This is the view of Vincent Taylor, "The Original Order of 'Q'," *New Testament Essays*, pp. 95-118; and "The Order of Q," *Ibid.*, pp. 90-4.

Further, Lindsey appears to have overstated the difference in the rate of verbal agreement between the triple and the double material. Scholars who have analyzed verbal agreements among the synoptic gospels have found that the rate of agreement in the double material is from 6-9% higher than in the triple.[29] Of course, there are pericopes in which the agreement rate is very high, but the difference in rate between the two kinds of material is not as striking to others as it appears to be to Lindsey. Unfortunately, he did not offer clear statistics on the matter and stated only that the rate of agreement between Matthew and Luke in pericopes found in all three gospels was often as low as 40%. Lacking citation of data, we can only judge that Lindsey has overstated the significance of the difference in the rate of verbal agreement.

In addition, the material that is parallel in Matthew and Luke and only there consists mostly of words of Jesus. It can be shown that there is generally a higher rate of agreement in reports of Jesus' teaching than in other categories of material. This is the case whether we compare Matthew with Mark, Mark with Luke, or Matthew with Luke.[30] Thus, the 6-9% difference in the rate of agreement is easily accounted for by reference to the nature of the material.

While Lindsey correctly assesses the situation in regard to the order of pericopes in the gospels, he has overstated the significance of the difference in the rate of verbal agreement. But this means that there is no Markan cross-factor. Matthew and Luke tend to agree with one another and with Mark on the order of pericopes in the triple tradition but not to agree on the order in the double tradition. This has been a commonly observed phenomenon, and it is about all that can be said.

Another factor that is important for Lindsey relates to language. He feels that the relative ease with which Luke can be translated into Hebrew provides evidence for Lukan priority. This might qualify as evidence if there is reason to think that a Hebrew document somehow lies behind our gospels. But has Lindsey given us good grounds for believing this to be the case? Does his ability to translate Luke into Hebrew require us to agree that there was a primitive Hebrew text? His claim runs counter to a number of observations about the semitic character of Mark and of Matthew.[31] Of course, Lindsey does not claim that the semitic character of Luke alone proves its priority. Rather, in concentrating on certain non-semitic stereotyped phrases frequently found in Mark and infrequently used in non-parallel passages in the Luke-Acts corpus, he asserts that Mark added them to his Lukan source. But is it more reasonable to think that Mark added them than to think that Luke eliminated them, or most of them? One can hardly avoid the impression that Lindsey opted for the view that Mark added them because he found the idea of a primitive Hebrew gospel

---

[29]Cf. Honore, "Statistical Study."

[30]Cf. Morgenthaler, *Statistische Synopse*, pp. 66-8, 82-3. Morgenthaler used three classifications for the material in the synoptic gospels: non-discourse material; words of Jesus and John the Baptist; and words of other characters. His calculations of verbal agreement show that, in every comparison (Matthew with Mark; Matthew with Luke; Mark with Luke), there is a higher rate of agreement in the discourse material than in the non-discourse material.

[31]Cf. e.g., E. P. Sanders, *The Tendencies of the Synoptic Tradition.*

congenial. If Lindsey is right about the possibility of translating Luke into Hebrew, the implication of Lukan priority is neither the only nor the most reasonable conclusion one might draw.

The issues which are related to the other theories — the two-document, the Farrer, and the Griesbach — are not so easily faced. In effect, however, it is possible to say that, with reference to the source criticism of Luke, the key issue is that of the relationship between Matthew and Luke.[32]

Proponents of the two-document hypothesis support their claim that Matthew and Luke were independent by citing not only the differences between the two in their arrangement of material but also the differences in their use of such important things as the birth stories, the genealogies, and the resurrection appearances. Farrer's attempt to find traces of a Matthean Hexateuchal pattern in Luke is not successful. He has finally to admit that Luke neither accepted nor rejected Matthew's pattern. If Luke was aware of Matthew's pattern, he removed Genesis from its first position, split up Exodus, enlarged Deuteronomy, and "rubbed faint" the rest. Farrer's analysis might be reasonable if we knew that Luke used Matthew, but it hardly provides evidence for his hypothesis. To say that Luke has rubbed Matthew's pattern faint really means that Matthew's pattern is not perceivable or only barely perceivable in Luke. If so, it can hardly serve as evidence that Luke used Matthew.

But the most important arguments in the debate about the independence of Matthew and Luke have been the argument about order and that about the minor agreements against Mark.

It is notable that Streeter and Farmer describe the same pattern of agreement and disagreement on the order of materials in the synoptic gospels and that they come to opposing conclusions. Streeter noted that Matthew and Luke almost never agree against Mark on the placement of a section which they share with Mark. He felt that this was convincing evidence that Mark offered to the other two gospels an outline which both generally followed and one almost always followed. Farmer felt, however, that this phenomenon can better be explained by putting Mark last rather than first. If Mark is first and Matthew and Luke are independent, then how can we understand Luke's procedure of departing from Mark's order *only* when Matthew followed it? But if Mark is third, then we can understand his procedure more readily. Mark followed the order of Matthew and Luke when the two agreed. When they did not agree, he followed the order of one or the other. At the very least, Farmer has shown that observations about order in the synoptic gospels do not inevitably dictate one conclusion.

E. P. Sanders has given serious consideration to the argument about order, and he claims that it does not support the independence of Matthew and Luke.[33] He took the statement about order as it was originally formulated by F. H. Woods

---

[32]The question of Proto-Luke is of secondary importance, for if it can be shown that Luke depended on Matthew, there is no necessity to suppose the existence of a document such as Proto-Luke.

[33]"The Argument from Order and the Relationship between Matthew and Luke," *NTS*, XV (1965), 249-61.

in 1886.[34] The important statements are reformulated by Sanders as follows:

(1) Both Matthew and Luke support Mark's order the greater part of the time.

(2) If Matthew or Luke disagrees with Mark's relative order, the other supports it. This point has corollaries:

(a) Matthew and Luke never place a Marcan passage in the same context which is different from its context in Mark.

(b) With one exception (Mark 3:31-35) no Marcan passage occurs in different contexts in all three gospels.

(c) No Marcan passage is ever rearranged be either Matthew or Luke while being omitted by the other. (It is not usually recognized that this last is a corollary to Woods's point three, but it is. If Matthew departs from Mark's order and Luke omits, neither has supported Mark's order; while the claim is that *one always supports Mark's order* except where both omit).

(3) Matthew and Luke never agree in the placement of Q material relative to Marcan material.[35]

Sanders states the problem as follows:

If Matthew and Luke generally agree with Mark (but not with each other against Mark) in the arrangement of the Marcan material, but disagree in the arrangement of the Q material, there is really only one explanation. Matthew and Luke have used two sources independently. Both generally followed the order of one source, but one or the other or both used the material from the second source without regard to its order. But any agreements, even minor ones, between Matthew and Luke on a point of order which cannot be attributed to their independent use of Mark and Q will argue strongly that there must have been some other contact between the first and third gospels.[36]

Sanders feels that scholars have had their attention drawn to the phenomenon of order by an examination of pericopes as defined by Tischendorf. But there are other ways to define pericopes, and if we look at units smaller than those defined by Tischendorf, we will discover certain agreements which are not explained by the hypothesis that Matthew and Luke are independent of one another. Thus, "the statement that both Matthew and Luke generally support Mark's order is a great over-simplification."[37] Sanders says:

It might lead to better comprehension of the phenomenon if we said that both Matthew and Luke support Mark's order three-fourths of the time after the entry into Jerusalem, but less than half the time before the entry, rather than that the greater part of Mark's order is confirmed by both Matthew and Luke.[38]

Sanders finds that Matthew and Luke do agree against Mark on the order of at

---

[34]"The Origin and Mutual Relations of the Synoptic Gospels," *Studia Biblica et Ecclesiastica*, ed. S. R. Driver, T. K. Cheyne, and W. Sanday, II, 60.

[35]Sanders, "Argument from Order," pp. 251-2. Sanders uses the term, 'Marcan material,' "to refer to a passage in Mark which is also in Matthew and/or Luke, without prejudice as to whether Matthew and Luke copied it directly from our Mark or not. Similarly, I [Sanders] use 'Q' only to indicate the tradition common to Matthew and Luke alone." (p. 251n).

[36]*Ibid.*, p. 252.

[37]*Ibid.*, p. 253.

[38]*Ibid.*, p. 254.

least four and perhaps as many as seven occasions. He finds five pericopes which are placed differently by each of the three evangelists, and he finds four places where one gospel relocates a Markan parallel while the other omits it. He also finds several places where Matthew and Luke agree on the location of Q material in Markan contexts. To Sanders, these observations weaken the hypothesis that Matthew and Luke are independent. He concludes: "The simplest explanation is that one knew the other; evidence not discussed here makes it likely that Luke used Matthew."[39]

Whichever interpretation appears to be more persuasive, we must agree that the character of agreements and disagreements in the order of pericopes does not require the explanation that Matthew and Luke are independent. But neither does it require the supposition that Matthew was a source for Luke.

The other argument which is used in current debates is that about the minor agreements of Matthew and Luke against Mark.[40] All scholars recognize that there are such agreements, and Streeter himself was aware of the potential problem which they might cause for the theory that Matthew and Luke are independent. He felt, however, that they could be easily explained. Some, he said, are irrelevant, and some are deceptive. Others occurred in the process of manuscript copying. Still others require the explanation that, at some points, Mark and Q overlapped. In those places Matthew and Luke combined Mark and Q, and sometimes both used the reading in Q rather than that in Mark.[41] Other scholars, such as Farrer and Farmer, are unpersuaded by these explanations, and they see the agreements as evidence of Luke's dependence on Matthew.[42] Farmer feels that it is precisely the minor, inconsequential, and sporadic character of the agreements that argues both for Luke's dependence on Matthew and for Mark's conflation of the other two gospels.

The major arguments, therefore, are reversible. The phenomena relating to order and the minor agreements may be understood as evidence for or against Luke's dependence on Matthew. We, therefore, stand at a time at which it must be said that *we have no dependable knowledge about the sources of Luke.*

It is possible, however, that some progress will be made toward a solution of the source problem by the application to individual synoptic pericopes of certain criteria which are intended to identify primary and secondary material. The criteria which are most frequently used were set forth by W. R. Farmer:

> That form of a particular tradition found in the Gospels, which reflects an extra-Palestinian, or non-Jewish provenance is to be adjudged secondary to a form of the same tradition which reflects a Palestinian or Jewish provenance.[43]

---

[39]*Ibid.*, p. 261.

[40]To date, the most comprehensive list of these agreements appears in Frans Neirynck, *The Minor Agreements of Matthew and Luke Against Mark.*

[41]Cf. Streeter, *Four Gospels*, pp. 293-332.

[42]B. C. Butler (*Originality*) built much of his case on agreements against. He said that there were agreements of each pair of gospels against the third, but there were fewer against Matthew than against either of the other two. He, therefore, claimed that Matthew was the earliest gospel, on the ground that writers who mutually but independently use a source will tend not to agree with one another against the source.

[43]Farmer, *Synoptic Problem*, p. 228.

> That form of a tradition which exhibits explanatory redactional glosses, and expansions aimed to make the tradition more applicable to the needs of the Church, is to be adjudged secondary to a form of the tradition which is free of such redactional glosses and expansions.[44]
> That form of a tradition which exhibits words or phrases characteristic of a redactor whose hand is clearly traceable elsewhere in the same Gospel is to be adjudged secondary to a form of the same tradition which is free of such words and phrases.[45]

Farmer also commended six principles which had originally been formulated by E. D. Burton:

> The following he regarded as evidences of secondary character: "(1) manifest misunderstanding of what stands in one document on the part of the writer of the other; (2) insertion by one writer of material not in the other, and clearly interrupting the course of thought or symmetry of plan in the other; (3) clear omission from one document of matter which was in the other, the omission of which destroys the connection; (4) insertion of matter the motive for which can be clearly seen in the light of the author's general aim, while no motive can be discovered for its omission by the author if he had had it in his source; (5) vice versa omission of matter traceable to the motive natural to the writer when the insertion (of the same matter in the other Gospel) could not thus be accounted for: (6) alterations of other kinds which conform the matter to the general method or tendency of the author."[46]

The *Journal of Biblical Literature* has recently carried two articles which have attempted to apply these criteria to a selected group of synoptic pericopes.[47] The two articles came to opposite conclusions. Charles Talbert and Edgar McKnight conclude:

> The results of our investigation have pointed to instances where Mark seems prior to Matthew, where Mark seems prior to Luke, where Luke seems prior to Matthew, *and where Luke and Matthew seem independent of one another.*[48]

George Buchanan felt that this conclusion was not justified and that equally good arguments could be offered in support of the Griesbach hypothesis.[49] The importance of these two articles is that they have shown that it is possible to approach the gospels without presupposing the correct solution to the synoptic problem and to compare parallel accounts in hopes of finding directional indicators, i.e., signs which show in which direction things are moving; thus, which is the earlier of two accounts. Their failure to agree means that scholars must face up to the fact that certainty in this matter is impossible, and they must

---

[44]*Ibid.*

[45]*Ibid.*

[46]*Ibid.*, p. 229. The reference is to E. D. Burton, *Some Principles of Literary Criticism and their Application to the Synoptic Problem.*

[47]Charles H. Talbert and Edgar V. McKnight, "Can the Griesbach Hypothesis Be Falsified?" *JBL*, XCI (1972), 338-68; George W. Buchanan, "Has the Griesbach Hypothesis Been Falsified?" *JBL*, XCIII (1974), 550-72.

[48]Talbert and McKnight, "Griesbach," pp. 367-8. Italics mine.

[49]Buchanan, "Griesbach," pp. 571-2.

begin to talk seriously about the more probable and the less probable solutions.[50]

The studies also indicate the need to test the proposed criteria. In his first edition of *The Synoptic Problem,* Farmer had included a principle which said, in effect, that secondary documents tend to be more specific than primary ones.[51] But in 1969 E. P. Sanders showed that the evidence is mixed in this regard.[52] Farmer was persuaded to abandon this criterion, and he omitted it in his second edition of 1976.[53] All of the returns are not in on the appropriateness of the other criteria, but enough is now known to show that there is a need for an intensive search for appropriate criteria.

Source Criticism and Redaction Criticism

Source criticism is not an end in itself. At best it is a tool which might be used in the interpretation of documents and in related historical studies. In the past two decades, redaction criticism has proven to be a highly useful method of interpreting documents such as the Gospel of Luke. It focuses attention on the work of the individual evangelists. They are pictured as redactors, i.e., as editors who make use of sources. As editors, they select the material they wish to use, arrange it in a particular order, and form transitions between sections. Perhaps they alter some of the expressions which they find in the source material, and they may include explanations, interpretations, or applications which they join to the source material. So, redaction critics presume that we can see the evangelist at work in his editorial activity. Thus, the interpretation of the Gospel of Luke is built upon an understanding of his redactional activity.

It is obvious that the redaction criticism of Luke can be done best if we know what source or sources he used. We can then separate source from redaction and see how Luke has worked. Because the two-document hypothesis has been the generally accepted solution to the synoptic problem, it should not be surprising to find that almost all redaction critical work on the Gospel of Luke has been done on the assumption that Luke used Mark, Q, and L. Perhaps the most influential work in this regard has been that of Hans Conzelmann, who claimed that Luke worked with a certain understanding of salvation history.[54] Other scholars have paid attention to the way in which Luke used his special material (L).[55] The treatment of the arrest and trial of Jesus has also come in for special

---

[50]Cf. M. Eugene Boring, "The Unforgivable Sin Logion Mark 3:28-29/Matt 12:31-32/Luke 17:10: Formal Analysis and History of the Tradition," *NovT*, XVIII (1976), 258-79. Boring begins without presupposing a solution to the source problem and proceeds to question the pericope in the effort to understand the literary and pre-literary relationships. Cf. also William O. Walker, Jr., "A Method for Identifying Redactional Passages in Matthew on Functional and Linguistic Grounds," *CBQ*, XXXIX (1977), 76-93. Walker's article is a stage in the identification of redactional characteristics in Matthew.

[51]Farmer, *Synoptic Problem*, p. 228.

[52]Cf. Sanders, *Tendencies.*

[53]See his note in the 1976 edition, p. 228.

[54]*The Theology of St. Luke.* For a critique, cf. Charles H. Talbert, "The Redaction Critical Quest for Luke the Theologian," in *Jesus and Man's Hope*, I, 171-222.

[55]Cf. e.g., Friedrich Rehkopf, *Die lukanische Sonderquelle.*

consideration, especially by scholars who believe that Luke had access to a non-Markan source for this material.[56] Still other scholars, notably Vincent Taylor, have studied Luke on the assumption that he combined Mark with Proto-Luke.[57] In all of these redaction critical studies, dependence on the two-document hypothesis is clear. In the near future we may expect scholars who have broken wiht the two-document hypothesis to produce redaction critical studies which rely on an alternative hypothesis.[58]

But if it is truly the case that we do not have reliable information about the sources of Luke and that we are unable to agree on the application of accepted criteria to the problem of sources, then either we must suspend redaction critical work on Luke or else reconceive it.[59]

A possibility for reconceiving redaction criticism is to understand Luke holistically. This means that we can treat Luke as an author — not only of the Gospel but also of the Acts — and approach his product as an intentional unity. Redaction criticism, then, would not simply concentrate on the editorial activity of Luke but would range over the entirety of his literary product. In brief, it would involve approaching Luke's gospel as if we knew nothing about his sources. Since we do not know anything, this would appear to be not only a necessary but also a legitimate approach. We could ask such questions as: Why has Luke arranged his material in the way that we have it here? What attention has he given to plot and characterization? How has he used his geographical and chronological references? What kind of readership has he presumed? Clearly these are questions which literary critics generally ask of documents, so we ought to be able to draw on their experience.[60] Of course, we cannot pretend to be blind to the existence of parallels in Matthew and Mark (and John), but we need not approach them as possible or alleged sources.

Such a holistic approach is new in gospel studies, although it has a tradition deeply rooted in humanistic studies. It is perfectly appropriate so long as we remain clear that its aim is to understand a literary document. It is not clear how or if a holistic study will lead to a resolution of the source problem. If it does we should regard that as a fringe benefit, for the very effort to understand the Gospel of Luke has intrinsic value.

---

[56]Cf. e.g., Vincent Taylor, *The Passion Narrative of St. Luke;* Paul Winter, *On the Trial of Jesus;* David R. Catchpole, *The Trial of Jesus;* Gerhard Schneider, *Verleugnung, Verspottung, und Verhör Jesu nach Lukas 22:54-71.*

[57]Cf. above, note 9.

[58]W. R. Farmer included some "Notes for a History of the Redaction of Synoptic Tradition in Mark," in his *Synoptic Problem*, pp. 233-83.

[59]Cf. Charles H. Talbert, "Shifting Sands: The Recent Study of the Gospel of Luke," *Int*, XXX (1976), 381-95. Talbert wrote: "Employing Mark as a control today is about as compelling as using Colossians and Second Thessalonians to describe Paul's theology" (p. 393). "The issue before us today is, How can one study the distinctive perspective of the Third Evangelist without assuming any source theories? In this regard the problem is the same as that faced with Mark and John all along" (p. 394).

[60]Cf. e.g., Roland M. Frye, "A Literary Perspective for the Criticism of the Gospels," *Jesus and Man's Hope* II, 193-221. Further suggestions will be made by Frye in a book to appear soon, published by Trinity University Press. The book will also contain responses and critical analyses of Frye's paper.

The Agreements That Exist Between John and Acts

F. Lamar Cribbs

Several recent comparative studies of the Gospels of Luke and John have disclosed the existence of a considerably larger number of verbal parallels between these two Gospels than had heretofore generally been recognized.[1] Thus E. Osty has identified over forty Lukan agreements with John in their passion narratives alone,[2] S. I. Buse has observed that while the passion agreements between Matthew and John are neither frequent nor decisive, those between Luke and John in their passion narratives are both numerous and quite exact,[3] Pierson Parker has claimed that John's "sharings with the Third Evangelist are enormous in their number and range,"[4] while Raymond E. Brown has written that some of the Lukan/Johannine passion agreements are "too precise to be accidental."[5]

These comparative studies of Luke and John are seemingly producing a

---

[1]Cf. e.g., E. Osty, "Les points de contact entre le recit de la passion dans saint Luc et dans saint Jean," *RSR*, XXXIX (1951), 146-54; S. I. Buse, "St. John and the Passion Narratives of St. Matthew and St. Luke," *NTS*, VII (1960-61), 65-76; Pierson Parker, "Luke and the Fourth Evangelist," *NTS*, IX (1962-63), 317-36; Raymond E. Brown, *The Gospel According to John XIII-XXI*, pp. 787-91, 805-96; F. L. Cribbs, "St. Luke and the Johannine Tradition," *JBL*, XC (1971), 422-50.

[2]"Les points de contact entre le recit de la passion dans saint Luc et dans saint Jean," pp. 151-4.

[3]"St. John and the Passion Narratives of St. Matthew and St. Luke," pp. 73-6.

[4]"Luke and the Fourth Evangelist," p. 335.

[5]*The Gospel According to John XIII-XXI*, p. 791.

developing awareness of the large number of verbal/conceptual agreements that exist between these two Gospels.[6] These numerous Lukan/Johannine agreements have not only led certain writers to posit some form of the hypothesis that Luke may have been acquainted with some of the traditions (either written or oral) that possibly lie back of the Gospel of John,[7] but they have also caused certain other writers to suggest that Luke may have been influenced by some *early form* of the developing Johannine tradition[8] in the composing of his Gospel. Thus E. Osty, on the basis of a number of Johannisms that he had identified in chs. 22-24 of Luke, has suggested that Luke may have been familiar with some form of the Johannine passion tradition.[9]   Similarly, Raymond E. Brown, in commenting on the many close Lukan/Johannine agreements that exist in their passion narratives, has written that "it is not impossible that Luke knew an early form of the developing Johannine tradition."[10] Then V. Taylor, in his recent study of the Lukan passion narrative, has observed that in a number of places in chs. 22-24 of Luke (e.g., Luke 22:3,53b; 23:6-15,22,53; 24:36) "some knowledge of the Johannine tradition is implied."[11] And in our recent studies of the agreements that exist between Luke and John,[12] we found a number of phenomena in Luke which seemingly suggest that the Third Evangelist, in the writing of his Gospel, was possibly influenced by some early form of the Johannine tradition rather than vice versa.[13] So before extending our comparative study of Luke and John to the Book of Acts, let us summarize some of the phenomena we have identified in our recent comparative examinations of these two gospels.

Among the phenomena we discovered in these studies, we regard the following as being especially significant.

*The existence of some fifty verbal parallels between Luke and John,[14] some

---

[6]Cf. e.g., M. -E. Boismard, "Saint Luc et la redaction du quatrieme evangile," *RB*, LXIX (1962), 185-211; *The Jerusalem Bible,NT*, 142; Robert T. Fortna, *The Gospel of Signs: A Reconstruction of the Narrative Source Underlying the Fourth Gospel,* pp. 75-85, 122-32.

[7]Cf. e.g., Pierson Parker, "Luke and the Fourth Evangelist," pp. 334-6; Robert T. Fortna, *The Gospel of Signs,* pp. 47, 124-9; Edwin D. Freed and Russell B. Hunt, "Fortna's Signs-Source in John," *JBL,* XCIV (1975), 574-9.

[8]There not only exists a sizable amount of evidence that behind the Gospel of John there stand historical traditions of considerable antiquity (C. H. Dodd, *Historical Tradition in the Fourth Gospel,* pp. 180, 243-6, 311-33; *The Jerusalem Bible,* NT, p. 142), but there also seems to exist a rather general consensus that the Fourth Gospel had a long literary history in the course of its development. Thus Frank M. Cross, Jr. ("The Dead Sea Scrolls," *IB,* XII, 662) could write of the "elaborate literary history" of St. John. Raymond E. Brown (*The Gospel According to John I-XII,* pp. xxxiv-xxxix) could posit five stages in the composition of the Fourth Gospel covering several decades. James M. Robinson ("The Miracle Sources of John," *JAAR,* XXXIX (1971), 339-48) could write of "the Johannine trajectory."

[9]"Les points de contact entre le recit de la passion dans saint Luc et dans saint Jean," pp. 146-54.

[10]*The Gospel According to John XIII-XXI*, p. 791.

[11]*The Passion Narrative of St. Luke*, pp. 44, 87-90, 101.

[12]"St. Luke and the Johannine Tradition," pp. 422-50; "A Study of the Contacts That Exist Between St. Luke and St. John," *SBL 1973 Seminar papers,* II, 1-93.

[13]Cf. "St. Luke and the Johannine Tradition," pp. 447-50.

[14]Cf. our study, "The Contacts That Exist Between St. Luke and St. John," pp. 88-90.

of which exhibit almost verbatim agreement between these two evangelists.[15]

*While Luke rarely disagrees with the factual information found in Mark/Matthew in any of those fifty-seven pericopes from the triple tradition that have no parallel in John,[16] in the 143 verses that comprise "the quadruple tradition"[17] there exist some forty instances in which Luke sides with the information found in John rather than with the differing data to be found in both Mark and Matthew[18] as well as some thirty additional instances in which Luke agrees with John in the omitting of important data that is to be found in the comparable passages of both Mark and Matthew.[19]

*Although Luke agrees with the Markan order of events with remarkable precision throughtout most of "the pure triple tradition,"[20] in the twenty-four pericopes that Luke shares with all three of his co-evangelists there exist some twenty instances in which Luke seems to be in agreement with the Johannine order of events[21] rather than with the differing order of events that is to be found in the comparable passages in both Mark and Matthew.

*St. Luke contains at least ten passages (3:16; 7:37-38; 22:3,58,59b,70;

---

[15]Cf. Luke 3:16a/John 1:26a; Luke 3:16c/John 1:27b; Luke 4:22b/John 6:42a; Luke 19:38a/John 12:13b; Luke 22:3a/John 13:27a; Luke 22:34/John 13:38; Luke 22:67/John 10:24b-25a; Luke 22:70b/John 18:37b; Luke 23:4b/John 18:38c; Luke 23:21/John 19:6b; Luke 23:33a/John 19:17b-18a; Luke 23:53c/John 19:41b; Luke 24:1a/John 20:1a; Luke 24:2/John 20:1c; Luke 24:36a/John 20:19c.

[16]Cf. Robert M. Grant, *Historical Introduction to the New Testament*, pp. 105-117; A. M. Perry, "The Growth of the Gospels," *IB*, VII, 61-7.

[17]I.e., those Lukan pericopes (3:15-16,21-22; 5:1-11; 7:36-39; 9:10-17,18-20; 19:36-40,45-46; 22:3-6,14-23,31-34,39-46,47-53,54-62,63-65,66-71; 23:1-5,6-12,13-19,20-25,32-38,44-49,50-56; 24:1-11) that have parallels in all three of the other gospels.

[18]Cf. "St. Luke and the Johannine Tradition," pp. 423-4; "The Contacts That Exist Between St. Luke and St. John," pp. 3-4.

[19]Thus Mark 1:6,9-10,14-15; 6:3; 8:1-10,27b; 11:10a; 14:2,19,21b,27,28,31,32a,37b,44,45,50,56,58,60,61a,63,64a,64b,69a,71; 15:1,4,8-9,11-12,19a,23,27a,29-30,34,35-36,46c; 16:5,7 (and the parallels in Matthew) are lacking in both Luke and John.

[20]E.g., of the eighty-seven pericopes Luke shares with Mark, eighty of these pericopes occur in the same relative chronological sequence in both Mark and Luke. As J. Jeremias (*The Eucharistic Words of Jesus*, p. 98) has written: "Whenever Luke follows the Markan narrative in his own gospel he follows painstakingly the Markan order, pericope for pericope. Up to the passion narrative there are only two insignificant deviations, Luke 6:17-19; 8:19-21." Even with regard to the sequence of events within pericopes, the agreement between Mark and Luke is quite exact (e.g., compare Luke 4:31-43 with Mark 1:21-29, Luke 5:12-6:11 with Mark 1:40-3:6; Luke 8:22-56 with Mark 4:35-5:43, or Luke 20:1-21:6 with Mark 11:27-13:2).

[21]E.g., in both Luke and John, Peter's confession comes after the feeding of the five thousand, the prediction of the denial comes *prior* to their departure from the upper room, the arrest of Jesus *follows* the sword incident, the Jewish accusations are brought to Pilate *before* he questions Jesus, Pilate's first affirmation of Jesus' innocence occurred right after his initial questioning of Jesus, a mocking of Jesus is placed midway in Jesus' trial before Pilate, Pilate's second affirmation is placed right after this mocking, Pilate offers to release Jesus *before* Barabbas is mentioned, the double cry occurs *just prior* to Pilate's third affirmation of Jesus' innocence, Pilate twice offers to release Jesus following the Barabbas incident.

23:22b;33,53b; 24:1) that seemingly contain examples of the possible conflation by Luke of differing Markan/Matthean and Johannine material (those Lukan verses in which a Markan/Matthean phrase not found in John and a Johannine phrase not found in Mark/Matthew are to be found woven together in a single statement in Luke).[22]

*While Luke exhibits a few more verbal parallels with Mark/Matthew in the twenty-four pericopes that comprise "the quadruple tradition" than he does with John,[23] in individual verses the percentage of verbal agreement between Luke and Mark/Matthew and Luke and John is often quite similar.[24]

*In certain instances Luke's degree of agreement/disagreement with John is also quite comparable to the degree of agreement/disagreement that exists between a number of Luke's parallels with Mark/Matthew.[25]

*The vast preponderance of the Lukan/Johannine agreements occur between their respective passion narratives. Thus most of the Lukan/Johannine sequential agreements, all but two of the examples of the possible Lukan conflation of Markan/Matthean and Johannine material, all but twelve of the Lukan/Johannine verbal parallels,[26] and over 80% of the Lukan factual agreements with John occur in chs. 22-24 of Luke.

*Luke also contains several verbal parallels and factual agreements with John in certain other of the basic narrative sections of his gospel[27] (i.e., the

_____

[22]Cf. "St. Luke and the Johannine Tradition," pp. 432-3, 445.

[23]Of the 143 verses found in the twenty-four pericopes that Luke shares with all three of his co-evangelists, fifty-nine of these Lukan verses (i.e., 3:16,21-22; 5:10-11; 7:36b-37; 9:10a,12-13a,14,16-20; 19:36,38a,45-46; 22:1-2,4-6,7,9-13,16,19,22,34,40b,42,45-47,50,52-53a,55b-56,59-60,62,69; 23:3,19,22b,25-26,33b,35,37-38,44-45,47,50,51b-53a; 24:1b,7) are found to contain verbal parallels with Mark/Matthew and fifty one of these same Lukan verses (i.e., 3:15-16,22; 5:5a,6; 7:38; 9:11,14; 19:37b-38a,45; 22:3,14a,23,33-34,39a,40a,50,53b-55a,58,59a.60b,64b,66c-67,70b; 23:2a,2d,3a,4,8c,9b,11b,13,14c.16.18,20b-22c,23a,33,34b,36,38,50a,52,53c,54a; 24:1a,2,4b,8,23b-24) are also found to contain verbal parallels with St. John.

[24]Thus if Luke shares eleven words out of fourteen with Mark at 22:19, thirteen out of eighteen at 22:22, eight out of sixteen at 22:34, ten out of seventeen at 22:50, eleven out of nineteen at 23:26, and eight out of eleven at 23:53a, it can also be observed that Luke shares eight words out of nine with John at 19:38a, nine out of sixteen at 22:34, eleven out of seventeen at 22:50, twelve out of seventeen at 22:67, ten out of seventeen at 23:4, nine out of fifteen at 23:16-18, and four out of six at 23:53b.

[25]Thus John 1:26a ("John answered them") is as close to Luke 3:16a ("John answered them *all*") as Mark 5:17 ("And they began to beg Jesus to depart from their neighborhood") is to Luke 8:37a ("Then *all* the people of the surrounding country . . . asked him to depart from them"); John 18:25c ("I am not") is as close to Luke 22:58c ("*Man*, I am not") as Matt 9:2c/Mark 2:5b ("My son, your sins are forgiven") is to Luke 5:29b ("*Man*, your sins are forgiven you"); and John 19:41c ("where no one had ever been laid") is as close to Luke 23:53c ("where no one had ever *yet* been laid") as Mark 11:2b ("on which no one has ever *yet* sat") is to Luke 19:30b ("on which no one has ever *yet* sat").

[26]Cf. "St. Luke and the Johannine Tradition," pp. 431-2.

[27]While Luke's verbal parallels with John occur almost entirely within those twenty-four pericopes that Luke shares with all three of his co-eangelists (the only real exceptions are Luke 4:22-24 and Luke 24:36-40), Luke elsewhere does possess some unusual

narratives describing John the Baptist, the calling of Peter, the anointing, the feeding of the five thousand, the entry). When the comparable eight pericopes in John[28] are joined with the seventeen Johannine passion pericopes that have Lukan parallels,[29] the resultant twenty-five Johannine pericopes would seem to resemble what could have been an early form of the Johannine kerygmatic proclamation.[30]

All of the foregoing considerations would seem to suggest that the relationship which may exist between the Gospels of Luke and John stands in need of careful re-examination. Indeed, it seems to this writer at the present time that possibly *a better explanation* of all these Lukan phenomena might well be the hypothesis that Luke was influenced by *some early form* of the developing Johannine tradition in his composing of certain sections of his gospel. This would seem to be especially true of the Lukan passion narrative, with the many close Lukan passion agreements with John suggesting the possibility that some form of the Johannine passion tradition may have been one of those sources with which Luke was acquainted and which seemingly exerted some influence upon Luke in his writing of his own passion narrative.[31] It shall therefore be the purpose of this study to continue our comparative examination of Luke and John by expanding it to include the Book of Acts, and thus to see if Acts contains many close verbal/conceptual agreements with John such as we have found in the Third Gospel, phenomena that could possibly be indicative of Luke's growing familiarity *with some early stage of developing Johannine thought.*

A Brief Survey of Recent John/Acts Research

While there probably exists today no major study dealing with the John/Acts

---

verbal/conceptual resemblances to Johannine material (e.g., compare Luke 1:45a with John 20:29b, Luke 10:16 with John 12:44, Luke 10:22b with John 10:15, Luke 11:28 with John 13:17, Luke 16:8b with John 12:36c, Luke 24:44b with John 1:45b, or Luke 24:48 with John 21:24a.

[28]John 1:19-25,26-29,30-34,35-42; 6:1-14,66-71; 12:1-8,12-19.

[29]John 13:21-30,36-38; 18:1-11,12-14,15-27,28-38,39-40; 19:1-5,6-12,13-16,17-22,23-27,28-30,38-42; 20:1-10,11-18,19-29.

[30]Cf. e.g., C. H. Dodd, "Le kerygma apostolique dans la quatrieme evangile," *RHPR,* XXXI (1951), 265-74; Raymond E. Brown, *The Gospel According to John I-XII,* pp. xli-xliii; Robert T. Fortna, *The Gospel of Signs,* pp. 221-3.

[31]There would seem to exist considerable agreement today that the passion narrative was the first extensive section of the gospels to acquire definite form in the development of early Christian tradition (cf. W. Marxsen, *Mark the Evangelist,* trans. James Boyce, p. 31; A. M. Perry, "The Growth of the Gospels," pp. 73-4; F. Filson, "The Literary Relationship Among the Gospels," *IOVC,* p. 1131). Thus even if the Gospel of John didn't gain its final form until 90-100 A.D., it is still not impossible that Luke may have been acquainted with some early form of the Johannine passion tradition (see above, notes 9-12). As D. Moody Smith, Jr. ("Johannine Christianity: Some Reflections on Its Character and Delineation," *NTS,* XXI (1975), 246) has written: "If the inner Jewish or Jewish-Christian setting of the Johannine community and tradition antedates the Roman War, as I think altogether possible, and even probable, then *a passion narrative* or something comparable would seem a likelihood for that earlier period."

parallels[32] comparable to some of the recent work that has been done on the parallels that exist between the Gospels of Luke and John, there nevertheless have appeared several recent studies on Acts that in different ways have called our attention to the existence of some of these John/Acts agreements.[33] Thus Johannes Munck, in his recent Commentary on Acts, noted in particular the conceptual parallelism that exists between the Johannine Jerusalem healing miracles (John 5:1-18; 9:1-17) and the Jerusalem healing miracle found in Acts 3.[34] Pierson Parker has also made a contribution to the John/Acts discussion by pointing out in his comparative study of Acts and our several Gospels that while there "are some forty areas where Mark and Acts stand far apart . . . , *John, however,usually sides with Acts, even when Luke's own gospel does not.*"[35] Then Robert T. Fortna, in the course of his reconstruction of his proposed Johannine Signs-Source, observed in particular the "astonishing number of lexical parallels" that exist between the Johannine account of the raising of Lazarus (11:1-45) and the account in Acts of the raising of Tabitha (9:36-43) as well as "the striking parallel" that exists between John 19:12 and Acts 17:7.[36] And Charles H. H. Scobie, in his recent study of Samaritan Christianity, has noticed that both John and Acts exhibit a definite interest in a mission to the Samaritans as well as possessing real similiarities to Samaritan theology including a distinctive Moses/Christ parallelism with the result that many of the themes that appear in Acts 3 and 7 are also to be found in the Gospel of John.[37]

This is not to suggest that the Gospel of John was one of the sources Luke used in his composing of his Acts' narrative, for there exist good reasons for questioning the hypothesis that Luke extensively used written sources in his writing of Acts.[38] On the other hand, it does seem possible to us that Acts in certain places seems to reflect a Lukan awareness of other early traditions,[39]

---

[32]E.g., compare Acts 2:22/John 3:2c; Acts 3:14a/John 6:69; Acts 3:15c/John 15:27a; Acts 4:15-16/John 11:47-48; Acts 4:20/John 3:32; Acts 5:32/John 15:26-27; Acts 8:6c/John 2:23; Acts 9:42b/John 11:45; Acts 10:38c/John 3:2a; Acts 10:39a/John 15:27a; Acts 10:43a/John 5:39c; Acts 13:25c/John 1:20; Acts 13:25d/John 1:27b; Acts 17:3c/John 20:31a; Acts 17:7c/John 19:12c; Acts 17:12a/John 11:45; Acts 19:2a/John 7:39; Acts 22:15/John 3:32.

[33]Cf. F. F. Bruce,*Commentary on the Book of Acts*, pp. 50, 336, 386; Johannes Munck, *The Acts of the Apostles*, pp. 25-6; Pierson Parker, "Mark,Acts, and Galilaean Christianity," *NTS*, XVI (1970), 295-304; Robert T. Fortna, *The Gospel of Signs*, pp. 74-84; Richard F. Zehnle, *Peter's Pentecost Discourse: Tradition and Lukan Reinterpretation in Peter's Speeches of Acts 2 and 3*, pp. 51-2; Charles H. H. Scobie, "The Origins and Development of Samaritan Christianity," *NTS*, XIX (1973), 390-414.

[34]*The Acts of the Apostles,* pp. 25-6.

[35]"Mark, Acts, and Galilean Christianity," pp. 298-300.

[36]*The Gospel of Signs*, pp. 84, 126.

[37]"The Origins and Development of Samaritan Christianity," pp. 391, 401-8.

[38]While we cannot here give a history of the recent source criticism of Acts, the reader is nevertheless referred to the excellent reviews of this critical history made by writers such as E. Haenchen (*Die Apostelgeschichte*, 5th ed., pp. 13-64), J. Dupont (*The Sources of Acts*, trans. Kathleen Pond), or Richard F. Zehnle (*Peter's Pentecost Discourse*, pp. 13-17).

[39]As Richard Zehnle (*Ibid.*, pp. 16-17) has written: "Recent critical inquiry into the speeches of Acts reveals widespread agreement on two points: First, there is a Lukan

historical traditions that appear to have exerted varying degrees of influence upon Luke in his writing of certain sections (e.g., the early Jerusalem narratives, the mission to Samaria in ch. 8) of Acts.[40] For example, there does seem to exist a number of verbal parallels between Acts and Mark (cf., e.g., Acts 6:14/Mark 14:58; Acts 9:40-41/Mark 5:41; Acts 10:37b/Mark 1:4; Acts 10:38b/Mark 3:11; Acts 13:24/Mark 1:4b; Acts 14:9b/Mark 5:34a) including at least three verbal resemblances with sections of Mark (cf. Acts 1:7/Mark 13:32; Acts 5:15/Mark 6:56; Acts 6:13/Mark 14:57) that are lacking in the Third Gospel. Thus Acts (by containing verbal parallels with Mark and by sharing in certain instances similar phraseology with Mark) would seem to reflect an awareness of the Markan tradition, a tradition that possibly exerted some influence upon Luke in his writing of the Acts' narrative. In a similar way, a comparison of Acts with St. John could possibly provide us with some data that might further our understanding with regard to the various questions relating to the traditions (or influences) that helped in the making of Acts, data that could also bring new insights to the various aspects of the Lukan/Johannine question. This study will therefore attempt to make a contribution to these questions by examining the agreements that seem to exist between John and Acts, noticing in particular the frequency and the preciseness of these various John/Acts agreements. Then after surveying the various areas of Acts that seemingly contain verbal/conceptual parallels with John, this study will then conclude by attempting to posit some possible explanations for the existence of these John/Acts phenomena.

The Portrayal of John the Baptist

The portrayal of John the Baptist found in Acts would seem to resemble the Johannine portrayal of the Baptist more than it does the Markan/Matthean.[41] In Mark/Matthew, John is *Elijah*,[42] the forerunner of the Messiah, the herald of the new eschatological age.[43] Contrariwise, St. John depicts the Baptist as denying that he is Elijah (1:21) and then consistently portrays him as being a witness to the messiahship of Jesus.[44] Mark/Matthew also explicitly describe the baptism of Jesus by John (cf. Mark 1:9-11/Matt 3:13-17) and portray John as preaching "a baptism of repentance" (cf. Mark 1:4b/Matt 3:6-8). Mark also depicts the Baptist as bringing forgiveness (1:4b), while Matthew alone among our evangelists depicts John as preaching, "Repent, for the kingdom of heaven is at hand" (3:2). All of these latter elements (the baptism of Jesus, repentance, forgiveness, the nearness of the kingdom) are lacking in John.

---

theology which orders and directs the author's two-volume work; second, Luke has used disparate materials in constructing his work. These are obviously not contradictory statements, but they define the tension existing in Acts research today."

[40]Cf. U. Wilckens, *Die Missionsreden der Apostelgeschichte,* p. 15; Eduard Schweizer ("Zu den Reden der Apostelgeschichte," *ThZ,* XIII (1957), 1-11; R. H. Fuller, *The New Testament in Current Study,* pp. 97-8; Richard Zehnle, *Peter's Pentecost Discourse,* pp. 59-60.

[41]Pierson Parker, "Mark, Acts, and Galilaean Christianity," pp. 300-2.

[42]Cf. Mark 1:2,6; 9:9-13; Matt 3:4; 11:14; 17:9-13.

[43]Cf. H. Conzelmann, *The Theology of St. Luke,* p. 22.

[44]Cf. John 1:15,29-30,32,34,36; 3:26-30; 5:33-36; 10:41.

Although Luke has parallels to several of the Markan/Matthean references to Elijah,[45] the Markan/Matthean portrayal of the Baptist has been somewhat modified by the Third Evangelist. Thus Luke, in his gospel proper,[46] has eliminated every Markan/Matthean passage that would seem to identify John with Elijah.[47] Even the Markan (1:6)/Matthean (3:4) description of John's mode of dress, which possibly could have been suggestive of the description of Elijah found in II Kings 1:8, is lacking in Luke as well as in John. Luke (like John) also lacks an explicit description of the baptism of Jesus by the Baptist, and contains the "anachronism of placing the arrest of John prior to Jesus' baptism."[48] Luke does agree with Mark/Matthew by referring in 3:3b to John's preaching a "baptism of repentance, " and also agrees with Mark 1:4b that John's baptism was for "the forgiveness of sins."[49]

Acts, however, departs even more than Luke does from the Markan/Matthean portrayal of the Baptist. Thus Acts not only agrees with Luke/John against Mark/Matthew in never identifying the Baptist with Elijah, but Acts also never suggests that "the Baptist brought forgiveness,"[50] never alludes to the baptism of Jesus by John, and never mentions Elijah. Acts does agree with the Synoptics by twice connecting "repentance" with John's baptism (cf. Acts 13:24; 19:4) and in twice referring to the promised baptism with the Holy Spirit (cf. Acts 1:5; 11:16). Otherwise, however, Acts seems to have largely departed from the portrayal of the Baptist found in the Markan/Matthean traditions.

On the other hand, Acts does contain several positive agreements with John in its treatment of John the Baptist. Thus Acts, like John, always refers to the Baptist with the simple designation "John" (ho Ioannes).[51] By contrast, Mark uses the designation "John the Baptizer" three times (1:4; 6:14, 24) while the term "John the Baptist" occurs twelve times in the Synoptic Gospels.[52]

Acts (13:25c) and John (1:20; 3:28) are also our only two NT writings that portray the Baptist as denying that he was the Messiah, with Acts 13:25c (ouk eimi ego) being quite comparable to John 1:20 (Ego ouk eimi ho Christos).

---

[45]Luke retains the Markan/Matthean references to Elijah only at 9:8 (the perplexity of Herod), 9:19 (Peter's confession) and 9:30-33 (the Transfiguration). Even the references to Elijah in the Markan/Matthean passion narratives (i.e., Mark 15:34-36/Matt 27:46-49) are lacking in Luke.

[46]Luke does contain one reference in his nativity narrative (1:17) that seemingly associates John with Elijah.

[47]Thus Mark 1:2,6; 9: 9-13 Matt 3:4; 11:14; 17:9-13 are all lacking in Luke. Luke even lacks Matt 11:14 (a "Q" passage) even though Luke 7:24-35 is otherwise quite comparable to Matt 11:7-19.

[48]See our remarks concerning this Lukan omission in our study, "St. Luke and the Johannine Tradition," pp. 429-30.

[49]Luke 3:3b not only agrees with Mark 1:4b that John's baptism of repentance brought "the forgiveness of sins," but this Lukan passage also stands in virtual verbatim agreement with its Markan parallel.

[50]Cf. Pierson Parker, "Mark, Acts, and Galilaean Christianity," p. 298.

[51]Cf. John 1:6,15,19,26,28,32,35,40; 3:23,24,25,26,27; 4:1; 5:33,36; 10:40,41; Acts 1:5,22; 10:37; 11:16; 13:24,25; 18:25; 19:3,4.

[52]Cf. Matt 3:1; 11:11,12; 14:2,8; 16:14; 17:13; Mark 6:25; 8:28; Luke 7:20,33; 9:19.

Acts also agrees with John by placing this denial of messiahship by the Baptist *immediately prior* to his proclamation of "the Coming One" (cf. Acts 13:25d; John 1:26-27). Moreover, the form of the Baptist's proclamation found in Acts 13:25d would seem to be closer to the form found in John 1:27b than it is to any of the synoptic versions (cf. Matt 3:11; Mark 1:7-8; Luke 3:16). Thus Acts 13:25d agrees with John 1:27b over against all of the synoptics in its use of the singular form of "sandal," in its use of "worthy" (*axios*) instead of "fit" (*hikanos*), in its omission of the phrase, "he who is mightier than I," and in the absence of any reference to the promised baptism with the Holy Spirit in its form of John's proclamation.[53] Observe also that the words, "I am not worthy" (*hou ouk eimi axios*), found in Acts 13:25d agree verbatim with the same phrase found in John 1:27b, so that despite the appearance of the phrase, "the sandal of his feet," in Acts 13:25d (a phrase that is peculiar to Acts), Acts' version of the Baptist's proclamation would seem to stand closer to John 1:27b than it does to any of the Synoptic versions.[54]

Then Acts 19:4 seemingly contains verbal/conceptual resemblances to both the Markan and the Johannine traditions, with Acts 19:4a ("John baptized with the baptism of repentance") being quite comparable to Mark 1:4b ("John . . . preaching a baptism of repentance") and Acts 19:4b ("telling the people to *believe* in the one who was to come after him, that is, Jesus") being comparable to such Johannine passages as 1:7 ("He came for testimony, to bear witness to the light, that all might *believe* through him") and 10:41 (everything that John said about this man was true").[55] As G. H. C. Macgregor wrote in the *Interpreter's Bible:*

> How far does this (Acts 19:4) correspond with the picture of the Baptist in the Synoptic Gospels? There also he preaches *repentance,* but *the one who was to come after him* is pictured rather as a stern judge who will "gather the wheat into his granary, but the chaff he will burn with unquenchable fire" (Luke 3:17). It is only in the Fourth Gospel that John consciously proclaims Jesus as the one in whom men are to believe for salvation.[56]

Thus John and Acts agree in depicting the Baptist as denying that he was the Messiah, in placing the Baptist's proclamation right after this denial, and in explicitly portraying the Baptist as calling on men to believe in Jesus of Nazareth.[57]

---

[53]Acts does contain two references elsewhere (1:5; 11:16) to this promised baptism even as John also contains such a reference at another place in his narrative (cf. 1:33).

[54]On the other hand, Acts 13:24 ("John had preached a baptism of repentence") resembles Mark 1:4 ("John . . . preaching a baptism of repentance") so that Acts 13:24-25 seemingly possesses verbal/conceptual parallels with both Mark 1:4 and John 1:20,27. But this is a phenomenon (i.e., a pericope in which Luke exhibits parallels to Mark/Matthew and John in successive verses) that is to be found elsewhere in Luke/Acts (cf. e.g., Luke 7:36-38; 22:3-6,66-71; 23:2-4,16-22,50-54; 24:1-4; Acts 9:36-43; 19:2-4).

[55]Cf. also John 1:29-32,36; 3:26-30; 5:32-34; Acts 13:23-25.

[56]"The Acts of the Apostles," *IB,* IX, (1954) 253.

[57]Cf. F. F. Bruce (*Commentary on the Book of Acts,* p. 386) who wrote: "The Synoptists do not expressly state that John directed his hearers to believe in the Coming One, as Paul here states (Acts 19:4); but Paul's statement is in thorough agreement with the Fourth Gospel (cf. John 1:26ff.; 3:25ff.)."

The Disciples as Witnesses

John and Acts also share in the frequent use of the term "witness" as a descriptive designation of the chosen followers of Jesus. Matthew and Mark never use the term "witness" in the sense of giving testimony to Christ and his gospel. In Luke, the word "witness" is apparently used in this sense only at 1:2b and 24:48.[58] But both John and Acts speak of "witness" and "witnessing" with great frequency.[59] As Michael Green has written:

> When we turn to the New Testament we find a good many occurrences of the ordinary sense of "witness" (meaning to attest facts or assert truths), but it is in Acts and the Johannine writings that we meet it in the special sense of Christian witness.[60]

But not only does the concept of "witness" occur with considerable frequency in both John and Acts, but these two NT writings also use this term in quite comparable ways. For example, both John and Acts speak of bearing "witness *to these things*" (cf. John 21:24a; Acts 5:32), of being witnesses *"from the beginning"* (cf. John 15:27b; Acts 1:21-22), of the Scriptures *bearing witness* to Christ (cf. John 5:39a; Acts 10:43a), and of bearing witness to what one *"has seen and heard"* (cf. John 3:32; Acts 22:15). With regard to Acts' treatment of the concept of witness, the following passages in Acts should especially be noticed.

*Acts 1:21-22. This passage which asserts that the disciple selected to take Judas' place must be one "of the men" who had followed Jesus "during all the time that the Lord Jesus went in and out among us, beginning from the baptism of John" would seem to be "in rather substantial agreement with the Johannine tradition that Jesus had gained his first disciples on the two days following the Baptist's witness to Jesus (cf. John 1:35,43) while John was still baptizing (cf. John 3:23) rather than with the Matthean/Markan tradition which asserts that Jesus did not call his first disciples until after John had been cast into prison (cf. Matt 4:12; Mark 1:14)."[61]

Acts 1:22a ("beginning from* the baptism of John") should also be compared with John 15:27b ("because you have been with me *from the beginning*") which, when taken together with John 15:26-27a, also teaches that "the qualification for

---

[58]Thus Luke 1:2b ("by those who from the beginning were eye-witnesses") can be compared with John 15:27 ("you also are witnesses, because you have been with me from the beginning") and Luke 24:48 ("You are witnesses of these things") can be compared with John 21:24a ("who is bearing witness to these things").

[59]Cf. John 1:7,8,15,32,34; 3:11,26,28,32; 5:31,32,33,36,37,39; 8:13,14,18a,18b; 10:25; 15:26,27; 19:35; 21:24; Acts 1:8,22; 2:32; 3:15; 5:32; 7:44; 10:39,41,43; 13:31; 14:3,17; 15:8; 22:15,20; 23:11; 26:16.

[60]*Evangelism in the Early Church,* p. 71.

[61]"St. Luke and the Johannine Tradition," p. 435. See F. F. Bruce (*Commentary on the Book of Acts,* p., 50) who wrote: "The statement that the Apostles had been companions of Christ from the days when John was baptizing agrees with the evidence of the fourth gospel, according to which nearly half the apostolic group began to follow Jesus in the days immediately following his baptism by John (cf. John 1:35ff.)."

'witness' is personal intimacy" from the beginning.[62] It is thus to be observed that the Lukan and the Johannine literature are the only sections of the NT that teach that Jesus had followers who were *witnesses* to him *from the beginning* (cf. Luke 1:2; John 1:35-50; 15:27; Acts 1:21-22; I John 1:1).

Acts 1:24b ("show which one of these two thou hast *chosen*"). Acts 1:21-26 describes the process by which Matthias was chosen to become with the eleven Apostles a witness to the resurrection. Luke uses this same word (*exelexato*) of Jesus' selection of the twelve at Luke 6:13 and Acts 1:2 as well as here in Acts 1:24.[63] This same verb ("to choose") is also the word John consistently used for referring to Jesus' selection of the twelve (cf. John 6:70; 13:18; 15:16,19). On the other hand, Mark/Matthew never use this verb of Jesus' selection of the twelve (Mark 3:14 uses the word "appointed" instead).

Acts 5:32 ("And we are witnesses to these things, and so is the Holy Spirit whom God has given to those who obey him"). In the NT, the twofold witness of the Holy Spirit and of the disciples to Christ in any single passage is to be found only here in Acts 5:32 and in John 15:26-27a. Acts 5:32b (which teaches that God gives the Holy Spirit "to those who obey him") would also seem to be in substantial conceptual agreement with John 14:15-16 which teaches that if a man keeps Christ's commandments, the Father will give him "another Counselor" who will remain with him forever.

Acts 22:15 ("you will be a *witness* for him to all men of *what you have seen and heard*"). In the NT, statements referring to witnessing (or speaking) of what one "has seen and heard" are to be found only in the Lukan and the Johannine literature (cf. Luke 7:22a; John 3:32; Acts 4:20; 22:15; I John 1:3). Thus John 3:32 ("He bears *witness* to *what he has seen and heard*") would seem to be quite comparable to Acts 22:15, with both passages using the word "witness" and similar wording in their phrase for having "seen and heard."[64] Luke 7:22a ("Go and tell John what you have seen and heard") and Acts 4:20 ("for we cannot but speak of what we have seen and heard") would also seem to be quite close to both John 3:32 and I John 1:3a ("that which we have seen and heard") with the verb for "seeing"[65] preceding the word for "hearing" in all five of these Lukan/Johannine passages.

The Treatment of Miracles in John and Acts

In Mark/Matthew, the miracles of Jesus are viewed basically as exhibitions of

---

[62]Cf. J. H. Bernard. *The Gospel According to St. John*, II, 500.

[63]Acts also uses a form of this word at 10:41 in the phrase, "to us who were chosen by God as witnesses."

[64]Thus John 3:32a (*ho heoraken kai ekousen touto marturei*) would seem quite comparable to Acts 22:15b (*hoti ese martus . . . hon heorakas kai ekousas*).

[65]The concept of "seeing" (esp. of "seeing" miracles) would therefore seem to be one that was significant for both Luke and John (cf. esp.Luke 5:26; 7:22; 8:34; 10:23-24; 17:15; 18:43; 19:37; 21:31; 23:8,47; John 1:46,51; 2:23; 3:3,11,32; 6:2,14,30; 9:25,39; 11:45; 12:45; 14:9; 19:35; 20:29; Acts 2:33; 4:20; 7:56; 8:6,13,18; 9:35; 13:12; 14:9,11; 22:9,15,18; 26:13,16; 28:4).

his power[66] or demonstrations of his compassion.[67] In Luke, while much of the Markan/Matthean treatment of Jesus' miracles as mighty works is retained,[68] Luke also exhibits a tendency to accentuate the reaction of the crowd to Jesus' miracles which in the Third Gospel usually takes the form of either an expression of praise to God[69] or an acclamation proclaiming Jesus as a prophet mighty in deed and word.[70] Mark/Matthew also often emphasize the role of faith in bringing about healing,[71] an emphasis that is likewise to be found with considerable frequency in Luke.[72] And even though Luke has seemingly modified the Markan/Matthean traditions by sometimes using these miracles as means to validate Jesus as "the one whom God has chosen to do his work" (cf. 7:16, 20-23; 8:39; 18:43),[73] there nevertheless does not seem to exist one clear example in any of the Synoptics of a miracle explicitly resulting in people coming to believe in Jesus.

Contrariwise, in St. John the miracles of Jesus are usually referred to as "signs"[74] that either result in belief in Jesus (cf. 2:11, 23; 3:2; 4:53; 6:14; 7:31; 9:38; 11:45; 12:11, 18) or which provide the setting for a major discourse by Jesus (cf. 5:19-47; 6:35-59). In the Synoptics, the word "sign" (except for Luke 23:8c) is never applied to the miracles of Jesus. Instead, they use this term only in those instances when the Jewish leaders came demanding that Jesus show them a "sign" as a proof of his authority (cf. Matt. 12:38-40; 16:1-4; Mark 8:11-12; Luke 11:16, 29-30) or in the Olivet discourse to refer to the "signs" that would immediately precede the destruction of the temple (cf. Matt 24:3; Mark 13:4; Luke 21:7) or the "signs" the false Messiahs would perform in "those days" (cf. Matt 24:24; Mark 13:22).

On the other hand, the Book of Acts often uses the word "sign" for referring to the miracles of Jesus or his disciples,[75] and in three of these instances (4:16, 22; 8:6) in Acts this term occurs singularly without any other accompanying words for miracles (see below) in a manner quite comparable to its usage in John. Acts also contains at least nine passages (4:2-4, 15-22; 5:12-14; 8:6-13; 9:33-35, 36-42; 13:12; 16:31-33; 19:11-18) in which it is stressed that miracles produced faith.[76] So while Acts certainly retains some of the Synoptic perspectives (e.g.,

---

[66]Cf. e.g., Matt 8:26-27; 9:6-8,18-25,32-33; 11:20-23; 13:54; 15:28-31; 17:18-21; Mark 1:27; 2:9-12; 4:39-41; 5:30,40-42; 6:2,5,14,51; 7:37-38; 9:25-29; 11:28-33.

[67]Cf. Matt 8:1-3,14-15; 9:27; 15:32; 17:15; 20:30-34; Mark 1:29-31,41; 3:1-5; 4:38; 5:19; 6:34; 8:2-3; 10:47-48.

[68]Cf. Luke 4:36,40-41; 5:9,24-26; 7:15-16; 8:24-26; 9:1,42-43; 13:17; 18:43; 19:37; 20:8.

[69]Cf. Luke 5:25-26; 7:16; 8:39; 9:43; 17:15,18; 18:43; 19:37; 23:47.

[70]Cf. Luke 7:16; 13:17; 24:19.

[71]Cf. e.g., Matt 8:2,13; 9:2,18,22,28-29; 13:58; 14:31; 15:28; 17:20; Mark 1:40; 2:5; 4:40; 5:23,34; 7:29; 9:23-24; 10:52.

[72]Cf. esp. Luke 5:12,20; 7:9; 8:25,48,50; 9:41; 17:19; 18:42.

[73]Cf. the article in this volume by Paul J. Achtemeier, "The Lukan Perspective on the Miracles of Jesus: A Preliminary Sketch," pp. 552-4.

[74]Cf. John 2:11,23; 3:2; 4:48,54; 6:2,14,26,30; 7:31; 9:16; 11:47; 12:18,37; 29:30.

[75]Cf. Acts 2:22,43; 4:16,20,30; 5:12; 6:8; 8:6,13; 14:3; 15:12.

[76]Thus Paul J. Achtemeier ("The Lukan Perspective on the Miracles of Jesus," p. 553)

the role of faith in healing,[77] the reaction of the crowd,[78] exorcisms[79]) in certain of its miracle pericopes, Acts also exhibits several impressive agreements with John in its treatment of miracles. Thus John and Acts are *our only NT writings* to use the term "sign" frequently for the miracles of Jesus or his disciples, to assert that "a sign" had led "many" to believe (cf. John 2:23; 6:14; 7:31; 11:45; 12:11; Acts 4:4; 5:14; 8:6; 9:35, 42), to urge that Jesus' miracles demonstrated that *"God was with him"* (cf. John 3:2c; Acts 10:38c), to teach that Jesus had appeared to his disciples "for many days" in Jerusalem (cf. John 20:19-29: Acts 13:31), or to use the description of a "sign" (cf. John 5:1-9; 6:1-14; Acts 3:1-10) as the historical setting for an important discourse (cf. John 5:19-47; 6:25-65; Acts 3:12-26).

With regard to Acts' treatment of miracles, the following passages should especially be observed.

Acts 2:22 ("Jesus of Nazareth, a man attested to you by God with mighty works and wonders and signs which God did through him *in your midst*"). When it is recalled that this speech of Peter was addressed to the "men of Judea and all who dwell in Jerusalem" (2:14), then it would seem that Acts 2:22 could be asserting that Jesus had performed "signs" in Jerusalem and Judea, a tradition that elsewhere in the NT is only to be found in John (2:23; 3:2; 5:1-9; 7:31; 9:1-12; 11:38-47).

Acts 3:1-10 (the account of the healing of a man "lame from birth"). This miracle in Acts exhibits some similarity to the Johannine Jerusalem healing miracles (cf. John 5:1-9; 9:1-12). Thus a comparison of these three pericopes would seem to disclose the existence of the following similarities between the Jerusalem miracles found in John and Acts:[80] (a) John 9 and Acts 3 both describe the healing of a man who had been afflicted from birth; (b) The setting is the same in both John and Acts (the temple and streets of Jerusalem); (c) In both John 5 and Acts 3 the healing is followed by a speech inferring Jesus to be a "prophet-like-Moses" (cf. John 5:45-47; Acts 3:22-26); (d) In both John and Acts the healings result in persecution (cf. John 5:16-18; 9:18-34; Acts 4:1-3); (e) Both John and Acts stress that the persecutions did not stop the preaching of Jesus or the Apostles (cf. John 5:19-47; Acts 4:5-12); and (f) in both John and Acts the healing is later referred to as a "sign" (cf. John 9:16; Acts 4:16).

Acts 4:16 ("What shall we do with these men? For that a *notable sign* has been performed through them is manifest to all the inhabitants of Jerusalem") would seem to be comparable to John 11:47b ("What are we do? For this man

---

could write that "it is rather clear in Acts that miracles were an effective device for turning people to faith."

[77]Acts 14:9 ("seeing that he had faith to be made well") would seem to be especially close to such synoptic passages as Matt 9:22b/Mark 5:34a/Luke 8:48 and Mark 10:52b/Luke 18:42b.

[78]Cf. Acts 3:9-10; 4:21c; 11:18; 14:11; 19:17b.

[79]Cf. Acts 5:16b; 8:7; 16:18c; 19:12b.

[80]See Johannes Munck (*The Acts of the Apostles*, pp. 25-6) to whom we are indebted for several of these John/Acts resemblances.

performs many signs."). The following similarities exist between these two passages: (a) Both John 11:47 and Acts 4:16 contain the singular usage of the word "sign" to refer to a great miracle (cf. also John 12:18);[81] (b) In both John 11:47a and Acts 4:15 a gathering of "the council" occurs shortly after the occurrence of this "sign" (cf. John 11:38-44; Acts 3:1-10); (c) In both John 11:47b and Acts 4:16a the council members are described as asking, "What are we to do?";[82] (d) In both John 11:47c and Acts 4:16b this question is followed by a reference to the "sign" and (e) both John 11:48 and Acts 4:17a reflect the fear of "the council" that this "sign" may influence "many" to believe.[83]

*Acts 8:6b ("when they heard him and saw the signs which he did") would also seem to be comparable to such Johannine passages as 2:23b ("when they saw the signs which he did"), 6:2b ("because they saw the signs which he did")[84] and 6:14a ("When the people saw the sign which he had done"). It is thus to be observed that Luke 23:8c ("Herod. . . . hoping to see some sign done by him"); John 2:23b; 6:2b, 14a; and Acts 8:6b are our only NT passages that speak of "seeing a sign done" by Jesus or one of his disciples, and that in three of these passages (i.e., John 2:23b; 6:14; Acts 8:6) it is also stressed that the "seeing of signs done" had led many to believe.

*Acts 9:36-42 (the miracle of the raising of Tabitha). This miracle pericope seemingly possesses close lexical resemblances to both the Synoptic account of the raising of Jairus' daughter (Matt 9:23-26; Mark 5:35-43; Luke 8:49-56) and the Johannine account of the raising of Lazarus (11:1-45). E.g., vss. 40-41 of Acts 9 seem to exhibit close parallels to both Mark 5:37-41 and Luke 8:51-55. Thus the phrase, "but Peter put them all outside," is quite reminiscent of Jesus' actions found in Mark 5:40a, while the words found in Acts 9:40b ("Tabitha, rise") are in close agreement with the Markan words (5:41), "Talitha cumi" (Little girl, I say to you, arise"), words which are lacking in Matthew's account and which are found in Greek in Luke 8:54 (compare also Acts 9:41a with Mark 5:41 and Luke 8:54). Contrariwise, Acts 9:36-42 also exhibits a number of verbal agreements[85] and a basic parallelism in format with John 11:1-45. Thus both John and Acts begin their accounts with similar wording (de tis en), and then after describing the serious illness of Lazarus/Tabitha, John 11:3/Acts 9:38b portray the "sisters"/"disciples" sending others to Jesus/Peter to inform them of the death/impending death of their loved one. After Jesus/Peter arrive at where the dead person lay, both John 11:33 and Acts 9:39 then depict many persons as weeping (klaiousai) over the death of Lazarus/Tabitha. Then after John (11:41-

---

[81]Anitra B. Kolenkow, in a paper ("The Contents of a Healing Controversy Gospel") delivered at the 1977 meeting of the SBL, has also called attention to Luke's singular use of "sign" in Acts 4:16 and to the several close parallels that exist between Acts 4:16-17 and John 11:45-47.

[82]John 11:47b (kai elegon, Ti pioumen) is thus quite comparable to Acts 4:16a (legontes, Ti poiesomen . . . .).

[83]Acts 4:4a ("But many of those who heard the word believed") would also seem to be somewhat comparable to John 4:41 ("many more believed because of his word.").

[84]While John 2:23b, John 6:2b, and Acts 8:6b all use different words for "seeing," the words ta semeia ha epoiei occur in verbatim form in all three of these passages.

[85]See Robert T. Fortna (The Gospel of Signs, pp. 84-5) for a complete listing of all the lexical parallels that exist between John 11:1-45 and Acts 9:36-42.

44)/Acts (9:40) describe the raising of Lazarus/Tabitha by Jesus/Peter, both John (11:45) and Acts (9:42) conclude their respective pericopes by asserting that this miracle had caused *"many"* to believe "in him"/"in the Lord."[86]

The Portrayal of Jesus in John and Acts

Certain resemblances would also seem to exist between John and Acts with regard to their portrayal of Jesus.[87] And while the extent of this study prohibits an extensive examination of the John/Acts christologies, the following similarities in particular should probably here be mentioned.[88]

*In contrast to the Synoptics, both John and Acts exhibit the titular use of "Christ" (*ho Christos*) with considerable frequency.[89] Contrariwise, Mark rarely uses this term: in fact there are no more than three instances in which Mark applies this term to Jesus.[90] This term does occur sixteen times in Matthew,[91] but seven of these Matthean usages have Markan parallels and four others occur in the Matthean nativity narrative (twice in the name "Jesus Christ") so that the Matthean titular use of "Christ" is still comparatively rare. In Luke, this term occurs eleven times,[92] but except for three occurrences in the Lukan nativity/resurrection narratives (2:11; 24:26,46), the titular use of "Christ" is almost as rare in Luke as it is in Mark. Yet this term occurs twenty-five times in Acts and twenty-one times in John, with the *frequent* assertion that "Jesus is (was) the Christ" being a trait common *only to John* (4:26; 7:26,41; 11:27; 20:31) *and Acts* (5:32; 9:22; 17:3; 18:5,28) in the NT.[93] Thus Acts 17:3 (*"This* Jesus ... *is*

---

[86]John 11:45 (*Polloi oun ek ton Ioudaion ... , episteusan eis auton*) is thus observed to stand verbally quite close to Acts 9:42b (*kai epistensan polloi epi ton kurion*).

[87]Cf. e.g., O. Cullmann, *The Christology of the New Testament,* trans. Shirley C. Guthrie and Charles A. M. Hall, pp. 36-9; Pierson Parker, "Mark, Acts, and Galilean Christianity," pp. 300-2; Charles H. H. Scobie, "The Origins and Development of Samaritan Christianity," pp. 393-408; J. A. T. Robinson, *Redating the New Testament,* pp. 267-9.

[88]In addition to the agreements mentioned in this section, John and Acts share in such other resemblances as "the kingship of Jesus" (cf. John 19:12; Acts 17:7), their *frequent* reference to "the name of Jesus" (cf. John 1:12; 3:18; 14:13,14,26; 15:16; 16:24-26; 20:31; Acts 2:38; 3:6,16; 4:10,12,18; 5:28,40; 8:12,16; 9:14,15,16,27; 10:48; 16:18; 19:5; 22:16), and in their comparable use and spelling of the term, "Jesus of Nazareth" (cf. John 1:45; 18:5,7; 19:19; Acts 2:22; 6:14; 10:38; 22:8; 26:9).

[89]Cf. John 1:20,25,41; 3:28; 4:25,29; 7:26,27,31,41,42; 9:22; 10:24; 11:27; 12:34; 20:31; Acts 2:31,36; 3:18,20; 5:42; 8:5; 9:22; 17:3a,3c; 18:5,28; 26:23.

[90]Cf. Mark 8:29; 14:61; 15:32. Mark also uses this term at 1:1 in the name of "Jesus Christ," as well as at 9:41; 12:35; and 13:21-22. But in none of these latter instances does this term apply unmistakably to Jesus of Nazareth.

[91]Cf. Matt 1:1,16,17; 2:4; 11:2; 16:16,20; 22:42; 23:10; 24:5,23,24; 26:63,68; 27:17,22.

[92]Cf. Luke 2:11; 3:15; 4:41; 9:20; 20:41; 22:67; 23:2,35,39; 24:26,46.

[93]Although Peter's confession, "You are the Christ" (Matt 16:16; Mark 8:29; Luke 9:20), and the question of the high priest, "Are you the Christ?" (Matt 26:63; Mark 14:61), are comparable in form, only John and Acts seemingly contain the assertion, "Jesus is (was) the Christ," with any frequency (cf. also Luke 22:67; I John 2:22; 5:1).

the Christ") can be compared with John 7:41 (*"This is the Christ"*),[94] Acts 18:5 ("testifying . . . that the Christ was Jesus") with John 11:27 ("I believe that you are the Christ"), or Acts 9:22 ("proving that *Jesus was the Christ"*) with John 20:31 ("that you may believe that *Jesus is the Christ"*).[95]

*Only John (6:69) and Acts (3:14) depict Peter as ascribing the title, "the Holy One" (*ton hagion*) to Jesus. Mark (1:24) and Luke (4:34) place this term in the mouth of a demon as a title for Jesus, but elsewhere in the NT this term is used as a designation for Jesus only at Rev 3:7.[96] But in Acts 3:14, Jesus is called "the Holy and Righteous One" by Peter just prior to his ascribing Deut 18:15 to him (Acts 3:22). Thus this title in Acts 3:14 would seem to be "a messianic epithet of the prophet like Moses."[97] However, John 6:69 also portrays Peter as ascribing this title, "the Holy One," to Jesus in an apparent Mosaic context. As Richard Zehnle has observed:

> The context is remarkable. Chapter 6 (of John) opens with the multiplication of the loaves by Jesus, and the crowd exclaims: "This is indeed the prophet who is to come into the world" (6:14). . . . Later there is a discourse on the bread of life which is filled with a Moses-Jesus contrast regarding the manna that Moses gave to the fathers in the desert. Thus, the whole chapter attests the combination of concepts: Moses-type, prophet, holy.[98]

John 6 and Acts 3 would thus seem to share some of the same themes: Mosaic motifs, "the promised prophet" (cf. John 6:14; Acts 3:22), Peter's confession of Jesus as "the Holy One."

*John and Acts would also seem to be our only NT writings that extensively attempted to interpret Jesus against the background of the promised "Prophet-like-Moses."[99] Thus Acts 3:22 applies Deut 18:15 to Jesus in the midst of a speech (3:12-26) in which a Moses/Christ parallelism appears to be quite prominent (cf. esp. 3:14,24), while Acts 5:31 describes Jesus in terms that are virtually equivalent to the manner in which Moses is described at Acts 7:35. Stephen's speech in Acts 7 seems also to have many contacts with Mosaic typology and Samaritan thought,[100] and Deut 18:15 is quoted again at 7:37.

---

[94]Thus Acts 17:3b (*hoti houtos estin ho Christos* . . .) would seem to be quite close to John 7:41 (*houtos estin ho Christos*).

[95]Acts 9:22 (*hoti houtos estin ho Christos*) would also seem to be comparable to John 20:31 (*hoti Iesous estin ho Christos*).

[96]"Holy" is also used a few times in the NT as an attributive adjective for the OT prophets (e.g., Luke 1:70; Acts 3:21) while in Sir 45:2 Moses is called "the equal of the holy ones in Glory."

[97]Cf. Richard Zehnle, *Peter's Pentecost Discourse*, p. 52.

[98]*Ibid.*, pp. 51-2.

[99]Thus O. Cullman (*The Christology of the New Testament*, p. 38) could write that "except for the Gospel of John and the first (Jewish Christian) part of Acts, no New Testament writing considers Jesus the eschatological Prophet who prepares the way for God."

[100]Cf. e.g., A. Spiro, "Stephen's Samaritan Background," in Appendix V, *The Acts of the Apostles*, by J. Munck, pp. 285-300; Charles H. H. Scobie, "The Origins and Development of Samaritan Christianity," pp. 391-400; M. H. Scharlemann, *Stephen: A Singular Saint*, pp. 36-51; Richard Zehnle, *Peter's Pentecost Discourse*, pp. 76-81.

Evidence is also accumulating that John's portrayal of Jesus likewise seems to have presented, at least in part, against the background of this same "Prophet-like-Moses" expectation.[101] Thus John describes Jesus as the one of whom Moses wrote (1:45; 5:46), and the same perspective is also to be found elsewhere in St. John (cf. esp. 4:25-29; 6:14; 7:40,52).[102] Considerable Mosaic typology is also to be found in John (esp. in the "manna discourse" in 6:25-51),[103] and if John 1:21 can depict the Baptist as denying that he was "the prophet," John 6:14 can portray the people as acclaiming Jesus as "the prophet who is to come into the world" (cf. also 4:19; 6:69; 7:40,52; 11:27).[104] In fact, even the description of the "Prophet-like-Moses" found in Deut 18:18 is virtually reproduced at several places in John,[105] so that even though John does not explicitly cite this OT passage,[106] Deut 18:15-18 nevertheless seems to have exercised a significant role in the Johannine interpretation of Jesus.[107] A Moses/Christ parallelism thus seems to have been an important trait of both the early Judean speeches in Acts (cf. esp. 3:12-26; 7:20-53) and the Johannine portrayal of Jesus.[108]

The Eschatology of John and Acts

Despite many differing evaluations, there would seem to be little doubt but

---

[101]Cf. e.g., T. F. Glasson, *Moses in the Fourth Gospel*, pp. 20-38; J. Bowman, "Samaritan Studies," *BJRL*, XL (1957-58), 298-329; J. Macdonald, *The Theology of the Samaritans*, pp. 420-46; W. Meeks, *The Prophet-King: Moses Traditions and the Johannine Christology*; Raymond E. Brown, *The Gospel According to John I-XII*, pp. lix-lx, 171-3.

[102]Cf. esp. Charles H. H. Scobie, "The Origins and Development of Samaritan Christianity," pp. 404-5; T. F. Glasson, *Moses in the Fourth Gospel*, pp. 20-30; J. R. Michaels, "The Johannine Words of Jesus and Christian Prophecy," *1975 SBL Seminar Papers*, II, 235-6.

[103]Cf. e.g., T. F. Glasson, *Moses in the Fourth Gospel*; R. H. Smith, "Exodus Typology in the Fourth Gospel," *JBL*, LXXXI (1962), 329-42; J. Macdonald, *The Theology of the Samaritans*, pp. 420-46; Raymond E. Brown, *The Gospel According to John I-XII*, p. lx.

[104]Cf. esp. T. F. Glasson, *Moses in the Fourth Gospel*, pp. 30-1; Raymond E. Brown, *The Gospel According to John I-XII*, pp. 172-3, 234, 325; J. R. Michaels, "The Johannine Words of Jesus," p. 236.

[105]Thus John 7:40 ("This is really the prophet") seemingly resembles Deut 18:18a ("I will raise up for them a prophet like you"), John 17:8 ("I have given them the *words* which thou gavest me") is comparable to Deut 18:18b ("I will put my *words* in his mouth"), and John 12:49b ("the Father who sent me has himself given me *commandment* what to say and what to *speak*") is comparable to Deut 18:18c ("he shall *speak* to them all that I *command* him").

[106]As writers such as C. K. Barrett ("The Old Testament in the Fourth Gospel," *JTS*, XLVIII (1947), 155-69) and F. -M. Braun (*Jean le Theologien II: Les grandes traditions d'Israel*) have shown, even though John contains relatively few explicit OT quotations, the Fourth Evangelist seems to have woven much of the OT into his system of thought.

[107]Cf. T. F. Glasson, *Moses in the Fourth Gospel*, p. 30; J. R. Michaels, "The Johannine Words of Jesus," p. 236; Charles H. H. Scobie, "The Origins and Development of Samaritan Christianity," pp. 402-5.

[108]As Charles H. H. Scobie (*Ibid.*, p. 404) has written, "It is becoming increasingly clear that a Moses/Christ parallelism dominates the christology of the Gospel."

that the Johannine eschatology is quite different from the Markan/Matthean.[109] Thus even though John does contain some futuristic elements (cf. esp. 5:25-29; 6:44,54; 14:3; 21:22-23),[110] the eschatology of John would still seem to be "predominantly 'realized' or 'realizing'."[111] Certainly, John possesses little of the apocalyptic element found in the Synoptics (even though the Markan/Matthean eschatology seems to have been modified at several points by Luke),[112] and outside of the few passages mentioned above, the Gospel of John apparently contains little futuristic material either.

An examination of the Books of Acts would seem to disclose that it also contains little apocalyptic or futuristic material. Pierson Parker has summarized the eschatological elements in Acts in this way:

> Acts devotes scarcely five sentences to any sort of futurist eschatology (Acts 1:11b; 3:20f.; 10:42b; 17:31a; 23:6b), and none of it sounds like Mark .... In this respect, as in its light treatment of the whole subject, Acts resembles the fourth gospel rather than any synoptic.[113]

Thus John and Acts (as well as Paul) both assert that it is *Jesus himself* who will judge all men (cf. John 5:22,26-29; Acts 10:42; 17:31),[114] and that it is *Jesus himself*, rather than the Son of man,[115] who will some day return (cf. John 14:3; 21:22-23; Acts 1:11; 3:20). On the other hand, the expectation of an "imminent parousia" is seemingly lacking in both John and Acts[116] in contrast to the frequency with which this concept is to be found in the Synoptics and Paul.[117] The familiar Synoptic term, "the kingdom of God," is also rare in both John and Acts,[118] and if John 12:32-34 clearly identifies Jesus with the Son of man, so does Acts

---

[109]Cf. e.g., M. -E. Boismard, "L'evolution du theme eschatologique dans les traditions johanniques," *RB*, LXVIII (1961), 507-24; Raymond E. Brown, *The Gospel According to John I-XII*, pp. cxv-cxxi; Wayne G. Rollins, "The New Testament and Apocalyptic," *NTS*, XVII (1971), 454-76; W. G. Kümmel, *The Theology of the New Testament*, trans. John E. Steely, pp. 283-306.

[110]Thus C. F. D. Moule ("The Individualism of the Fourth Gospel," *NovT*, V (1962), 182) has urged that "the Fourth Evangelist's eschatology is much more normal than is often assumed."

[111]See James H. Charlesworth, "A Critical Comparison of the Dualism in 1QS III: 13-IV: 26 And the 'Dualism' Contained in the Fourth Gospel," *NTS*, XV (1969), 407.

[112]Cf. Fred O. Francis, "Eschatology and History in Luke-Acts," *JAAR*, XXXVII (1969), 52-3; S. G. Wilson, "Lukan Eschatology," *NTS*, XVI (1970), 330-47.

[113]"The 'Former Treatise' and the Date of Acts," *JBL*, LXXXIV (1965), 58.

[114]Cf. also Rom 2:16; 2 Cor 5:10

[115]Cf. e.g., Wayne G. Rollins, "The New Testament and Apocalyptic," *NTS*, XVII (1971), 465-7, 474-6.

[116]Thus S. G. Wilson ("Lukan Eschatology," p. 347) has written that "Luke's eschatology does not appear to be the same in the Gospel and Acts. In the Gospel there is a tension between the delay and imminent expectation; in Acts there is no imminent expectation."

[117]Cf. e.g., Matt 4:17; 10:23; 16:28; 24:34; 26:64; Mark 1:15; 9:1; 13:29-30; 14:62; Luke 9:27; 12:41-48; 18:8; 21:32; Rom 13:11-12; I Cor 15:51-57; Phil 3:20-21; 4:5; Col 3:4; I Thes 1:10; 3:13; 4:13-18.

[118]Cf. John 3:3,5; Acts 1:3; 8:12; 14:22; 19:8; 28:23,31.

7:55-56.[119]

Both John and Acts also emphasize "believing,"[120] "salvation,"[121] and the crucial importance of the life, death, and resurrection of Jesus of Nazareth.[122] Thus John and Acts speak of "believing"/having "faith *in his name*" (cf. John 1:12; 3:18; Acts 3:16), refer to Jesus' "glorification" by God (cf. esp. John 17:1-5,22; Acts 3:13b), and frequently write of the *"many"* who had believed in Jesus (cf. esp. John 2:23; 4:39,41; 7:31; 10:42; 11:45; 12:11,42a; Acts 4:4a; 6:7b; 8:6a; 9:42; 14:1b; 17:12a; 18:8b; 19:18; 21:20b). Indeed, some of these latter John/Acts resemblances would seem to be quite close. Let the following three examples of this phenomenon suffice:

Acts	John
"and many believed in the Lord"[123] (9:42a)	"Yet many . . . believed in him" (7:31a)
"Many of them therefore believed" (17:12a)	"Many of the Jews therefore . . . believed in him" (11:45)[124]
"Many of the Corinthians hearing Paul believed" (18:8b)	"Many Samaritans . . . believed in him because of the woman's testimony" (4:39a)

John and Acts also share in urging that Jesus of Nazareth was the fulfillment of the writings of Moses and the prophets (cf. John 1:45; 5:39,46; Acts 3:24; 26:22; 28:23c),[125] and in emphasizing that Jesus was "the promised One" (cf. John 4:25; 6:14; 7:40,52; 11:27; Acts 3:22-24; 7:52; 13:25; 18:28; 19:4). John and Acts thus seem to stand close together in their emphasis on the present significance of the great acts of Christ as well as in their almost complete lack of any real apocalyptic material.

Summary and Conclusions

The length of this article prohibits an examination of all the areas of agreement that seem to exist between John and Acts. Nevertheless, mention should probably at least be made of the following additional areas in which these

---

[119]Thus both John 12:32 and Acts 7:55 first clearly identify the one "lifted up"/"standing at the right hand of God" as Jesus of Nazareth, and then only after making this identification do they ascribe the title, "the Son on man," to this personage (cf. John 12:34; Acts 7:56).

[120]Of the 241 occurrences of the word "believe" in the NT, ninety-eight of these occurrences are to be found in John and thirty-eight of them are to be found in Acts.

[121]Cf. esp. John 3:17; 4:42; 5:39; 7:38; 10:9,28; 12:47; 20:30-31; Acts 2:40,47; 4:12; 11:14; 13:23,26; 15:1,11; 16:17,30; 28:28.

[122]Cf. John 1:12-18; 10:7-18,24-30; 12:31-36,44-50; 17:1-23; 20:30-31; Acts 2:32-36; 3:13-15; 4:10-12; 5:30-31; 10:34-43; 13:23-39; 17:1-4; 18:5-11; 26:4-23; 28:23-31.

[123]Thus Acts 9:42a (*kai episteusan polloi epi ton kurion*) would seem to be quite comparable to John 7:31a (*de polloi episteusan eis auton*).

[124]Acts 17:12a (*polloi men oun eks auton episteusan*) is thus observed to be verbally quite similar to John 11:45 (*Polloi oun ek ton Iondaion . . . episteusan eis auton*).

[125]Cf. also Luke 16:29, 31; 24:27, 44b.

two writings seem to stand in rather close agreement: (a) Both John and Acts seem to possess a strong "anti-temple sentiment" in possible Samaritan contexts (cf. John 4:21-24; Acts 6:13-14; 7:47-50); (b) Both John 4:4-42 and Acts 8:4-25 seemingly reflect a keen interest in a mission to Samaria;[126] (c) Both John and Acts contain extensive teachings relating to the Holy Spirit, mainly in Jerusalem settings;[127] (d) Both John and Acts use the term, "the Jews," with great frequency in quite comparable ways; [128] (e) Both John and Acts inform us that the people (esp. "the Jews") were sometimes divided with regard to their opinion of Jesus or his disciples;[129] and (f) John and Acts agree that the *chief* opposition to Jesus and the early church in Jerusalem came from the chief priest.[130]

Our examination of the various John/Acts agreements have disclosed the

---

[126]Thus both John 4 and Acts 8 tell of Jesus (or Philip) going to "a city of Samaria" (cf. John 4:28,39; Acts 8:5) and teaching many people there. Both John 4:41 and Acts 8:6 also reflect a successful mission among the Samaritans, and it is in Samaria that John 4:35 depicts the fields as being "already white for harvest" (cf. also Charles H. H. Scobie, "The Origins and Development of Samaritan Christianity," p. 403). Both John and Acts also place this Samaritan mission immediately after their description of an earlier mission by Jesus or his apostles to the people of Jerusalem and Judea (cf. John 2:13-3:36; Acts 1:8; 2:1-8:1), so that the same geographical progression (Jerusalem-Judea-Samaria) is to be found in the early chapters of both John and Acts.

[127]Cf. esp. Pierson Parker, "Mark, Acts, and Galilean Christianity," pp. 297,301. But not only do most of the teachings in John and Acts relating to the Spirit occur in Jerusalem settings (cf. John 3:5-8; 7:37-39; 14:16-26; 15:26-27; 16:7-13; 20:21-23; Acts 1:2-9; 2:1-4,33-38; 5:32; 11:16-17), but there are also important agreements in these teachings between John and Acts. Thus John 14:16,26 agrees with Luke 24:49 and Acts 2:33 that it is "the Father" who sends "the Spirit," John 15:26b and Acts 5:32b both depict "the Spirit" as a "witness" to Jesus, while Acts 19:2 ("Did *you receive* the Holy Spirit when *you believed*?") would seem to be verbally and conceptually comparable to John 7:39 ("Now this he said about the Spirit, which those *who believed* in him were *to receive*").

[128]Of the 168 occurrences of the term, "the Jews," in the NT, seventy-three of them are to be found in John and fifty-seven of them in Acts. This term also occurs twenty times in the earlier letters of Paul (Rom, 1-2 Cor, Gal, 1 Thes), but is rare elsewhere in the NT. John and Acts also use this term in quite comparable ways. Thus Acts 21:20b can be compared with John 11:45; Acts 9:23 with John 5:18; Acts 14:19 with John 10:31; or Acts 17:11 with John 11:36.

[129]Thus John 9:16 informs us that "there was a division" among the Pharisees concerning Jesus, John 10:19 tells us that "there was again a division among the Jews because of these words," while Acts 23:7 asserts that "a dissension arose between the Pharisees and the Sadducees" concerning Paul (cf. also John 7:11-12:43; 11:45-46; Acts 14:4; 28:24).

[130]Thus in Acts 5:17 we learn that it was the high priest and the party of the Sadducees who "arrested the apostles" (cf. also Acts 4:1-6; 9:1; 24:1; 26:10). Similarly, John also indicates that the main opposition to Jesus had come from the high priest/chief priests. Thus John asserts (11:49-50; 18:14) that it was "Caiaphas" who had advised the Council that it was expedient for them to put Jesus to death, while in the Johannine passion narrative it was "the chief priests" who were usually depicted as the leaders of the movement that was seeking the death of Jesus (cf. esp. John 18:3,35; 19:6,15). And while John (like the Synoptics) frequently refers to the opposition of the Pharisees, whenever they are mentioned with the chief priests, it is always the chief priests who are listed first (cf. John 7:32b,45; 11:47,57; 18:3).

existence of certain phenomena that might be summarized as follows:

(1) There appear to exist some forty areas (e.g., the Baptist's proclamation of the Coming One, the Baptist as witness, the disciples as witnesses, the disciples as "chosen" by Christ, the emphasis on "seeing miracles," the use of "signs" for miracles, the importance of "seeing signs done," the proclamation of the messiahship of Jesus, being a witness to what one has "seen and heard," signs as a means of producing faith) in which Acts seemingly sides with John against the Markan/Matthean traditions and some twenty-five of these same areas (e.g., the Baptist's denial of messiahship, the Holy Spirit as a witness to Jesus, miracles a source of faith, the frequent usage of "Christ," a Moses/Christ parallelism, an interest in a mission to Samaria, extensive teachings concerning the Holy Spirit, the frequent usage of such terms as "believing," "salvation," "the Jews," "signs," "witness") in which Acts stands closer to John than it does even to the Third Gospel.

(2) Acts also possesses some thirty verbal agreements with St. John, some of which exhibit almost verbatim agreement between these two NT writings. Let the following five examples suffice:[131]

Acts	*John*
Blepein ta semeia ha epoiei	*etheoroun ta semeia ha epoiei*
(8:6b)	(6:2b)
hoti houtos estin ho huios tou theou	*hoti houtos estin ho huios tou theou*
(9:20b)	(1:34b)
hoti houtos estin ho Christos	*hoti Iesous estin ho Christos*
(9:22b)	(20:31b)
hoti ho theos en met autou	*ean me e ho theos met autou*
(10:38a)	(3:2c)
hou ouk eimi axios	*hou ouk eimi axios*
(13:25e)	(1:27b)

(3) There also exist a number of concepts and terms (e.g., "seeing signs done," "witnessing to what one has seen and heard," "signs" leading many to believe, the two-fold witness of the disciples and the Holy Spirit, a Moses/Christ parallelism, no "imminent eschatology") that in the NT are limited only or mainly to John and Acts.[132]

---

[131]In addition to these five Acts/John parallels herein listed, the reader is referred to the following additional verbal agreements that seem to exist between these two writings: Acts 3:14a/John 6:69b; Acts 4:4a/John 4:41; Acts 4:16a/John 11:47b; Acts 4:20/John 3:32; Acts 5:32a/John 21:24a; Acts 7:55b/John 11:40b; Acts 8:5a/John 4:5; Acts 9:39c/John 11:33b; Acts 9:42b/John 11:45; Acts 10:39a/John 21:24a; Acts 10:42b/John 5:27a; Acts 10:43a/John 5:39b; Acts 13:25c/John 1:20b; Acts 14:4a/John 7:43; Acts 17:3b/John 7:41; Acts 17:7b/John 19:12b; Acts 17:12a/John 11:45; Acts 18:8c/John 4:39a; Acts 19:2a/John 7:39; Acts 19:4b/John 1:36; Acts 21:20b/John 12:11; Acts 22:15/John 3:32.

[132]Among other NT terms that are to be found only in John and Luke-Acts are such words as "rulers" (Luke 18:18; 23:13,35; 24:20; John 3:1; 7:26,48; 12:42; Acts 3:17; 4:5,8,26; 13:27), "Annas" (Luke 3:2; John 18:13,24; Acts 4:6), "Solomon's Porch" (John 10:23; Acts 3:11; 5:12), and another disciple named "Judas" (Luke 6:16; John 14:22; Acts 1:13).

(4) While the parallels between Luke and John are limited basically to their passion narratives and a few other key pericopes (see the Introduction to this study, esp. n. 28), Acts' parallels with John are with far more sections of the Fourth Gospel than is true of the Lukan/Johannine parallels (e.g., Acts has verbal/conceptual agreements with such varied sections of John as 1:20a,27,34; 2:23b; 3:2c,32; 4:29,39,41; 5:1-18,39c,46; 6:2b,14,69b; 7:31a,39,41a,43; 11:27,45,47b; 14:16,26; 15:26c-27; 19:12b; 20:31a; 21:24a).

Our examination of the John/Acts agreements has seemingly disclosed a number of areas where John and Acts stand in quite close agreement. Indeed, it seems to us that some of these agreements are too precise to be merely accidental. Especially when one adds the numerous Lukan/Johannine parallels to these John/Acts agreements, then the number of verbal/conceptual agreements that exist between Luke/Acts and John would appear to be quite considerable indeed. Certainly, many solutions for these Lukan/Johannine phenomena (e.g., John was influenced by Luke-Acts, both Luke and John knew common or similar early traditions, Luke had become familiar with some early form of Johannine thought) remain possible, with not all of these options being necessarily mutually exclusive.

Nevertheless, it seems to us that these various John/Acts agreements (esp. those areas where Acts stands closer to John than it does even to Luke) suggest the possibility that Luke, in his writing of Luke-Acts, had become acquainted with some early form of the developing Johannine tradition. We would therefore like to conclude this study by making the following three tentative suggestions: (1) The evidence suggests that when Luke wrote Acts, early Christian tradition had become very fluid, diverse, and complex; (2) Acts' modifications of Luke and Acts making so much greater use than Luke of such concepts as "witness," "signs," and "believing" suggests that a time interval of some length intervened between Luke's writing of his Gospel and Acts;[133] and (3) during this time period in which he wrote Luke and Acts, the Third Evangelist possibly had become familiar with *some early form of Johannine thought.* At the least, these John/Acts agreements suggest that here is an area of NT study that calls for considerable investigation and discussion.

---

[133]Similarly, S. G. Wilson ("Lukan Eschatology," p. 347) has written that "it seems quite probable, purely on the basis of his eschatology (in Acts), that Luke wrote Acts a considerable time after the Gospel, and that in the interim period his views developed and changed."

The Last Volume of Luke: The Relation of Luke-Acts to the Pastoral Epistles[1]

Jerome D. Quinn

The abrupt ending of Acts still provokes questions. The author of this work well knew how to end one volume and begin another as the transition from Luke to Acts illustrates.[2] Moreover as one reads the final chapters of Acts, with their third narration of Paul's conversion, the lengthy storm scene, the double arrival in Rome (28:14, 16), and the like, one comes away with the impression that the author, with full deliberation, has been filling up the roll and bringing this volume to precisely the conclusion he wanted. Yet the final note that Paul stayed on "for two years" under house arrest implies that there was more that the author could have told.[3]

Is it conceivable that the ending of Acts is really part of a larger problem? Is there a literary relation between the works which we call Luke-Acts and that little collection of letters to Titus and Timothy that purport to be Pauline and which tor

---

[1] The hypothesis being offered here grew out of discussions in a 1968 seminar for the Catholic Biblical Association of America and has been used since (cf. "Ministry in the New Testament," *Lutherans and Catholics in Dialogue*, eds. P. Empie and T. A. Murphy, p. 96, n. 107, reprinted in *Biblical Studies in Contemporary Thought*, ed. M. Ward, as well as "P46 — The Pauline Canon?" *CBQ*, XXXVI [1974], 385, n.36) as I have prepared my commentary for the Doubleday Anchor Bible, volume 35, *I and II Timothy and Titus*.

[2] In this paper, the term "Luke" will be used as a synonym for the author of the compositions that will be designated as Luke-Acts.

[3] E. Haenchen, *The Acts of the Apostles*, pp. 724, 726.

convenience we dub the Pastoral Epistles?[4]

Common Characteristics

Luke-Acts and PE share certain characteristics for all their evident differences. Thus both literary *corpora* come from the second Christian generation, i.e., sometime between A. D. 70-100, and both employ sources, both oral and written.[5] Again Luke-Acts does not explicitly name its author and the name of Paul, prefixed to each of the PE, has not settled the question about his actual authorship of the text that follows. Thirdly, both collections have been explicitly addressed to individual persons — a "Theophilus" who has never been identified with any individual known otherwise among the Christians of the first two generations; and Timothy and Titus, known on other grounds as collaborators with Paul in the first Christian generation but whose actual relationship to the PE is as problematic as the nature of the Pauline authorship of this little collection.[6]

It is in their literary form that these two blocks of composition appear in the sharpest contrast. Luke-Acts is quite evidently a theological narrative cast in a biographical form that has been interlarded with sayings and speeches that interpret for the reader the events and activities that engage the persons who are being written about, from the father and mother of John the Baptist through Jesus and his apostles to Paul under house arrest in Rome. The PE are in the epistolary genre, and thus are meant to be received as part of a dialogue, a conversation in writing, in which a person's observations and directives have been given a form that transcends the limits in which space and time confine a man. The content of the PE as well as their peculiar lexical and syntactical character already signal that these letters were meant to be read in tandem, and probably in the order Titus — I Tim — II Tim.[7] They were published as a single collection of three letters, and

---

[4]Hereafter, "PE": This abbreviation and terms 1-2 Tim, Titus, when they occur in this essay, designate the literary composition(s) unless the context unequivocally refers to these persons.

[5]Not only the source materials (the Jewish scriptures; Mark, Jesus' logia; hymns, prayers, credal professions, etc.) but even the manner in which they are redacted show resemblances. There is no space for further analysis here. In particular one must forego examining the question of the relation of PE to a correspondence from "the historical Paul" in the sixties of the first century. I hold that there was an *epistolē systatikē* behind Titus 1:1, 4-5 and 3:12-15 as well as a personal note (or notes) behind what is now 2 Tim 1:1-2, 15-18; 4:6-22 and other scattered verses, but the argument for these is reserved for the commentary cited in n. 1.

[6]On authorship and date: see the commentaries of Jeremias (NTD), Spicq (E Bib), Kelly (HNTC) versus N. Brox (RNT), Dibelius-Conzelmann (HNT), C. K. Barrett (New Clarendon Bible) for an early origin in the Pauline entourage versus pseudonymous authorship in the second or even the third Christian generation.

[7]Cf. W. Doty "The Classification of Epistolary Literature" *CBQ*, XXXI (1969), 183-199, esp. 192-8, as well as *Letters in Primitive Christianity,* esp. pp. 8-9.

The following facts argue for the order of PE proposed here: the very lengthy introduction of Titus 1:1-4 which is discussed below; the way in which the content of Titus is repeated and redacted in 1 Tim; the way in which 1-2 Timothy telescope into one another (cf. the abrupt "conclusion" of 1 Tim 6:20-21a [Doty, *Letters,* p. 40, n. 48] and the disturbed

thus resemble the single *biblion* of seven letters that opens Rev (1:11) more than I—II Thess or I—II Cor. But if the PE are indeed a dialogue between Paul and his co-worker-successors, preserved in the genre of the "unreal letter,"[8] then their link with the speeches of Acts as well as their Pauline "biographical" interest bring them closer to Luke-Acts than the dramatic difference in form would at first lead one to suspect. Actually each composition in its own genre complements the other as both alike set out to exalt the Pauline apostolate and transmit the Pauline teaching.

Evidences for Relationship

Are there hard data for a relationship between these two literary *corpora*? Already in 1830 H. A. Schott suggested a common author for Luke-Acts and PE, the Luke of II Tim 4:11. In recent decades a series of studies have made the case more credible. In this essay, a selection of data under three headings are proposed from which one could infer a literary relationship between Luke-Acts and PE.[9]

Linguistic Data

The essays of C. F. D. Moule and A. Strobel have laid the groundwork in lexical and syntactical analysis which illustrate the bonds between Luke-Acts and PE.[10] The work has been critiqued by N. Brox and W. G. Kümmel.[11]

Though one could qualify one or another entry in Strobel's lists,[12] his base can in fact be effectively broadened by considering the proper names which in the NT are found only in the PE and Luke-Acts. Thus in the NT only these compositions

---

text of 6:21b where B. Metzger, *A Textual Commentary on the Greek NT*, p. 644, opts for the plural, against J. K. Elliott, *The Greek Text of Timothy and Titus*, p. 110; the appropriateness of a final position of 2 Timothy with its last testament of Paul; the fact that this is the order in which they are listed in the *Muratorianum*, 59-64. The "canonical" order represents an arrangement on a quite different principle and some time after the original publication of the PE (see below and *CBQ supra*. n. 1, pp. 379-85).

[8]W. Doty, *Letters*, pp. 6-7; 65-71.

[9]The evidence will be fully marshalled in the commentary cited in n.1.

[10]C. F. D. Moule, *The Birth of the NT,* pp. 220-1, and "The Problem of the PE: a Reappraisal," *BJRL*, XLVII (1965), 430-52; A. Strobel, "Schreiben des Lukas? Zum sprachlichen Problem der Pastoralbriefe," *NTS*, XV (1969), 191-210, who also cites the authors since Schott who had favored Lukan intervention in the production of PE.

[11]N. Brox, "Lukas als Verfasser der Pastoralbriefe?" *JAC*, XIII (1970), 62-77; W. G. Kümmel, *Introduction to the New Testament,* trans. A. J. Mattill, Jr., p. 374.

[12]Strobel, "Schreiben des Lukas?" p. 194-5, one could add at apotheisthai, Acts 7:27,39; at sōphrosynē, 1 Tim 2:15; at sōphrōn, Titus 1:8; at hyponoein, Acts 25:18. Again, neōteroi also occurs at 1 Peter 5:5 and that entry accordingly might well move into Strobel's second list of terms that are found frequently in Luke-Acts-PE but comparatively rarely in the remainder of NT. If symparaginesthai is for textual reasons not to keep its place in the former list, then paraginesthai might well appear in the latter, for 29/36 NT uses are in Luke-Acts-PE, versus one in the remainder of the Paulines (1 Cor 16:3).

name Pilate "Pontius" (Luke 3:1; Acts 4:27; 1 Tim 6:13) or "Crete" and "Cretans" (Acts 2:11; 27:7, 12, 13, 21; Titus 1:5, 12) or Miletus or Pisidian Antioch, Iconium, and Lystra to which we shall return below.

Strobel's inferences from vocabulary[13] can be strengthened. Every word found in Luke-Acts is, in a real sense, the choice of the author, whether he picked it from a source or not. The same is true of the vocabulary of PE. Where the vocabulary stock of these two literary *corpora* coincides, every term has to be weighed in evaluating a possible relationship, no matter how many times a term can be documented elsewhere in the NT or in other first century compositions. Terms found only in Luke-Acts and PE will be particularly persuasive, but ultimately all the words that they have in common must be considered.[14] To the commonality in vocabulary that has surfaced from these studies, one must add the numerous grammatical and syntactical coincidences between these two *corpora,* including the notable use of compound words (861 in Luke-Acts; 135 in PE).[15] Though all these phenomena suggest an actual relationship between Luke-Acts and PE, they do not of themselves demonstrate it nor do they offer an explanation of the resemblances that have emerged.

Common Materials

Do the coincidences in content, i.e., in the subjects treated by these two bodies of literature, clarify the relationship that vocabulary and syntax suggest? The delicacy of the question becomes apparent when one recalls that all Christian literature has precipitated from the relation of believers with Jesus Christ. The fact that his name occurs more frequently than any other in the PE or in Luke-Acts indicates the attachment of the author(s) to that person rather than any literary relationship between the compositions. Again, certain persons who were historically members of the Pauline entourage, e.g., Titus, figure in PE and are otherwise named only in the other Pauline documents. Others who figure in PE, such as Paul, Timothy, Tychicus, and Apollos, are found not only in the other Paulines, but also in Acts (and in the case of Paul and Timothy even in 2 Peter and

---

[13]Strobel's statistics on the common terms shared by PE with Luke-Acts can be schematized as follows:

Vocabulary of PE, apart from proper nouns 848

NT *hapax legomena* in PE 175

Terms in PE that also occur in Luke-Acts 493

Terms in PE that also occur in the ten other Paulines 540

Terms that are exclusively or typically Lukan .... c. 65

Terms that are exclusively or typically Pauline .... c. 50

[14]On the NT literature as an integral part of a larger pool of documentation, Christian (orthodox and heretical), Jewish, and pagan, see H. Koester, "New Testament Introduction: a Critique of a Discipline," *Christianity, Judaism, and Other Greco-Roman Cults,* ed. J. Neusner, I, 1-20, esp. 9ff.

[15]Strobel, "Schreiben des Lukas?" pp. 197-201. The materials on style, now in N. Turner, *A Grammar of New Testament Greek,* IV, 45-63; 101-5 are important, as well as G. D. Kilpatrick, "What John Tells Us About John," *Studies in John,* ed. W. C. van Unnik, pp. 75-87, esp. 79-81 and cf. n. 26.

Hebrews). The PE name places such as Rome, Corinth, Ephesus, and even Troas that are noted in the other Paulines as well as in Acts. The coincidence becomes striking when 2 Tim 3:11 writes of the Pisidian Antioch, Iconium, and Lystra which are otherwise documented in first-century Christian compositions only in Acts 13-14, 16. Both *loci* offer the same order for the names and both cite the persecutions that Paul suffered in those cities. Most striking of all, both compositions draw the same theological lesson out of that content.

In contemporary scholarship about Acts it is commonplace to note that there is an indisputable and curious silence about Paul's correspondence. There is not a hint that the apostle dispatched a single letter to a church or to an individual, although other correspondence is noted.[16] On occasion a few words in Acts can be paralleled with a text in Rom or Gal. Not so often noted has been a corresponding phenomenon in PE, which for all their veneration of Paul never actually quote from his letters. At best one can find, on two or three occasions, as many as three words running which might be cited from Rom (Titus 1:15; 2 Tim 2:20-21) or Phil (2 Tim 4:6).[17] In a word, the PE document Paul's literary remains to roughly the same extent as Luke-Acts.

Theological Relationships

In the light of such coincidences in language and content, coincidences in the theology of Luke-Acts and PE become significant;[18] and in fact the way in which PE reflect upon and articulate the relation of the one God of Israel to men in Christ bears some striking resemblances to the approach of Luke-Acts. There is in both bodies of literature an interest in hymns, prayers, and credal compositions whose theological vocabulary and conceptualization are notably similar,[19] at times surprisingly so.[20] Moreover, both language and content issue in the same

---

[16]See the treatment of the "unreal letter" below for fuller discussion with citations.

[17]The way in which 1 Clem cites 1 Cor would illustrate the contrast with PE. The extent to which the correspondence with the Corinthians, embedded in the Acts of Paul, adduces texts from the Pauline letters is also notable (cf. E. Hennecke, *New Testament Apocrypha*, II, 374-77, with an introduction to its problems, 340-42).

[18]Methodologically the historico-critical questions about the relationship of these two literary *corpora* are prior to questions of the theology or theologies that underlie them. These compositions are not in the genre of scientific theological tracts any more than in the form of scientific history or of an actual correspondence. Accordingly if it becomes historically possible or probable that Luke-Acts and PE originated from the same author, then any theology which they possibly or probably presuppose has to be disengaged from analyzing the whole composition, not by denying or simply ignoring the literary relationship between its parts, a procedure that has dominated the treatment of Luke-Acts since 100 A.D.

[19]Thus one notes the association of the *sōtēria* and *epiphaneia* terminology with the events surrounding the birth of Jesus (rather than with the passion-resurrection or the final judgment) in both Luke 1-2 (cf. R. Brown, *The Birth of the Messiah*, pp. 360, 439, 460) and in Titus 2:11-14; 3:4-7; 1 Tim 1:15; 2 Tim 1:8-10. C. F. D. Moule, "The Christology of Acts," *Studies in Luke-Acts*, eds. L. Keck and J. Martyn, pp. 159-185, esp. 176-7, offers many evocative observations.

[20]Thus the solemn Christian prayer of Acts 4:24 addresses God as *despota* as did the

theologoumena. Thus what happened to Paul in the Galatian cities included not only persecutions (diōgmous) but also the Lord's rescue, and from this experience the author of PE infers in Paul's name, "Indeed, all who desire to lead a godly life in Christ Jesus will be persecuted (diōchthēsontai) while evil men and imposters will go from bad to worse, deceivers and deceived" (2 Tim 3:11-13). When the author of Acts describes the return of the persecuted "apostles" (Acts 14:4, 14), Barnabas and Paul, to the same Galatian cities which had almost destroyed them and their mission, the author has them exhort the believers to persevere, "saying that through many tribulations (thlipseōn) we must enter the kingdom of God" (Acts 14:22). The three-fold coincidence here, in terminology, in persons and events described, and in theological inference is particularly notable.[21]

The resemblances noted are not unique. Stephen Wilson's introductory study on the relationships between the image of the apostle Paul in the PE and Acts maps out similar currents flowing between the two bodies of literature.[22] Again the similarity between the concepts of the Kingdom of God in PE and Luke-Acts is notable,[23] as well as the way in which the PE provide the "security" that is the anounced object of the author of Luke-Acts (Luke 1:1-4).

Hypotheses

But what is the *Sitz im Leben* of the PE? How does their picture of the community of believers, its administration, its teaching, its life and problems, relate to the picture in Acts?[24]

Such questions have to be answered in terms of the hypothesis that one proposes to account for the similar data that have been sampled above. Such a hypothesis could assume three basic patterns that are not mutually exclusive.

1) PE and Luke-Acts came from two different authors in the second Christian generation. Resemblances between them are explained in terms of a common temporal and theological horizon as well as written sources and similar oral reports to which both had access.

2) PE and Luke-Acts come from two different authors, one of whom used

---

aged Jewish Simeon (Luke 2:29) but not as "Father" which one might have expected after Luke 11:2. Indeed David is "our father" in Acts 4:25. The PE similarly address God as "the King of ages" (*basilei*: 1 Tim 1:17; cf. 6:15-16) though they too know the title "Father" (Titus 1:4; 1 Tim 1:2; 2 Tim 1:2). Cf. the essay of A. A. Trites in this volume.

[21]The more general correlation with the way in which Luke-Acts links Jesus and the gospel with both salvation and catastrophe also ought to be noted: thus compare the canticles and oracles of Luke 1-2 (Brown, *Birth of the Messish*) with Luke 3:4-9 and Acts 28:23-28, as well as 2 Tim 3:12-13.

[22]S. Wilson, "The Portrait of Paul in Acts and the Pastorals" *SBL 1976 Seminar Papers*, ed. George MacRae, pp. 397-411, as well as his *The Gentiles and the Gentile Mission in Luke-Acts*, pp. 116-7, and his *Luke and the Pastoral Epistles* (to be published). R. F. Collins, "The Image of Paul in the Pastorals," *LTP*, XXXI (1975), 147-73, is the more persuasive for the fact that it was written without a view to the thesis argued here.

[23]Cf. 2 Tim 4:1, 18 with Luke 22:29, 30; 23:42; Acts 14:22; 28:23, 31.

[24]Cf. Kümmel, *Introduction to the NT*, p. 374.

the other's composition. That relationship could be either:

a)   the author of Luke-Acts used the PE as one of his sources, and thus resemblances to the PE are due to a conscious adoption and adaptation of their teaching; or

b)   the author of PE used Luke-Acts and fashioned his "Pauline epistolary" to supplement and continue what he felt was lacking in Luke-Acts. On this hypothesis the PE are the earliest answer to the abrupt conclusion of Acts, and its silence about Paul's correspondence.

3)   A third hypothesis would submit that one author was responsible for Luke-Acts and PE.

On this hypothesis, the two literary *corpora* could be regarded as:

a)   completely separate compositions at quite different times; or

b)   they could also be considered as one long composition originally published in three consecutive papyrus rolls or volumes with Luke-Acts followed by the single roll containing Titus — 1 Tim — 2 Tim in that order. The data will be reviewed in the light of this hypothesis, reserving the full discussion of all the options for another work.[25]

Epistolary Appendices

Is it even conceivable that there was an epistolary appendix that concluded a composition in another genre? The author of Acts was already an innovator in publishing his second volume as a complement to his gospel. He was moreover the most versatile stylist in the NT with wide ranging interests in his reading and associations.[26] He was on the theological alert, listening to the problems of his generation and refracting them through what had been done and said by Israel, Jesus, and the first generation churches.   But would it have occurred to him, in the latter decades of the first Christian century, to have written his work in such a mixed genre?

The Hebrew Bible once bears the trace of such an appendix to several volumes of narrative when 2 Chron 36:23 draws to a close with the written proclamation of Cyrus authorizing the return to Jerusalem and the restoration of the temple there. One must wait, however, until the Hellenistic period of the LXX collection to find the Jeremiah corpus (re-)arranged in the order: the prophetic book; the book attributed to the disciple, Baruch; then the little collection of poems that we call Lamentations; and finally the so-called "Epistle of Jeremiah" (to the exiles).[27] The rather later Latin translations of this collection witness to another form of this arrangement in which Jer-Lam-Baruch have the Epistle of

---

[25]Cf. *supra*, n. 1.

[26]N. Turner, "The Quality of Greek in Luke-Acts," *Studies in New Testament Language and Text*, ed. J. K. Elliott, p. 387, citing A. Plummer. Is this versatility the reason for the PE belonging, on Kilpatrick's criteria (*supra*, n. 15), in the stylistic lumber room of the NT, along with Mark, John, and Revelation, whereas the narrative of Luke-Acts is of high stylistic quality?

[27]Cf. D. R. Hillers, *Lamentations*, p. xviii. Note that the Vg Esther puts the letter of

Jeremiah suffixed to Bar as its closing chapter.

In the same period, in Jewish pseudepigraphical composition, this closing of a more or less lengthy composition with an "epistle" was occurring in both Aramaic and Greek. A pre-Christian Enoch collection was in five Aramaic "books" that could be distributed in separate scrolls or volumes. Certain works seem to have moved in and out of the collection (e.g., the third "Book of the Giants").[28] This loose-leaf pentateuch of apocalyptic concluded with "the Epistle of Enoch". The work was not only translated for Greek-speaking Jews, but there is no question that the "epistle" was *de facto* detached and read separately by both Jews (4Q En ^{9}) and Christians. The latter read it together with still other works, e.g., the sermon on the Passover by Melito of Sardis.[29] Even this "epistle" is apparently a composite.[30]

Just as notable is the pseudepigraphical Apocalypse of Baruch that appeared in the Hellenistic world in the last decades of the first Christian century.[31] The last nine chapters of this work profess to be one of two epistles that the successor to Jeremiah wrote as a testament to the dispersed people of God. Again this "epistle" became detached and remained afloat when the rest of the work sank into a twelve-century oblivion.

Even outside the Jewish and Christian communities and in the first part of the third century when Diogenes Laertius compiled "The Lives and Opinions of Eminent Philosophers in Ten Books" he concluded a dozen of these sketches with one or more letters, usually to individuals, and his *Vita* of Epicurus ended with three long, doctrinal letters.[32]

Thus there is evidence that points to the last pre-Christian century and the first Christian centuries as precisely the period in which this combination of genres would occur to an author, particularly one versed in the Hellenistic Jewish tradition. There is accordingly nothing antecedently improbable in the author of

---

Artaxerxes last. The LXX Esther 10:3^l refers to a letter. MT has no letter. Whoever put 2 Chr at the end of MT added apparently the brief letter (edict or proclamation of Cyrus) borrowed from Ezr 1:1-3. Also see C. A. Moore, *Daniel, Esther and Jeremiah: the Additions*, pp. 259, 325-28.

[28] J. T. Milik, *The Books of Enoch* on whose introduction these paragraphs have been based.

[29] See the C. Bonner and F. Kenyon editions cited by Milik, p. xiii, and his own analysis of the "epistle", pp. 47-58.

[30] Milik, pp. 55-7.

[31] J. H. Charlesworth, *The Pseudepigrapha and Modern Research*, pp. 83-6 for a summary and bibliography, and the edition by P. Bogaert *L'Apocalypse syriaque de Baruch*, who in volume 1, pp. 67-8, 120-6, discusses the "epistle" as part of this work, as well as the epistolary "testament" in the service of apocalyptic composition.

[32] Conveniently available in the Loeb Classical Library, edited by R. D. Hicks, this *Vita* has an additional appendix of forty maxims. I owe this reference to C. H. Talbert, whose observations on the pattern in which Diogenes arranges his lives (founder-successors-summary of teaching) illuminates the hypothesis being argued here: see his *Literary Patterns, Theological Themes and the Genre of Luke-Acts*, pp. 125-40; his observations on PE on pp. 95-6 could also square with this hypothesis.

Luke-Acts composing and publishing the final volume of his work as an appended epistolary.

An Epistolary Appendix for Luke-Acts?

What are the actual probabilities for such a composition? Since 1836 and K. A. Credner, through Spitta, Goguel, and Zahn,[33] it has been noted that Acts 1:1 speaks of the third gospel as the author's "first work" (*prōton logon*) not "the former work" (of two: *proteron logon*); and thus the terminology itself could suggest that a further volume was projected after Acts. *Prōton* certainly can be the Hellenistic equivalent of *proteron*. Yet that does not eliminate all basis for taking the language of the author who penned the elegant prologue of Luke 1:1-4, in the superlative sense in which it has been written.[34] When one reads the opening of Acts in conjunction with the abrupt ending noted above, the text begins to speak for some such reconstruction of the work that the author projected.

In the Lukan prologue the author explicitly proposed that his composition give "security" (*tēn asphaleian*) to the catechesis that "Theophilus" had received (Luke 1:4). That term and its cognates are particularly Lukan in the NT.[35] The PE do not employ the terminology, yet precisely as "non-real letters" they fulfill that purpose.

Already in the LXX addition to the MT of Esther, "epistles" were interspersed to confirm the authenticity of what was being narrated (thus the text of an edict) and give it credibility.[36] Recent studies have submitted that the "non-real letter" (like the non-real speech) had not only the apologetic function of authenticating the directives that came over the author's signature but that they also served to satisfy the curiosity of the community about the personalities of the past and to purvey edifying biographical information about them.[37]

The way in which the author of Acts used "letters" (*grammata: epistolē*) is notable in this connection. In Acts 9:2 the Jewish *epistolas* authorize Paul's persecution (cf. 22:5); in Acts 15:30, the *epistolē* is the Jerusalem decree (cf. vs. 22-29) for the gentile converts; in Acts 23:25, 33 the reference is to the dispatch from Claudius Lysias in Jerusalem down to the governor Felix in Caesarea ("quoted" in vss. 26-30), to explain why he was sending Paul on to his superior. In Acts 28:21 the Jews of Rome say, "We have received no letters (*grammata*) from Judea about you . . ." *Epistolē* for this author designates letters (Jewish, Christian, Roman) that were in some way authoritative and directive for action; the only two

---

[33]E. Haenchen, *Acts*, pp. 16-8, 137 n. 1.

[34]Cf. F. Blass, A. Debrunner, R. Funk, *A Greek Grammar of the New Testament,*#62 with #464.

[35]Acts 5:23; adjective, Acts 21:34; 22:30; 25:26; verb, Acts 16:24; adverb, Acts 2:36; 16:23. There are half a dozen other NT uses, including 1 Thes 5:3; Phil 3:1.

[36]O. Eissfeldt, *The Old Testament*, pp. 591-2, and cf. Moore, *Daniel, Esther, and Jeremiah*, pp. 153-4, 165-6, 190-9, 232-8.

[37]W. Doty, *Letters in Primitive Christianity*, pp. 6-7; 65-71 and the literature cited there, with K. Berger, "Apostelbrief und apostolische Rede" *ZNW*, LXV (1974), 190-231 and Bogaert, *L'Apocalypse syriaque de Baruch,* as in n. 31.

that are quoted profess to emanate from the Jerusalem church and from the Roman imperial service.[38]

Regardless of the literary relation between Luke-Acts and PE, this use of correspondence in the composition of Acts still signals what the composer of a collection of non-real letters would intend that genre of composition to communicate. The Paul of PE comes on the scene as transmitting directives as authoritative as those of the Jerusalem church. His letters come out of his task or mission in an imperial service. In the hypothesis submitted here, the PE really aimed to give further "security" to Theophilus in several ways, by rehabilitating the Pauline apostolate and teaching (as the author understood it). He wrote for the benefit of a generation that had allowed Paul to fall into oblivion. Along with Acts, this correspondence aimed at lifting the cloud from the apostle who had probably been betrayed finally by some of his Christian brothers (cf. 2 Tim 1:15; 4:10-11, 14-16),[39] who had been executed after due process (cf. 2 Tim 4:16) as a Roman citizen, who was an embarrassment to his very successors (cf. 2 Tim 1:8; 2:8-9). One or another church doubtless still read a single letter or even a pair that the previous generation had received from Paul. There is no evidence that anyone in the decades following his martyrdom set out to collect the surviving correspondence, much less to circulate it.

Now in the eighties, Acts aimed to restore confidence in the Pauline apostolate and the PE to ensure its continuation in the second Christian generation. Both the speeches of Acts and the PE intend to summarize and transmit the Pauline teaching. Both accordingly put it into written form to give it evidentiary weight.[40] Even the division and repetitions of the evidence between two witnesses (i.e., Titus and Timothy) and the three documents serve further to verify its authenticity according to the norms of the Torah (cf. 1 Tim 5:19). Moreover, the concluding letter, 2 Timothy, is also a Pauline last will and testament. Letters often enough served this purpose in the Hellenistic world;[41] and the testamentary genre, common enough in the pseudepigrapha,[42] has been

---

[38]In Luke 16:6-7 *grammata* are receipts for goods received and in Acts 26:24, human learning. PE do not use *epistolē*, and *grammata*, qualified as *hiera,* refer to the Jewish scriptures (2 Tim 3:15). Only in 1 Tim 3:14 do PE use *graphein*, and there in a "disclosure formula" it refers to Paul writing this composition to his coworker (cf. J. L. White, *The Body of the Greek Letter*, pp. 45-6, 49-51 for the parallels from the papyri to this verse). The noun, *graphē*, in PE certainly refers to the Jewish scriptures and perhaps to a collection of Jesus' sayings (1 Tim 5:18; 2 Tim 3:16).

[39]O. Cullmann, *Peter*, trans F. V. Filson, pp. 91-110 has argued for this, particularly from 1 Clem 5:2,5, and it has been received favorably since (cf. S. Wilson, *SBL 1976 Seminar Papers,* p. 401).

[40]For the concern of the author of Acts with the laws of evidence and witnesses, see A. A. Trites, "The Importance of Legal Scenes and Language in the Book of Acts" *NovT,* XVI (1974), 278-284, and *The New Testament Concept of Witness*, pp. 66-77, 128-153, and particularly on PE, 207-212.

[41]Doty, *Letters in Primitive Christianity,* p. 5.

[42]Charlesworth, *The Pseudepigrapha and Modern Research, passim* for bibliography, and E. Stauffer, *New Testament Theology,* trans. J. Marsh, pp. 344-7 for a comparative listing and classification of data.

documented elsewhere in the NT, not to mention Acts and PE.[43] The very point of the testamentary form is the lawful transmission of an inheritance from father to son, from the exalted and venerable patriarch to his lesser descendants. That is precisely what is at stake in PE, the authentic transmission of the Pauline inheritance; i.e., his work and his teaching, to his real children (cf. Titus 1:4; 1 Tim 1:2,18; 2 Tim 1:2; 2:1-9).

But do PE, beginning with Titus, actually complement Acts? To put the question at the point where it is most acute, does Titus 1:1-4 (as an introduction to the *whole* correspondence that follows) read out of Acts 28 in a literarily satisfying fashion? The narrative of Acts concluded with that solemn scene in which Paul, still under arrest, conferred with the members of the Roman synagogues, bearing witness to (*diamartyromenos*, 28:23) and proclaiming (*kēryssōn*, 28:31) the kingdom of God (*tēn basileian tou theou*), warning his Jewish hearers as they balk that ". . . this salvation of God has been sent to the Gentiles" (*tois ethnesin apestalē touto to sōtērion*) (28:28). The narrative then concludes (Acts 28:30-31) with the emphatic assurance that this two-year house-arrest did not halt the Pauline *kērygma* or *didachē*, his mission to unbelievers and believers; that, in fact, he continued to teach "about the Lord Jesus Christ quite openly" in public (*meta pasēs parrēsias*) and "without let or hindrance" (*akōlytōs*). With this technical legal term[44] Acts concludes. *Ex hypothesi* the reader now opened the third volume or roll of Luke's work, the epistolary appendix, and began reading the sixty-six words of the solemn introduction to Titus (1:1-4). Only the letters to the Galatians and the Romans surpass this opening in length, and, comparatively speaking, it is the longest in the Pauline corpus. Is this flamboyant, baroque entrance to a mere three chapters of text no more than a nervous apology for a pseudonymous composition? If Titus is indeed the opening document of the third roll, then the reader is encountering the solemn prologue to the last volume of Luke-Acts and the abrupt shift in form calls for just such a full-dress introduction to the three-letter volume that follows. Moreover, the key terms of Titus 1:1-4 also appear to run back into the last verses of Acts with that change of key which would be expected in a different genre. Thus the Paul that Acts described as *kēryssōn* now speaks of the *kērygma* that has been entrusted to him (Titus 1:3). "This *salvation of God* " in Acts 28:28 (cf. 31) becomes a reference to *tou sōtēros hēmōn theou* (1:3) and to *Christou Iēsou tou sōtēros hēmōn* (1:4). The *apestalē* of the same saying now becomes *apostolos . . . . Iēsou Christou* of Titus 1:1. The solemn and explicit authentication of Paul as apostle and as one who penned a correspondence, which hardly figured in Acts, now comes into focus for a lengthy treatment in the evidentiary letters that follow.

The ending of Acts had assured the reader that Roman house arrest put no legal hindrance on Paul's preaching or teaching. With the opening of the PE, the reader meets the apostle free once more, journeying, (Titus 1:5; cf. 3:12) still

---

[43]J. Munck, "Discours d'adieu dans le NT" *Aux sources do la tradition chrétienne: Mélanges Goguel*, ed. J. J. von Allmen, pp. 155-70, and J. Dupont, *Le discours de Milet*.

[44]Not otherwise documented in LXX, NT, or the apostolic fathers but in Testament of Job 45:4, and six times in Philo and Josephus. Wisd 7:22 uses the adjective of the Spirit of Wisdom. Beginning in ii/A.D., legal documents employ the term often (J. Moulton and G. Milligan, *The Vocabulary of the Greek Testament*, p. 20).

preaching and teaching the Word, and now pictured as directing his coworkers in their continuing care of congregations that Paul had founded or visited. The final cycle or "missionary journey" had begun that would culminate in Paul's last arrest, imprisonment, and death.[45]

As noted above, the repetitions of materials within the PE (e.g., qualifications for apostolic ministers repeated from Titus 1:6-9 to 1 Tim 3:2-7) ought to be understood as the testimony of "two or three witnesses" in a quite Lukan mode of composition. The two lists of apostles (Luke 6:14-16; Acts 1:13), the two narratives of the Ascension (Luke 24:50-52 and Acts 1:9-12), and of the vision of Peter (Acts 10:9-16 and 11:5-10) as well as the three accounts of Paul's conversion illustrate this. Moreover the same materials in a new setting have a new meaning and the predominantly Jewish Christian churches in which Titus is conceived to be working are not the congregation at Ephesus.[46] The repetitions from Acts to PE, e.g., the Antioch-Iconium-Lystra vignette exploited above, or the two "testaments" of Paul in Acts 20 and 2 Tim, are similar illustrations of the author's mode of composition.

But are there not actually glaring contradictions between Acts and PE? How can one, e.g., reconcile an author twice noting Paul's saying to the presbyter-bishops of Ephesus that none of them will see his face again (Acts 20:25, 38) with the notation placed on Paul's lips in the opening of 1 Timothy, "As I urged you when I was going (*poreuomenos*) to Macedonia to remain at Ephesus . . ." (*se prosmeinai en Ephesōi*)? It is a counsel of despair to begin by saying a responsible author forgot what he said. The Greek of this whole passage (1 Tim 1:3-7) is in "utter chaos"[47] and the anacoluthon may well indicate that the author of PE was straining over this very difficulty. He may have had, on the one hand, what was to his mind an incontrovertible tradition that Paul had made such a prediction at Ephesus on his last trip to Jerusalem in the latter fifties and, on the other hand, equally incontrovertible data for a later trip of the apostle through this very area in the mid-sixties. He was reluctant to say the apostle's prophecy was not fulfilled.[48] He accordingly referred very obliquely and awkwardly to a later visit of Paul to Ephesus. Indeed the tortuous text actually does not state that Paul stopped in Ephesus on the journey (from Crete?) to Macedonia (to Nicopolis?)

---

[45]Cullmann,*Peter*, pp. 82-3; 104 has suggested that Acts ends as it does so that the author does not have to rehearse the scandalous betrayal of the apostle, not to mention his execution by due legal process (cf. Haenchen, *Acts*, pp. 731-32). On that interpretation, the shift into the epistolary genre in the final roll is quite intelligible, for the final message of Paul can thus dominate the composition and significant materials from the end of his life be obliquely transmitted while the details of troublesome events can be ignored without qualm.

[46]Luke portrays Paul as habitually beginning evangelization by addressing his fellow Jews and he actually closes Acts with such a scene. He accordingly could open the epistolary volume with Paul's directives for predominantly Jewish Christian congregations; then in 1 Timothy turn to a church that was of predominantly gentile origin (note the mention of the gentiles in 1 Tim 2:7; 3;16; 2 Tim 4:17 but not in Titus); and finally close with Paul's last will and testament in 2 Timothy.

[47]Blass, Debrunner, Funk, *Greek Grammar*, # 467.

[48]Though it is evident from 1 Cor 15:51 that a first century believer might be accustomed to some slippage between an apostle's prophecy and the ensuing course of events.

being envisioned in this correspondence, but that, while he was en route (*poreuomenos*)[49] through the area, he instructed his coworker to stay on (*prosmeinai*) at Ephesus. Then in 1 Tim 3:14-15, he says: "I hope to come to you soon but I am writing these instructions so that, if I am delayed, you may know how one ought to behave . . ." This also is to be read in the light of Acts 20:25, 38 and it thus becomes a poignant reminder that Paul's prophetic word had been fulfilled. Accordingly the PE deliberately complement and supplement the previous narrative of Acts, functioning in much the way that the Ascension narrative of Acts does in its reworking of traditions that were articulated differently in the conclusion of the third gospel, where one also encountered a last testament, that of Jesus to his disciples.

The separation of the rolls of Luke's work for individual circulation must have occurred within a decade or so of their composition. Thus the Greek manuscript tradition never copied Luke-Acts together, and accordingly they were not read together, i.e., in accord with the author's purpose.[50] The ancient sources venture no explanation or defense of this, but that is not surprising in view of the history of other compositions distributed over separate rolls. In this light one can understand why there was, likewise, no ancient notice that the PE were read as the third roll of a single work that began with Luke-Acts. In another study it has been suggested that this dismembering of Luke's work was occasioned by a technological advance in bookmaking that the Christians made their own in the last decade of the first century, the codex.[51] With Goodspeed it is still feasible to propose that the publication of Luke-Acts galvanized Christian interest in the historical Paul.[52] But how would a work that offered not a hint that Paul wrote anything motivate a search for and collection of his letters? *Ex hypothesi*, it was the final volume by Luke, the PE, that was the catalyst which prompted a search for, and finally, between 90-100 A.D., a collection of actual letters of Paul to the churches. If Zuntz is correct, an Alexandrian edition (that included Hebrews) swept the field around 100 A.D.[53] In this process the very success of Luke-Acts-PE became its undoing as a single work. Luke had written his master synthesis to give "security" to the second Christian generation. He had proposed a Paul for that generation much as he had proposed an edition of Mark. Instead of sweeping the field, his great work actually prompted the assembling of collections like his. Four "gospels" from the second generation were gathered into codices and Luke's was now read in series with Matthew, Mark, and John.

---

[49]Cf. Rom 15:24 where the *hōs an poreuōmai eis tēn Spanian* is then specified as *diaporeuomenos* of Paul actually passing through Rome. I suggest that on his final journey in the East Paul got no closer to Ephesus than Miletus (2 Tim 4:20; the only other NT mention of the city is Acts 20:15, 17!).

[50]Cf. *infra*, n. 54.

[51]Cf. "P⁴⁶ — The Pauline Canon?" adding T. C. Skeat, "Early Christian Book-Production: Papyri and Manuscripts" *The Cambridge History of the Bible*, II, 54-79.

[52]Cf. "P⁴⁶ — The Pauline Canon?" p. 385 n. 36, for the literature.

[53]G. Zuntz, *Opuscula Selecta*, p. 270, and his earlier *The Text of the Epistles*, p. 279. See H. Gamble, *The Textual History of the Letter to the Romans*, pp. 96-142, who has persuasively argued for the way in which various "editions" of the original sixteen chapter text of Romans began to circulate in the second Christian generation. He finds (p. 120) less salvageable from Goodspeed than the hypothesis offered here.

Acts became a quite separate work,[54] perhaps meant to be read as a sort of Deuteronomy concluding a Pentateuch that began with the four gospels.[55] The Pauline collection of letters to the churches was now complemented by taking the PE as a collection of letters to individuals and prefixing (or suffixing) the letter to Philemon.[56] The harvest looked different from the seeds that had been sown.

If, on the hypothesis just argued or a variant of it, Luke-Acts is in a close literary relationship to PE, then a reorientation is in order of historical, literary, and theological studies of the second Christian generation. A review of the whole question of what is meant by the pseudonymity of PE is called for.[57] The purpose of Luke-Acts must be recovered and re-evaluated in the light of its epistolary appendix. One must reckon with the fact that the second Christian generation for whom these works were written ignored their purpose while honoring their constituent parts. That Pauline apostolate and its teaching, whose continuation this body of literature sought to authenticate, was, in the final analysis, the scale on which Luke-Acts-PE were weighed.

---

[54]The first reasonably certain citations of Acts begin with Justin (Haenchen,*Acts*, pp. 8-9). It is hard to come by any ancient notice that Luke-Acts were read in tandem. This is vividly illustrated by the Muratorian Fragment where Acts is described (34-39) completely apart from and after the four gospels but before the Pauline letter collection(s). There is no hint of a literary relation to the Third Gospel (2-8) though the dedication to Theophilus is noted (35-36). For the *Muratorianum,* the Third Gospel was written by Luke *ex opinione* (6) whereas Acts was penned *quia sub praesentia eius singula gerebantur* (36-37). The *Muratorianum* then notes that Acts contains no notice of Peter's martyrdom or Paul's trip to Spain because Luke was not present for these events. Does this imply that he was present for Paul's final journeys and martyrdom as PE presuppose them? Did the author of *Muratorianum* understand 2 Tim 4:11 (in its context) as supplying what Acts did not?

The "Anti-Marcionite" prologue to Luke closes with only a perfunctory mention of Acts, but it is striking to see the purpose of the Third Gospel articulated in the terminology of PE (Titus 1:14; 1 Tim 1:4; 2 Tim 2:18). Is this a faint memory of the part Luke had in all these compositions? An important study on the purpose of Acts is that by V. Pfitzner, "Continuity and Discontinuity: the Lucan View of History in Acts," *Theologia Crucis: Studies in Honor of H. Sasse,* ed. H. Hamann, pp. 33-49.

[55]Perhaps even this five-fold arrangement was suggested by the five "books," Luke Acts-Titus-1 Tim-2 Tim. The collection of compositions into groups of five was popular in Jewish circles (the Pentateuch; the five books of Psalms; and later the five Megillot [cf. Hillers, *Lamentations,* pp. xvii-xviii]; Henoch) as well as Christian (e.g., the five books of Papias and of Irenaeus).

[56]The early second century with its varied collections of both LXX and Christian literature in the newly adopted codices had its own problems which Marcion sought to solve with drastic theological surgery that, in this instance, killed the doctor and precipitated the process that eventually issued in a Christian biblical canon.

[57]Cf. N. Brox, *Falsche Verfasserangaben zur Erklärung der frühchristlichen Pseudepigraphie*, with bibliography cited on pp. 151-2, as well as J. Ménard, "Pseudonymie," *DBSup,* IX, 245-52.

The Value of Acts as a Source for the Study of Paul

A. J. Mattill, Jr.

Of what value is Acts in the study of Paul's life and work? To what extent can Acts be used in the reconstruction of Paul's thought? Or should Acts be used at all? To approach the historical Paul should we disregard the Paul of Acts and restrict ourselves to the Pauline Epistles?

In the history of criticism, four major answers have been given to these questions. Each of these four solutions has necessarily entailed a study of Luke's composition, sources, traditions, and tendencies (the name Luke" is used without prejudice as to authorship). We shall describe each of these positions generally and methodologically (1,2) and then show what valid information this methodology lays bare in Acts on the chief aspects of Paul's life and thought (3,4,5,6):

1. GENERAL DESCRIPTION, including methodology in respect to the use of Acts and Epistles and their relative value in the reconstruction of the historical Paul.

2. METHODOLOGY used to distinguish tradition from redaction in the Pauline portions of Acts.

3. CURSUS VITAE: place of birth (9:11; 21:39; 22:3; cf. 9:30, 11 25); the name "Saul" (7:58; 13:9); Roman citizenship (16:37-38; 22:25-29; 23.27; 25:10-12); Gamaliel's pupil (22:3); letters of extradition (9:2; 22:5; 26:10,12) locale of Paul's persecution of the church (9:13; 26:10); site of conversion (9:3; 22:6; 26:13); apostleship (14:4,14); journeys (9:26-30; 11:25-30; 12:25; 13:1-14:28; 15:36-18:22; 18:23-21:17; 23:31-35; 27:1-28:16); appeal to the Emperor (25:10-12,21,25; 26:32; 28:19); personality.

4. THE SUPERNATURAL: miracles which happen to Paul (9:1-9, 17-19; 22:5-

16; 26:12-18; 16:23-34; 28:3-6); miracles which Paul performs (13:6-12; 14:3,8-10; 15:12; 16:16-18; 19:6,11-12; 20:9-12; 28:8-10); visions which Paul sees (16:9-10; 18:9-10; 22:17-21; 23:11; 27:23-24); visions which others see about Paul (9:10-16); prophecies uttered by Paul (20:23,25,29-30; 27:10,22); prophecies involving Paul (11:27-28; 21:4,10-11); divine guidance (13:2,4; 16:6,7; 17:15D; 19:1D,21).

   5. PRACTICES AND PRINCIPLES: Paul's custom of preaching first to Jews and when rejected to Gentiles (13:5,14,46; 14:1; 17:1-2,10,17; 18:4,6,19; 19:8-9; 28:28); Jewish rites (16:3; 18:18,21D; 20:6,16; 21:17-26); the Apostolic Decree (15:20,29; 16:4; 21:25); Paul's relationship to the Jerusalem church (9:27-30; 15:1-35).

   6. DOCTRINE: Paul the Pharisee (23:1-10); Paul's speeches (13:10-11,16-41,46-47; 14:15-17; 17:22-31; 20:18-35; 22:1-21; 23:1-6; 24:10-21; 26:2-29; 28:17-20,25-28); one-verse summaries of Paul's speeches (9:20,22; 14:22,27; 15:12; 16:31; 17:18; 24:25; 28:31).

The One-Paul View of The School of Historical Research[1]

   1. GENERAL DESCRIPTION. In Acts and Epistles there is only one Paul, for the Paul of Acts is basically consistent with the Paul of the Epistles in principle and practice. The Paul of Acts is the Paul of the Epistles in attitude to the Law, the Jews, and manual labor, and in respect to divine calling and adaptability to all sorts and conditions of men and situations.

   Acts and Epistles are reliable and sufficient sources for the study of Paul and they mutually illuminate one another. For knowledge of Paul's thought, Acts may be said to be secondary to Epistles, since Acts is at best one step removed from Paul's mind. Yet it is Acts which gives us the perspective for Paul. In fact, for Paul's external history, Acts is the leading and most productive source. It enables us to sketch his life-history in that it gives us a connected (but not complete) representation of his life from the stoning of Stephen until his Roman imprisonment. Without Acts the Epistles are incomplete. Thus to obtain a historically accurate picture of Paul we must combine the narratives of Acts and

---

[1]J. R. Oertel, *Paulus in der Apostelgeschichte*; R. B. Rackham, *The Acts of the Apostles*; A. Wikenhauser, *Die Apostelgeschichte und ihr Geschichtswert*; F. F. Bruce, *The Acts of the Apostles. The Greek Text*; Bruce, "Paul and Jerusalem," *TB*, XIX (1968), 3-25; Bruce, "The Speeches in Acts — Thirty Years After," *Reconciliation and Hope: New Testament Essays on Atonement and Eschatology Presented to L. L. Morris on his 60th Birthday*, ed. R. Banks, pp. 53-68; Bruce, "Paul and the Athenians," *ExpTim*, LXXXVIII (1976), 8-12; Bruce, "Is the Paul of Acts the Real Paul?" *BJRL*, LVIII (1976), 282-305 (here Bruce so qualifies Luke's picture of Paul that we may regard Bruce as having moved from School I toward, if not to, School II: "Without Paul's letters we should have a very inadequate and one-sided impression of him, . . ."; see especially pp. 290-2, 300, 305); W. W. Gasque, "The Speeches of Acts: Dibelius Reconsidered," *New Dimensions in New Testament Study*, ed. R. Longenecker and M. Tenney, pp. 232-50; Gasque, *A History of the Criticism of the Acts of the Apostles*. H. H. Evans (*St. Paul, the Author of the Acts of the Apostles and of the Third Gospel*) regards both Acts and Epistles as primary sources, the work of one mind, Paul. Evans points out that with any person there are three distinct individualities: the objective A, as he appears to B; the subjective A, as he appears to himself, A; and the real A, as he truly is. In Acts and Epistles we have the subjective Paul, as he appeared to himself (208).

Epistles, determining as exactly as possible the order of events and the proper light in which to view them. Acts and Epistles are to be used simultaneously, not successively.

Undesigned coincidences between Acts and Epistles, similarities in thought and diction between Paul's speeches in Acts and Paul's Epistles, and confirmation from studies in geographical, historical, and archeological sources so establish the substantial truthfulness of Acts that Acts may be regarded as a witness of the first rank which is not in any significant degree unhistorical. The agreements between Acts and Epistles are so numerous that when Luke gives data which cannot be checked by the Epistles we may have confidence in these data, which, after all, come from Paul's own traveling companion, Luke the physician. Hence we may from the outset approach Acts with confidence in its picture of Paul.

If any discrepancies between Acts and Epistles do exist, they are simply due to gaps in Luke's knowledge. Tradition and redaction do not basically distort Acts' picture of Paul, for Luke as Paul's friend had reliable traditions, and his own editorial work and composition were checked by his desire to give an accurate historical report. Therefore both Luke's traditions and redaction are dependable and are indispensable for the study of Paul. Hence the task of separating tradition from redaction is not an urgent one when it comes to getting back to the real Paul.

2. METHODOLOGY. The linguistic character of Acts is so uniform that the linguistic criterion for the separation of sources is not decisive. Also of only limited value is the criterion of roughnesses, hiatuses, seams, clumsy or artificial transitions, and disharmonies, for these are found in all parts of Acts, and what may be impossible for a modern author is not necessarily impossible for an ancient one. Many unevennesses, moreover, may be traced to Luke's negligence and to scribal tampering with the text.

The most important datum of Acts, so far as tradition, redaction, and historical reliability of the Pauline portions are concerned, is the "we" of the "we-section," which is best explained as Luke's announcement of his own eye- and ear-witnessship. Thus in Acts 16-28 Luke was in a favorable position to obtain information and was not forced to use free composition or even written sources but was able to rely almost exclusively upon oral tradition which he gathered during his own experiences and contacts with Paul and other witnesses and participants.

At the basis of the earlier Pauline units where Luke was not present, such as Paul's conversion, first missionary journey, and apostolic council (9:1-31; 13-14; 15:1-35), lie oral traditions from eyewitnesses. The uniformity of accounts (Paul's arrival, preaching to Jews, turning to Gentiles, success of his activity, and reason for departure; 9:19-25; 13:14-52; 17:1-10; 18:1-18) indicates Luke's absence, whereas the thoroughness, exactness, and diary-like nature of the we-sections suggest Luke's presence.

Clues as to the existence and identity of Luke's informants are found in references to such persons as Barnabas, James, Manaen, Mark, Mnason, Philip, Rhoda, Silas, Sopater, and Timothy. Details scattered throughout Luke-Acts point to oral information about the Herod family (Luke 3:1; 8:3; 9:9; 13:31-33; 23:6-12,15; Acts 4:27; 13:1; 25:13-26:32). The data of the Epistles (Rom 1:8; 1 Thes

1:2-8; 2 Cor 3:1-3, etc.) indicate that Luke did have access to traditions about the Apostles and early churches.[2]

This School, then, minimizes, if not denies, Luke's use of written sources in the Pauline parts of Acts. This extensive oral tradition, however, may have been fixed rather than fluid. But in either case, it is reliable material, for it is based on first-hand reports, is colored by transmission only in secondary points, and has not been distorted by Luke's interests and redaction. That Luke did not invent details is indicated by the fact that only twice does he disclose the definite number of the faithful (2:41; 4:4) but otherwise is indefinite in the absence of exact numbers in the tradition (13:43; 14:1,21; 16:5; 17:4,34).

Yet Luke, though not using large written sources which themselves were intended for publication, such as the supposed "Acts of Paul," very probably used his own written notes of a non-literary nature, which he would have needed as memory-aids when writing in Rome: shorthand notes of speeches, lists of names (13:1), chronological notices, numbers, names of lesser persons, and such a wealth of details which would exclude total reliance upon memory. Luke expanded these notes with information from other trustworthy witnesses.

As for the Pauline speeches, difficult features, such as 23:5, point to reliable tradition which none would have invented. The proximity of several speeches to the we-sections implies earwitness tradition. The Pauline echoes in vocabulary, style, and thought do the same. Moreover, just as Luke in his Gospel is not unfaithful to sayings and speeches in his Markan source, so also we may suppose he has been no less faithful to his speech sources in Acts.

On the other hand, the brevity of the speeches and their Lukan style indicates Lukan redaction. Yet Luke's omission of speeches at such appropriate occasions as 28:16 suggests he had no tradition for such speeches and freely composed none.

The isolation of tradition in Acts is complicated by the lack of any parallel to Acts comparable to the Synoptic parallels. Yet within Acts itself there are parallel reports. When these are compared, signs of tradition and redaction emerge:

(a) According to 9:26-30, Paul leaves Jerusalem because of a threat from Hellenists; according to 22:17-21 because Christ sends him to the Gentiles. 9:26-30 reflects a source which knew only of the murder attempt. Luke either heard Paul speaking at 22:17-21 or obtained his information from an earwitness. Hence Luke passes on both traditions without showing that the two can be reconciled.

(b) When Agabus' prophecy (21:11) is compared with 21:31-33, it is seen that events did not turn out exactly as prophesied: Paul was bound by Romans, not by Jews; he was not handed over by Jews but was taken from them by force. An inexact prophecy thus indicates reliable tradition reported accurately by Luke without conforming the source to later events also reported by him. He remained true to the wording of the prophecy which he himself heard or which was transmitted to him (so also 11:28, for the famine involved only Judea, not the

---

[2]See W. W. Gasque, "Did Luke Have Access to Traditions about the Apostles and the Early Churches?" *JETS*, XVII (1974), 45-8, based upon J. Jervell, "The Problem of Tradition in Acts," in his *Luke and the People of God.*

whole world).

(c) Likewise Claudius Lysias' letter (23:26-30) contains two falsifications: Lysias' knowledge of Paul's Roman citizenship was a later discovery, not the cause of his rescue of Paul (23:27; 21:38; 22:29), and Lysias, because of secrecy surrounding Paul's removal to Caesarea, had not yet given the instructions of 23:30 to Paul's accusers (23:12-15,20-24). Here again Luke has faithfully reproduced his sources.[3]

(d) For Felix, Paul must have spoken about the proceedings before the Sanhedrin in detail for Felix to understand, but Luke can shorten Paul's statement (24:20-21) because the reader already knows the situation (23:1-10). In other words, redaction is indicated when a brief summary (which is intelligible to the reader because he has already read the earlier parallel account) replaces what must have been a detailed explanation if the original audience was to understand.

(e) Similarly, at 28:17-20 Luke has summarized Paul's remarks for the sake of readers, who already are oriented about the course of events. The brevity shows that the wording is Luke's (note the similarity between 28:17b and 21:11). Actually Paul was not delivered by the Jews to the Romans (Felix and Festus) but was snatched by the Roman soldiers from the Jews who wanted to lynch him and was secretly sent by Lysias to Caesarea. Nor did the Romans show willingness to release Paul before his appeal to Caesar (25:11) but only after it (25:18,25; 26:32). Thus Luke's hand is revealed when a later parallel account is a summary in Luke's style and is not in strict harmony with the earlier detailed accounts.

(f) There is at least one parallel between Gospel and Acts (Luke 23:50-53; Acts 13:27-29). According to the former, Joseph of Arimathea took Jesus down from the cross and buried him, whereas according to the latter, it was those living in Jerusalem and their rulers. Here Luke can report unchanged his tradition of Paul's speech because Luke knows his readers are more precisely informed of events.

In short, comparison with parallel accounts in Luke-Acts, relevant portions of the Pauline Epistles, and secular historical sources shows that Luke has faithfully reproduced an abundance of oral, eyewitness, reliable reports about Paul's life and thought.

3. CURSUS VITAE. With this dependence upon the reliability of Luke's tradition and composition, the School of Historical Research finds no sufficient reason to doubt the data of Acts on such matters as Paul's birthplace, Roman citizenship, rabbinic education under Gamaliel,[4] persecution of the church in Jerusalem, and appeal to the Emperor. The name "Saul" is undoubtedly correct, for papyri indicate that double names were common, and according to Rom 11:1 and Phil 3:5 Paul was from the tribe of Benjamin, the tribe of King Saul. Gal 1:17 suggests that Paul's conversion was in or near Damascus. Paul did receive

---

[3]J. M. Lister ("Claudius Lysias," *ExpTim*, XII [1900-1901] 336) seeks to save "this honest soldier" from diplomatic lying by translating: ". . . I . . . rescued him. Having learned that he was a Roman, and wishing to know the cause, . . ." (23:27-28).

[4]See E. F. Harrison, "Acts 22:3 — A Test Case for Luke's Reliability," *New Dimensions*, pp. 251-60.

letters of extradition from the high priest, for in a certain sense the Sanhedrin exercised judicial authority over all Jewish congregations in the world, though direct authority only in Judea. How far a congregation would follow the direction of the Sanhedrin depended upon the good will of that particular congregation.

For Luke, Paul is not merely equal to the other Apostles (14:4,14), but he is the greatest of the Apostles, the church-planting missionary par excellence.[5] According to the evidence of the Epistles, Acts sets forth accurately the itinerary and sequence of Paul's journeys.[6] Research shows that Luke is well-nigh without error in topographical, political, historical, and nautical details of these journeys, a precision which could be obtained only by an eyewitness.[7] So far as the course of Paul's mission, his missionary work, and the founding of churches are concerned, Acts surpasses Epistles in abundance of materials.

In respect to Paul's personality, the question is not, "Does Acts portray Paul in all his greatness?" but, "Is that which Luke reports true, or does he give a false picture of Paul?" Acts in fact is a marvellous illustration of Paul's self-knowledge as set forth in 1 Cor 15:10.

> The characterization of Paul in *Acts* is so detailed and individualized as to prove the author's personal acquaintance. Moreover, the Paul of *Acts* is the Paul that appears to us in his own letters, in his ways and his thoughts, in his educated tone of polished courtesy, in his quick and vehement temper, in the extraordinary versatility and adaptability which made him at home in every society, moving at ease in all surroundings, and everywhere the centre of interest, whether he is the Socratic dialectician in the agora of Athens, or the rhetorician in its University, or conversing with kings and proconsuls, or advising in the council on shipboard, or cheering a broken-spirited crew to make one more effort for life. Wherever Paul is, no one present has eyes for any but him.[8]

In Acts the figure of Paul rises clearly above that of other persons. Paul is sketched much sharper and more individually than Peter. The reader receives a rather clear, concrete picture of Paul. Acts vividly portrays the fanatical hate of Paul the persecutor, and more concretely than do the Epistles. Against this dark background is contrasted the enthusiastic, sacrificial love of Paul for Christ and his work after his conversion. One sees clearly Paul's towering significance, his inexhaustible zeal, and his no mean success as a missionary. In the Miletus address is the deepest revelation of the secret of Paul's soul: the indefatigable pastor living only for his flock. 20:36-38 is "a picture drawn with Luke's inimitable command of pathos, which reveals the apostle's wonderful power in attracting personal affection and devotion." Hints of Paul's frequent depression (2 Cor 1:8-

---

[5]Cf. E. Fudge, "Paul's Apostolic Self-Consciousness at Athens," *JETS*, XIV (1971), 193-8.

[6]T. H. Campbell, "Paul's 'Missionary Journeys' as Reflected in His Letters," *JBL*, LXXIV (1955), 80-7. "Certainly Paul's letters are our primary sources for a resconstruction of his career, whereas Acts is at best a secondary source *except* at those points where the author is writing as an eye-witness or using the journal of an eye-witness" (81) D. Moody ("A New Chronology for the Life and Letter of Paul," *PRS*, III [1976], 248-71) proposes a Pauline chronology based upon Acts' quinquennial chronology. School I frequently identifies Acts 11:27-30 with Gal 2:1-10.

[7]See A.N. Sherwin-White, *Roman Society and Roman Law in the New Testament.*

[8]W.M. Ramsay, *St. Paul the Traveller and the Roman Citizen,* pp. 21-2.

9; 2:12-13) are found at Acts 17:15; 18:4; 20:1; 23:11; 28:15.[9]

4. THE SUPERNATURAL. Paul's supernatural experiences are possible and credible, else Paul could not have appealed to them himself (Rom 15:17-19; 1 Cor 12:9-10,28; 2 Cor 12:1-12; Gal 2:2; 3:5). A great religion does not establish itself in Asia without marvellous preliminaries. Luke as a physician was especially qualified to apply the correct standard to the miracle accounts which he received and to seek out trustworthy authorities.

5. PRACTICES AND PRINCIPLES. Paul's preaching in synagogues is in line with Gal 2:8-10 (geographically interpreted); Rom 1:16; 9:3; 1 Cor 9:20; and 2 Cor 11:24 (Paul's submission to synagogue punishment, which suggests that Paul not only preached in synagogues but also submitted to the Law), and provided him contact with Gentiles who frequented synagogues. Acts 16:13 (we-section) indicates that the missionaries had sought in vain for a synagogue.

Because of Jewish and Christian strains in his own thought and because of his law of liberty and love, Paul could permit Jewish Christians, including himself, to observe the Law (freely without the intent of winning divine favor) and yet he could defend freedom from the Law for Gentile Christians. Gal 5:11 suggests that there must have been something in Paul's preaching and/or practice which gave rise to the charge that he was preaching circumcision.

Paul did approve, circulate, and enforce the Apostolic Decree, for it was only temporary and localized for a special emergency. Since it was not permanent or universal Paul did not mention it in his Epistles. The Decree added nothing to Paul, for Paul in his missionary wisdom had introduced these regulations in his mixed congregations long before the Council of Jerusalem. Some members of the Historical School would contend that the Decree is not mentioned in Galatians because Galatians was written before the Council of   Acts 15.

The harmony pictured in Acts between Paul and the original Apostles and James is in accord with the Epistles, which also show Paul and the Twelve at one in faith, love and proclamation. The conflict over the Law was between Paul and the Judaizers. Neither Acts nor Epistles depict Paul as subservient to Jerusalem but rather as in brotherly communion with one another.

6. DOCTRINE. In saying, "I am a Pharisee" (23:6), Paul is as little untrue as in Phil 3:5. Paul reduces the formal charge of blaspheming the Law to the great principle at issue, the resurrection of Christ (23:6). Although the Pharisees (23:9) granted that a spirit had appeared to Paul, they would not have acknowledged that spirit to have been the Messiah.

The speeches of Paul in Acts are not verbatim reports but are based upon reliable tradition (cf. 2. above), summaries of speeches given by Paul on the occasions indicated, compressed into Luke's style but Pauline in subject matter and line of thought, trustworthy reproductions of what Paul actually said. In Acts, as in Epistles, Jesus' atoning death appropriated through faith is the center of the Gospel (13:28-39; 20:28).

Luke's dependable tradition and redaction, then, immeasurably enrich our

---

[9]Wikenhauser, *Apostelgeschichte,* pp. 285-6; Rackham, *Acts,* pp. 300-1, 324, 360, 370-1, 396, 435, 498.

knowledge of the course of Paul's life, the role of the supernatural in his experience, his participation in Jewish rites, and his theology.

The Lopsided-Paul View of the School of Restrained Criticism[10]

1. GENERAL DESCRIPTION. Although there is no absolute divergence between the Paul of Acts and the Paul of the Epistles, each alone is a one-sided Paul. Since the complete Paul is to be found neither in Epistles nor Acts, Paul ought no longer to be judged so exclusively by his own writings. Acts fills the gaps left by the Epistles, and there are dozens of places where Acts stands the test of the Epistles. Often we can learn more clearly from Acts than from the Epistles, though the facts in Acts may be frequently deduced from the Epistles. No one yet has been able to draw a convincing portrait of Paul from his Epistles alone.

Since Paul was a party-man in conflict, there is a possibility that Acts is correct when it contradicts the Epistles.[11] The Epistles, however, are the primary source, a control and check on Acts, and are to be preferred, when rightly interpreted, if they stand over against Acts, which is a secondary, generally less trustworthy source, yet containing much valuable material, which is especially useful when corroborated by the Epistles or when found in the we-sections of Acts. If we possessed only Acts we would be essentially worse off than if we had only the Epistles.

Acts' one-sided picture of Paul is grounded in Acts' apologetic purposes (such as making Paul acceptable to Jewish Christians) and Paul's own defective self-portrait grows out of his polemics (such as proving Gentiles free from the Law, when he naturally omits or tones down his own Jewishness). Yet Luke's

---

[10]M. Schneckenburger, *Ueber den Zweck der Apostelgeschichte;* A. Harnack, *Luke the Physician;* Harnack, *The Acts of the Apostles;* Harnack, *The Date of the Acts and of the Synoptic Gospels;* G.H.C. MacGregor, "The Acts of the Apostles," *IB,* IX, 1-352; J. Munck, *The Acts of the Apostles;* Mattill, "The Purpose of Acts: Schneckenburger Reconsidered," *Apostolic History and the Gospel: Biblical and Historical Essays Presented to F.F. Bruce on His 60th Birthday,* ed. W. Gasque and R. Martin, pp. 108-22. P.-G. Miller ("Die 'Bekehrung' des Petrus: Zur Interpretation von Apg 10, 1-11," *HK,* XXVIII [1974], 372-5) reports on Professor F. Mussner's 1973 summer seminar on Acts 10:1-11:18, which abandoned the "primitive Catholicism thesis" that Luke "domesticated" Paul. In our categories, there was a shift from School III toward School II. C. Burchard ("Paulus in der Apostelgeschichte," *TLZ,* C [1975], cols. 882-95) reviews three 1973 books on Luke's Paul (Löning, Stolle, Michel) and finds that Luke has a better understanding of Pauline concepts than is commonly supposed. Also in E. Grässer's extensive survey of recent study of Luke's Paul and of the speeches in Acts ("Acta-Forschung seit 1960," *TR,* XLI [1976], 275-90; XLII [1977], 35-51, 56-7) some movement is descernible from School III toward School II in that some of the more extreme positions of School III have been modified.

[11]E. Meyer (*Ursprung und Anfange des Christentums,* I, 28) contends that "even when there is conflict with the Pauline epistles, Luke must sometimes be preferred. On theological grounds it has been judged that Paul must always be right. But historically speaking—well, what sort of portrait could be painted on the basis of preferring, let us say, Napoleon's ideal picture of himself to that drawn by an intelligent onlooker?" More recently, J. Parkes (*Judaism and Christianity,* p. 85) contends that the Epistles are of primary importance, yet, accepting the general accuracy of Paul's defense speeches in Acts, we shall not rightly understand the Epistles "until we have found an interpretation consistent with Paul's own belief that he was throughout a loyal and observant Jew."

picture of Paul is disfigured by no unworthy trait.

Luke had many good traditions available, traditions close to events, traditions which he on the whole transmitted faithfully. But his selection from them and his redaction of them have been affected by his purposes, and he used his artistic licence to adapt them, rearrange them, and touch them up. Hence both tradition and redaction must be used cautiously. We must avoid contempt for what Acts does offer us and also shun forced harmonization of Acts and Epistles.

2. METHODOLOGY. Luke's prologue (Luke 1:1-4), plus his use of Mark, make it a priori probable that written sources lie behind Acts. But since vocabulary and style are everywhere the same, they are not a criterion for distinguishing these sources. Discrepancies, inaccuracies, imprecisions, and gaps are also inadequate criteria, for they are found in all parts of Acts and indicate Luke's negligence. Thus it is impossible to analyze the unit of 15:36-28:31 into sources. But it is probably not based upon written sources, for Luke as Paul's companion had access to oral reports of himself and others, such as Aristarchus, Gaius, James, Mark, Paul, Philip and family, Silas, Timothy, and Titus, reports which Luke himself first reduced to writing. References to obscure persons are hints of sources. Luke used personal notes or his own travel journal for events when he was with Paul and completed these notes with information from other witnesses.

The we-sections are the key to the source analysis of the Pauline portions of Acts. Detailed linguistic studies show that the we-sections are the most Lukan parts of Luke-Acts, which means that here Luke is writing in his own style, reporting his own experiences, whereas in the rest of Acts he is dependent on oral and written tradition, whch markedly influences his style and vocabulary. As expected, then, the nearest in style to the we-sections are those parts of the last half of Acts in which "we" does not occur, for here Luke had neither written sources nor fixed oral tradition and hence could let himself go. Luke's interests, such as medicine and Paul's practice of going first to synagogues, also appear in the we-sections. Thus on the basis of style and interests it is plain that Luke did not edit and incorporate an original document from someone else into his work.

9:1-30 appears to be a separate Pauline source, based upon the criterion of person (in contrast to setting). Or possibly since 26:12-18 is more easily harmonized with Galatians 1 (for the commission of 26:16-18 is given directly to Paul by Christ and not through Ananias) it approximates most nearly the story in Luke's source and constitutes the original out of which Luke built up the other two accounts (9:1-9; 22:5-16).

According to the criterion of setting, 12:25-15:35 may be part of a Jerusalem-Antiochean source, partially, if not wholly, stemming from Silas.

Chs. 13-14 may be another special Pauline source, a written document, as indicated by the fullness and accuracy of detail, the register of names (13:1), the mention of Barnabas and Saul as if for the first time (13:1), and the change of Saul's name to Paul (13:9).

The letter of 15:23-29 is Lukan in style, but some such encyclical may have been issued and Luke followed the outline of the original. Since Luke thinks of the Decree as applicable to all Gentile Christians (16:4; 21:25), the fact that he limited the address of the letter to Syria and Cilicia (15:23) proves he was influenced by a fixed tradition.

Since Luke loves nothing better than to relate wonders, he would certainly include miracles described in his sources. Thus proof that Luke kept close to his sources is found in the fact that the most sober narratives in Acts are not in the we-sections but in Paul's visits to Thessalonica-Berea (17:1-15), Athens (17:16-34), Corinth (18:1-17), and Jerusalem (21:19-40), where Luke did not add miracles.

An example of Luke's own share in composition is seen in Acts 21:25, which gives the impression that Paul hears of the Decree for the first time, an erroneous impression gained because the statement is not James' but Luke's to the reader to exonerate Paul from any suggestion he is implicating Gentile Christians in the minutiae of Jewish ceremonial.

Felix' question about the province to which Paul belongs (23:34) is an example of good tradition. Luke can have had no possible reason for recording this detail unless he was himself present (oral tradition) or had access to the papers in the case (written tradition). Similarly, the letter 23:26-30 was perhaps heard by Luke in court. It is in Luke's style, for the original was in Latin, but Luke gives the general tenor, just what we would expect from a subordinate (Claudius Lysias) seeking to place his own conduct in the best light.

28:30-31 is Lukan redaction, for it has the appearance of a postscript and is in Luke's style, agreeing in construction with Luke's other statements concerning the duration and character of Paul's ministry in large centers (11:26; 18:11; 19:9,10; 24:23,27).

3. *CURSUS VITAE.* With its methodological confidence in Luke's general trustworthiness, the School of Restrained Criticism finds no difficulty with Acts' data on the place of Paul's birth, his Roman citizenship, the locale of Paul's persecution of the church,[12] and the site of his conversion (on 9:1-9; 22:5-16; and 26:12-18 see 2. above). Hellenistic Jews had two names and often these two were as much alike as Saul and Paul; a Roman citizen was even more likely to have two names. Paul was Gamaliel's pupil but Paul did not mention him in his letters because the name would have meant nothing to Gentile Christians. 1 Macc 15:15 shows that the Romans had granted to the high priest the right of extraditing to Jerusalem Jewish malefactors who had fled abroad; this would cover Christians who had fled from Jerusalem to Damascus; certainly not enough is known about the matter of such letters of authority to reject Luke's account.

As for Paul's apostleship, Luke wrote to defend Paul's apostolic claims, and to place him on an equality with the Twelve. Paul is an apostle not only in the sense of one sent out as a missionary (14:4,14) but also in the sense of one who has seen the Lord and has been commissioned directly by him (22:21; 26:17-18). It is Paul who most nearly fulfills the commission of 1:8. Luke (especially Acts 14:3) like Paul (Rom 15:19; 2 Cor 12:12; Gal 3:5) regards Paul's signs and wonders as a part of his legitimation as an apostle. Paul, like some passages in Acts (1:21; 13:31) excludes himself from the number of the Apostles (1 Cor 15:5; cf. Rom 16:7). And according to Acts 1:21, not even the Twelve would qualify as apostles,

---

[12]Paul did persecute the church in Jerusalem according to A.J. Hultgren, "Paul's Pre-Christian Persecutions of the Church," *JBL,* XCV (1976), 97-111.

for they were called later than John's baptism (Mark 1:16; Luke 5:1-11).[13]

The general outline of Paul's missionary career in Acts is confirmed by coincidences between Acts and Epistles. Yet certain readjustments may have to be made (11:27-30 and 15:1-35 may be doublets of one visit, or 11:27-30 may equal Gal 2:1-10). That Luke stuck to tradition and did not invent Pauline trips is suggested by Luke's silence about the period between Paul's conversion and the first missionary journey (see also 2. above).

Paul appealed to the Emperor because he feared imminent conviction by Festus and because he desired not to be handed back to Jewish jurisdiction.

Although Acts is not a mirror enabling us to gaze into the very soul of Paul, the Paul of Acts is not a colorless personality but drawn from life by an intimate friend (2. above). Paul's frankness and self-assertion, for example, crop out in 15:36-41; 16:37; 22:28; 23:3; 27:21. His love of his churches is shown in 20:18-35, and throughout Paul's story we see his peculiar combination of mystical and practical elements.

4. THE SUPERNATURAL. An a priori denial of miracles is refuted by Paul himself (2 Cor 12:12). Moreover, the we-passages of Acts manifest interest in the miraculous as does the rest of Luke-Acts (on Luke's restraint in reporting miracles see 2. above). In a favorable environment the growth of legend may begin with the earliest reports of what happened. We cannot expect a credulous physician endowed with spiritual gifts of healing to draw a clear line between science and magic. Cures by suggestion are recorded at all times. Since Luke is as likely to have believed in miracles as a later redactor, the presence of the supernatural in the narrative is no proof it is not primitive and authentic. We may distinguish differing degrees of credibility, from miracles of the first degree (the less spectacular miracles of the we-sections) to those of the second degree (chs. 1-15).

5. PRACTICES AND PRINCIPLES. Acts's description of Paul's relations with Judaism is in essential agreement with Paul's Epistles. As for preaching first to Jews, there is no basis for rejecting this feature of Acts nor of limiting Paul's ministry to Gentiles (Rom 1:16; 9:1-3; 10:1; 1 Cor 9:19-23). Paul's Jewish practices in Acts do not go beyond what is consistent with Paul's principles (1 Cor 9:20). In indifferent matters, considerations of practical wisdom disposed Paul to a practical accommodation to the adherents of the Law. Since Paul with his doctrine of the status quo (1 Cor 7:18-24) did not contend for freedom from the Law for Jewish Christians, he could perform Jewish functions with a clear conscience. A person of so many sides as Paul could combine a number of attitudes and practices which to us seem irreconcilable.

Since the Decree was not a new imposition upon Gentile Christians (for most of Paul's Gentile converts were "God-fearers" who were already observing these rules from Lev 17-18), but the charter of liberty for Gentile Christians against the demands of the Judaizers, Paul circulated the Decree among his churches because he hoped it would be a more effective defense against the Judaizers than his own authority. Some of this School find that the obstacles clustered

---

[13]Cf. C. Burchard, *Der dreizehnte Zeuge: Traditions- und kompositionsgeschichtliche Untersuchungen zu Lukas' Darstellung der Fruhzeit des Paulus.*

around the Decree are removed if the moral interpretation of Codex D is accepted. (On 15:23-29; 16:4; and 21:25 see 2. above)

Acts' picture of Paul's peaceful but subordinate relationships with the primitive Jerusalem church is substantially correct. There was basic harmony between Paul and the Twelve, who should not be identified with the "false brethren" (Gal 2:4). The struggle was not between Paul and his followers and Peter and his followers, but between the Judaizers, on the one hand, and Paul and the Gentile Christians, on the other. Paul in Galatians exaggerated his independence of Jerusalem, for all Christendom, including Paul, recognized the authority of the Mother Church; Paul went up to Jerusalem, not Jerusalem down to Antioch to meet Paul (Gal 2:1-10). A balanced concept of Paul's independence includes Jerusalem as the court of ultimate appeal for all Christians.

6. DOCTRINE. As for Paul and the Pharisees (23:1-10), historical fact has been altered only slightly because of Luke's tendence of making Paul inoffensive to Jewish Christians. It is possible that Paul spoke as here indicated, for he could claim to be a Pharisee just as he could represent himself as a worshipper of the unknown God, and he could say that he was charged concerning the resurrection even as Luther declared he was questioned concerning Christ. Paul and his fellow Jewish Christians were the only true Pharisees, because they recognized Jesus as Messiah, who alone was able to effect the resurrection. This minimization of Paul's divergence from the Pharisees, if unauthentic, must have come from a later time, when there was a rapprochement between Christianity and Pharisaism. But as time passed there was a mutual desire to stress the gulf between Jews and Christians. Hence the probability is that Paul himself used this line of defense.

Although Paul's speeches are designed to show Paul as a pious Israelite, they are not Luke's free inventions, for he had heard Paul speak, not with full comprehension, but well enought to ensure a relative Paulinism. The Epistles indicate Paul would have spoken to Jews, Gentiles, and converts in substance as in the discourses at Antioch, Athens, and Miletus, and the speeches of chs. 22-28 must be based upon a tradition that seemed trustworthy to Luke, else one speech would have sufficed. Paul was not so "Pauline" as is often supposed.[14]

These abundant data of Acts, which are anchored in good traditions and are on the whole faithfully transmitted, enable us, when we properly check them by the Epistles, cautiously to round out the one-sided Paul found in Acts or Epistles alone and to construct a well-proportioned Apostle.

The Two-Paul View of the School of Creative Edification[15]

---

[14]For similarities, especially in eschatology, between Paul in Acts and Epistles, see P. Borgen, "From Paul to Luke. Observations toward clarification of the theology of Luke-Acts," *CBQ*, XXXI (1969), 168-82; and Mattill, "*Naherwartung, Fernerwartung,* and the Purpose of Luke-Acts: Weymouth Reconsidered," *CBQ*, XXXIV (1972), 276-93.

[15]E. Zeller, *The Contents and Origin of the Acts of the Apostles;* J. Knox, *Chapters in a Life of Paul;* P. Vielhauer, "On the 'Paulinism' of Acts," *Studies in Luke-Acts,* ed. L. Keck and J. Martyn, pp. 33-50; E. Haenchen, "Tradition und Komposition in der Apostelgeschichte," *ZTK,* LII (1955), 205-25; Haenchen, "The Book of Acts as Source Material for the History of Early Christianity," *Studies in Luke-Acts,* pp. 258-78; Haenchen, *The Acts of the Apostles;*

1. GENERAL DESCRIPTION. In Acts and Epistles there are two Pauls, the historical Paul of the authentic Epistles and the legendary Paul of Acts. These two different figures are basically inconsistent with each other, and all attempts at reconciliation are futile. Acts annihilates Paul's peculiar Gospel and gives us a new sketch of a new Paul, so that for Paul's ideas, personality, journeys, and chronology, the Epistles constitute our only primary, reliable source.

The credibility of Acts must be judged by the Epistles, and when so judged Acts yields no weighty, reliable information about Paul. We can by no means be certain that a report in Acts about Paul corresponds to the facts, even if such a report is in itself consistent and seems to offer a precise report. Even a clear hint in the Epistles is of more value than the most explicit statement in Acts which contradicts it. Acts is so remote from Paul in theology and chronology that it cannot be used to correct the Epistles. Acts even incorporates anti-Pauline traditions. Hence Acts can be trusted only at such points as are directly confirmed by the Epistles.

The historical Paul can be found only by disregarding the Lukan Paul. Paul must be redeemed from Acts by examining the Epistles entirely apart from Acts, that is, Epistles and Acts are to be used successively, not simultaneously, and are not to be synthesized. No one in Galatia or Corinth would have recognized in Acts the Paul they had heard or read. Insofar as attempts to enhance the historical reputation of Acts are successful, there inevitably follows a corresponding depreciation of the historical value of the Pauline Epistles, as is illustrated by the School of Advanced Criticism (see below).

The reason for the unhistorical nature of the Lukan Paul is found in (a) Luke's conscious tendency to Petrinize or to neutralize the real Paul, or (b) in Luke's non-tendentious attitude toward tradition and composition, whereby he, upon the basis of fragmentary traditions, uses his imagination to create a fictional Paul after the image of his own epoch for the edification of the church, for what is historical cannot be edifying. Luke's Paul serves to assure Gentile Christians of their legitimate participation in the promises to Israel.

In short, Luke's own creativity in structure and content is so great that Acts is of little or no use in the study of Paul. Tradition and redaction in Acts have produced a legendary Paul in opposition to the historical Paul of the Epistles. Tradition is at a minimum and redaction is at a maximum, and both are historically unreliable.

P.E. Howard, *The Book of Acts as a Source for the Study of the Life of Paul;* G. Klein, *Die zwölf Apostel. Ursprung und Gehalt einer Idee;* J.C. Hurd, Jr., *The Origin of 1 Corinthians;* Hurd, "Pauline Chronology and Pauline Theology," *Christian History and Interpretation: Studies Presented to John Knox,* ed. W. Farmer *et al.,* pp. 225-48; E.R. Goodenough, "The Perspective of Acts," *Studies in Luke-Acts,* pp. 51-59; S. Sandmel. *The Genius of Paul;* M.S. Enslin, *Reapproaching Paul;* Enslin, "Luke, the Literary Physician," *Studies in New Testament and Early Christian Literature: Essays in Honor of Allen P. Wikgren,* ed. D. Aune, pp. 135-43; C.K. Barrett, "Acts and the Pauline Corpus," *ExpTim,* LXXXVIII (1976), 2-5; R.L. Jeske, "Luke and Paul on the Apostle Paul," *CurTM,* IV (1977), 28-38; B.E. Shields, "The Areopagus Sermon and Romans 1:18 ff.: A Study in Creation Theology," *RQ,* XX (1977), 23-40; G. Bowman (*Das dritte Evangelium,* p. 63) finds the Paul of Philemon to be closely related to the Paul of Acts; S.G. Wilson ("The Portrait of Paul in Acts and the Pastorals," *Society of Biblical Literature 1976 Seminar Papers,* ed. G. MacRae, pp. 397-409) argues that the image of Paul in Acts and Pastorals is similar enough to support the hypothesis that the author of Luke-Acts also wrote the Pastorals.

2. METHODOLOGY. The basic methodological principle of this School was set forth by Zeller, who, after noting that vocabulary and style are insecure evidence for sources in view of the linguistic unity of Acts, continues:

> Similarly, little can be proved by the connection, or want of connection, of individual paragraphs with those preceding and following, because on [the] one hand a fixed plan pervades the whole; on the other, the abruptness of a narrative may be owing, not only to the use of a fresh source, but quite as likely to omissions in the material derived from it, or from the intervention of free fiction in the midst of traditional material. The surest index is still the purport and tendency of the individual paragraphs. The more conspicuously a speech or a story represents our author's peculiar standpoint and serves the peculiar object of his book, and the slighter the probability of its historically faithful transmission, so much the more is there to recommend the hypothesis that it proceeds from our author himself; the less it can be explained from these points of view, the more are we obliged to fall back on extraneous sources. But neither in this way is a certain result always to be attained, for it is also possible that the author metamorphosed traditional material from his own standpoint, and employed it for his own object; hence the results so obtained must always be very uncertain in detail.[16]

As applied by Zeller to the we-sections, this principle means that the exactness of description and incomparable picturesqueness of the narrative cannot be explained by the object of Acts and therefore the we-sections are a record in the first person (by Luke) incorporated into Acts by the fianl author, with the following additions and revisions which cannot be traced to an eyewitness: the expulsion of the demon (16:16), questionable because of its connection with the miracle of 16:25-34; the raising of Eutychus (20:9-12), which too much resembles OT restorations; 20:16, which is open to suspicion of unhistorical pragmatism; 27:21-26, which can be omitted without interrupting the context and which appears to be a tendentious *vaticinium ex eventu*; similarly 27:34, which is in suspicious affinity with Luke 21:18; the incredible miracles at Melita (28:8-10); and the improbable saying of the aborigines (28:6).[17] Pointers to tradition and redaction, then, are the presence of the miraculous, pragmatism, interruption of the context, *post eventum* prophecies, and parallels to other OT and NT accounts.

Others of this School have found the word "we" in itself insufficient to determine a we-source and have posited an itinerary-document which contained names of stations where Paul stopped on his journeys, notes of his journeyings and activities in evangelizing, a document which served as a framework for 13:1-14:28; 15:35-21:16. Still others reject the itinerary theory, for the "we" is the author's attempt to give the reader the impression he himself is sharing in the events.

Zeller's basic principle has issued in what we may term the "spin-off" theory of composition: from his theological ideas, interests, data of Paul's Epistles, and fragmentary traditions of various dates and origins, Luke spins off new details, stories, speeches, scenes, and successions of scenes, indeed, an apostolic history, for the edification of the church. This theory is, of course, opposed to the view that Luke's composition was based on personal experience or was limited to

---

[16]Zeller, *Acts,* II, 302-3.

[17]Zeller, *Acts,* II, 318-9.

uniting extensive traditions (written or oral) which were really "mini-Acts" before Acts. Since the Apostles and other Christian preachers did not proclaim their own words and deeds there were no synoptic-like traditions about the Apostles and early churches.[18]

A corollary of this spin-off theory is that Lukan redaction and composition are found where we can identify a spin-off, at the basis of which may be a reliable tradition, if this basis agrees with the Epistles, or an unreliable (or even anti-Pauline) tradition, if it disagrees with the Epistles. Clues as to the existence of spin-offs are found where one detects Luke's ideas and interests, especially in conjunction with disagreements with Epistles or where Acts supplements Epistles, or where there are variations between parallel accounts in Acts. Some general results of the spin-off theory follow.

There is no detail in Acts of Paul's pre-Damascus days which Luke could not have spun off from the Epistles (this approach is simpler than the quest for sources). Luke's fertile imagination discovers answers to his questions by making explicit what was at best implicit in the Epistles (Enslin).

Acts' pattern of three misionary journeys, each of which has its beginning and ending in Antioch or Jerusalem, is a spin-off from Luke's concept that Paul works under the authorit of the Twelve, a spin-off which distorts Luke's sources (Knox).

Luke's statements about travel in his itinerary are reliable, but the episodes attached to this itinerary are of lesser value, their connection to a particular city of still less value, and their connection with a particular visit to a particular city of the lowest value of all (Hurd). Redaction is indicated by artificiality: adventures (which may be based upon traditions of questionable historicity) occur on Paul's first visit to a city.

Paul's miracles are spin-offs from Luke's idea that Paul was a holy man who must have performed wonders.

Paul's speeches, with their striking resemblances to the speeches of Peter and Stephen, their contradictions to Paul's theology, and their absence of Pauline peculiarities of doctrine and language, are spin-offs from Luke's own tendency and theology, occasionally incorporating kerygmatic and liturgical formulae.

In connection with the speeches, we especially see Lukan composition expressed through three literary devices:

(a) Luke imparts information to his readers, not by his own didactic exposition, but by putting it into the mouths of his protagonists. Pointers to this technique of composition are (1) the probability that the information is directed toward the reader, not the original audience; (2) the improbability that the speaker would have spoken thus; and (3) variations in parallel accounts. Examples: the exchange between the Lord and Ananias (9:10-16) is a spin-off from Luke's desire to inform readers of the sudden change in Paul's life; 22:17-21 is a spin-off from Luke's wish to tell readers that Paul's Gentile mission is not of human but of divine origin.

---

[18]Haenchen, *Acts,* p. 84, rejects Bultmann's 1959 theory of an extensive Antiochene source.

(b) Interruptions (17:32; 22:22; 23:7; 26:24): Luke leaves what is important until his intended end of the speech and emphasizes it by means of the contradiction of the listeners.

(c) A Greek proverb in Jesus' mouth (26:14), which is a spin-off from Luke's intention to show the reader how completely Paul is in Jesus' power.

We now list some results of the spin-off theory in reference to specific passages:

9:1-9; 22:5-16; 26:12-18. — The three accounts of Paul's conversion are so similar that they cannot be traced back to different sources but are spin-offs from Gal 1:13-16; 2 Cor 11:32, and ecclesiastical tradition that Paul was healed of blindness caused by Christ's appearance at Damascus and was baptized by Ananias.

9:3; 22:6; 26:13. — Luke's statements about the site of Paul's conversion and the locale of his persecution of the church (9:13; 26:10) are spin-offs from Luke's conception of Paul's life as centered in Jerusalem, spin-offs which distort Luke's sources (Knox).

11:27-30. — This journey is not based on history or legend but is a spin-off from the following: Luke's interest in appeasing Jewish Christians by interrupting Paul's years of absence from the center of the theocracy; similarities to other accounts (ch. 15, visit of Paul and Barnabas to Jerusalem; collection visit; 21:10, Agabus; knowledge of famine under Claudius). Hence arises the principle:

> When a record is thus related to other accounts, it justifies the suspicion that it arose by doubling the same event; and if this same record, by its inconsistency with a better accredited one (that of the Epistle to the Galatians), bears the negative mark of inaccuracy on its front, the suspicion is raised by such coincidence to a high degree of probability.[19]

13:1-14:28. — As judged by Lukan style and resemblances to other passages in Acts, this unit originally "must have been separate notes, perhaps taken from a more comprehensive work, from which he [Luke] spun out the record before us."[20]

15:1-35. — Luke's account of the Council is a spin-off from Gal 2:1-10, in Luke's language, with Luke's speeches and Luke's resolutions.

16:9. — Paul's vision at Troas is a spin-off from Luke's theory that the spread of Christianity was controlled by revelation.

16:19-40. — This prison narrative was spun out of a general notice like 1 Thes 2:2.

18:19a. — "And he left them there" points to a written source, which originally read, "and he left them there, but he himself sailed away from Ephesus" (19a, 21b). Thus 19b-21a stands out as a spin-off from Luke's aim to make Paul the founder of the church at Ephesus. Hence a roughness in the text may point to a written tradition, and a Lukan interest (such as magnifying Paul) in conjunction with that roughness may indicate redaction.

---

[19]Zeller, *Acts,* II, 15.
[20]Zeller, *Acts,* II, 321.

25:14-26:32. — This scene is not an eyewitness report of Paul's companion but Luke's free spin-off, untrammelled by tradition, from Luke's desire to prove that Roman authorities treated Christian missionaries kindly and acknowledged them to be politically harmless.

We have noted that the School of Creative Edification finds anti-Pauline traditions in Acts. These include: The story of Ananias (9:10-19) is the kind of story against which Paul protests in his Epistles. 9:20-22 is directed against Galatians ("straightway" of 9:20 is aimed at Gal 1:16; "destroyed" of 9:21 is influenced by Gal 1:23). 9:26-30; 26:20 is a tradition of Paul's opponents in Galatia, who held Paul was dependent upon Jerusalem in his preaching, that all that Paul taught correctly he owed to the Apostles in Jerusalem, and thus was not a true apostle, but from the start was under the moral protection of the original Apostles. Luke does not think of Paul as a witness of the resurrection but places in his mouth words which Paul himself would have repudiated (13:31). 15:1-35 represents an understanding of Paul's relationship to the Jerusalem apostolate which Paul himself corrects in Gal 2:1-10. 16:3 is a slanderous rumor, perhaps the very one referred to in Gal 5:11 (thus Luke hardly invented 16:3 but naively received a tradition from Paul's Judaistic opponents). In Acts Paul preaches the childlike milk of a non-sacramental Jewish Christianity calling men to repent, to be baptized, to believe Jesus has risen, and to await his return, whereas the geniune Paul put a curse upon anyone who should preach such a Gospel (Gal 1:6-9). The entire Acts is the kind of letter of recommendation which Paul scorned (2 Cor 3:1).

We have observed that the School of Historical Research and, to a lesser extent, the School of Restrained Criticism stress the historical study of antiquities (geography, history, archeology), whereas the School of Creative Edification is characterized more by critical speculation. Possibly the clearest example of this methodological contrast is Ramsay's defense of the account of Paul's release from prison (16:19-34) upon the basis of his (Ramsay's) knowledge of Aegean earthquakes, Turkish prisons, and the Oriental mind, as compared with Haenchen's conclusion that "an earthquake able to shake off a prisoner's chains has never yet occurred. On the other hand, the quaking of a house as a divine response to prayer had been told frequently in pagan Hellenism."[21]

3. *CURSUS VITAE.* Further implications of this School's methodology surface as we look at the various aspects of Paul's life. Tarsus as the place of Paul's birth and Saul as his other name are historical, for Luke had no reason on the basis of his interests in Jerusalem, the Twelve, and the political innocence of Christianity to invent them, nor had Paul any need to mention them (Knox). We may infer, then, that these references to Tarsus and Saul are based on reliable tradition and not upon Luke's unreliable imagination. When details in Acts are not found in the Epistles and do not conflict with the Epistles or other traditions and did not grow out of Luke's interests, and when there is no reason why Paul should have mentioned them, then we have reliable tradition.

On the other hand, Tarsus as the place of Paul's birth may be regarded as Luke's invention based on Gal 1:21 and the name Saul as deduced from Phil 3:5; Rom 11:1 (Enslin; see 2. above).

---

[21]Ramsay, *Paul,* pp. 222-3; Haenchen, "Acts as Source Material," p. 273.

Paul's Roman citizenship is doubted or denied on the grounds that Paul does not mention it (cf. 2 Cor 11:25), it fits Luke's conception of the political inocuousness of Christianity and the cosmopolitan character of Paul, and it would mean that this tentmaker came from one of the greatest families in the East.

Paul's study at the feet of Gamaliel is suspected or denied because it serves Luke's interests; Paul would be expected to mention it; Paul thinks differently from the Tannaim; and it is simply Luke's explanation of why the Tarsan Jew was in Jerusalem at the time of Stephen's death. The historicity of the letters of extradition is improbable, being Luke's conjecture to explain why Paul was in Damascus at the time of his conversion. Paul did not persecute the church in Jerusalem and Judea, and his conversion occurred in Damascus,[22] not as he approached Damascus. Here there is a clear conflict between Acts and Galatians (1:22-23) and therefore Acts must be rejected out of hand.

Acts has either removed Paul's apostolic office altogether or does not regard him as an apostle of equal standing with the Twelve. He could not meet the requirements of 1:21, and is not called an apostle except in 14:4,14, which probably means that Paul was a missionary sent out by the church at Antioch (13:1-3), not by Christ himself. Or, Paul in Acts is so obviously not an apostle that he can be called one in 14:4,14 without anyone's taking it seriously.

As spin-offs (2. above), Paul's journeys as depicted in Acts must either be radically rearranged, so as to eliminate doublets, or be declared largely unhistorical (there may be a historical fact lying behind this or that event, but the narratives are Luke's conscious creations).

Although we cannot be entirely certain about Paul's appeal to the Emperor, there is no reason to distrust this detail.

The Paul of Acts is only a generalized apostolic figure, lacking the distinctive features of the real Paul. Without Acts we would know as much about the personality and thought of Paul as with Acts. For any knowledge we can gain of Paul's ideas and inward aspects of his personality his Epistles constitute our only reliable source. The informed student simply disregards Acts as a source for Paul's inner life. The Paul of Acts is quite a different man from the Paul of the Epistles.

> If the Acts of the Apostles is really correct in its portraiture of St Paul, if this colourless rhetorical representative of average Christianity is the genuine Paul, then I can no longer resist the baleful attraction of the hypothesis proclaimed by the school of Leyden: that Paul the great epistolary writer is a later fiction, an ideal form, which an unknown artist has elevated upon eagle's wings out of the lowly circumstances of the real Paul into heavenly heights . . . Those, however, for whom the Paul of the four great epistles abides the most certain, the most unimpeachable thing in the whole New Testament, must describe the portraiture of St Paul in the Acts as woefully deficient and poor, just because it preserves absolutely nothing of the peculiar characteristics of the man: and if one who for

---

[22]S. Sabugal ("La conversion de S. Pablo en Damasco," *Aug*, XV [1975], 213-24) takes Gal 1:15-17; Acts 9:1-19a; 22:3-16; and 26:1-18 to mean that Paul's conversion occurred in the region of Qumran, referred to figuratively as "the region of Damascus."

many years was a companion, a friend, indeed a fellow-worker of St Paul — as was St Luke — in spite of the multitude of reminiscences which even in unimportant matters stood at his disposal, and in a writing where a picture of the genuine Paul was above all things called for — if such a one could not introduce into his portrait even one of the grand and noble characteristics of the Apostle, then indeed it is altogether vain to expect, or even to cherish a modest hope, that the Gospel historians, who depend entirely upon the testimony of others, present us with anything more than notices concerning external events in the life of our Lord and an artificial scheme of His ministry. how can we expect to receive from them genuine words from the lips of Jesus, or to feel through them the breath of His spirit pass upon us! If one of St Paul's most intimate friends tells us (Acts xxi. 20ff.), without the slightest hesitation, that the Apostle when in Jerusalem was ready, merely for the sake of peace and by a premeditated and elaborate act of hypocrisy, to convince the Jews that he walked now as before in strict observance of the Law; and if this piece of information, alleged to be given by a friend who must have known St Paul's real attitude towards the Law, deserves to be described as good tradition, then all trust in an intelligent tramsmission of actual history in the Primitive Church sinks to nothing, and we can no longer oppose with confidence the negation even of the best-attested statements.[23]

4. THE SUPERNATURAL. Since miracles are impossible and incredible, the accounts in Acts are either legendary or free compositions (inventions, spin-offs; 2. above). The religious dialectician of the Epistles who battles only with words, who accomplishes his work through sufferings and temptations, and who boasts only in his weakness, is supplanted in Acts by the miracle worker and magician who blinds his opponents and heals at a distance through handkerchiefs which had been in contact with his body. Paul in Acts no longer lives in the sphere of the cross but of glory.

5. PRACTICES AND PRINCIPLES. In Acts, where Paul preaches first to the Jews, he is primarily Apostle of the Jews, only secondarily Apostle of the Gentiles. Paul could never have followed the principle of not turning to Gentiles until Jewish unbelief had entitled him to do so, for according to Paul, his commission from his conversion on was only to Gentiles, and he never refers to his preaching to Jews or entering a synagogue. Paul's Jewish practices belong to the incredible side of Acts, for Paul held external ceremony to be absolutely irreconcilable with salvation. Paul neither observed the Law himself nor permitted his Jewish or Gentile converts to do so. The motives which Acts gives him for these compromising actions impugn Paul's character; the actions themselves violate his principles; and both together involve him in reprehensible hypocrisy. In the face of arguments to the contrary, Luke's tendency is to prove Paul loyal to the Law. Without violating his principles, Paul could not have approved nor executed the Decree nor remained silent about it if it had ever existed (on 15:1-35 see 2. above).

Contrary to Acts' idyllic picture of harmony between Paul and Jerusalem, the Epistles reveal two hostile parties, preaching two hostile Gospels, promoting two hostile missions, headed by two hostile apostles, Peter and Paul. There was a rude antagonism between the universalism of Paul and the narrow Judaizing views of the Twelve. Paul's independence of Jerusalem in Galatians contradicts

---

[23]A. Jülicher, *Neue Linien in der Kritik der evangelischen Überlieferung*, quoted by Harnack, *Date*, pp. 36-7.

his dependence in Acts (2. above), for the real Paul from his conversion on went his own independent way, avoiding all contacts with the older Apostles.

6. DOCTRINE. 23:1-10 is a fictitious account composed by Luke to place Paul in as close a relation as possible to Judaism, thereby distorting Paul's character, involving him in duplicity, and reducing him to a mendacious quibbler.

As suggested by the practice of ancient historians and borne out by other considerations (2. above), the speeches attributed to Paul in Acts are Luke's free compositions, dramatic messages for the readers, serving Luke's apologetic purpose of Petrinizing Paul or naively reflecting the deutero-Paulinism of an age theologically distant from Paul. The Paul of Acts is pre-Pauline in his Christology and post-Pauline in his natural theology, concept of the Law, and eschatology. From Acts, specifically Pauline ideas are missing, as justification and the atoning power of Jesus' death. Hence we cannot cite any of Paul's words in Acts as if they were Paul's own. The Paul whose speech was "contemptible" (2 Cor. 10:10) has been transformed by Luke into an eloquent orator. We can use Paul's speeches in Acts only if they agree with the Epistles, and in that case they are superfluous. We must not allow Paul's speeches composed by Luke to obscure the Epistles composed by Paul. It is necessary to erase the picture of the Paul of the speeches of Acts if the value of the underlying itinerary document is to be rightly estimated.

In sum, when we stress Luke's free creativity and use various pointers to tradition and redaction, we find that the Pauline portions of Acts generally represent Luke's standpoint, serve Luke's interests, and consequently picture Luke's Paul.

The Three-Paul View of the School of Advanced Criticism[24]

1. GENERAL DESCRIPTION. In Acts and Epistles there are three Pauls: (a) The historical Paul, the missionary of the travel narrative, a wandering Jew who preaches in many regions "the things concerning Jesus"; a disciple among disciples, with no essential difference in faith and life from them. (b) The legendary Paul, the hero of the "Acts of Paul" (2. below), who as a Christian reformer exposes the new principles of a universal religion emancipated from Judaism, who in a special sense is guided by the Holy Spirit, who is entrusted with "the gospel of the grace of God" (20:24), and whose life is full of supernatural events. This legendary Paul was further developed in the Epistles into the advocate of justification by faith. (c) Luke's (the final, mid-second-century redactor of Acts) Paul, the Paul, who, next to Peter is the founder of the Catholic Church, and who combines the principles of the primitive disciples ("the things concerning Jesus") with those of the Christians ("the Gospel of God's mercy"). For Luke there were no differences between Peter and Paul. By giving to Peter "Pauline touches" and to Paul Petrine "words and tints," Luke put Peter and Paul even closer together than they already were in the "Acts of Peter" and the "Acts of Paul."

It is the reliable tradition of the travel narrative which gives us the historical Paul in contrast to the redactional and legendary Paul. Van Manen tried to answer

---

[24]W. C. van Manen, "Paul," *Encyclopaedia Biblica*, III, 3603-6, 3620-38; and Mattill, *Luke as a Historian in Criticism since 1840*, pp. 207-36.

the question, "What does Acts teach us about Paul and Paulinism apart from the Epistles?" And he found that the representation of the historical Paul in the we-sections of Acts is nearer to the real Paul than the legendary Paul in the Epistles, for in the latter, "Paulinists" worked up the material of Acts under the influence of a tendency. All of the Paulines are pseudepigrapha, literary weapons aimed at anti-Pauline disciples.

It is arbitrary to assume the genuineness and reliability of the principal Epistles and that Acts accordingly must be tested by them. Rather we must estimate the value of what has come down to us through Acts and Epistles, compare them, arrange them, bring them into consistent and orderly connection, and thus see how the figure of Paul was repeatedly recast. The Epistles, which are patched, interpolated, and incomprehensible, set forth a much more unnatural picture of relationships within the church than does Acts. Confusing is the representation in Galatians of Paul's separation from the original Apostles, for in Galatians he receives his Gospel entirely from supernatural revelation and comes forth at once with all that was great and new in his preaching. But how natural is the picture of Acts, where Paul begins as an assistant to Barnabas and maintains a harmonious relationship to the Twelve, finally establishing his independence by force of his personality. Both the picture of Paul's missionary journeys and of his relations to his churches are unintelligible in Galatians. Equally confusing is the character of the Paul of the Epistles: radical, conservative; bold, weak; firm in small things, yielding in great things. The most natural view is that Acts gives what is historically most authentic, whereas the Epistles draw an imaginary picture. Hence the investigation of Acts must be carried on independently of the Epistles and vice versa.

2. METHODOLOGY. Acts is no loose stringing together of fragments derived from various sources. Yet in spite of the over-all unity there appear interruptions of the continuity, contradictions, and various conceptions of one and the same event which betray the fact that the author only with effort and his own interpretation arranged the reports lying before him. We must "distinguish between the original historical datum, the valuable substance of a trustworthy tradition, and the one-fold, two-fold,three-fold or it may be manifold clothing with which this has been invested by later views and opinions, and in too many cases, unfortunately, concealed them, in such a manner that it is not always possible...to discriminate...between truth and fiction."

Using these criteria, van Manen isolated these sources: the travel narrative (the oldest foundation of Acts), the Acts of Paul, the Acts of Peter, oral tradition, Josephus, and a few details from the Pauline Epistles. According to the original form of the journey narrative (which was completely revised by the author of the Acts of Paul), Paul traveled to Rome as a free man, for he is treated as such on ship, not as a prisoner. Furthermore, at least part of those who accompanied Paul to Jerusalem (20:4; 21:16) set out with him for Rome (27:2), which fact suggests a short stay at Caesarea, not a two years' imprisonment. Luke used details from Josephus to invent unhistorical scenes in Acts. Luke's mention of the Egyptian (21:38) and of Felix, Drusilla, Festus, Agrippa, and Bernice is explained by the fact that Luke knew the works of Josephus and did not scruple to use them in his description of Paul's life.

3. CURSUS VITAE. The historical Paul was a younger contemporary of Jesus'

disciples, and probably a Jew and native of Tarsus, a tentmaker. Originally hostile toward the disciples, he later joined them and spent the remainder of his life as a wandering preacher in Syria, Asia Minor, Greece, and Italy. He may have been one of the first to preach to Jews and Gentiles outside of Palestine (11:19-20). He seldom or never came into contact with the disciples of Palestine, and on a visit to Jerusalem narrowly escaped death for contempt of the Temple. There is reasonable certainty about only one great journey of Paul, and that toward the end of his life, the external conditions of which are dryly and exactly set forth in the we-source: Troas-Philippi-Troas-Assos-Mitylene-Samos-Miletus-Rhodes-Patara-Tyre-Ptolemais-Caesarea-Jerusalem-Caesarea-Sidon-Myra-Fair Havens-Melita-Syracuse-Rhegium-Puteoli-Rome (16:10-7; 20:5-15; 2l:1-18; 27:1-28:16). Acts provides no certain knowledge about the details of this journey. Paul reckons according to the Jewish calendar (20:6; 27:9), and is taken up as one of their own by the disciples in Tyre (21:3), Ptolemais and Caesarea (21:7-8), Jerusalem (21:17), Sidon (27:3), Puteoli (28:14), and Rome (28:15).

4. THE SUPERNATURAL. All of the supernatural elements in Acts' account of Paul are legendary, being a good distance along the road toward the apocryphal Acts.

5. PRACTICES AND PRINCIPLES. The real Paul engaged in Jewish practices, remaining in his own consciousness a Jew, a faithful attender of Temple and synagogue, who had not outgrown the Law any more than other Jewish Christians. Paul, Peter, and the original Apostles were scarcely distinguishable from Jews. Paul in Acts is not too Jewish but too Gentile. The historical Paul stood in a peaceful relationship to the Jerusalem church. Any struggles would have broken out after Paul's life-time (20:29-30), for while he lived it is impossible to guess what a quarrel could have been about.

6. DOCTRINE. Luke's creative activity is seen in the speeches of Paul, for Paul, like all other speakers in Acts, expresses Luke's own ideas as he pleads the cause of Christianity in the same fashion as the other speakers. The preaching of the real Paul was virtually identical with that of the Twelve, who also preached "the things concerning Jesus."

This, then, is the authentic Paul whom we discover by regarding the travel narrative of Acts as the primary source for the reconstruction of Paul's life and thought.[25]

Conclusion

This survey reveals how closely the evaluation of Acts as a source for the study of Paul is related to the estimation of the we-sections. The traditional view of the we-sections results in a high regard for Acts' data (Schools I and II). Non-traditional views are associated with distrust or rejection of this data (School III) or with a use of only a fraction of it (School IV). In this light, studies of the we-

---

[25]In contrast to these four schools which use Acts and Epistles together or place the Epistles above Acts or vice versa, B. Bauer (Die Apostelgeschichte) regards both Acts and Epistles as unhistorical, so that the real Paul is to be found in neither. In a similar vein, A. Loisy (Les Actes des Apôtres) finds that the redactor of Acts has turned the original historical Acts into legend; neither can Paul's Epistles be trusted, for they too are tendentious, and Paul did not necessarily conform to all the theories of his own writings.

sections assume unusual importance.[26]

As of today School IV is dead. School I is strong among conservative scholars. School III is dominant overall, and has succeeded in putting the burden of proof on others. Intrerpreters not only cannot ignore the work of School III, but usually must begin with its conclusions and proceed to build upon, modify, or reject them. School II "follows afar off." But the situation now appears to be changing. If there is a shift in opinion from Schools I and III to or toward School II (see footnotes 1 and 10), then it is from within this fluid situation that significant developments in Lukan studies will most likely emerge.

---

[26]J. Dupont, *The Sources of the Acts*; P. Pokorný, "Die Romfahrt des Paulus und der antike Roman," *ZNW*, LXIV (1973), 233-44; V. K. Robbins, "The We-Passages in Acts and Ancient Sea Voyages," *BR*, XX (1975), 1-14; Robbins, "By Land and by Sea: A Study in Acts 13-28," *1976 Seminar Papers,* pp. 381-96; Robbins, "The We-Sections in Acts," in this volume; E. Grässer, "Acta-Forschung seit 1960," *TR*, XLI (1976), 188-94. Cf. also A. J. and M. B. Mattill, *A Classified Bibliography of Literature on the Acts of the Apostles*, # 1053, 2118, 2124, 2140, 2144, 2145, 2153, 2161, 2179, 2200.

The Role of the Prologues in Determining the Purpose of Luke-Acts

Schuyler Brown

Any hypothesis concerning the purpose that the author of Luke-Acts may have had in writing must, if it is to lay serious claim to acceptance, be based on the work as a whole. One of the weaknesses of the redaction-critical method, as it is sometimes employed, is its concentration on certain "key" texts from which the author's entire theological program is inferred. We may wonder whether the texts selected for this use were really as crucial to the author as they are to his modern interpreter. It may well be beyond the ingenuity of any New Testament exegete to suggest a purpose for Luke-Acts, or even for either part of the work, for which no "Achilles' heel" can be found in the form of some passage or saying which appears to contradict such a suggested purpose. Indeed, we may legitimately ask whether Luke *must* have had one and only one overriding purpose in writing. Furthermore, even if he *did* have such a purpose, it is hazardous to assume that he was entirely consistent in eliminating or editing *all* traditional material which could not be made to serve this purpose.

If the form-critics erred in viewing the evangelists as mere "collectors," it may be that the redaction-critics have gone too far in urging their independence and "creativity" in the use of tradition. "The 'process of redaction' can have taken place in several steps, over a rather long period of time and with the involvement of an entire circle of persons."[1] The contribution of the final author would, in this case, be considerably more modest than has sometimes been assumed, and the

---

[1]A. Weiser, *Die Knechtsgleichnisse der synoptischen Evangelien*, p. 241. See our review in *Bib*, LIV (1973), 578-81.

gospels, as well, perhaps, as other New Testament books, would have to be viewed as imperfect unities.

But whatever value such cautionary observations may have, the search for Luke's overall purpose will certainly continue, and in this search the textual starting point that the exegete selects is of considerable importance. One obvious starting point is the two prologues,[2] particularly the prologue to the gospel, in which the author explicitly *states* his purpose in writing (Luke 1:3-4). Unless we are to suppose a discrepancy between the author's *declared* purpose and his *real* purpose, it would seem reasonable to expect that all hypotheses concerning Luke's purpose be related somehow to what the author himself says. To be sure, the meaning of these verses is far from obvious, and one's interpretation of them will inevitably be influenced by the understanding of Luke's purpose obtained from the rest of the work. Nevertheless, the introduction of a "hermeneutical circle" is clearly necessary: we must allow Luke's work to provide the commentary for his stated purpose and then check our interpretation of the work against the author's statement in Luke 1:3-4.

The former task, of allowing the individual exegesis of the gospel and Acts to cast light on Luke 1:3-4 and on any statement of purpose that may be implied in Acts 1:1-8, must be left to the authors of commentaries on these two works. Our concern in this article is restricted to the latter half of the circle. We will take the principal hypotheses which have been proposed concerning Luke's purpose and see what basis they have in the two prologues.

Charles H. Talbert has given us a convenient summary of the alternative options from which we have to choose in determining the purpose of Luke.[3] Today Talbert's categories still cover most suggestions as to Luke's purpose, even those which have been proposed in the interim. If we omit the last alternative,[4] which has played no major role in recent discussion, the remaining options may be listed[5] as follows:

1. The rehabilitation of Paul

2. An apology directed to the Roman state

3. The evangelization of the non-Christian world

4. The solution of a theological problem

5. A defence against heresy[6]

Obviously, options four and five are closely related, as long as they are proposed in this generic way.

---

[2]We are presuming the authenticity of the prologue to Acts, which some critics have assigned to a redactor. See. E. Haenchen, *The Acts of the Apostles: A Commentary*, pp. 144-6.

[3]*Luke and the Gnostics*, chapter 7, "The Alternatives."

[4]That of J. Knox in *Marcion and the New Testament*, treated by Talbert on pp. 108-9.

[5]We have reversed the sequence of Talbert's second and third options and described options one, four, and five more generically than he does, in order to make them as comprehensive as possible.

[6]Option five is the proposal of Talbert himself, who identifies the heresy in question as Gnosticism.

One preliminary question which has a direct bearing on two of these options is whether the purpose stated in Luke 1:3-4 is to be taken as extending to both volumes of Luke's work or whether it simply gives his purpose in writing the gospel. In other words, is Luke 1:1-4 the prologue to the gospel alone or to the entire two-volume work?

The first option, that Luke's purpose is the rehabilitation of Paul, is possible only if the *former* alternative is true. For obviously Paul has no place in the gospel, and consequently, if Luke 1:1-4 expresses the theme of *both* volumes, option one is excluded as the purpose of *either*. Only if Acts was written as an afterthought, with a different purpose from the one expressed in the prologue to the gospel, does option one have any plausibility.

On the other hand, if Luke 1:1-4 is taken to be the prologue for *both* volumes of Luke's work, this would give considerable support to option four. For an intent to write the story of Jesus and the story of the church as two parts of one "historical"[7] work suggests an originality of theological outlook which would set Luke apart from all the other evangelists, including John. "Thereby Christ's death and resurrection became one point in a series of fulfilled prophecies."[8] The Christ-event no longer has the same climactic significance as in the other evangelists.

Unfortunately, this question about the literary function of Luke 1:1-4, which is so important for Luke's purpose, is probably not capable of being answered definitively. To be sure, it was the custom in antiquity to prefix to the first volume of a work a preface to the whole.[9] But this really does not resolve the question. It shows that Luke 1:2-4 *can* can be the preface for both the gospel and Acts but scarcely that it *has* to be. For if Acts *were* an afterthought, Luke might still have wished to refer back to the earlier work when he commenced the later one. The prologue to Acts is "secondary" in the sense that it recalls the content of the earlier volume, but this does not establish its function in the volume in which it stands.

For us the primary objection to regarding Luke 1:1-4 as the preface to both volumes lies in the introductory clause. If "the things which have been accomplished among us" are taken to include the contents of Acts, then Luke would be affirming that he had "many" predecessors not only in writing his gospel but also in composing his second volume, something that few contemporary critics would be prepared to admit.[10] However, we must admit that this

---

[7]Whether or not Luke intended to write strict history depends, as far as the prologues are concerned, on how one interprets his use, particularly in Luke 1:3, of expressions found in contemporary Hellenistic historiographers. See D. J. Sneen, "An Exegesis of Luke 1:1-4 with Special Regard to Luke's Purpose as an Historian, *ExpTim*, LXXXIII (1971-72), 40-3. We believe that "Acts cannot be called an historical work in the proper sense, because what Luke intends to present is not human history but salvation history." (A. Wikenhauser and J. Schmid, *Einleitung in das Neue Testament*, p. 351.) The same statement could be made about Luke's gospel.

[8]E. Lohse, "Lukas als Theologe der Heilsgeschichte,"*EvT*, XIV (1954), 265.

[9]H. J. Cadbury, "Commentary on the Preface of Luke," *The Beginnings of Christianity*, II, 491.

[10]Luke's pioneer role in the composition of Acts is independent of the question whether

consideration may not be absolutely decisive.[11]

Another general question concerning Luke 1:1-4 which has a bearing on Luke's purpose is the secularity or *Sachlichkeit*[12] which it exhibits. The use of *pragmata* (vs. 1) and of the hapax legomenon *autoptai* (vs. 2) instead of *martures*, and perhaps the absence of any reference to *pistis* in vs. 4 may be taken as examples of this tendency. But the phenomenon can be interpreted in more than one way. The more obvious explanation would seem to favor option two or three: Luke prefers the language of Greek historiography to the language of faith because he is writing for non-Christians. However, Luke's secular style in the prologue has also been explained as the expression of a theological position,[13] rather than as an accommodation to his readers.

There is no need for us to show how Luke 1:1-4 can be understood as an apology directed to the Roman state, since this task has long ago been done.[14] Furthermore, as we have said already, the first option, the rehabilitation of Paul, has no relationship to the prologue of the gospel. Consequently, in considering the exegesis of Luke 1:1-4 we will be concerned with options three, four and five. In this connection it will not always be possible to distinguish clearly between options four and five, since the indications in the prologue that Luke is pursuing a theological purpose do not permit us to say definitively whether this was in response to the threat of false teaching.

Before Luke expresses his own purpose in writing, he states where he stands in relation to the previous tradition.[15] To what extent Luke is to be understood as setting himself off *against* this tradition depends on how much force is given to *epecheirēsan* (vs. 1). Obviously, Luke does not regard his own work as superfluous. But if he is claiming to undertake a task which his predecessors have attempted *unsuccessfully*, then this suggests an inner-Christian polemic which would give support to option four or five.

Those who consider Luke to be "the theologian of salvation history" will be inclined to see the theological notion of "fulfilment" behind the word *peplērophorēmenōn*.[16] A glance at the concordance will show the interest Luke has in the theological concept expressed by *(sum)plēroō*. However, it can be questioned whether this interest is announced here in the prologue. First of all, as we have already noted, the prologue is very sparing in the use of specifically

---

or not there were available *traditions* concerning the life of the early Christian communities. See J. Jervell, "The Problem of Traditions in Acts," *Luke and the People of God.*

[11]G. Klein ("Lukas 1:1-4 als theologisches Programm," *Zeit und Geschichte*, ed. E. Dinkler) admits that the work of Luke's *predecessors* did not include the history of the early church (p. 205), but he sees an allusion to Acts in *pasin* and *kathexēs* [vs. 3] (pp. 210-1).

[12]H. Flender, *Heil und Geschichte in der Theologie des Lukas*, p. 61.

[13]Klein, "Lukas 1:1-4," p. 214: "Luke waives the use of a *lingua christiana* in order to express the objective verifiability of the contents of faith."

[14]H. J. Cadbury, "The Purpose Expressed in Luke's Preface." *Exp*, XXI (1921), 431-41.

[15]Klein (p. 211) divides the prologue into a *Standortbestimmung* (vss. 1-2) and a *Zweckbestimmung* (vss. 3-4).

[16]Lohse, "Lukas als Theologe," p. 261: "The full-sounding participle . . . points to the fact that God has caused events to be fulfilled whose significance extends into the future and therefore has a fundamental character for the church."

Christian conceptions.[17] More important, it is difficult to see how *events (pragmata)* can be *fulfilled* in a theological sense. They can be the *fulfilment* of God's promises, but this is clearly not what Luke is saying here. A non-theological interpretation of the participle therefore seems preferable.[18]

The first person plural pronoun *hēmin* in vss. 1,2 raises once again the relation of Luke 1:1-4 to Acts. If these verses form an introduction to both volumes of Luke's work, then these two pronouns may somehow be related to the "We" passages in Acts.[19]

We have already mentioned the principal argument in favor of restricting the *pragmata* to the events narrated in the gospel. If this argument is accepted, the question arises: why does the author use the first person plural pronoun in connection with events at which he was clearly not present in person? A certain analogy is found in the Johannine prologue (John 1:14,16), and it is of no great importance for our present concern whether the first occurrence of *hēmin* is called "ecclesiastical" or "eschatological."[20]

In the *hēmin* in vs. 1 Luke associates himself with the accomplishment of the *pragmata*. In the *hēmin* in vs. 2 he associates himself with the *polloi*. Had he wished to suggest that his own task was radically different from that of his predecessors, we would expect to find *autois* as the indirect object of *paredosan*.[21] This consideration must be balanced against any polemical intent which might be read out of *epecheirēsan*. Positively, Luke's association of himself with his predecessors offers a basis for the view that *diēgēsis* is not simply Luke's designation for what the *polloi* have written but also expresses what Luke understood his own *prōtos logos* (Acts 1:1) to have been.[22]

If the phrase *hoi ap' arches autoptai kai hupēretai genomenoi tou logou* (vs. 2) refers to the apostles—the Twelve,[23] then we have here a Lukan theological leitmotiv: the *traditio apostolica*. Elsewhere[24] we have defended the thesis that in Luke's view the church rests on the *fides apostolica*, understood not merely as

[17]About the only exception to the rule of secularity in the prologue is the use of *logos* in vs. 2.

[18]Arndt & Gingrich (*A Greek-English Lexicon of the New Testament and Other Early Christian Literature), ad verb.*, offer the translation "the things that have been accomplished among us."

[19]See H. J. Cadbury, "'We' and 'I' Passages in Luke-Acts," *NTS*, III (1956-57), 128-32, and E. Haenchen, "Das 'Wir' in der Apostelgeschichte und das Itinerar," *ZTK*, LVIII (1961), 329-66.

[20]See H. Schürmann, *Das Lukasevangelium: Erster Teil*, p. 8.

[21]*Ibid.*, p. 8, n. 44.

[22]See W. Marxsen, *Mark the Evangelist: Studies on the Redaction History of the Gospel*, trans. J. Boyce, p. 25.

[23]For Klein this indentification is suggested by the comparable formulation in Acts 13:31. There were "eye-witnesses from the beginning" who did not *become (genomenoi)* "servants of the word" (see Acts 1:21-22), and there were "servants of the word" who had not been "eye-witnesses from the beginning" (see Acts 26:16), but the two concepts *coincide* only in the Twelve. For the details of Klein's somewhat complex argument, see pp. 201-5.

[24]*Apostasy and Perseverance in the Theology of Luke.*

the continuity of the apostles' testimony but also as their unbroken faith during the Age of Jesus. Of course, the prologue does not tell us *why* Luke has recourse to the *traditio apostolica.* Is he concerned with the problem of tradition in itself (option four): how is the church connected with its origins?[25] Or is he appealing to the concept of the *traditio apostolica* to ward off some teaching that he considers to be dangerous (option five)?

If this theological conception is the presupposition for Luke's statement of purpose, then the *hēmin* in vs. 2 takes on special force. The *traditio apostolica* was not simply the source for the work of the *polloi* and of Luke himself. It is the ultimate norm for the church (ecclesiological *hēmin*).

A "canonical" intent on Luke's part may be suggested by the phrase *edoxe kamoi* (vs. 3), particularly when we recall the similar phrase in Acts 15:28: *edoxen gar to pneumati tu hagio kai hemin.* Luke's omission of any reference to the holy spirit is in keeping with his secular style, but it offended some scribes who added the words "and to the holy spirit,"[26] thereby underlining the parallel with the text in Acts. For Luke the apostolic decree was the definitive document which consolidated the relationship between the Gentile Christians and the Jewish Christians.[27] Does his use of *edoxe kamoi* suggest that he attributed an analogously definitive significance to his own gospel? In any case, the *kamoi* underlines Luke's solidarity with his predecessors and, through them, with the *traditio apostolica* which they incorporated into their writings.[28]

In what sense Luke's work may have gone *beyond* that of his predecessors could be suggested by the distinction between *ap' archēs* and *anōthen.* The two expressions occur together in Acts 26:4-5, and *anothen* may designate an *earlier* point in time than *ap' archēs.*[29] According to Acts 1:22 (*arxamenos apo tou baptismatos Iōannou*), the *arche* in question would seem to be the beginning of the *traditio apostolica,* i.e. the baptism of John. It seems reasonable, therefore, to suppose that *anōthen* in Luke 1:3 includes the infancy narrative, which follows immediately upon the prologue.[30]

If this is the case, what is the reference of *pasin?* An explanation of the word as a solecism for *pasais,* referring to *diēgēseis* (understood),[31] would make

---

[25]Klein, "Lukas 1:1-4," p. 214: "The question of how the connection with the beginning is to be preserved."

[26]B. M. Metzger, *A Textual Commentary on the Greek New Testament,* p. 129.

[27]Klein, "Lukas 1:1-4," p. 215.

[28]Cf. W. C. van Unnik, "Opmerkingen over het doel van Lucas' Geschiedwerk (Luke 1:4)," *NedTTs,* IX (1955), 330, n. 1: "From the *kamoi* it is clear that verse one levels no criticism against predecessors but rather that Luke lines himself up with them."

[29]Klein, "Lukas 1:1-4," pp. 208-10.

[30]See Schürmann, *Das Lukasevangelium,* p. 11: "Here Luke has us consider that his . . . careful investigation went beyond the traditions derived from the legitimated apostolic eye-witnesses (vss. 1-2), *ap' archēs,* i.e., that it brought to light the 'prehistories' of Luke 1-2." Cadbury ("Commentary," p. 502) cautions us: "There appears to be no warrant for assigning to the word [*parēkolouthēkoti*] the sense of deliberate investigation." Therefore, even if *anōthen* is taken to include the infancy narrative, the prologue does not oblige us to suppose that Luke had special sources or informants for his first two chapters.

[31]This possibility is mentioned but rejected by Schürmann, *Das Lukasevangelium,* p. 10.

Luke's task correspond *precisely* with that of his predecessors. On the other hand, an interpretation of the word to include what Luke narrates in Acts [32] seems to overlook the probable reference to the *pragmata* in vs. 1.[33] Furthermore, the parallel use of *pantōn* in Acts 1:1 makes clear, through the phrase that follows, that Jesus' ascension (*anelemphthē*) (vs. 2) is the *terminus usque ad quem*.[34] If Luke is claiming here to be more comprehensive than his predecessors *a parte post* as well as *a parte ante*, then perhaps the *pasin* is to be thought of as including Jesus' conversations with his apostles after the resurrection (Luke 24:1ɔ-49; Acts 1:3-8).

Luke's use of *panta* in both prologues may have a polemical thrust, a possibility which would favor option five. "Luke underlines the completeness of the apostolic witness in various ways at decisive points in Acts, evidently taking a position against growing pseudo-Christian secret tradition."[35] In other words, Luke is telling his readers *all* there is to tell, and he does so by going beyond the work of his predecessors, including an infancy narrative and post-resurrection conversations. Can we conclude from this that these two loci served as sources for the secret teaching which Luke opposed?

"It is not completely impossible that Luke may have known about the heretical danger of such *logoi apokruphoi,* and that his reaction against this danger . . . was an influence in limiting the appearances to forty days."[36] It is possible that the Gospel of Thomas intends to give the reader the words of the *risen* Jesus,[37] and apocryphal infancy narratives were used to convey unorthodox teaching.[38]

---

[32]Klein, "Lukas 1:1-4," p. 210.

[33]Grammatically speaking, *pasin* can be either masculine or neuter. If masculine, it would refer to either to *polloi* (vs. 1) or to *autoptai kai hupēretai* (vs. 2). This would yield two possible interpretations for *parēkolouthēkoti . . . pasin:* 1. Luke has *studied* all the earlier writers. 2. Luke has *accompanied* all the "eyewitnesses and servants of the word." The former interpretation corresponds with Luke's dependence on Mark and Q, according to the Two-Source Theory. The latter is the apparent basis for the view in the early church that Luke was "a follower and disciple of the apostles" (Irenaeus, *Against Heresies,* 3.10.1). If *pasin* is neuter, the reference is to *pragmata* (vs. 1), and this interpretation seems to be the simplest. This would make it possible for *pasin* to include the events treated in chaps. 1-2, since *pragmata,* which occurs before the comparative clause in vs. 2, is not, of itself, restricted to the events following the *archē* of the *traditio apostolica.* On the other hand, to understand this reference to *pragmata* as somehow bypassing the *traditio apostolica* and its incorporation in the literary efforts of the *polloi* seems unwarranted. For the opposing view see Klein, "Lukas 1:1-4," pp. 206-7: "For him [Luke] his own discovery of truth replaces recourse to the apostolic tradition."

[34]However, in Acts 1:1 *pantōn* is limited by the phrase "that Jesus began to do and teach," so that *here* the *arche* of the *traditio apostolica* is the *terminus a quo,* i.e., the infancy narrative cannot be included. If *pasin* (Luke 1:3) and *panton* (Acts 1:1) do in fact have a different comprehension, this is not necessarily due to any deliberate intention on the author's part.

[35]Schurmann, *Das Lukasevangelium,* p. 11.

[36]J. M. Robinson, *"Logoi Sophōn:* Zur Gattung der Spruchquelle Q," in *Zeit und Geschichte,* p. 84, n. 27.

[37]*Ibid.*

[38]O. Cullmann, "Infancy Gospels," *New Testament Apocrypha,* ed. E. Hennecke and W. Schneemelcher, trans. R. McL. Wilson *et al,* I, 367: "It is the Gnostics who appear to have

However, any assumption that the literary genres used to circulate heresy in the post-Biblical period were already being used for this purpose in Luke's day must remain extremely tentative.

Whatever the precise reference of *pasin* (Luke 1:3), it is not necessary to understand it in such a way to to *exclude* the *diēgēseis* of Luke's predecessors.[39] The normative character that the *traditio apostolica* has for Luke is suggested by *hēmin* (vs. 2), and this tradition is accessible to him only through the works of his predecessors, in which it is incorporated. *Pasin* can therefore be taken to refer *both* to *diegeseis* and to *pragmata*, so that both senses of *parakoloutheo* are brought into play. By "following what is read" in the works of his predecessors Luke "keeps in touch with"[40] "the things accomplished among us."

The adverb *akribos* may sharpen the polemical tendency implied in *pasin*. It is not clear whether it is to be taken with *parēkolouthekoti* or with *grapsai,* but its position may suggest that it goes with both.

The word *kathexēs* has been used as a basis for ascribing a theological purpose to Luke (option four). For a study of the gospel shows that "Luke does not give us an order which represents the historical sequence of events more accurately than Mark. Consequently, his program to write everything 'in the correct sequence' *(kathexēs)* cannot designate a strictly chronological order."[41] If Luke's order is not chronological,[42] is it perhaps theological? Such a reference to theological order could be connected with Luke's "geographical theology,"[43] but it could also signify the joining together of two phases of salvation history, the Age of Jesus and the Age of the Church.[44] To be sure, this latter suggestion has force only if we presuppose that Luke 1:1-4 is the prologue for *both* books.[45]

But it may be that the notion of "order"—whether chronological or theological—is not in *kathexēs* at all. If the correct translation is simply "as follows," then the purpose which Luke expresses in vs. 4 would be achieved not

---

been especially interested in infancy stories and to have encouraged the collection of all kinds of material.

[39]Klein, "Lukas 1:1-4," p. 206: "The predecessors were concerned with the traditional *diegēsis* of events. Luke, on the contrary, wants to get back to the events themselves."

[40]See Cadbury, "Commentary," pp. 503-4.

[41]J. Schmid, "Lukasevangelium," *Lexikon für Theologie und Kirche;* ed. J. Hafer and K. Rahner, VI, 1208.

[42]Schürmann, *Das Lukasevangelium,* p. 12 insist that *kathexes* means a "chronologically correct sequence" but then adds: "To be sure, Luke is thinking more in terms of salvation history than 'historically.' " But an order that is governed by considerations of salvation history would seem to be more theological than chronological.

[43]Lohse, "Lukas als Theologe," p. 260: Luke "points to the geographical way which was taken by the sequence of events that he describes."

[44]Klein, "Lukas 1:1-4," p. 211. It is this "follow-up" to the Age of Jesus which, in Klein's opinion, Luke missed in the words of his predecessors.

[45]Klein seems to presuppose what his interpretation of *kathexes* is intended to prove. *If,* when Luke announced his intention to Theophilus to write "one thing after the other" (see Klein, "Lukas 1:1-4," p. 211, n. 99), he had already determined on a sequel to the gospel, *then* the notion of succession in *kathexēs* might be given the significance that Klein assigns to it.

by any sort of order but simply by the accuracy *(akribōs)* of what he writes.[46]

More important than the insoluble question of the *personal identity* of Theophilus[47] is the question of *whom he represents*.[48] Considered in terms of options three through five, this question can be rephrased: was Theophilus a "person who had received ecclesiastical instruction"[49] or was he someone "on the brink of Christianity"?[50] The question of Luke's purpose is closely related to the question of his addressees. Was Luke writing to Christians or to well-disposed non-Christians?

This question becomes crucial for the interpretation of the final verse of the prologue. Does *katēchēthēs* suggest a process of formal catechetical instruction or does the verb have the general meaning "to inform"?[51] A possible connection between *logoi* in vs. 4 and *logos* in vs. 2, suggesting that the plural form is the concretization of the singular,[52] might favor the former alternative, since *logos* is clearly the apostolic preaching (cf. Acts. 6:2,4).

If *logoi* refers to catechetical instruction,[53] then *asphaleia* cannot refer to faith,[54] which Theophilus, as an instructed Christian, would already possess. It could signify *objectively* the security or protection provided by Luke's work itself

---

[46]J. Kurzinger, "Luke 1:3: . . .*akribōs kathexēs soi grapsai*," *BZ*, XVIII (1974), 249-55. See also M. Völkel, "Exegetische Erwagungen zum Verständnis des Begriffs *kathexēs* im Lukanischen Prolog," *NTS*, XX (1973-74), 289-99. Volkel translates *kathexēs* as *"continua serie."* Unlike Kurzinger, he believes that the word has a relation to Luke's purpose. Luke endeavors "to represent them [*pragmata*] in such a way that the connecting sense of the event that he describes becomes clear and thus . . . contributes to *epignosis* in relation to the *asphaleia* of the teaching" (p. 298).

[47]The fact that "Theophilus" appears in Josephus (*Ant.* 18.123) as the name of a Jew would have significance for those who think that Luke is addressing Jewish-Christians.

[48]Klein, "Lukas 1:1-4," p. 213: "Luke does not compose his work with a view to convincing an historical individual . . . . In Luke's mind, the intended effect on Theophilus represents the effect of the work on each reader."

[49]Schurmann, *Das Lukasevangelium*, p. 13.

[50]W. C. van Unnik, "The 'Book of Acts' — the Confirmation of the Gospel," *NovT*, IV (1960), 59.

[51]Arndt & Gingrich, *Greek-English Lexicon, ad verb.*, cite parallels for the general meaning as well as for the meaning "teach, instruct . . . in our literature only of instruction in religious matters." In Acts 21:21,24 the verb must have the generic meaning, since it is used of the *mis*information that has been circulated about Paul. In Acts 18:25, however, the connotation is religious: Apollos had been "instructed *(katechēmenos)* in the way of the Lord." The specific sense of *catechetical* instruction is found in 2 Clement 17:1.

[52]The problem of the relationship between "the word" and "the words" is a familiar one in contemporary theological discussion.

[53]Klein's suggestion (213) that the *logoi* are "the pre-Lucan literature" seems quite unfounded. It rests on the parallel between the plural forms *polloi* (vs. 1) and *logoi* (vs. 4). Robinson's article (see n. 36) gives the history of the plural usage.

[54]Flender, *Heil und Geschichte*, p. 63: "Not one word suggests that . . . [Luke's] presentation is supposed to call forth faith." Klein, "Lukas 1:1-4," p. 216 comes close to suggesting that Luke intends that *asphaleia* should *replace* faith. One senses that systematic concerns are finding expression here.

for the church's catechesis.[55] This interpretation would support option five, since it suggests the presence of a threat to faith which Luke's work is intended to counter.[56] But *asphaleia* could also be taken *subjectively* to designate Theophilus' reflex certitude concerning what he had already come to believe.

On the other hand, if Theophilus is a well-disposed non-Christian, then his acknowledgment *(epignōs)* of the reliability *(asphaleian)* of the matters *(logon)* about which he has been informed (*katēchēthes*) would be the act of faith itself. This strange circumlocution would come from Luke's concern to avoid the use of Christian language in addressing readers who were not yet Christian.

From our limited perspective, which is confined to the prologue, it is not easy to choose between option three, on the one hand, and option four or five, on the other. The style of Luke 1:1-4 does seem geared to win over the readers of the gospel to Christianity. On the other hand, the appeal to the *traditio apostolica* as the ultimate authority appears to presuppose that Luke's readers are already Christians. Can the theological (or anti-heretical) tendency be brought together with the evangelical tendency, so that both can be seen as expressions of one and the same purpose? An affirmative answer to this question has been given. "The same impetus which, with respect to the past, led to a new type of certitude concerning the facts of salvation history led, with respect to the present, to the characterization of Christianity as an intellectual movement capable of holding its own in competition."[57]

But even if such a formulation could show how the two tendencies of the gospel stem from the same impetus on the part of the *author*, does it explain how Luke's work could have been addressed to a *single audience*? Why would Christians need to be shown that Christianity was an attractive intellectual option, and, conversely, why would those whom Luke was seeking to win over by such a demonstration require a *new* type of certitude? The double tendency in Luke *does* seem to presuppose two circles of readers,[58] and perhaps some thought should be given to the question: what plausible *Sitz im Leben* in early Christianity might have given rise to a book with such diverse potentials?

The prologue to Acts can be dealt with much more briefly, since its bearing on the purpose of the author is limited. Even if we understand the prologue to extend as far as Jesus' final words with his disciples, i.e. through Acts 1:8, there is nothing in it to correspond to Luke's explicit statement of purpose in Luke 1:3-4. This could be seen as an argument in favor of the view that Luke 1:1-4 was intended by the author to introduce *both* works. But Acts 1:1-8 may contain an *implicit* expression of Luke's purpose, which would deserve consideration.

---

[55]From a Roman Catholic confessional standpoint, "motives of credibility" do not undermine the nature of faith, since they neither *cause* it (subjectively) nor *prove* it (objectively). A similar "motive of credibility" can be seen in 1 Cor 15:6. See my "Response to Professor Peter — II," *CTSA Proceedings*, XXIX (1974), 279.

[56]To continue the parallel from the previous note, Paul's appeal to living witness of the risen Lord in 1 Cor 15:6 is made in response to a clear danger to the faith of his community (1 Cor 15:14, 17).

[57]Klein, "Lukas 1:1-4," pp. 212-13.

[58]*Ibid.*, p. 212: "It is not that a message is being delivered here to two different groups of readers."

The prologue to Acts is at one with the prologue to the gospel in its utilization of contemporary literary forms. Luke's second prologue, then, provides additional evidence of the author's intention to represent Christianity as a world religion and not as a Palestinian sect.[59] As we have already noted, this tendency supports the view that the author's purpose was evangelization (option three).

In the first two verses the author resumes the content of his earlier work and then proceeds immediately to a summary description of the forty days (vss. 3-5), which serves as a transition to a new scene, Jesus' last conversation with his apostles before his ascension (vss. 6-8). If the prologue to Acts is taken narrowly, so as to exclude these last three verses, then the author gives us no preview of the contents of the book that he is beginning. However, this function is fulfilled by Jesus' prediction and implicit command in vs. 8.

If Luke 1:1-4 is understood to be the prologue to both the gospel and Acts, the most that we might hope to find at the beginning of the second volume would be some confirmation of the author's purpose as already expressed at the beginning of the gospel. If Luke's purpose is to present a "geographical theology," then the reference in Acts 1:8 to the triumphant advance of the apostolic witness "in Jerusalem and in all Judea and Samaria and to the end of the earth" could be seen as spelling out the implications of kathexēs in Luke 1:3. If, on the other hand, Luke hopes to bring Theophilus and the group of readers whom he represents to believe in the Christian preaching, then the fact that this preaching has reached "the end of the earth," i.e. Rome, the capital of the Greco-Roman world, could be taken as confirmatory evidence of its reliability (asphaleia).

If the author's purpose is to appeal to the traditio apostolica, this appeal is surely strengthened by Jesus' promise concerning the territorial expansion of the apostolic witness. If Luke invokes the traditio apostolica in order to combat dangerous doctrine, then the forty-day period of instruction by the risen Lord on the subject of "the things about the kingdom of God" (vs. 3), i.e., the content of Christian teaching, serves to exclude any appeal to secret teaching which might be in conflict with the traditio apostolica. If, on the other hand, the theme of tradition was introduced in the prologue to the gospel precisely as a theological problem, then Acts 1:6-7 may be raising a complementary theological problem. The problem of tradition is how to preserve the connection with the beginning. The problem of Acts 1:6-7 could be phrased: how to preserve the expectation of the end (basileia), despite the church's ignorance of the time of its coming (Ouch humon estin gnonai chronous e kairous)? Acts 1:8 would then be seen as an answer to this problem: the church's ignorance as to when the end will come is rendered tolerable by its reception of the spirit and its engagement in its missionary task.[60]

If we assume that Luke-Acts represents a single work with a single purpose, then we must raise with respect to Acts the same question that presented itself for the gospel: do the evangelical and theological tendencies expressed in the

---

[59]Haenchen, Acts, pp. 137-8.

[60]H. Conzelmann, Die Apostelgeschichte, p. 22: "The delay of the parousia is transformed into something positive, from the standpoint of salvation history." But there is really nothing in these verses to suggest that the problem is the delay of the parousia.

work presuppose two groups of readers, and, if so, what may this suggest concerning the historical circumstances in which the work was written?

We have discussed the possibility of interpreting Acts 1:1-8 as a confirmation of the author's statement of purpose in Luke 1:3-4. But what if Acts was written as an afterthought, in response to a *different* problem and in order to achieve a *different* purpose.[61] As we have noted, there is no *explicit* statement of purpose at the beginning of Acts. Nevertheless, the fact that the expansion of the apostolic witness (Acts 1:8) appears as a prediction and a command on the lips of the risen Lord could suggest an *implicit* purpose on the author's part.

If the outward movement from Jerusalem to Rome is understood quantitatively, so as to suggest the *growth* of the Christian mission, then the fact that this growth is the fulfilment of Jesus' promise and command might serve "to spur his (Luke's) community to missionary effort at a time when external pressures made such effort extraordinarily difficult."[62] If, on the other hand, the emphasis is *qualitative*, so as to suggest the *transition* from the Jewish-Christian community in Jerusalem to the center of the Gentile world, then Acts 1:8 could be intended to represent the Gentile mission "as being the result not of any human decision but of God's direct intervention."[63]

Finally, if Acts was written as an afterthought, 1:8 could be taken as support for option one, the rehabilitation of Paul. The fact that the promise made by Jesus to the apostles (Acts 1:8) comes to fulfilment in the person of Paul (Acts 28:30-31) is a very forceful way of associating him with the *traditio apostolica*.[64]

The purpose of this paper has been strictly limited. We have not attempted to propose all the exegetical alternatives for the interpretation of the two Lukan prologues, since only a limited number of these alternatives are related, directly or indirectly, to the question of the author's purpose. Nor have we tried to list all the hypotheses concerning Luke's purpose or purposes, since such hypotheses depend on the interpretation not only of the prologues but of the entire work.

---

[61]A shift in Luke's purpose between the gospel and Acts would seem more likely if he were addressing Christians in both works than if he were addressing well-disposed non-Christians. The needs of Christians could shift between the composition of the two volumes, but if he were addressing non-Christian readers, Luke's purpose would remain basically the same, i.e., the conversion to Christianity. Hence the adoption of option three seems more compatible with viewing Luke-Acts as a single work written with a single purpose than it does with the contrary hypothesis.

[62]S. Brown, "Precis of Eckhard Plümacher, *Lukas als hellenistischer Schriftsteller,*" *SBL 1974 Seminar Papers,* II, 112.

[63]*Ibid.,* p. 110. Haenchen's suggestion (*Acts,* p. 143) that the problem of the Gentile mission is already alluded to in Acts 1:6 depends on his restrictive interpretation of "Israel" in that verse. Jervell, *Luke and the People of God,* p. 60 argues, to the contrary, that "the addition of the Gentiles is part of the restoration of Israel." The point of Acts 1:8 could not be that "salvation is not *restricted* (emphasis ours) to Israel" (Haenchen, *Acts,* p. 144) if Luke considers the Gentiles to be associate members of Israel.

[64]G. Klein, *Die Zwölf Apostel,* p. 210. M. Bourke has gone so far as to suggest (The University Seminar for Studies in the New Testament, Minutes of the Meeting of Nov. 22nd, 1974, p. 11): "It has always seemed to me that Luke must consider Paul as an apostle because Paul is the only one who actually fulfills the commission in Acts 1:8 ('to the end of the earth')."

Nevertheless, we have shown the interconnection between the exegesis of the prologues and the principal hypotheses concerning the purpose of Luke-Acts. Clearly, this purpose cannot be determined solely by an analysis of the prologues, since the prologues can be read in such a way as to support any one of the main hypotheses which have been proposed. What is needed is some new activity in the other direction of the hermeneutical circle. For only thus can light be shed on the fundamental question: to what extent was Luke a self-conscious author and to what extent was he the representative of a wider tradition which he only imperfectly succeeded in making his own?

Poor and Rich:
The Lukan Sitz im Leben

Robert J. Karris, O.F.M.

What do we know about Luke's *Sitz im Leben?* That is a question I recently asked myself and was surprised by the answer, "not much."[1] That answer becomes an embarrassment when I realize that some twenty years of redaction critical work have issued in the paltry result of "not much" and when I glance at what colleagues have been able to determine with considerable probability about the *Sitz im Leben* of John's Gospel and Matthew's Gospel. The goal of this paper is to challenge us to step up our pursuit of the Lukan *Sitz im Leben.*

In what follows I will examine, in a brief way, one prospect of getting at the concrete Lukan Sitz im Leben — the theme of poor and rich.[2] In developing this prospect, I will doggedly raise the question of *Sitz im Leben.* Answers to that interrogation will hint at the complexity of the Lukan *Sitz im Leben.*

Definition of Terms

I follow Jacques Dupont in defining the poor as the indigent, those who lack

---

[1]That "not much" is reflected in the "official" scorecard of NT research. Werner G. Kümmel lists the following "purposes" for Luke's Gospel: 1) Luke answers the question of how the church of his time can remain in continuity with the period of Jesus which belongs to the past; 2) Luke is combatting Gnostic and especially Docetic false teaching. He lists eight "goals" for Acts without relating them to the Lukan *Sitz im Leben. (Introduction to the New Testament*, pp. 146-47; 163-64. See also Kümmel's "Current Theological Accusations Against Luke," *ANQ* XVI (1975), 131-45 (142-45).

[2]The sheer mass of material on poor and rich in Luke-Acts intimates that we can get at least a peek at the Lukan *Sitz im Leben* by studying this them. The theme must have been of some importance within Luke's situation for him to have preserved so much material on it.

the necessities, those who need alms.[3] The rich are those who have considerable possessions or money. I disassociate my definition of poor from that of Joachim Jeremias, who, while having many helpful comments on Luke 4:18, 6:20, and 7:22, gives a definition of poor which is so broad that it is not serviceable as a means of discriminating between the various materials on poor and rich: "Jesus used 'the poor' in this wide sense that the term had acquired in the prophets . . . the hungry, those who weep, the sick, those who labour, those who bear burdens, the last, the simple, the lost, the sinners."[4]

Previous Studies on the Theme of Poor and Rich in Luke-Acts

In this section I will whet our appetites for pursuit of the Lukan *Sitz im Leben* by summarizing and evaluating studies which make representative or major contributions to our thematic. I will underline what these authors have to say about the Lukan *Sitz im Leben.*

1. A MERE "CONCERN." It seems that many studies on Luke devote a number of pages to his "concern" for the poor. Quite often these discussions fall into the literary category of spiritual nosegay and betray not the slightest trace of an interest in relating this theme to the *Sitz im Leben* of Luke.[5]

2. HENRY JOEL CADBURY. As in so many other instances, Cadbury had a

---

[3]*Les beatitudes, Tome III: Les évangélistes,* pp. 42-3.

[4]*New Testament Theology: The Proclamation of Jesus,* pp. 109-13 (113). In Jeremias' definition the concept of the poor is swallowed up by the rubric of concern for the outcasts and sinners. Luke lays heavy stress on the Jesus who had table fellowship with toll collectors and sinners. This theme, however, should not be confused with the theme of poor and rich. Similarly, it is important to investigate Luke's picture of Jesus as a miracle worker as a theme in its own right and not neutralize the importance of that study by subsuming Jesus' miracles under the rubric of "care for the poor." The various Jewish traditions about the poor are complex. In the OT one can note these four strains of tradition: 1) in pre-monarchic Israel there were clan egalitarianism, redistributional land tenure, and the ideal of a brotherhood where there was no poor person (see Deut 15:4; cf. Acts 4:34); 2) poverty as a scandalous condition. Clan egalitarianism is weakened by the power elite. See Amos 8:4-6. The King, as Yahweh's vicar, should care for the widows, orphans, and other needy; 3) poor person as a symbol for one's attitude towards God; poverty as a spiritual childhood or religious ideal of humility. See Isa 66:2; Zeph 3:12; 4) the wisdom literature stresses the dangers of wealth (Sir 31:5), but also states that self-incurred poverty and beggary are hateful to God; riches can be a sign of God's blessing (see Prov 10:4,15; 14:20; Sir 31:1-11). At Qumran the poor person is the humble one who acknowledges his sinfulness and is saved by God's grace. Also at Qumran there was sharing of community goods and almsgiving. Martin Hengel summarizes the position of Rabbinic literature in this wise: "Jewish piety, which took its stamp from the message of the prophets and the social commandments of the Torah, did its utmost to eliminate or at least to alleviate the particularly abrupt contrast between the rich and poor in the Hellenistic Roman period" (*Property and Riches in the Early Church,* p. 19). Hengel also notes on p. 21 that the rabbis continued one facet of the wisdom tradition as they esteemed wealth highly and despised poverty. In apocalyptic literature, e.g., *I Enoch* 97, there is condemnation of the rich who think that their wealth is a sign of God's favor.

[5]Is Kümmel representative when he writes about the "human, moving features of Jesus?" (*Introduction,* p. 139) Note also that Kümmel conflates "poor" with sinners and outcasts.

profound insight into the material on poor and rich. Some 50 years ago he wrote: "It is to possessors, not to the dispossessed, that Jesus speaks on alms and on the cares and pleasures of property." "But the rebuke of wealth . . . betokens a concern for the oppressor rather than pity for the oppressed . . . ."[6] Cadbury makes no statement about the Lukan *Sitz im Leben.*

3. HANS-JOACHIM DEGENHARDT.[7] I make two points. First, Luke separates the *laos* from the *mathetai,* the *mathetai* from the *apostoloi.* The admonitions to renounce wealth/possessions are given to the disciples who are the *Amtstragern* of Luke's community — traveling apostles, missionaries, evangelists, wandering preachers, charismatic prophets, and resident community leaders. These are the ones who must follow the radical statement of Jesus about renunciation of possessions.[8] Further, there is also the danger and tendency among Luke's church leaders to become greedy, pleasure-seeking, and forgetful about almsgiving.[9]

My second point is that Degenhardt hedges on the primary *Sitz im Leben,* outlined above, and introduces another.[10] By means of his modifications of the inherited traditions behind Acts 2:41-47 and 4:31c-35, Luke confronts Gentile Christians who because of cultural conditioning have little or no concern for love of neighbor and almsgiving. Unless this cultural conditioning is confronted and transformed, the very existence of the Christian community as a fraternity will be in jeopardy. Moreover, Luke has to show these Gentile Christians that possessions can separate them from union with Christ (see Luke 12:21; 11:41; 12:15; 14:14; 18:18-27; cf. 12:16-20).[11]

Methodologically, Degenhardt's work is deficient because he does not deal with the Magnificat and the Zacchaeus story;[12] because it is not possible to separate the "disciples" from the "people" and the twelve (apostles) with any type of consistency;[13] and especially because Degenhardt does not sufficiently discuss other material within Luke-Acts which deals with church leaders and thus does not provide a control for his methodology and conclusions.

While there are problems with some aspects of Degenhardt's monograph, he has made many valuable points. I single out two: 1) he takes very seriously the

----

[6]*The Making of Luke-Acts,* pp. 262-63.

[7]*Lukas, Evangelist der Armen: Besitz und Besitzverzicht in den lukanischen Schriften.* See also his "Die Liebestätigkeit in den Gemeinden der apostolischen Zeit," *Volk Gottes. Festgabe für Josef Höfer,* pp. 243-53.

[8]If one asks Degenhardt why Luke does this, he responds that Luke inherited these radical traditions and had to make contemporary use of them. See *Lukas,* pp. 41, 214-5.

[9]*Lukas,* pp. 215-16.

[10]For minor, additional examples of hedging: in Luke 16:14-31 Luke is arguing against libertine, Gnostic opponents (*Lukas,* p. 135 n. 20); in Luke 12:13-21 Luke has rich Christians in mind besides church leaders (*Lukas,* p. 80).

[11]*Lukas,* pp. 221-23.

[12]See Dupont, *Beatitudes,* III, 152 n. 3.

[13]See I. Howard Marshall, *Luke: Historian and Theologian,* pp. 207-09, esp. 207 n. 1.

fact that Luke preserved radical material about possessions and asks the question why; 2) he surely is on to something very significant when he notes that Luke has to counter a cultural tendency within his Greco-Roman community, a tendency, which if left unchallenged, would lead to the abandonment of the poor.

4. GERD THEISSEN.[14] While Degenhardt argues that Luke has preserved the "radical" Jesus material on possessions for church leaders, Theissen argues that Luke has preserved this radical material only to have Jesus rescind it in Luke 22:35-36. This rescinding reveals Luke's *Sitz im Leben*: he is arguing against the descendents of the first itinerant charismatics who plague his church. For Luke there were only twelve legitimate apostles, the great itinerant missionaries of the earliest days.

It is highly questionable that Luke 22:35-36 rescinds all the radical material in Luke's Gospel. I cannot deem Theissen's proposed *Sitz im Leben* plausible until more evidence is offered.

5. JACQUES DUPONT.[15] Dupont enters the discussion of our thematic via the beatitudes and woes. He argues that the beatitudes are addressed to the Christian community which is persecuted for its faith, poor, suffering deprivation. The woes are not addressed to Christians, but to people outside the Christian community. These people are incredulous Israel. The passages about the dangers of wealth show how wealth can lead to blindness, a blindness characteristic of incredulous Israel. Riches are also a very great danger about which Luke must warn his Christian community.

It is hard to understand why Luke has to warn his poor and persecuted community about the dangers of wealth. How could the message about the dangers of wealth really be relevant for these poor? Moreover, on page 202 he explains the vitally important Luke 12:33, 14:33, 5:11,28, and 18:22 in one paragraph by subsuming them under the rubric of placing all one's security in God and not in mammon. Furthermore, he does not take into account Acts 2:41-47 and 4:31-35 about which he had written so perceptively in a previous article.[16] Lastly, Dupont seems to think of the Lukan community in monolithic terms, that is, the beatitudes and the woes cannot be addressed to the same community. This view must be challenged.[17]

---

[14]"Itinerant Radicalism: The Tradition of Jesus Sayings from the Perspective of the Sociology of Literature," *Radical Religion*, II (1975), 84-93 (91) — "Wanderradikalismus. Literatursoziologische Aspekte der Überlieferung von Worten Jesu im Urchristentum." *ZTK*, LXX (1973), 245-71.

[15]*Beatitudes*, III, 19-206, esp. 149-203.

[16]"La Communauté des biens aux premiers jours de l'Eglise (Actes 2,42. 44-45; 4,32. 34-35," *Etudes sur les Actes des Apôtres*, pp. 503-19.

[17]I do not find persuasive the view of F. Hauck, *Die Stellung des Urchristentums zu Arbeit und Geld*, p. 96 (as quoted in Degenhardt, *Lukas*, p. 210) that there were not many rich people in the community or else there would not be so many Jesus words about the difficulty of the rich entering the kingdom. Space allows only the briefest comments on a provocative section in Schuyler Brown, *Apostasy and Perseverance in the Theology of Luke*, pp. 98-107. Brown argues that in the Age of the Church "the readiness of *all* Christians to dispose of their property, however small it might be, for the benefit of the community corresponds to the totality of actual renunciation during the Age of Jesus" (p. 101 n. 417). Even granting the validity of the theological significance which Brown places

In summary we may say that, with variations, Cadbury, Degenhardt, and Theissen agree that members of Luke's community had possessions. Cadbury and Degenhardt (at times) suggest that Luke's community was composed of a certain number of rich Christians. Dupont is the only author to champion the view that Luke's community was composed solely of poor Christians. Thus, these studies provide us with sound clues in our pursuit of the Lukan *Sitz im Leben*. The main clue is that Luke is more concerned with possessors than with the poor. In what ensues I will discuss the most important Lukan passages on poor and rich to see whether we can follow up on the clues of the previous studies, especially in the area of the Lukan *Sitz im Leben*.

Lukan Passages on Poor and Rich

1. Acts 2:41-47 and 4:31c-35. Degenhardt, Theissen, and Brown are quite accurate in granting major significance to these summary passages. I presuppose that these passages open the window onto the *Sitz im Leben* behind the Lukan theme of poor and rich.

Obviously, it is impossible to treat all the problems attendant on these verses. The following points must suffice. For some time now scholars have recognized the Greco-Roman philosophical utopian parallels to our passages.[18] Plümacher[19] and Charles H. Talbert[20] interpret these parallels as evidence of Luke's idealization of the primitive community as free from heresy and schism. It seems to me that they have read the summary passages of Acts 2 and 4 too narrowly. Luke uses the terminology of friendship to show that what was longed for, but rarely, if ever, realized has been realized in the Christian community. Luke's primary point is that Christians treat each other as friends. And because and when they do, they share what they have (give alms), and no one is in need. Put another way, Luke, by the use of Greco-Roman philosophical terminology of friendship, modifies his inherited tradition[21] in order to make it comprehensible to his Greco-Roman audience which does not share the Christian/Jewish concern for the neighbor in need and for the poor. Luke's point, then, is: the Christians aid the neighbor in need and the poor in the community because they view each other as friends.

In order for us to fathom the significance of Luke's modifications in Acts 2:41-47 and 4:31c-35, it is vital that we appreciate the general Greco-Roman cultural

---

on the two Ages, I do not see how actual renunciation of possessions is a universal or even constant prerequisite for discipleship in the Age of Jesus. As I read Luke 5:11,28, I notice that Peter and Levi *voluntarily* left all; they were not commanded by Jesus to leave all. One cannot too quickly read 5:11,28 in the light of the troublesome 14:33.

[18]See Eckhard Plümacher, *Lukas als hellenistischer Schriftsteller: Studien zur Apostelgeschichte*, pp. 16-18 on 2:44-45 and 4:32; the most complete parallels are found in Dupont, "Communauté."

[19]*Schriftsteller*, p. 18, esp. n. 61.

[20]*Literary Patterns, Theological Themes and the Genre of Luke-Acts*, pp. 101-2.

[21]In Acts 2:41-47 Luke uses this terminology in 2:44 to interpret his source's *koinonia* (2:42); see Dupont "Communauté," pp. 505-9. In 4:31c-35 he uses the same type of terminology in 4:32bc to interpret his source material in 4:34; see Degenhardt, *Lukas*, pp. 170-2 and "Liebestätigkeit," pp. 247-9.

background on the poor and on almsgiving.[22] While it may not be possible to develop an absolutely pure typology, the evidence is considerable that almsgiving is not known among the Greco-Romans whereas it is a cultural expectation for those from an Egyptian/Jewish (oriental) background. The Greco-Romans would not come to the aid of a non-citizen; they would help a friend in need, but only to collect IOU's against future contingencies.[23]

In sum, what emerges from the summary passages of Acts 2 and 4 is mission theology: how to make the Christian/Jewish teaching about the necessity of almsgiving and about fellowship intelligible to converts who come from a widely different cultural expectation. If the Christian community in Jerusalem, composed of so many different people, treated each other as friends, so too should the recent converts of Luke's own time. Luke's *Sitz im Leben* consists of propertied Christians who have been converted and cannot easily extricate themselves from their cultural mindsets. It also consists of Christians in need of alms. Luke takes great pains to show that Christians treat each other as friends and that almsgiving and care for one another is of the essence of the Way. If the converts do not learn this lesson and learn it well, there is danger that the Christian movement may splinter.[24]

In what follows I will examine passages in the Gospel where Lukan redaction is most manifest to see whether analyses of these passages may give greater specificity to the *Sitz im Leben* detected behind the Lukan redaction of Acts 2:41-47 and 4:31c-35.

2. Luke 3:1-9:50.[25] a) Luke 4:18+7:22; 5:20-26. Almost all Lukan scholars

---

[22]This background is supplied by Hendrik Bolkstein, *Wohltätigkeit und Armenflege im vorchristlichen Altertum: Ein Beitrag zur Problem "Moral und Gesellschaft"* and A. R. Hands, *Charity and Social Aid in Greece and Rome.* Degenhardt, *Lukas*, pp. 180-1 has a most useful summary of Bolkestein's findings.

[23]In Acts 2 and 4 Luke does not argue against this reciprocity ethic. See below on Luke 14:12-14.

[24]You might grant that my suggested *Sitz im Leben* for Luke's redaction of Acts 2:41-47 and 4:31c-35 seems plausible enough and may even help to explain the materials in the Gospel. However, you muse, why does Luke spend so little time on this theme in the rest of Acts if it is so key for him? I would contend that Luke does devote space to this theme in Acts, but that it is not his only missionary concern. See the following passages, whose significance is little noticed in the literature, even by Haenchen: 1:18 (Judas); 3:2-10 (Peter and John do not have silver and gold to give as alms); 5:1-11 (an illustration of the "mortal danger present in the attachment to the world effected through possessions and riches" [S. Brown, *Apostasy*, p. 107]; 6:1-6 (care for widows); 8:18-25 (simony); 9:36 (the almsgiving of Tabitha); 10:2,4,31 (Cornelius is favored because of his almsgiving); 11:29 (relief sent to the famine-stricken brethren in Judea); 20:28-35 (Degenhardt, *Lukas*, pp. 174-6, rightly emphasizes this passage for it singles out Paul as a model for church leaders, not least because Paul worked with his hands [Acts 18:3; 20:35] and because "to give" can be interpreted to mean "give alms"); 24:17 (Paul brings alms and offerings). The above passages indicate that poor and rich is a theme which is also present in Acts. Space limitations dictate that we can merely allude to these passages here.

[25]I omit 1:5-2:52; 3:10-14; 6:27-36; 8:3 because of space limitations. My surmise is that Luke 1:5-2:52, esp. 1:46-55, has much to say about our thematic. I make this most tentative suggestion: one way of looking at the Magnificat is to see it addressed to the rich Christians in Luke's community who feel that their riches are a sign of God's favor. To these

would agree that 4:16-30 is programmatic: it describes Jesus' nature and mission. Also, it is clear that 4:18 is closely related to 7:22. But it is not clear who the poor are on the redactional level. I question whether it is totally legitimate to interpret the "poor" of 4:18 (7:22) on the basis of what that term might mean in Isaiah. I suggest that we turn to 6:20-26 in our quest to give content to the word "poor" on the redactional level.

I agree with Dupont's analysis that 6:20-23 refers to the Christian community of Luke's day. They are poor, suffering deprivation and persecution for their faith.[26] Thus, if we interpret the "poor" of 4:18 and 7:22 via 6:20-23, they are Christians of Luke's own time who suffer want and are persecuted for their faith. Jesus brings good news to them.

When it comes to an identification of who the rich are (6:24,26), the question is not as easy as Dupont thinks. I am not convinced that the rich are incredulous Israel.[27] Dupont's argument that Luke does not conceive of the recipients of the woes as present is not valid on the redactional level of analysis. If the woes are meant to be injunctions to repentance, is it intrinsically improbable that they be addressed to rich members of Luke's community? The rich members may be tempted to compromise their faith rather than suffer persecution and possible deprivation of property (see Hebr 10:34). They may be afraid to befriend their persecuted fellow Christians.[28]

Thus, it seems that one aspect of the Lukan *Sitz im Leben* is deprivation occasioned by persecution. This persecution may be seen as a real possibility for all times (see Acts 14:22) or something which the community has recently experienced or is experiencing. Within this *Sitz im Leben* Luke's purpose is to console the poor of his community. Luke *may* also be concerned with the rich members of his community whom persecution unmasks as too attached to their possessions. Luke edits the woes to warn them of the life-and-death decision which faces them. This proposed *Sitz im Leben* adds one factor to the *Sitz im Leben* suggested for Acts 2:41-47 and 4:31c-35, namely, persecution.

B) Luke 5:11,28. As mentioned above in note 17, I find no evidence in these texts that abandonment of possessions is the prerequisite for following Jesus. Peter and Levi are examples, in much the same way as Barnabas in Acts 4:36-37, and show what some people may do in response to the call to become disciples. At this point of the investigation this contention cannot be proven. We need the additional evidence of Luke 18:18-30, especially 18:28.

C) Luke 9:1-6; 10:1-12; 22:35-36. It seems best to treat these three passages together, especially since 22:35-36, although addressed to the apostles, refers

---

individuals it is said that God's concern is for the lowly like Mary. I immediately concede that *tapeinosis* (1:48) and *tapeinoi* (1:52) do not necessarily have to bear the full weight of my definition of "poor." The *tapeinoi* need not be materially poor at all.

[26]See also Heinz Schurmann, *Das Lukasevangelium, Erster Teil: Kommentar zu Kap. 1:1-9:50*, pp. 338-9.

[27]Schurmann, *Lukasevangelium*, pp. 338-9, sees the woes in a different light: 6:24-26 mirrors opponents who are also attacked in Acts 20:29-30.

[28]It is obvious that the identification of the rich suggested for this passage needs confirmation from other Lukan passages. These other passages will at least show that there are rich members in Luke's community.

not to 9:3, but to 10:4. As we have seen above, Theissen stakes a huge claim on his interpretation of 10:4 and 22:35-36. Analysis will not allow his claim.

Luke 10:4 points to the total Christian hospitality shown to all traveling brothers and is not advocating an ascetic renunciation of worldly goods. "The disciples are to take nothing along *since they can have anything they need from those with whom they stay.*"[29] Luke 22:35-36 refers to a situation of persecution during which the Christian missionaries must finance themselves. Degenhardt is especially insightful on this passage. "Both injunctions, that of 10:4 and that of 22:36 have continued validity during the time of the church, each for a special situation. Luke 10:4 obtains during the peaceful development of the church and 22:36 for a time of persecution."[30]

Thus, these passages are concerned with the theme of poor and rich as it applies to Christian missionaries. The passages are not explicit on how the missionaries are to finance themselves during the times of persecution. Perhaps, the "missionary" Paul is their model.[31] These passages, especially 22:35-36, supply additional evidence that the Lukan *Sitz im Leben* is one in which persecution is operative.

3. Luke 9:51-19:44 — TRAVEL NARRATIVE. After laboring industriously for decades on the Travel Narrative, scholars must admit that it has not given up its secrets.[32] We may be able to eavesdrop on this section as we study its materials on poor and rich. To use Kümmel's terminology, why does Luke have Jesus equip his disciples with so much teaching about poor and rich in this section?[33]

C) Luke 11:41. This passage is Lukan redaction. In it Luke surely underscores the importance of giving alms.[34] Yet such an observation does not do full justice to the verse. I believe that this passage will not yield its full meaning until Lukan scholarship clearly identifies the Lukan "Pharisees." It is obvious that Luke is not talking about the historical Pharisees in this passage which is set within the context of a meal (see 5:27-32; 7:36-50; 14:1-24; 15:1f.; Acts 11:2; 15:5; cf. Luke 16:14). Perhaps Jacob Jervell is on the right track when he observes: "Almsgiving is important for Luke, and only for him among the New Testament

---

[29]David L. Dungan, *The Sayings of Jesus in the Churches of Paul*, p. 45; emphasis his.

[30]*Lukas,* pp. 67-8. We must beware of the temptation to imagine the Lukan community as some monolithic mass. In such a reconstruction of the data, the instructions for peaceful missionary work and beleagured missionary work must be handled by some hypothesis as Conzelmann's Age of Jesus (peaceful) and Age of the Church (troubled). What happens if our reconstruction envisions a missionary community which experiences both peaceful and beleaguered missionary endeavors — as described in Acts! — and has both rich and poor members? We must allow for seeming contradictions to exist side by side without trying to force them into a convenient reconstruction, whose convenience may only reveal our reluctance to cope with such apparent contradictions and our desire to put everything into pigeonholes where there may be great order, but no life.

[31]See Acts 20:33-35 and Dungan, *Sayings,* pp. 72-4.

[32]See Kümmel, *Introduction,* pp. 141-2.

[33]I cannot treat 11:13; see Wilhelm Ott, *Gebet und Heil: Die Deutung der Gebetsparänese in der lukanischen Theologie*, pp. 108, 111. I also omit 11:21-22; see S. Legasse, "L' 'Homme fort' de Lc 11:21,22," *NovT,* V (1962), 5-9.

[34]See Degenhardt, *Lukas,* p. 59.

writers, as a sign of true adherence to the law (11:41; 12:33; Acts 9:36; 10:2,4,31; 24:17)."[35]   *Maybe* the "Pharisees" represent those people within Luke's community who think they know what God's will is, those who know under what conditions a person should be invited to (full) table fellowship. Almsgiving may be raised to the level of a first principle by which other regulations of the law, like ritual cleanliness, must be judged. Proper participation at a meal is open to those who have given alms to the needy.

B) Luke 12:13-21,33-34. Luke 12:13-34 should be interpreted as a unit. By means of the framework Luke gives to the parable of 12:16-20, he interprets it.

Luke is responsible for the barbarous Greek of 12:15; he adds *ek tōn hyparchonton auto* to leave no doubt that abundance means abundance of possessions.[36] Dupont makes a viable case that 12:21 must be seen as a Lukan composition based on 12:33.[37] The rich fool is reproached because he did not transform his goods into heavenly capital, i.e., did not distribute them to the poor. Thus, by means of the framework he provides, Luke interprets the parable to mean: possessions are meant to be given in alms to those in need.

The *Sitz im Leben* behind 12:13-34 must be one where the members of Luke's community do have possessions, can be tempted to avarice, and can be admonished to store up treasure by giving alms. The conduct of the rich fool is to be eschewed like a cobra, for he neglected his obligations to the poor. This material is addressed to the rich within Luke's community who are tempted to believe that true life consists in the abundance of their possessions and who neglect the Christian poor.[38]

C) Luke 14:12-24; 14:25-33. Luke 14:1-24 is the Lukan symposium. At first blush, 14:12-24 seems to be concerned with the theme of God's call, which is addressed to and accepted by the poor and those excluded from cult. Those who were called are rejected.[39] This interpretation is compelling until one reflects seriously on the implications of 14:12-24, especially 14:12-14. For this latter passage to make sense it must mean that there are members in Luke's community who have the wherewithal to host festive meals. Luke 14:12-14 is addressed to them and goes against the common Greco-Roman reciprocity ethic: put your friends in your debt, so that at some future time you can cash in on their IOU's.[40] The affluent "Pharisees" are to invite in the poor and can expect no earthly return for their sharing. These same Pharisees are present for the teaching of the parable of 14:16-24, which does not highlight the divine maker of the guest list, but the excuses people proffer for not responding to the invitation to the banquet. These excuses betray overattachment to worldly concerns and are

---

[35]*Luke and the People of God: A New Look at Luke-Acts*, p. 140.

[36]Degenhardt, *Lukas*, pp. 73-4.

[37]*Beatitudes* III, 184-5, based on the argumentation of 115-7.

[38]See Degenhardt, *Lukas*, p. 80.

[39]See J. A. Sanders, "The Ethic of Election in Luke's Great Banquet Parable," *Essays in Old Testament Ethics: J. Philip Hyatt, In Memoriam,* ed. James L. Crenshaw and John T. Willis, pp. 245-71.

[40]See W. C. van Unnik, "Die Motivierung der Feindesliebe in Lukas 6:32-35," *NovT*, VIII (1966), 284-300 (293-300); cf. above on Acts 2:41-47 and 4:31c-35.

the typical excuses church people of Luke's time made to avoid conversion.[41] Thus, 14:12-24, especially 14:16-24 does not espouse a miniature theology of salvation history, but contains lessons for the rich and propertied in Luke's community: treat the poor as your friends; don't be seduced into supposing that care lavished on possessions is of greater value than deepened conversion.[42]

This analysis brings us to the doorstep of the awesome 14:33. Our entry into the meaning of 14:33, however, is barred unless we view it in its context. Dupont makes a sound case that 14:25-33 is related to 14:16-24 by means of the common theme of the detachment which is necessary for a lasting response to the call of the kingdom.[43] Luke 14:33 follows upon 14:28-32 and means in that context that Christians must show fidelity to what they have undertaken.[44] Now we are in a favorable position to enter into the interpretation of 14:33. This verse is clearly Lukan composition. Its verbs show that the proper translation should go: all disciples must be *ready* to renounce their possessions. The context (14:26-27) also suggests the situation behind Luke's redaction of 14:33. It is a persecution situation during which the Christians may have to suffer loss of possessions if they are to complete the walk with Jesus which they have undertaken.

In sum, 14:25-33, especially 14:33, is an important passage for any interpretation of the theme of poor and rich in Luke. As 14:16-24, especially 14:18-20, has already indicated, accepting the call to be a disciple and persevering in that call are not facile or petty matters for the Christian with possessions. Luke 14:25-33 points to the "cross" aspect of that discipleship, particularly in 14:26-27. This persecution context is abetted by the two parables of 14:28-32 and issues in the final discipleship admonition of 14:33. The members of the Lukan community who have posessions must be ready to forego them if they stand in the way of their fidelity to Jesus Christ. Thus, Luke 14:12-33 provides further evidence that Luke's community had a somewhat high proportion of fairly prosperous members, who had to be exhorted to remember the poor Christians who were their friends. They also had to be advised that the cost of discipleship had been drastically increased because of persecution. This last point correlates well with the identification of the rich suggested above for 6:24-26.

d) Luke 16:1-31. It seems that the tendency in past scholarship has been to consider the two parables of this chapter in relative isolation from one another and from 16:14-18 or to single out 16:16 as if the rest of the chapter did not exist. I presuppose that ch. 16 forms a unity. My main question is: how is Luke 16:14-18 related to 16:1-13 and 16:19-31? I will fashion my answer by summarizing and

---

[41]See Jacques Dupont, Les béatitudes, Tome II: La bonne nouvelle, pp. 262-72.

[42]I do not have space to show how "wife" of 14:20 (see 14:26; 18:29) accords with the interpretation suggested here. See A. Stoger, "Armut und Ehelosigkeit — Besitz und Ehe der Jünger nach dem Lukasevangelium," GL, XL (1967), 43-9, known to me only through NTA, XII (1968), 197.

[43]Dupont, Beatitudes, II, 262-72.

[44]In this and what follows I am dependent on Dupont, "Renoncer a tous ses biens (Luc 14,33)," NRT, XCIII (1971), 561-82.

criticizing the viewpoints of Dupont[45] and Degenhardt.[46]

(1) Dupont makes two major points. First, 16:14 is a Lukan redactional introduction to 16:19-31. Dupont virtually eliminates 16:15-18 from his discussion of the relationship of 16:1-13 to 16:19-31. Secondly, in relating 16:19-31 to 16:14,9,13, Dupont makes these observations. Luke 16:14 shows the Pharisees' negative reaction to the teaching of 16:1-13 on the use of money. Luke 16:1-13 provides the positive statement on the conduct which evidences repentance/conversion (16:30,31). Luke 16:9 spotlights the conduct of a rich man who is attentive to the teachings of Moses and the prophets and gives alms to the poor. Contrast the rich man in 16:19-31, who should have made Lazarus his friend by giving him alms. Finally, 16:13 shows that the rich man of 16:19-31 needs a radical conversion because he worships mammon.

(2) Relative to 16:14-15, Degenhardt makes the valuable point that there are no Pharisees in Luke's Gentile community. Luke addresses himself to opponents in his church. He warns the greedy not to put their stock in their social position, for all depends on God's estimation of them. The opponents might view riches as evidence of God's favor. The sayings material of 16:14-18 might be continued in 17:1. If this is so, 16:19-31 may make a single point, analogous to that of 16:18, namely, the law (OT) of helping the poor still obtains.

These authors present a courageous, initial scouting report on the relatively unexplored question of how Luke 16:14-18 is related to 16:1-13 and 16:19-31. I would judge that Dupont has made a very plausible case for the connexion between the two parables. Unfortunately, he did not pause long enough to scout 16:15-18 adequately. I would take Degenhardt's sound interpretation of the Pharisees of 16:14 a step further. My scouting suggests that the rich (Pharisees) in Luke's community think that almsgiving is not important, perhaps because these folk maintain that Jesus abrogated the law and the prophets and their teaching about almsgiving. A corollary of their position, attacked in 16:15, is that riches are a sign of God's favor. In combatting them, Luke introduces the *pas* of 16:16: the kingdom of God is not just for some or the rich. Luke 16:19-31 provides him with additional armament for his combat: the poor who ostensibly are not blessed participate at the heavenly banquet while the favored rich suffer. Luke 16:19-31 also upholds the validity of the teaching about almsgiving contained in Moses and the prophets (see 16:16-17), a teaching which is continued in the preaching about Jesus (= kingdom of God in 16:16) who preached good news to the poor (4:18; 6:20; 7:22).

In summary, if my scouting report bears up under subsequent explorations, then 16:1-31 furnishes additional insights into the Lukan *Sitz im Leben*. The rich members of Luke's community strive to discern God's will and favor, and appeal to their wealth as a sign of that favor. Needless to say, this element of theological discernment complicates the Lukan *Sitz im Leben* considerably. It is not just a situation where the greedy rich have failed to give alms to the Christian poor. The rich seem to have found theological justification for their self-centeredness. Thus, the *Sitz im Leben*, suggested by our analyses of Acts 2:41-47 and 4:31c-35 and augmented by subsequent analyses, might be modified further. Luke is not

[45]Dupont, *Beatitudes*, III, 162-82.
[46]Degenhardt, *Lukas*, pp. 113-35.

just arguing against rich Christians whose cultural conditioning blinds them to the needs of their brothers and sisters and who have too much to lose in the face of persecution.　He may also be arguing against Christians whose cultural conditioning has been reinforced by theological speculation.

e) Luke 18:18-31. In this section it suffices to share and build upon the outstanding insights of S. Légasse.[47] Légasse's major contribution lies in his examinations of Luke's redaction. In 18:24-30 the rich ruler does not depart, but is present for what transpires: the rich ruler presents a moral case, a problem within the community. The attentuated response in 18:27 is rather severe; Luke omits "all things are . . . ." The *ta idia* of 18:28 is not just a stylistic variation for *panta* of 18:22. Acts 4:32 must be taken most seriously as its interpretive parallel. "What Luke means here is not so much total dispossession as it is renunciation of that which is one's own for the sake of the ecclesial koinonia . . . ." (104). "To the rich of the church Luke proposes the example of Peter and the apostles . . . . The apostolic group, which abandoned *ta idia*, along with the mother church of Jerusalem described in Acts, are for Luke types of his own ideal and the mediators of his message" (106).

In 18:18-30 Luke is addressing current problems about rich people in his community. Luke 18:28 refers back to 5:11 (5:28) and ahead to Acts 4:32 and shows one of Luke's major answers to the problems of possessions: voluntary sharing of *ta idia* for the sake of the poor in the community. Thus, we note again the pivotal importance which Luke ascribes to Acts 2:41-47 and 4:31c-35. The possessors in Luke's community can escape from the chains of their cultural tunnel vision by imitating the examples of the apostles and the primitive Christian community of Acts 2 and 4.[48]

f) Luke 19:1-10. The key to the interpretation of this passage is found in 19:8, Luke's modification of the traditional story.[49] As Grundmann rightly notes, this modification makes the Zacchaeus story a contrast to 18:18-30. But Grundmann does not detail the content of this contrast. This redacted story contrasts to 18:18-30 as it shows that there may not be one dominant answer to the problems of possessions in the Lukan community. Zacchaeus is not required to sell all; nor does he voluntarily give all to the poor. It suffices that he donate half of his possessions to the poor.

The *Sitz im Leben* behind this passage is the problem of how a rich person should deal with his possessions. Luke answers that it is not necessary for a rich person to sell everything. Thus, the response which Peter and the apostles (18:28-30) gave to Jesus' invitation is not the only one possible. Zacchaeus' response is also a legitimate one. In sum, Luke's *Sitz im Leben* is one in which there are rich Christians. Their continued adherence to the Lord does not necessitate that they sell all. It does, however, necessitate that they give a

---

[47]*L'appel du riches (Marc 10:17-31 et paralleles): Contribution a l'etude des fondements scriptuaires de l'etat religieux*, pp. 97-110.

[48]It is not suficiently clear to me that Luke is also attacking a view which regarded wealth as a sure sign of God's favor. He inherited "Who can be saved?" (18:26) from Mark. Of course, the new context which Luke provides for this eyepopping question clearly shows that he disagrees with its implications.

[49]See Walter Grundmann, *Das Evangelium nach Lukas*, pp. 358-60.

genuine sign that they are not so attached to their possessions that they neglect the Christian poor.[50]

Conclusion

It is time to assemble the pieces of the puzzle of the theme of poor and rich in Luke to see whether they fit into a clear picture of the Lukan *Sitz im Leben*. Luke's community clearly had both rich and poor members. Luke is primarily taken up with the rich members, their concerns, and the problems which they pose for the community. Their concerns, as evidenced in 18:18-30 and 19:1-10, revolve around the question: do our possessions prevent us from being genuine Christians? The concerns of the rich are multiplied by the onslaught of sporadic, unofficial persecution (see 6:24-26 and 14:25-33). The rich Christians do not become conscious of their concerns in isolation from the rest of the Christian community. Luke confronts them with the problems which they raise for the Way and for the poor: your cultural conditioning inhibits you from easily helping the poor in the community and thus living up to Christian ideals (Acts 2:41-47 and 4:31c-35). Your view of who your fellow Christians are is unacceptably narrow (Luke 14:10-12). You are still too attached to your possessions (12:13-34 and 14:16-24) as our present persecution situation makes shamefully manifest (6:24-26 and 14:25-33). Riches are not an infallible sign of God's favor; Jesus did not abrogate the teachings of the law and the prophets on almsgiving (16:1-31). Repent before you lose your invitation to the heavenly banquet (14:16-24 and 16:1-31). This proposed *Sitz im Leben* has its greatest probability as it confirms Cadbury's insight that Luke's theme of poor and rich is principally addressed to possessors within his community. High probability must be assigned to the element of persecution in Luke's *Sitz im Leben*. There is strong probability that all possessors in Luke's community had the same concerns. Likewise, it is probable that all possessors caused problems for Luke's community. It is less probable that all possessors were theologically facile in discerning that riches are a sign of God favor (16:1-31).

In this article I have relentlessly pursued the Lukan *Sitz im Leben* behind the theme of poor and rich. You can well challenge me: Show us the city which is reflected in Luke-Acts! Show us that city's social structures! How did Christianity make inroads among the rich? What Jesus tradition was first preached to them? And I could challenge both you and myself by asking: could it be that the accounts of the non-Jewish converts in Acts are not mere apologetic stage-props, but contain genuine reflection of the fact that these first converts were rich, e.g., Simon Magus, the Ethiopian eunuch, Cornelius, Sergius Paulus? Could it be that Luke has scoured hill and dale to discover more material on poor and rich so that he can better address himself to the nobleman(= rich?) Theophilus' problems? Perhaps Theophilus is not so much concerned with peddlars of spurious Christological traditions as he is with the true meaning of possessions, especially in the teeth of persecution.

Admittedly, there are problems in pursuing the implications of this article's thesis. Yet I am comfortable with these problems because they are the problems

---

[50]This analysis concludes our study of the Gospel passages on poor and rich. Space does not permit a study of 21:1-4.

of growth in research and do not have veto power over the pursuit itself. Luke's sun does not rise and fall with his theme of poor and rich. It is one theme among many. Nevertheless, it does expose his community in broad daylight. If this article has attained its goal of spurring us to discuss the Lukan *Sitz im Leben* with greater frequency and clarity, then it has been a success. Maybe through similar studies and discussions we can reverse the verdict on the Lukan *Sitz im Leben* from "not much" to "quite a bit."

Luke's Method in the Annunciation Narrative of Chapter One

Raymond E. Brown, S.S.

For Roman Catholicism the narratives of Jesus' birth and infancy found in Matthew and Luke may well constitute the last frontier to be crossed by biblical criticism. The Roman Church has taken a somewhat liberal position regarding the composition of the gospel accounts of the ministry of Jesus: they are *not* literal, chronological reports of his words and deeds.[1] But even with such an official directive it has been difficult to move Catholics from a literalistic view. The church has taken no official position on the birth narratives in the gospels; and so *a fortiori* it is and will be more difficult to correct the general impression that Matthew and Luke preserve literal family histories of Jesus' origins. True, some Catholic writers, particularly in Europe, have stressed the OT atmosphere and midrashic character of the infancy narratives; but most often even informed clergy and laity treat the birth stories as if they had the same historical value as the passion stories. Sentimentality, emotion, and doctrinal fears have discouraged forays across the last frontier.

While Protestant biblical criticism breached this frontier a long time ago, it never really settled the territory and made the desert bloom. Early in this century most Protestant scholars recognized that the two infancy stories were different in kind from the rest of the gospel material and sometimes in conflict with it — indeed, sometimes in conflict with each other. But the popular character of such narratives, featuring magi, a birth star, the wicked king, angelic messengers and

---

[1]For information on the 1964 statement of the Roman Pontifical Biblical Commission, see *JBC*, article 72, §§8, 35.

choruses, led to debunking and almost to a contempt whereby such material was deemed unworthy to be a vehicle of the pure gospel message. Thus, the frontier territory of Jesus' birth, once it had been "scouted" by critics, was judged capable of only marginal scholarly cultivation, and likely to be settled only by primitives and romantics.[2]

Through a commentary on the infancy narratives of Matthew and Luke,[3] I have argued the case that, although of different origin and historical character from the rest of the gospel, these stories are truly gospel, integrated into the purposes of the respective evangelists, and proclaiming vividly the good news of salvation. This essay treating the two annunciation scenes in Luke 1 is a small gesture in that direction. Let me begin with a few background reminders.

If we assume that Mark was written before Matthew and Luke, it is clear that the gospel narrative once began with the public ministry of Jesus, inaugurated by the baptism. No matter how early they circulated in a popular setting, it was only late in the century that the birth stories came to be included as part of the gospel account (and even then perhaps not in all churches). A late dating for the birth stories in their present form is harmonious with the modern approach to christology, for they reflect a "higher" and more developed christology. While formulas found in the Pauline letters and in the sermons in Acts associate Jesus' divine sonship with the resurrection, and while the body of the gospels associates divine sonship with the beginning of the ministry (the baptism), the infancy narratives associate divine sonship with conception in the womb of Mary. Jesus is clearly God's Son from the first moment of his earthly existence. Granting all of this, we are still faced with particular problems about the Lukan infancy narrative. There is no real doubt that the author we call Luke,[4] who wrote the body of the gospel and the book of Acts, wrote the two chapters of infancy narrative.[5] But did he write the infancy narrative before or after he wrote the rest of his two-volume work? The very solemn passage that is now Luke 3:1 may once have served as the opening of the Lukan narrative of Jesus; there are good parallels in Josephus and Thucydides for such an opening, as H. J. Cadbury has pointed out. Acts 1:1 and 1:22 may be interpreted to mean that the Lukan Gospel once began with the baptism of Jesus, so that it was the story of what Jesus did and taught as attested by those who were with him from that baptism. But whether Luke began his work

---

[2]Proportionately, the infancy narratives often receive little attention in introductions to the NT or in seminary courses.

[3]*The Birth of the Messiah* (1977). Because that commentary carries complete bibliography, I shall not take up space here with long bibliographical footnotes. For those unfamiliar with the literature on the Lukan infancy narrative, the writings of the authors to whom I refer can be tracked down in B. Metzger, *Index to Periodical Literature on Christ and the Gospels*, covering articles up to 1961, and in the cumulative index to *NTA* (1956-71).

[4]I use the common designation without deciding the question whether the author had been a companion of Paul, specifically Luke the physician. The theory that he was such a companion has often been accompanied by the thesis that, while in Palestine during Paul's imprisonment at Caesarea (ca. A.D. 58-60), Luke uncovered the sources from which he composed the infancy stories, e.g., the "Baptist source" and the "Marian source" to be mentioned below.

[5]Marcion's form of the Gospel of Luke did not include the infancy narrative, but this omission scarcely reflects manuscript tradition; it probably resulted from Marcion's excision of material which had such strong OT background.

with 3:1 and only at the end of his labors added chs. 1-2 (as I incline to think)[6] or he began with the infancy narrative so that the present order represents the order of composition, it is important for ths discussion that the material in the body of the gospel was preached and known before the infancy narrative was made a part of the consecutive message about Jesus.

Did Luke himself compose the material in the infancy narrative, or for the most part did he take over and touch up material already shaped (in whole or in part)? The latter possibility, which implies a source or sources, has been defended on the grounds of theology, language, and content.

First, theology. In his famous analysis of Lukan thought and plan H. Conzelmann virtually ignored chs. 1-2 wherein he found a theology different from and even contrary to that of the rest of the gospel. For instance, Conzelmann maintained that in proper Lukan theology John the Baptist (henceforth J Bap) belongs to the period of the law and the prophets, not to the period of the preaching of the kingdom of God (Luke 16:16). But in the infancy narrative the birth of J Bap is clearly part of the good news of salvation, fulfilling the prophets (1:20, 70, 77). Other writers on Lukan theology, like H. Oliver, W. Tatum, and G. Voss, while accepting Conzelmann's general analysis, have sought to work the infancy narrative into that analysis. Still others, like J.-P. Audet, P. Minear, and H. Songer, have used the infancy narrative to challenge the validity of the Conzelmann analysis. They have insisted that the infancy narrative is a true introduction to the main themes of the gospel and is thus harmonious with Luke's theology.

Second, language. The Greek of the infancy narrative is more Semitized than that of much of the gospel; it is similar to the more Semitized sections of Acts. Accordingly, some have suggested that Luke drew upon and translated written or oral sources in Aramaic (M. Dibelius, W. Michaelis, A Plummer, F. Spitta, B. Weiss), or in Hebrew (G. A. Box, G. Dalman, P. DeLagarde, H. Gunkel, R. Laurentin, B. Streeter, C. Torrey), or in both languages (P. Winter). On the other hand, many scholars have denied the necessity of positing extended Semitic sources for the main infancy narrative and have explained the Semitized Greek by Luke's deliberate use of a Septuagintal style when he was composing a narrative imitative of the OT (P. Benoit, H. Cadbury, M. Goulder and M. Sanderson, A. von Harnack, N. Turner, J. Wellhausen).[7]

Third, content. There have been complicated theories about pre-Lukan

---

[6]Additional arguments include: (a) The placing of the genealogy in ch. 3 rather than in ch.1. Seemingly the genealogy was already part of the gospel before the infancy narrative was prefixed but had to be adapted to the thesis of virginal conception after the addition of 1:26-38, whence the parenthetical insertion of "as was supposed" in the description of Jesus as the son of Joseph. (b) The many similarities between the Lukan infancy narrative and the opening two chapters of Acts, especially as regards prophecy and the Spirit. Both were probably composed after the gospel proper (in which the influence of Mark had been a guiding factor).

[7]Notice that I have spoken of sources for the main infancy narrative. Many who deny the existence of such sources allow a source for the three hymns: the *Magnificat,* the *Benedictus,* and the *Nunc Dimittis.* Personally I think that substantially these hymns came to Luke from early Jewish Christianity, perhaps from the Jerusalem community. Luke edited them, made additions, and inserted them into his narrative, almost as appendages in the respective scenes.

material, with an many as seven or more sources posited (K. L. Schmidt; H. Schürmann); but, as regards ch. 1,[8] the debate often centers around whether or not there was a "Baptist source" and a "Marian source." Let me stress that I am talking about a *source*, meaning an oral or written consecutive narrative, rather than scattered bits of information. Many scholars who deny the existence of sources admit that Luke picked up items of tradition, historical or non-historical, from which he shaped the present narrative; but they insist that it was Luke who composed the consecutive story.

The Baptist source is sometimes thought to have had Christian origins but more often to have been composed by followers of J Bap.[9] Indeed, it is posited that the Baptist source once contained not only the material in Luke 1 that now refers to J Bap but other material that has been shifted in application to Jesus. For instance, some have proposed that originally there was an annunciation to Elizabeth (as well as to Zechariah) but this has been reshaped into or replaced by an annunciation to Mary. A more popular suggestion (with some minor textual backing) is that the *Magnificat* was originally the song of Elizabeth, corresponding to the *Benedictus*, the song of Zechariah, but has been shifted to Mary. A prominent reason for positing a Baptist source is the contention that the view of J Bap in Luke 1 is different from Luke's own view of him as represented in the gospel proper (see the reference to Conzelmann's theory above) and that, with the deletion of certain small Lukan touches, the portrait of J Bap that emerges from Luke 1 is not subordinate, so that in the source he may have been the principal salvific figure, the prophet, etc.

The Marian source has its advocates today almost entirely in Roman Catholic circles; usually it posits an oral communication of Mary's experiences to Luke, either directly or indirectly (through family).[10] The basic argument is that, since Mary is pictured alone on the occasion of the annunciation, only she could be the source of the dialogue found therein. Leaving aside the simplistic aspects of such an argument,[11] including presuppositions about historicity, I would point out that there is something to be said in favor of the priority of the annunciation to Mary when that annunciation is compared to the annunciation to Zechariah. The two annunciations share so many common features[12] that in their present form

---

[8]I omit from this discussion ch. 2 which may have had very different origins from ch. 1. See note 30 below.

[9]Followers who were anti-Christian and maintained that J Bap, not Jesus, was the Messiah; or followers who simply did not become Christian; or even followers who did become Christian. The last suggestion is similar to the thesis that the Baptist source had its origins in early Jewish Christianity.

[10]See note 4 above.

[11]The whole account could be the product of Luke's creative imagination. The theory grows more simplistic when it is claimed that the *Magnificat* was composed by Mary on the occasion described, so that she is the source of the hymn as well.

[12]Note the following (a) both annunciations have an introduction that mentions the husband, the wife, and the tribal origin; (b) in both the angel is identified as Gabriel; (c) in both Gabriel addresses the visionary by name and urges "Do not be afraid"; (d) the phrasing of the messages in 1:13 and 1:31 about the birth and naming of the son is very similar; (e) each message is followed by a poetic passage predicting the future greatness of the child; (f) in turn, this prediction is greeted by a "How?" question posed by Zechariah and by Mary respectively; (g) the "How?" question is answered by a sign from the angel showing the power of God.

they cannot have arisen independently of each other in two different sources. Luke has shaped the parallelism by making one match the other or by composing both of them. The scholars who favor the Baptist source maintain that Luke found therein an annunciation of the birth of J Bap and that he composed an annunciation of the birth of Jesus to match it. A contrary suggestion has been made by Benoit that Luke had a tradition of an annunciation of the birth of Jesus and that he freely composed an annunciation of the birth of J Bap to match that. This theory is not easily dismissable as Marian piety once we bring Matthew's gospel into consideration. In an account that betrays no dependence on Luke. Matthew tells of an annunciation (to Joseph) of the birth of Jesus. This is explicable if, anterior to both Matthew and Luke, popular interest in Jesus' origins had produced a tradition of an annunciation of the birth of Jesus by an angel,[13] a tradition that Matthew and Luke each used in his own way. Matthew fitted it into a narrative that patterned Joseph the father of Jesus on the Genesis model of the patriarch Joseph, using the two prominent aspects of that story, namely, that revelation came to Joseph in dreams and that Joseph went down to Egypt.[14] Luke filled out the annunciation tradition in a manner to be discussed below and fitted it into a narrative set up on a parallelism between J Bap and Jesus.[15] For Luke, Mary was a more important figure than Joseph, even as she is more important than Joseph in the body of the gospel story of Jesus' ministry. Each evangelist in his own way succeeded in making the story of the annunciation (and birth) a miniature gospel and thus brought popular traditions into the service of the good news of salvation.

Working with this hypothesis that an annunciation pattern (of the birth of Jesus) was pre-Lukan, *first* I shall seek to show that Luke filled out this pattern with christological statements from Christian preaching and with a portrait of Mary known to him from the body of the gospel (the account of Jesus' ministry). Thus, I maintain that there is no need to posit a Marian source in the sense of a narrative stemming from Mary concerning her conversation with the angel and her feelings on that occasion. *Second*, I shall propose that in imitation of the annunciation of Jesus' birth Luke shaped an annunciation of the birth of J Bap. While he may have had some items of historical information (the names of J

---

[13]We shall see below that the OT supplied very close antecedents for angelic annunciations of the births of salvific children.

[14]The narative continued by comparing the baby Jesus to the baby Moses (since it was Moses who led Israel back from Egypt), with Herod playing a role patterned on that of the wicked Pharaoh who, in Jewish tradition, sought to kill Moses and so ordered the killing of all the Hebrew male children.

[15]The logic seems to have worked thus: for Luke the conception and birth of Jesus had become a proclamation of the good news of salvation (2:10-11); historically, J Bap had a ministry before Jesus began his ministry of proclaiming this good news; and so if now the good news was to be attached to Jesus' birth, his birth should be preceded by the birth of J Bap. J Bap came first, before God's voice at the baptism proclaimed Jesus to be His Son; an annunciation of the birth of J Bap should come first, before an angel announces the birth of Jesus as God's Son. We can trace through the gospels a development in the church's thought about J Bap, increasingly subordinating him and his ministry to Jesus. In the infancy narrative Luke goes farther than elsewhere in the gospels in the process of Christianizing J Bap: he makes J Bap a relative of Jesus, something difficult to reconcile with the baptismal story (cf. John 1:31).

Bap's parents: the fact that they were of priestly stock),[16] I see no need to posit a J Bap source in the sense of an already composed annunciation narrative. I shall briefly sketch how the angelic statements about the future of J Bap in 1:13-17 could have been composed by Luke out of what is found in the body of the Lukan gospel about J Bap, especially from Luke 3:1-20 and 7:18:35.

The Annunciation of the Birth of Jesus

It is well known that the OT supplies us with a virtually stereotyped pattern for the annunciations of the forthcoming births of famous figures in salvation history,[17] narratives obviously written in retrospect after the figure had become famous. Regularly there are five features in the pattern:

— Appearance of an angel or of God, sometimes greeting by title the subject of the vision.
— Fear or prostration on the part of the subject confronted with this supernatural presence.
— The annunciation message, sometimes prefaced by the injunction not to fear and the mention of the visionary's name. The basic message contains the following items:
    (a) the woman is or is about to be with child;
    (b) she will give birth to the child;
    (c) the name by which the child is to be called;
    (d) an etymology interpreting the name;
    (e) the future accomplishments of the child.
— An objection on the part of the visionary as to how this is to come about.
— The giving of a sign to reassure the visionary.

In comparing Matthew and Luke's accounts of the annunciation of the birth of Jesus (to Joseph and to Mary, respectively), we find that Matthew preserves three of the features while Luke preserves all five. Thus, many items in Luke's account of the annunciation are simply the stereotyped features of the OT pattern for which he needed no special source, Marian or otherwise: the angelic appearance in 1:26; the angelic greeting in 1:28 (cf. Judg 6:12); Mary's being startled in 1:29; the "Do not be afraid" in 1:30; the message of conception in 1:31; Mary's "How can this be?" in 1:34; a sign given by the angel in 1:36-37. But there remain three major aspects of the Lukan scene which cannot be explained simply from the OT annunciation pattern: (1) the content of the description of the child and his future; (2) the idea of a virginal conception; (3) Mary's reaction. Let us discuss these one by one.

---

[16]This seems less demanding on the imagination than the theory mentioned by Goulder and Sanderson wherein the identification of J Bap as the Elijah-figure of Malachi brought in an association with the priesthood (since Malachi directs his words to priests) and the name Zechariah (the prophet who precedes Malachi in the canon); and the fact that Jesus' mother was named after Moses' sister Miriam gave Luke the idea of naming J Bap's mother after Aaron's wife Elizabeth.

[17]Good comparisons for the study of Luke 1 can be found in the annunciations of the birth of Isaac (Gen 17:1,3,15-16,17,19) and of Samson (Judg 13:3a,22,3b-5,20). The pattern has been studied minutely by X. Leon-Dufour among others.

(1) *The content of the description of the child and his future.* This is embodied in two angelic pronouncements (1:32-33 and 1:35), semi-poetic in their structure. First Pronouncement:

> 32a: He will be great and will be called Son of the Most High.
> 32b: And the Lord God will give him the throne of his father David;
> 33a: and he will be king over the house of Jacob forever,
> 33b: and there will be no end to his kingdom.

Second Pronouncement:

> 35b: A Holy Spirit will come upon you.
> 35c: and power from the Most High will overshadow you.
> 35d: Therefore the child to be born will be called holy — Son of God.

The first angelic pronouncement in Luke clearly echoes the promise of Nathan to David (2 Sam 7:8-16), the promise that came to serve as the foundation of messianic expectation:

> 9: I shall make for you a *great* name . . .
> 13: I shall establish *the throne of his kingdom forever.*
> 14: I shall be his father and he will be *my son* . . .
> 16: And your *house* and your *kingdom* will be made sure *forever.*

The second angelic pronouncement in Luke echoes in its wording (and in its sequence to the first) a creedal formula of the type that Paul quotes in Rom 1:3-4, where he describes Jesus Christ, God's Son:

> 3: Descended from David according to the flesh;
> 4: and *designated Son of God* in *power* according to a *Holy Spirit* [Spirit of Holiness] by resurrection from [of] the dead.

(In citing both 2 Samuel and Romans I have italicized verbal parallels to the first and second Lukan pronouncements.) Just as the pre-Pauline formula in Romans speaks first of the son of David and then of the Son of God, the Lukan annunciaton pronouncements deal first with Jesus as the fulfillment of the Davidic promise and then with Jesus conceived as the Son of God. In Paul the two are contrasted: through human origin Jesus is the son of David, while through resurrection, Holy Spirit, and power, Jesus is designated as God's Son in a special way. For Luke there is no contrast: the Son of the Most High in whom the Davidic promise is fulfilled is the child to be called the Son of God, conceived through the Holy Spirit and power.

This difference is understandable if we reflect on the development in christology separating the pre-Pauline creedal formula (pre-58 A.D.) and the Lukan infancy narrative (final form in the 80s?). The pre-Pauline formula, like other echoes of early preaching, makes the resurrection the christological moment[18] when God begot Jesus as His Son, exalted him at His right hand, and

_____

[18]A still earlier christology, leaving only faint traces in the NT, may have made the parousia the christological moment: Jesus would be the Messiah, the Son of Man, when he would return again — but that is not of importance for our purposes here. What does it mean to an orthodox Christian that there were different christologies in the NT, some of them, especially the earlier ones, clearly inadequate in the light of later faith? It means that the full appreciation of Jesus' divinity took time. Each of the christologies had positive value in emphasizing the importance of a particular moment (the parousia, the resurrection, the baptism, the conception) but did not express the full truth about Jesus.

bestowed on him the name Lord (Acts 2:36; 5:31; 13:33; Phil 2:9). The ministry before the resurrection was accordingly considered a ministry of lowliness (Phil 2:7). Intermediary between this early christology and that of the infancy narratives was the christology evident in the body of the gospels (Mark written in the late 60s?) where the christological moment has moved back to the baptism of Jesus where God's voice declares Jesus to be His Son[19] and the *Holy Spirit* descends on him so that he can begin his ministry with *power* (Luke 4:14 — note the same terminology formerly attached to the resurrection). Consequently, the ministry becomes less and less a ministry of lowliness as we progress through Matthew, Luke, and John: and the fact that Jesus is God's Son, not simply His servant, becomes more apparent in the pages of the gospel story.

But for many Christians the moving of the christological moment from the resurrection to the baptism still did not solve the mystery of who Jesus was, and in the prefaces of the later gospels we see two parallel further movements of the christological moment. In John it is moved back to pre-existence before creation;[20] in Matthew and Luke it is moved to conception.[21] And particularly in Luke 1:35 terminology drawn from the early creedal formulas is also moved back to the conception. By giving two angelic pronouncements, one phrased in the language of Nathan's prophecy to David, the other in the language of Christian christological proclamation and creed, Luke is showing that the fulfillment matches the promise: God told David that David's offspring would be His son, and through the power of the Holy Spirit the son of David comes into the world as the Son of God.

(2) *The idea of a virginal conception.* If Luke needed no special Marian source for the content of the angelic proclamation about the child and his future, did he need personal information stemming from Mary for the idea of a virginal conception? Elsewhere at length[22] I have discussed this subject and found nothing in the OT, in pagan sources, in Jewish Hellenistic mysticism, or in early Christian preaching that would explain convincingly why both Matthew and Luke maintain that Jesus was conceived of a virgin without the intervention of a human

---

[19]In the Western text of Luke 3:22 God *begets* Jesus at His Son at the baptism. In all the gospels I am assuming that the heavenly voice is the evangelist's way of communicating to the Christian reader God's revelation about who Jesus was; it is not a historical revelation to Jesus or to bystanders at the baptism who heard God speaking.

[20]Christological development is not strictly chronological, for pre-existence christology antecedes John's Prologue and is found in Paul. But John's Prologue is the first clear example of a theory of pre-existence before creation, since Phil 2:6 can refer to a pre-existence of an Adam-like figure (Adam was in the image of God but grasped at being equal to God), and Col 1:15 has Jesus pre-existing as the first-born of all creation. (See also 1 Cor 8:6).

[21]Although the subsequent church quickly combined pre-existence christology and conception christology by having the pre-existent Word take flesh (John) in the womb of the virgin Mary (Matthew, Luke), originally these were two different answers to the same problem. In particular, I interpret Luke 1:35 to mean that Jesus *became* God's Son by being conceived through the action of God's Holy Spirit. His being "called" God's Son means his being recognized for what he is. I find no suggestion of pre-existence in the Matthean or Lukan infancy narratives.

[22]R. E. Brown, *The Virginal Conception and Bodily Resurrection of Jesus.* Also "Luke's Description of the Virginal Conception," *TS*, XXXV (1974), 360-2.

father. Others who have come to similar results from their investigations have concluded that therefore the virginal conception is either a pure theologoumenon in the sense of a dramatization and historicizing of a theological statement (e.g., Jesus is the Son of God, therefore not the son of a man) or else a historical reminiscence passed down through family tradition stemming from Mary. The theologoumenon approach suffers from the difficulty that there is no real evidence that the theology of Jesus as God's Son would lead *Jews* to conclude that he had no human father — and the pre-Matthean story especially, with its Joseph/Moses pattern, suggests Jewish Christian not Gentile Christian origin.[23] The family-tradition approach faces a formidable difficulty in explaining why such a memory left no traces in *any* of the early NT writing and preaching outside the infancy narratives[24] and indeed seems to have been totally unknown to Mark writing in the 60s (Mark 6:2-3; see also footnote 28 below).

Perhaps it is possible to explain the origin of the idea of a virginal conception by combining the suggestions of theological conclusion and historical fact (without resorting to intimate family tradition for the latter). The marriage situation envisaged in Matthew and (seemingly) in Luke where Mary has conceived or will conceive before living with Joseph implies that Jesus was born at a *noticeably* early period after his parents came to live together. This could have been a historical fact known to Jesus' followers and opponents. (I cannot believe a Christian freely invented the awkward marriage situation posited in Matthew, or that a Christian would not have denied it if opponents had invented it.) The Jewish opponents of Christianity eventually accused Jesus of being illegitimate[25] — their interpretation of the fact of his noticeably early birth — but Christians rejected any implication of sin in Jesus' origins as part of their theology that Jesus was totally free of sin (2 Cor 5:21; 1 Pet 2:22; Heb 4:15; 1 John 3:5) and that his parents were holy and righteous (Matt 1:19; Luke 1:42). And so interpreting the historical fact in the light of a theology of sinlessness and divine sonship Christians concluded that the child was conceived of the Holy Spirit before Mary lived with Joseph.[26] I mention this very tentative hypothesis to demonstrate that positing a historical basis for the virginal conception does not necessarily imply a Marian source.

(3) *Mary's reaction to the annunciation.* A key argument for a Marian source has been the understanding that we have Mary's *ipsissima verba* in 1:38: "Behold the handmaid of the Lord; let it be done to me according to your word." Rather, I

---

[23]Many who speak of the Hellenistic origins (or even Gentile Christian) origins of the infancy material base themselves on the christological language found therein and do not distinguish the possibility that the christological interpretation of the virginal conception may be one of the latest factors in the infancy narrative, indeed the factor that caused the story of Jesus' conception to be seen as gospel. Often too there is insufficient allowance for the fact that the idea of a virginal conception arose long enough before Matthew and before Luke to be able to be fitted into two very different annunciation stories.

[24]The case against a secret family tradition has been argued strongly by the Catholic scholar A. Vogtle, *BLeb*, XI (1970), 51-67.

[25]For hints of this accusation in the gospels, see Brown, *The Virginal Conception*, p. 66.

[26]The veracity of this conclusion cannot be scientifically proved. This is an area where one's acceptance of divine inspiration and of the authority of traditional church teaching will play a deciding role.

propose, we have here a Lukan echo of the one scene in which Mary appears in the common synoptic tradition of the ministry.[27] As this scene is narrated in Mark 3, it has two parts. First, in 3:20-21 "his own"[28] go out to seize him because the frenzied pace of his ministry is provoking charges of madness; second, in 3:31-35 his mother and his brothers arrive and stand outside the place where he is, asking for him; but Jesus responds that the listeners seated around him who do the will of God are his mother and his brothers. The first part of the Markan scene reveals the attitude of Jesus' relatives toward him and it is scarcely one of belief. Luke and Matthew do not report this first part of the Markan scene, so that the closest parallel is John 7:5, "Even his brothers did not believe him." The second part of the Markan scene reveals Jesus' attitude toward family relationship. His real family is established through a relationship to God, not by human origin. (The Johannine parallel is in 2:4 where Jesus resists his mother's interference, seemingly because she has no role in the coming of his "hour.") When the two parts of the Markan scene are read together, the impact of 3:33-34 is very strong: "And Jesus replied, 'Who are my mothers and my brothers?' And looking around on those who sat about him, he said, 'Here are my mother and my brothers!'" — it is a replacement of his natural mother and brothers and can even be read as a rejection of his family altogether.

Be that as it may, Luke's parallel scene is quite different.[29] Luke omits not only the first part of the Markan scene (Mark 3:20-21) but also the lines just quoted from the second part. The scene in Luke 8:19-21 reads as follows:

> Then his mother and his brothers came to him, but they could not reach him because of the crowd. He was told, "Your mother and your brothers are standing outside, desiring to see you." But he said to them, "My mother and my brothers are those who hear the word [*logos*] of God and do it."

This is not to be read as if the hearers of the word of God replace Jesus' mother and his brothers as his real family (so Mark), but as a statement that his mother and his brothers are among his disciples: the physical family of Jesus is truly his family because they hear the word of God. Luke preserves Jesus' insistence that hearing the word of God and doing it is what is constitutive of his family, but Luke thinks that Jesus' mother and brothers meet that criterion. Luke is quite logical, then, in reporting that among the 120 "bretheren" who constituted the believing community after the resurrection-ascension were "Mary the mother of Jesus and his brothers" (Acts 1:14).

---

[27]Mary is mentioned but does not appear in Mark 6:3 where Jesus returns to Nazareth. There is a parallel in Matt 13:55 and John 6:42, but not in Luke 4:22 which mentions Joseph but not Mary.

[28]*Hoi par' autou,* literally "those from him," which theoretically could mean emissaries. But we must consider the sequence in Mark where "they set out to seize him" in 3:21 is followed shortly by "his mother and his brothers came and, standing outside, sent to him" in 3:31. It seems likely that Mark understood the *hoi par' autou* to be his mother and his brothers. However, the absence of an equivalent for Mark 3:21 in Matthew and Luke, plus the fact that the Johannine parallels are widely separated (John 7:4; 2:4), raises the possibility that Mark has joined two once independent traditions. The Johannine parallel confines disbelief to the Jesus' brothers; in the NT his mother is never mentioned by name as a disbeliever.

[29]Matt 12:46-50 follows Mark 3:31-35 closely, so that Luke's differences are probably to be attributed to his editing.

It is this Lukan tradition that Jesus' mother was one of "those who hear the word of God and do it" that supplied the response placed on Mary's lips at the end of the annunciation scene: "Behold the handmaid of the Lord; let it be done to me according to your word [rēma]" (1:38). Luke needed no special source nor Mary's reminiscence for this response; he needed only to make the picture of Mary in the infancy narrative consistent with the picture he had of her from her sole appearance in the common Synoptic tradition of the public ministry.

This conclusion is reinforced if we press beyond the annunciation to the visitation which is the last long description of May in the infancy narrative.[30] It is noteworthy that the Lukan account of the public ministry has not just one saying abut Jesus' mother (the parallel to Mark 3:31-35) but a second saying for which there is no parallel in the other gospels, namely Luke 11:27-28:[31]

> As Jesus said this, a woman in the crowd raised her voice and said to him, "Fortunate is the womb that bore you and the breasts you sucked." But he said, "Fortunate rather are those who hear the word [logos] of God and keep it."

This may be a doublet of the first saying since it has the same contrast between family relationship and hearing the word of God. (Curiously, although found only in Luke, it is more negative in thrust than the Lukan adaptation of Mark 3:31-35.) This second Lukan saying provided the background for Elizabeth's reaction to Mary in the visitation (1:42,45):

> Blessed are you among women,
> and blessed is the fruit of your womb . . . .
> Fortunate is she who believed that the Lord's word to her would be fulfilled.

Like the woman in the crowd, Elizabeth praises Mary's physical motherhood; but since Elizabeth is the vehicle of the prophetic spirit, she continues by praising Mary's real value as the one who hears the word of God with persevering belief — the value Jesus praised in 11:28 in response to the woman. Once again Luke seems to have found his material (and this time even the form of the material, a macarism) in what he knew from the public ministry.

The Annunciation of the Birth of John the Baptist

Space limitations imposed for contributions to this volume do not permit me to show in detail that Luke used this same technique of borrowing from the public ministry (especially from Luke 3:1-20 and 7:18-35) for his description of the future of J Bap in the annunciation of Gabriel to Zechariah in 1:13-17. But lest I tantalize unduly, let me at least list my key suggestions in this area with the hope that I shall be able to develop them elsewhere.

---

[30]Mary's role in 2:1-40 is very brief; nothing there presupposes a virginal conception or an annunciation. The story in 2:41-51 is almost certainly a tradition independent in origin of ch. 1, and is perhaps an early reflection of the tendency to shape stories about Jesus' precocious boyhood that we find in the apocryphal gospels. The Mary of 2:48-49 does not seem to be the Mary who was told about Jesus by an angel or even the Mary who heard from the shepherds' reports of an angelic proclamation about Jesus. I would be more inclined to posit a narrative source behind some of the material in Luke 2.

[31]In what follows I translate makarios by "fortunate" and a word related to eulogētos by "blessed" to signal the distinction between the macarism and the benediction. See R. E. Brown, *The Gospel According to John,* XIII-XXI, p. 553.

1:13 – In constructing an annunciation of birth for J Bap (in imitation of a pre-Lukan tradition of an annunciation of Jesus' birth), Luke follows the standard pattern discussed above.

1:14 – Joy and gladness greet the salvific event of the resurrection-ascension-gift of the spirit in Luke 24:41 and Acts 2:28. In the infancy narrative the salvific event has been moved forward to the conception and birth of Jesus, and the same reactions appear (see also Luke 2:10).

1:15 – "Great before the Lord" = 7:28.

– "Drink no wine or strong drink" = theme of J Bap's asceticism in 7:33, adapted to an infancy format in free imitation of the infancy narratives of Samson and Samuel (Judg 13:14; 1 Sam 1:15).

– "Filled with a Holy Spirit" hints at the prophetic role of J Bap.[32] In the OT the *spirit* of the Lord and the *word* of the Lord are equivalent descriptions of the divine source of prophecy. Here Luke uses the former of the two for J Bap; in 3:2 he uses the latter for J Bap.[33]

1:16 – "Turn many of the sons of Israel to the Lord their God" = standard OT terminology for the repentance of a people, sometimes in relation to the word of a prophet moved by the spirit of God (2 Chr 15:1,4). Thus the ending of 1:15 and 1:16 simply spell out in OT language that J Bap is a prophet, nay more than a prophet (7:26).

1:17 – "In the spirit and power of Elijah." Despite the oft-stated claim that Luke reserves the Elijah role for Jesus not J Bap, in 7:27 Luke applies to J Bap the classical Elijah passage from Malachi.[34]

> "To turn the hearts of the *fathers* to the *children*
> and the *disobedient* to the wisdom of the *just.*"

This is more Elijah language from Mal 3:24 (4:6) and Sir 48:10. However, there is a peculiar twist in the second line of Luke's adaptation of the Elijah motif. Malachi speaks reciprocally of "the hearts of the fathers to their

---

[32]Scholars often trace to a non-Christian Baptist source the association of the Holy Spirit with J Bap in 1:15, precisely because the Christian tradition distinguishes between J Bap's baptism with water and Christian baptism with the Holy Spirit (Luke 3:16; Acts 1:5; 19:2). The Holy Spirit attached to Christian baptism is the Spirit of Jesus communicated by him after the resurrection; obviously that cannot be associated with J Bap. But in the infancy narrative we are dealing with the prophetic spirit that Christians knew of from the OT, and that is quite appropriate for J Bap.

[33]Compare Luke 3:1-2 with the opening description of the career of the prophet Zechariah, remembering that Zechariah is the name of J Bap's father. Luke's stress in 1:15 that J Bap was filled with a Holy Spirit "even from his mother's womb" is reminiscent of the opening of Jeremiah's prophetic career which also began in the womb (Jer 1:5). A parallelism with Samson is also echoed here (Judg 16:17).

[34]Unfortunately Conzelmann has persuaded many that Luke was a highly systematic theologian shaping all things toward a master goal. Luke has an overall plan but has not leveled out all the inconsistencies in what he reports. In many passages he casts Jesus in an Elijah or prophet role (perhaps an older christology); but even in the body of the gospel he leaves traces of the thesis that J Bap had an Elijah role. In the infancy narrative, composed after the body of the gospel and with an even higher christology, there is a contrast between Jesus who is conceived as the Son of God and J Bap who is conceived as an Elijah-like prophet.

children *and the hearts of the children to their fathers"*; Sirach speaks of "the hear of the father to the son *and to restore the tribes of Israel."* But Luke, if taken in strict synonymous parallelism, identifies the fathers with the disobedient whereas the children seem to be the just whose wisdom is noted.[35] Is it coincidental that most of this language echoes Lukan passages concerning J Bap in chs. 3 and 7? In 3:8 J Bap warns those who claim that Abraham is their *father* that they can be replaced by new *children* to Abraham (3:8). In 7:33-35 Jesus says that, in contrast with those who criticize J Bap, *wisdom is justified by her children.* A possible interpretation of 1:17 is to see the children who have the wisdom of the just as those who accept the challenge of the kingdom which the disobedient fathers will refuse, so that J. Bap's task is to break down this refusal on the part of those who claim to be descended from father Abraham.

To conclude, I think that in composing ch. 1 Luke had some items that came to him from tradition, e.g., the names of J Bap's parents and that they were of priestly origin; the songs of an early Jewish Christian community (at Jerusalem?) now adapted as the *Benedictus* and the *Magnificat*; the tendency to compare the conception of Jesus to the conception of OT salvific figures by the use of an annunciation pattern; the idea of a virginal conception. He combined and fleshed out these traditions with a Christian creedal formula about Jesus as Son of God and with portraits of J Bap and Mary gleaned from the gospel account of the public ministry. The two chapters of the infancy narrative were meant by Luke to provide a bridge from the OT to the gospel story of Jesus (even as the first two chapters of Acts were meant to provide a bridge from the gospel story of Jesus to the story of the church). Those dramatis personae in the infancy narrative who appear in the gospel (J Bap, Mary) were shaped from the gospel portraits; those who do not (Zechariah, Elizabeth) were shaped from OT portraits (Abraham, Sarah, Hannah). The infancy narrative, then, is a key to the Lukan conception of salvation history.

---

[35]This identification is so startling that many interpreters want to see a chiastic relation of the terms: father = just; children = disobedient.

The Composition of Luke, Chapter 9

Joseph A. Fitzmyer, S.J.

The ninth chapter of the Lukan Gospel reveals certain interests of the evangelist that ought to be more fully considered.* It is not simply that this is the part of the Third Gospel into which the elaborate so-called Travel Account or Central Section is introduced, which makes this gospel quite distinctive among the Synoptics; but in his own way Luke has here woven into it a subsidiary treatment of Jesus of Nazareth to which one should perhaps more closely attend. It is an identification of him that gradually builds up, with titles and other elements, that makes it a crucial section in the Gospel as a whole, especially since this identification serves in its own way as an important prelude to the Travel Account and to the function which this part of the Gospel has.

Aside from the usual treatment of this section of the Lukan gospel in standard commentaries, it has not been the object of much detailed study;[1] hence I would like to reconsider it. My discussion will have four parts.

I

A few preliminary remarks are in order to clear the air on certain issues that are presupposed in the following discussion. First of all, if I refer to chap. 9 of Luke, my discussion is obviously not tied to the medieval chapter and verse

---

*This is a revised form of a paper read at the SBL meeting in Los Angeles, 1972.

[1]See J. G. Davies, "The Prefigurement of the Ascension in the Third Gospel," *JTS, ns VI* (1955), 229-33; C.H. Talbert, "The Lukan Presentation of Jesus' Ministry in Galilee," *RevExp,* LXIV (1967), 482-97; W. Wilkens, "Die Auslassung von Mark. 6:45-8:26 bei Lukas im Licht der Komposition Luk. 9:1-50," *TZ,* XXXII (1976), 193-200.

divisions, as if the evangelist had himself so designated this portion of his narrative of what Jesus did and taught. I am referring specifically to the series of episodes in the Lukan Gospel that begins with that about Herod's perplexity (9:7-9); this and the succeeding pericopes serve as a climax to Jesus' Galilean ministry and a prelude to the Travel Account (9:51-18:14). In a sense, one could even include the mission of the Twelve (9:1-6), since it is also part of that climax and prelude, being a mission charge that formulates a series of church-rules out of sayings attributed to Jesus; its advice for early church missionaries and other Lukan concerns relate it remotely to the Travel Account.[2] But the more specific development to which I refer begins with the episode of Herod's perplexity.

Secondly, in the discussion which follows I shall be presupposing the Two Source Theory as a practical solution to the Synoptic Problem, i.e., the priority of Mark and "Q" over the Lukan Gospel. The reasons for this position have been set forth by others many times over, and I have myself attempted a resurvey and a reordering of the reasons elsewhere;[3] there is no need to retail them here. However, no little part of the distinctive character of the Lukan portrait of Jesus at this point in the Gospel is seen precisely in the comparison of it with the earlier tradition, especially Markan.

Thirdly, two crucial modifications of earlier Synoptic materials are made by Luke within the compass of what we now call chap. 9. In the development of his narrative up to this point Luke has been working with several blocks of Markan material.[4] Though he has on occasion transposed an episode,[5] he has by and large been faithful to the Markan order in reproducing the Markan material. But into the Markan material Luke has made two interpolation of non-Markan matter: a "small intepolation" (Luke 6:20-8:3, largely the Sermon on the Plain and other material from "Q" or "L") and a "big interpolation," the Travel Account (Luke 9:51-18:14). The latter is one of the two crucial modifications which occur in chap. 9. The other is the so-called "great omission," i.e., the dropping of what ocrresponds to Mark 6:45-8:26, and it occurs precisely at Luke 9:17. This omission has always been puzzling, but whatever reason may be assigned for it,[6] the important element here is not so much the omission itself of significant

---

[2]Certain commentators look upon Luke 9:1 as the place for a secondary break in the Third Gospel, regarding it as the beginning of the fourth section of the Galilean Ministry. Thus, e.g., A. Plummer, *A Critical and Exegetical Commentary on the Gospel according to S. Luke,* 5th ed. p. 238; E. E. Ellis, *The Gospel of Luke,* rev. ed., p. 135. Similarly, in a sense, H. Schürmann, *Das Lukasevangelium: Erster Teil: Kommentar zu Kap. 1:1-9:50,* pp. x, 498. We are not trying to suggest that a structural division should be recognized at the beginning of the Herod episode.

[3]See P. Feine, J. Behm, W. G. Kümmel, *Introduction to the New Testament,* 14th ed., trans. by A. J. Mattill, Jr., pp. 33-60; J. A. Fitzmyer, "The Priority of Mark and the "Q" Source in Luke " *Jesus and Man's Hope,* I, 131-70.

[4]For details, see my article, "The Priority of Mark," 136.

[5]*Ibid.,* 138.

[6]It is hardly likely that Luke is dependent on a form of *Urmarkus* which did not have 6:45-8:26. A commonly espoused explanation is Luke's geographical perspective, i.e., his concern to move Jesus from Galilee to the City of Destiny without distraction; consequently, he omits these Marcan episodes that depict Jesus leaving the Galilean area for other parts. For a discussion of the various reasons, see H. Conzelmann, *The Theology of St Luke,* pp. 52-5; W. Wilkens, "Die Auslassung," pp. 195-7.

episodes as the resultant shape of chap. 9. For Luke's story at this point turns out to be not merely a truncated version of the Markan tradition, but the combination of the "great omission" and the "large interpolation" serves to produce a picture of Jesus that is distinctively Lukan.

Fourthly, an aspect of the distinctive Lukan portrait of Jesus is produced by a Lukan transposition. The story of Herod Antipas' imprisonment of John the Baptist (Mark 6:17-29), which follows upon the Markan story of Herod's reaction to the reports about Jesus and his beliefs that Jesus is none other than a resurrected John the Baptist, "whom I beheaded" (vss. 14-16), is transposed by Luke to an earlier part of his Gospel. Indeed, Luke introduces the account of the Baptist's imprisonment even prior to the narrative of the baptism of Jesus (3:19-20), undoubtly intending to finish off thereby the basic story of the Baptist before the account of Jesus' ministry is begun.[7] This transposition, however, leaves the episode of Herod's perplexity in a different form and with a different function in the Lukan Gospel. Indeed, one might wonder why the evangelist ever retained the episode itself, once he had decided to transpose and curtail radically the more important story of the Baptist's imprisonment. The Herod episode no longer serves the same innocent purpose of introducing this ruler and the subsequent story about him (the lengthy account of the imprisonment and beheading of the Baptist) such as one finds in the Markan *Vorlage*. In the brief transposed two-verse notice of the Baptist's imprisonment in Luke 3:19-20, we never learn of the ultimate fate of John; there Luke was content to note the climax of Herod's evil deeds as the shutting up of John in prison. Only here in 9:9 does Luke, following his Markan source, make Herod admit that he has "beheaded" John. This detail, borrowed from Mark 6:16, is scarcely distinctive in the Lukan account, which concentrates rather on Herod's reaction to Jesus' reputation among the people.

This discussion, however, of the Lukan transposition of the Baptist's imprisonment, which creates a minor omission of Markan material in chap. 9, is already transitional to the main points in my discussion; for it raises the question of the character and the purpose of the episode of Herod's perplexity in the Lukan narrative, to which we now turn.

II

At first sight, the Herodian episode (9:7-9) is innocent-looking. The significant aspect of it, however, is not its mere retention despite the omission of the following Markan tale about Herod's imprisonment and beheading of John, but rather the peculiarly Lukan reformulation of the episode.[8] This indicates that Luke's composition here is noteworthy. Whereas Mark had simply recorded Herod's impression of Jesus as one of several reactions to him — in fact, it sounds there like a guilty conscience merely repeating a popular reaction — Luke dramatizes the Herodian involvement. Mark wrote:

---

[7]This demarcation of the stories of John the Baptist and Jesus agrees in part with H. Conzelmann's treatment (see *Theology*, 21). But I should also want to leave room for the important modification of Conzelmann's views set forth by W. Wink, *John the Baptist in the Gospel Tradition*, pp. 55-6. The striking thing about the earlier episodes is that, once John is imprisoned, the baptism of Jesus is narrated in the Third Gospel without any mention of him.

[8]See further T. Schramm, *Der Markus-Stoff bei Lukas: Eine literarkritische und redaktionsgeschichtliche Untersuchung*, p. 128.

> King Herod heard of it; for Jesus' name had become known. Some said, John the baptizer has been raised from the dead; that is why these powers are at work in him. But others said, "It is Elijah." And others said, "It is a prophet, like one of the prophets of old." But when Herod heard of it he said, "John, whom I beheaded, has been raised." (6:14-16)

Whereas Luke, following Mark's order, writes instead:

> Now Herod the tetrarch heard of all that was done, and he was perplexed, because it was said by some that John had been raised from the dead, by some that Elijah had appeared, and by others that one of the old prophets had risen. Herod said, "John I beheaded; but who is this about whom I hear such things?" And he sought to see him. (9:7-9)

We note the following changes introduced into the Lukan reformulation of the episode: (1) The identification of Herod as *ho tetraarchēs*. Though it is a minor agreement of Luke with Matthew against Mark in the Triple Tradition,[9] it is of no significance in the development of the Lukan story. (2) The object of what Herod has heard about Jesus is given as *ta ginomena panta,* "all that was going on" (or "all that was being done"). The object is thus more generically and more vaguely formulated than either the object-less, absolute use of *ēkousen* in Mark 6:14 or the Matthean specification, *tēn akown Iesou,* "Jesus fame" (14:1). Mark's text had related the verb of hearing directly to the immediately preceding account of the disciples' preaching and curing (with a subsequent specification). But the Lukan reformulation, *ta ginomena panta,* is at once more vague and relates Herod's reaction to an even broader perspective. (3) Only Luke among the Synoptists has introduced the mention of Herod's perplexity, *kai dieporei dia to legesthai hypo tinon hoti . . . ,* "And he was puzzled by what was being said by some that . . . ." It is a reformulation of the Markan bland statement, *kai elegon hoti . . . ,* "and they were saying . . . ."[10] But the Lukan reformulation, highlighting Herod's perplexity, foreshadows the question that Herod is made to ask at the end of the episode (vs. 9c). (4) For some reason Luke omits here all reference to Jesus' miracles (*dynameis*), which in the Markan account eventually specifies in detail what Herod had been hearing, and the omission of this detail heightens the vagueness of the intial *ta ginomena panta.* In dependence upon Mark, Luke introduces the popular reaction that Jesus might be Elijah, "that Elijah had appeared," and rephrases the saying about "one of the prophets of old" arising. He thus achieves an elegant threefold parallel subject-clause, introduced by *hoti* which functions as the subject of the passive infinitive *legesthai.* After the borrowed and slightly modified Markan phrase about the beheading of John, we come to the significant Lukan reformulation of the episode. (5) Luke puts on the lips of Herod the dramatic question, "Who is this about whom I hear such things?" (*tis de estin houtos peri hou akouō toiauta,* vs. 9c). The question is distinctively

---

[9]See my article, "The Priority of Mark," pp. 142-7; cf. T. Schramm, *Markus-Stoff,* pp. 72-7, 128 (independent correction of Mark by Luke and Matthew); F. Neirynck, "La matiere marcienne dans l'evangile de Luc," *L'Evangile de Luc: Problèmes littéraires et théologiques: Mémorial Lucien Cerfaux,* pp. 157-201, esp. 195-6.

[10]A variant in some important mss. reads *elegen* (i.e., Herod) instead of *elegon.* Though it may be owing to a confusion of the majuscule E and O, it may also be a reason why Luke modified the Markan source. Herod's own statement is made in the following vs. 16 (with *elegen*).

Lukan, being found neither in the Markan nor the Matthean parallels. It sums up Herod's perplexity in vs. 7. But it also serves to pinpoint the function of the following episodes in chap. 9. Herod is made to ask the crucial question, and the answer to it is provided in many ways in the episodes that follow; the question and the answers act as a prelude to the Travel Account itself and to its function in the Lukan Gospel. Thus the transposition of the story of the Baptist's imprisonment has produced, along with various Lukan modifications, a form of the Herodian episode that has its own peculiar function in the Third Gospel.[11] (6) Finally, vs. 9d, "and he sought to see him," is a Lukan foreshadowing of 13:31 and 23:8.

Before turning to the answers that chap. 9 provides to Herod's question, we may note that the question itself has been foreshadowed earlier in the Gospel. It is similar to that posed by the disciples in 8:25, after Jesus "rebuked the wind and the raging waves," *tis ara houtos estin hoti kai tois anemois epitassei kai to hydati, kai hypakouousin autō,* "Who then is this that he commands even winds and water, and they obey him?"[12] There Luke's formula for the question in the main clause was derived directly from Mark; here in the Herod episode its phrasing is slightly different and is, indeed, closer to other Lukan questions (cf. 5:21; 7:49).

III

When we look at the following episodes in chap. 9, we find that they either implicitly or explicitly answer Herod's question. This is the purpose of the Lukan literary presentation at this point in his Gospel. In looking at the episodes, however, it is important that we keep in mind the concatenation of them and the resultant series brought about by the modifications in the order of episodes that we have already mentioned. However, at the outset we admit that not every one fits into this scheme as perfectly as the others; and yet, enough of them do to make this interpretation of the series plausible.

The episodes which follow that of Herod's perplexity are nine, including the specific Lukan introduction to the Travel Account: (1) the Feeding of the Five Thousand (vss. 10-17), (2) the Confession of Peter and the First Announcement of the Passion (vss. 18-22), (3) Sayings of Jesus about the Conditions of Discipleship (vss. 23-27), (4) the Transfiguration (vss. 28-36), (5) the Cure of the

---

[11]The pericope actually ends with a Lukan comment, "And he sought to see him." This is a clear foreshadowing of the later comment in 23:8 (H. Schürmann, *Das Lukasevangelium,* pp. 506-8, calls attention to the echo of *ta ginomena panta* in *semeion ginomenon*). However, this last comment of the evangelist has little to do with the development in chap. 9.

[12]H. Schurmann (*Das Lukasevangelium,* p. 505) notes that the question was already alive since 7:16, 19-20, 49; 8:25, 28. Save, however, for the places which we have noted above, it has not been presented in this form. The fact that it is not repeated after chap. 9 is an indication that it is being answered here. In the Infancy Narrative a similar question is asked of John the Baptist (1:66, "What then will this child be?"). Thought the contrast of John and Jesus there might suggest to the reader the same question about Jesus, it is never so formulated of him in the Infancy Narrative. In any case, the use of such a question there as well as in the Gospel proper shows a concern in the evangelist's mind to raise the question of identity in the reader's mind.

Possessed Boy (vss. 37-43a), (6) the Second Announcement of the Passion (vss. 43b-45), (7) the Strife of the Disciples about Greatness (vs. 46-48), (8) the Saying of Jesus about the Strange Exorcist (vss. 49-50), and finally (9) the introduction to the Travel Account, the visit to Samaritan Villages (vss. 51-56).

The break in Luke's Gospel at the beginning of the Travel Account is acknowledged by most commentators; the reference to Jesus' being taken up and to his setting his face toward Jerusalem (9:51) introduces a distinctive development in the structure of the Gospel and shifts the emphasis to a new concern. When one considers the distinctive form of the Herod episode and reflects on the episodes that Luke has retained from the Markan source (with modifications) and has strung together between that question of Herod and the Travel Account, it seem clear that they are mainly intended to answer Herod's question and to serve as a christological climax of what has preceded as well as a prelude to the Travel Account itself. The answers in these episodes are not all presented in equal fashion; in some instances, it is a matter of titles being used of Jesus which may already have been present in the pre-Lukan tradition; in others, there are titles only found in Luke; and in still others, the answer to the question is implicit in the narrative and derived from the Lukan retention and re-use of the narrative-forms.

Obviously, we cannot analyze all nine episodes here in great detail. But we can at least examine them for the general intent of the evangelist and for the answers that they provide to Herod's question. Both the question and the subsequent answers sketch a christological portrait of Jesus upon which the Travel Account builds.

The first episode after Herod's question is the miracle story of the Feeding of the Five Thousand (9:10-17). Derived from the Markan source, it is retained by Luke as an implicit miraculous answer to Herod's question.[13] The retention of traditional pre-Lukan material here does not include a specific title; but Jesus' preaching of "the kingdom of God" (9:11) and the miracle-story, telling of an act of Jesus described in formulas with eucharistic overtones of a later vintage and with symbolic nuances (e.g., "he looked up to heaven, blessed, broke, and gave" [eucharistic formulation]; "twelve baskets of fragments" [symbolic nuance], clearly identifies Jesus as a person in whom God's message, activity, and creative presence are revealed.[14] The Lukan explanation of the episode is not formulated here; in fact, it is striking that the first episode after Herod's question should be one related to the *dynameis* of Jesus whereas Luke has omitted precisely all reference to them in the Herod episode itself. But the mentality that is behind the retention of this episode and its concatenation with the others is manifested in an explanation of Jesus' identity that Luke has penned elsewhere. In Peter's speech in Acts there is a Lukan explanation of Jesus' miracles: "Jesus of Nazareth, a man attested by God with mighty works and wonders and signs which God did through him in your midst" (Acts 2:22). Such an explanation underlies the use of the miracle-story of the Feeding of the Five Thousand as an

---

[13]The would-be similarities between this Lukan passage and its Matthean counterpart (14:13-21) listed by T. Schramm (*Markus-Stoff,* p. 129) are not really close enough for one to conclude to *Traditionsvarianten* and to another source independent of Mark here.

[14]See further W. Wilkens, "Die Auslassung," p. 194.

implicit answer to Herod's question.

The second episode is that of Peter's Confession, a scene which provides an explicit answer to Herod's question (9:18-21), but in a formulation that is Lukan. Between the preceding episode of the Feeding of the Five Thousand and this Confession of Peter intervenes what we referred to above as the "great omission," the material of Mark 6:45-8:26 not used here. Whatever may be the reason for that omission, the proximity of Peter's Confession to Herod's question is now noteworthy. Luke's omission of the geographical locality of the scene, Caesarea Philippi, has often been explained in terms of his geographical perspective.[15] This may still be a valid reason, but it is just as likely that the collocation of Peter's Confession in the present lineup of chap. 9 is also a reason for the omission. There is no need for a geographical setting because the episode serves the purpose of answering a larger literary question, that of Herod.[16] One cannot help but note the typically Lukan setting of Jesus at prayer "alone" (9:18).[17] True, the episode does contain a pre-Lukan question, which is also answered: "Who do the crowds say that I am?" Though it is Lukan in its use of *hoi ochloi* instead of the *hoi anthrōpoi* of Mark 8:27, "Who do men say I am?",[18] this question is clearly derived from Mark. And yet, it is really secondary in the Lukan use of the episode. It introduces the popular answers, "John the Baptist," "Elijah," and "one of the prophets of old has arisen." Though these popular answers repeat the substance of the Markan formulas, the third one echoes precisely a phrase in the Herod episode, "one of the prophets of old has arisen" (*prophetes tis ton archaion aneste*). The connection, then, between this Lukan form of Peter's Confession and the earlier Herod episode is thus established; the echo of the phrase is literal. It relates the questions posed here to that of Herod the ruler. The real answer to Herod's question, however, is given through another pre-Lukan question asked of Peter, "Who do you say I am?" In this case Luke borrows the phraseology word for word from Mark. But the answer differs slightly: "God's Messiah" (or "the Anointed One of God"). Luke's account has nothing of the additional Matthean material (16:16b-19) or of the rebuke of Peter found in the earlier Markan source (8:32-33). But Peter's answer, identifying Jesus as "God's Messiah," goes far beyond the answers of the "crowds." It is puzzling, however, that Luke retains Jesus' charge to the disciples that they tell no one about Peter's answer — a detail that certainly suits the Markan theme of the messianic secret much better than the concern of Luke in his Gospel to make known the identity of Jesus. H. Conzelmann may be right in relating this charge to an understanding of the Passion.[19] In any case, this truncated Lukan form of Peter's Confession

---

[15]See H. Conzelmann, *Theology*, p. 55. Cf. K. H. Rengstorf, *Das Evangelium nach Lukas*, 9th ed., pp. 119-20. Luke's mention of Bethsaida (9:10 — cf. Mark 6:32, but also 45) would suggest that that is where Peter's confession is to be located. It takes place not way up north, but in a town opposite Galilee. See further W. Wilkens, "Die Auslassung," p. 196.

[16]E. E. Ellis (*The Gospel of Luke*, p. 139) thinks rather that Luke wanted to connect Peter's Confession with the feeding miracle and he compares John 6:14, 68-9. There may be something to this, but it may also be reading a Johannine connection into Luke.

[17]Cp. Luke 3:21; 5:16; 6:12, 9:28, 22:41. See H. Flender, *St Luke: Theologian of Redemptive History*, p. 53.

[18]*Ibid.*, p. 47.

[19]However, his way of expressing it is unclear. He says, ". . . by altering his sources and

seems better understood as an answer to Herod's question than as an episode concentrating on the role of Peter, an emphasis that seems more appropriate for the Markan or Matthean form. In the Lukan Gospel this passage is much less one that enhances Peter's role.[20]

The end of the episode of Peter's Confession, which includes the First Announcement of the Passion, explains that the Son of Man must suffer many things. This pre-Lukan element, retained in modified form from Mark,[21] serves basically the same purpose in Luke that it has in Mark, as a corrective to the acknowledged messiahship of Jesus. The corrective, however, is far more closely linked to Peter's confession in Luke and provides a still further answer to Herod's question. Put on the lips of Jesus, it says in effect that he may be the Messiah, but he is such *as* the suffering Son of Man: He will be recognized as Messiah insofar as he is seen as the one destined for suffering and death as Son of Man.

The fourth episode is the Transfiguration (9:28-36), a scene that Luke has again derived from his Markan source and modified for his own purposes.[22] There the answer given to Herod's question is both implicit and explicit. The explicit answer is provided by the heavenly voice from the overshadowing cloud, "This is my Son, my Chosen One" (9:35).[23] He may be God's Messiah and suffering Son of Man, but he is also "Son" and "Chosen One." The implicit answer, and indeed a subsidiary and minor one, is contained in the narrative itself, viz., in the appearance of Moses and Elijah in glory with him, as they discuss with him his "departure" (*exodos*), his transit through passion and death to him who calls him "Son."[24] Their eventual disappearance and their leaving him "alone," together with the charge from the heavenly voice, "Listen to him" (probably an echo of Deut 18:15), clearly identifies Jesus as the one who now has to be heard in place of Moses and Elijah. In effect, he is the New Moses and the New Elijah. The "New

---

introducing variations of Markan motifs . . . he turns Mark's Messianic secret into a misunderstanding of the Passion" (*Theology*, p. 56). What is not clear here is the "misunderstanding of the Passion" that is supposed to be in this Lukan text. Luke has related Jesus' charge to the Passion, provided that *touto* in 9:21 is to be understood as referring to what follows — which could be defended. But does what follows constitute a "misunderstanding" of the Passion? After all, this is the first announcement of it, and one wonders whether there has yet been in Luke's narrative a chance for a misunderstanding. See note 23 below, and the place to which it refers in the text.

[20]See further W. Dietrich, *Das Petrusbild der lukanischen Schriften*, pp. 94-104.

[21]Luke uses *tē̃ tritē̃ hemera egerthēnai* (cf. Matt 16:21), whereas Mark has *meta treis hemeras anastēnai;* for the rest Luke borrows from Mark. Luke has a pronounced preference for *anastēnai* (see T. Schramm, *Markus-Stoff*, p. 30); so his change here is striking and is perhaps due to an independent tradition.

[22]See H. Schürmann, *Das Lukasevangelium*, pp. 552-67, for details; cf. F. Neirynck "Minor Agreements Matthew-Luke in the Transfiguration Story," *Orientierung an Jesus: Zur Theologie der Synoptiker: Für Josef Schmid*, ed. P. Hoffmann et al., pp. 253-65; T. Schramm, *Markus-Stoff*, pp. 136-9 (he thinks the Lukan account is dependent on another tradition).

[23]An allusion to Isa 42:1 most probably.

[24]See further below, p. 150.

Moses" is really not an operative motif in the Third Gospel, as it is in the First;[25] it is found here because it is retained from the Markan source (9:4, with the same charge used there). The appearance of Elijah, however, is different. Even though he already was present in the pre-Lukan source, his appearance fits a theme of the Third Gospel in which Jesus is presented in a role similar to Elijah, or possibly even as a "New Elijah."[26] In addition to the popular identification of Jesus as such (recorded in Luke 9:9, 19), the evangelist plays on the relation of Jesus to Elijah in several places in the Gospel (4:25; 9:54, 62). What is puzzling in this regard, however, is Luke's omission of the Saying about the Coming of Elijah found in the Markan source (Mark 9:9-13). It is an episode that creates its own problems, which need not detain us now; we can speculate about the Lukan omission of it,[27] but in any case the omission heightens the identification of Jesus as the New Elijah implicitly suggested by this episode; it too supplies an answer to Herod's question. The christological affirmation here is that all that Moses and Elijah meant for Israel of old is now summed up in Jesus and that he is now the one — as Messiah and suffering Son of Man — to whom all must now listen. The Transfiguration scene reveals Jesus for what he is; heaven identifies him. And the irony of it all is that the disciples, having heard the instruction, "Listen to him," "kept silence and told no one in those days anything of what they had seen" (9:36).

The fifth episode is another miracle-story, the Cure of the Possessed Boy (9:37-43a), an episode that Luke has probably borrowed from Mark.[28] It is greatly reduced in its form by Luke and confined to essentials; what has interested Luke in it is not the depiction of Jesus as a great thaumaturge coping with demon-sickness, but the essentials of the story again supply an implicit answer to Herod's question (in a way similar to that of the Feeding of the Five Thousand): Jesus is one in whom God's salvific power is manifested; or to put it more closely in the words of the episode itself, Jesus is the one in whom the majesty of God is made manifest. "And they were all astonished at the majesty of God" (*epi tē megaleiotēti tou theou,* (43a).[29] This is again a distinctively Lukan comment,

---

[25]*Pace* J. H. Davies, "The Purpose of the Central Section of St. Luke's Gospel," *Studia evangelica,* II, 164-9, esp. 165.

[26]There is actually a double treatment of Elijah in the Lukan Gospel, one which presents Jesus with Elijah's traits, and another which reverses the roles of John and Jesus, depicting John as Elijah. As J. A. T. Robinson has shown, the latter is undoubtedly a more primitive tradition (see "Jesus, John, and Elijah: An Essay in Detection," *NTS,* IV (1957-8), pp. 263-81; reprinted, *Twelve New Testament Studies,* pp. 28-52. The Lukan identification of John and Elijah is found in the Infancy Narrative (1:17), where it is introduced with hindsight. Striking is the omission of the identification of John and Elijah in the Third Gospel, which one finds in Matt 11:14; likewise the omission of the entire episode of Mark 9:9-13. Whatever the reason for this may be, it is an oversimplification to say that Luke does not know or use the identification of John with Elijah in his gospel; those who so present Lukan thought never seem to reckon with 7:26-8, where the identification is certainly implicit.

[27]See Conzelmann, *Theology,* p. 59.

[28]The similar reduction of the episode in Matthew raises questions about the independent origin of this particular episode. T. Schramm (*Markus-Stoff,* pp. 139-40) concludes that it "steht deutlich unter dem Einfluss einer Traditions-variante." That may be, but it still does not exclude the probability that the passage is basically Markan.

[29]This phrase is singularly devoid of comment in most commentaries on the Lukan

present in neither the Markan nor the Matthean parallels.

The sixth episode, the Second Announcement of the Passion (9:43a-45), is another pre-Lukan identification of Jesus, again most likely derived from Mark (9:30-32) in its substance, and is undoubtedly retained by Luke as part of the triple announcement in the gospel tradition. It also supplies a further answer to Herod's question: He is the Son of Man who is to be handed over to his enemies (*anthrōpon*). Noteworthy is the Lukan modification of the episode, which eliminates the reference to Galilee (Mark 9:30),[30] emphasizes the incomprehension of the disciples,[31] and strips away the mention of his death and resurrection. Coming after the impression that was made by the Cure of the Possessed Boy, it obviously serves again as an answer corrective to the crowd's astonishment. Contrast also the "handing over" of Jesus here with his prayer on the cross (23:46).

The seventh episode, the Strife of the Disciples about Greatness (9:46-48), gives no explicit answer to the question of Herod. It is retained from the Markan source (9:33-37) and abbreviated; it at most identifies Jesus as "someone sent," indicating that he is to be welcomed with the openness of a child.[32] The use of traditional material here and the farther one gets from the question of Herod both make it more difficult to see the episode as a direct answer to it.

Similarly, the eighth episode, the Saying about the Strange Exorcist (9:49-50), is retained because of the Markan source, although Luke does adapt it. The one title that it contains, "Master" (*epistatēs*), used of Jesus by John (son of Zebedee), replaces the Markan counterpart, "Teacher" (*didaskalos*), a title that

---

Gospel. Those commentators who do say something about it normally understand it of wonder at what Jesus has done as an agent of the God of might or majesty (thus, e.g., W. F. Arndt, *The Gospel according to St. Luke*, p. 266; W. Grundmann, *Das Evangelium nach Lukas*, 2nd ed., p. 195; H. Schürmann, *Das Lukasevangelium*, p. 570 ("In Jesu Machttaten wirkt Gott — 'denn Gott war mit ihm' (Apg 10, 38) -, so dass nun alle nicht über die Macht Jesu, sondern über die Grosse Gottes ausser sich geraten")). While this may well be the sense of the Lukan phrase which should be retained, there is one small problem that seems to have gone unnoticed and perhaps has been passed over because of the normal way in which vs. 43 is divided up. This phrase in vs. 43a is usually read with the preceding episode, and vs. 43b with the following. If, however, one reads them together and notes the absence of a specific subject to the third singular verbs (*epoiei, eipen*) in vs. 43b, which obviously refer to Jesus and look back to a third singular that precedes in vs. 43a, the word *theos* that is there is the only referent. Is it just possible that Luke is making use here of *ho theos* as a title for Jesus himself? Prima facie, *ho theos* designates the Father in the Synoptic Gospels. Yet the time comes in the NT writings when that title is given to Jesus (at least in John 1:1; 20:28; Heb 1:8-9; see further R. E. Brown, "Does the New Testament Call Jesus God?" *TS*, XXVI (1965), 545-73). Would it be impossible for Luke, writing ca. A.D. 85-90, to refer to Jesus in this way? Cf. Acts 20:28 and the discussion raised by that verse. The suggestion is tantalizing, but it is by no means certain. If it were, it would be another answer to Herod's question. But at least an implicit miraculous one is provided in the narrative itself as one in whom the majesty of God is present.

[30]See H. Conzelmann, *Theology*, p. 60.

[31]Contrast the explicit statement of the evangelist here about the misunderstanding of the disciples with the absence of it in 9:21-2. See note 14 above.

[32]See R. Leaney, "Jesus and the Symbol of the Child (Lc 9:46-48)," *ExpTim*, LXV (1954-5), 91-2.

Luke does not eschew for Jesus (see 9:38), but which he has altered for one that he uses elsewhere and that is used by him alone (5:5; 8:24; 45; 9:33; 17:3). Though it is not a significant title for NT christology nor a real answer to Luke's identification of Jesus, it does imply some authority that he has. Falling into the line-up of other identifications, it serves in its own small way as an identification of him and an answer to Herod's question.

The ninth episode is the introduction to the Travel Account itself (9:51-56). This is the first pericope of the new section in the Third Gospel and is distinctively Lukan, not only in its formulation but also in the future reference that it gives to the Lukan story of Jesus' ministry from now on. The mention of his "being taken up" (9:51) refers at least to the Ascension (see Acts 1:11),[33] but should undoubtedly be understood in the larger sense of the whole complex of Passion-Death-Resurrection-Ascension in the Lukan story — Jesus' transit to glory. Moreover, the mention of the City of Destiny, Jerusalem,[34] introduces an element in the narrative that has not been present up to this point. In itself, the episode tells of the disciples' reaction to the Samaritans and Jesus' comments on it. The narrative *in se* does not further answer Herod's question, for it is the beginning of a new element in the Gospel. But a title does appear in it, *Kyrie* (9:54), and in the light of the lineup of other titles in chap. 9, it probably ought to be considered. In the *Sitz im Leben Jesu,* which it may remotely reflect, it would have no more of an implication than "Sir," but its use here in the evangelist's composition, in the *Sitz im Evangelium,* may also carry the connotation that it has elsewhere in the Gospel, "Lord" (see 5:8,12; 6:46; 7:6,13,19).[35] In the evangelist's literary context it is not without some significance.

This rapid survey of the episodes of chap. 9 between that of Herod's perplexity and the beginning of the Travel Account has sketched in broad outline the picture of Jesus that Luke has sought to present at this point in his Gospel. It has aimed at an identification of him in terms of answers given to the question dramatically posed by Herod (9:9), "Who is this about whom I hear such things?" Luke's answer, achieved by various modifications of the Markan source, has produced what H. Conzelmann has called "a series of Christological statements which Luke harmonizes one with the other by altering his sources and introducing variations of Marcan motifs."[36] Thus Luke has here presented Jesus as someone

---

[33]See J. G. Davies, "The Prefiguration," pp. 229-33; E. E. Ellis, *The Gospel of Luke,* p. 150.

[34]H. Conzelmann (*Theology,* p. 63) regards Jesus' journey in this section to be not so much a progress toward Jerusalem (because 'he never really makes any progress,' p. 61, quoting K. L. Schmidt) as a "progress towards the Passion." This may, indeed, be true, but the writing off of the Central Section of the Lukan Gospel as no travel report is a little too much. This is not the place to debate the issue; the Travel Account has a literary purpose, and that is all that matters at the moment.

[35]See I. de la Potterie, "Le titre *kyrios* appliqué a Jesus dans l'évangile de Luc," *Mélanges biblique en hommage au R. P. Béda Rigaux,* ed. A. Descamps et A. de Halleux, pp. 117-46; D. L. Jones, "The Title *kyrios* in Luke Acts," *Society of Biblical Literature 1974 Seminar Papers,* ed. G.W. MacRae, II, 85-101; cf. J.A. Fitzmyer, "Der semitische Hintergrund des neutestamentlichen Kyriostitels," *Jesus Christus in Historie und Theologie: Neutestamentliche Festschrift für Hans Conzelmann zum 60. Geburtstag,* ed. G. Strecker, pp. 267-98.

[36]*Theology,* p. 56.

related to John the Baptist (9:19), as someone related to Elijah or the New Elijah (9:19, 30, 36), as someone related to the prophets of old (9:19), as "God's Messiah" (9:20), as the suffering Son of Man (9:22, 44), as Heaven's Son and Chosen One (9:35), as a New Moses (9:30, 36), as a Teacher (9:38), a Master (9:33, 49), and as one in whom "the majesty of God" is manifest (9:43a).[37] Some of the answers are explicit, some only implicit; some of the explicit answers are not exclusively Lukan, being derived from pre-Lukan material. Some of the answers are given by way of a miracle (9:10-17, 37-42); others are ascribed to various individuals: Peter (9:18-21), Jesus himself (9:22, 44-45), a heavenly voice (9:35). At least one comes from the evangelist (9:43a). This line-up of titles reminds one of the similar piling up of identifications of Jesus found in John 1:19-51; the difference is that there they appear early in the Gospel. But as there, the titles are not confined to this section alone. It is clear, however, that the Peter episode and the Transfiguration stand out above all in the christological affirmation about Jesus. They prepare the reader for the Passion-Death-Resurrection ending of the Jesus-story. Thus chap. 9 is crucial in the Lukan Gospel, as a sort of climax of all that has preceded, but also transitional to the Travel Account and all that it means in the Lukan writings.

This series of christological statements about Jesus, made through the literary device of a question and various implicit or explicit answers to it, precedes the Travel Account proper which also begins in chap. 9. It is not my intention to rehash here the problem of the Travel Account and the various interpretations that have been given to it (historical, geographical, literary, and theological).[38] They have sought to present an understanding of the purported journey of Jesus to Jerusalem (the goal being called to the reader's mind several times over during the course of it: 9:51, 53; 13:22, 33; 17:11; 18:31; 19:11, 28), which is otherwise composed of episodes that inevitably distract the reader from the idea of a journey at all. This "central section" of Luke's Gospel, made up of a "completely amorphous" collection of sayings and a few deeds of Jesus,[39] has a built-in

---

[37]Or as *theos*, if there is any merit in the suggestion made in note 29 above.

[38]A convenient survey of the various interpretations can be found in A. Denaux. "Het lucaanse reisverhaal (Lc. 9:51-19:44)," *Collationes brugenses et gandavenses*, XIV (1968), 214-42; XV (1969), 464-501. See further P. Benoit, "La section 9:51-18:14 de saint Luc," *RB*, LX (1953), 446-8; J. Bligh, *Christian Deuteronomy (Luke 9-18);* J. Blinzler, "Die literarische Eigenart des sogenannten Reiseberichts im Lukas-Evangelium," *Synoptische Studien Alfred Wikenhauser zum siebzigsten Geburtstag . . . dargebracht, pp. 20-52; reprinted, Gesammelte Aufsatze,* pp. 62-94; W. H. Cadman, *The Last Journey of Jesus to Jerusalem,*" *BVC*, XI (1955), 69-87; W. Gasse, "Zum Reisebericht des Lukas," *ZNW,* the Central Section of St. Luke's Gospel," *Studia evangelica,* II, pp. 164-9; C. F. Evans, "The Central Section of St. Luke's Gospel," *Studies in the Gospels: Essays in Memory of R. H. Lightfoot,* ed. D. E. Nineham, pp. 37-53; I. Fransen, "Cahier de Bible: La montée vers Jérusalem," *BVC,* XI (1955),   69-87; W. Gasse, "Zum Reisebericht des Lukas," *ZNW,* XXXIV (1935), 293-9; D. Gill, "Observations on the Lukan Narrative and Some Related Passages," *HTR,* LXIII (1970), 199-221; L. Girard, *L'evangile des voyages de Jesus: Ou la section 9:51-18:14 de saint Luc;* M. D. Goulder, "The Chiastic Structure of the Lucan Journey," *Studia evangelica,* II, pp. 195-202; W. Grundmann, "Fragen der Komposition des lukanischen 'Reiseberichts,' " *ZNW,* I (1959), 252-70; J. C. Hawkins, "Three Limitations to St. Luke's Use of St. Mark's Gospel," *Studies in the Synoptic Problem,* ed. W. Sanday, pp. 27-94, esp. 29-59 ("The Disuse of the Marcan Source in St. Luke 9:51-18:14"); J. Leal, "Los viaies de Jesus a Jerusalen segun San Lucas," *XIV Semana biblica espanola (21-26 Sept.*

tension between its form and its content. Whatever the correct analysis is, the Travel Account does serve a literary purpose of depicting Jesus training in his own ministry those "who came up from Galilee to Jerusalem, who are now his witnesses to the people" (Acts (13:31). In the first part of the Gospel the "Galileans" were assembled,[40] but here the instruction of them by him who is the Teacher par excellence is intended by Luke as the preparation of the witnesses, those "who were chosen by God as witnesses" (Acts 10:41), those who were "witnesses to all that he did both in the country of the Jews and in Jerusalem" (Acts 10:39), as he taught "throughout all Judea, from Galilee even to this place" (Luke 23:5).[41] It is important, then, that the picture of Jesus that immediately precedes this instruction be presented as of one with authority, and this is why the episodes from the Herod pericope on serve precisely as the christological prelude to the Travel Account.

Underlying all of this is the stated purpose of Luke in his prologue to the Gospel, that Theophilus — and others like him — may know the assured basis (*asphaleia*) of the things in which he has been instructed (Luke 1:4). The emphatic position of *asphaleia* at the end of that sentence reveals Luke's concern for assurance, security. He strives to show that what the church of his day is teaching is rooted in the instruction of the earthly Jesus, and that the Christian movement in its varied developments was not only God-ordained but Jesus-inspired. And the link is the witnesses instructed by Jesus en route to Jerusalem. To make sure that the authority behind it all is not missed, Luke has Herod, a man of authority, pose the crucial question, "Who is this about whom I hear such things?"[42]

The mission and authority of those sent out by Jesus in 9:1-6 is thus guaranteed; it is rooted in the sending and authority of Jesus himself.[43] In the

---

1953), pp. 365-81; E. Lohse, "Missionarisches Handeln Jesu nach dem Evangelium des Lukas," *TZ*, X (1954), 1-13; C. C. MacCown, "The Geography of Jesus' Last Journey to Jerusalem," *JBL*, LI (1932), 107-29; "The Geography of Luke's Central Section," *JBL* LVII (1938), 51-66; X. de Meeus, *La composition de Lc 9:51-18:14; G. Ogg, "The Central Section of the Gospel according to St Luke," *NTS*, XVIII (1971-2), 39-53; B. Reicke, "Instruction and Discussion in the Travel Narrative," *Studia evangelica*, I, pp. 206-16; W. G. Robinson, Jr., "The Theological Context for Interpreting Luke's Travel Narrative (9:51ff.)," *JBL*, LXXIX (1960), 20-31; J. Schneider, "Zur Analyse des lukanischen Reiseberichtes," *Synoptische Studien*, pp. 207-29; F. Stagg, "The Journey toward Jerusalem in Luke's Gospel. Luke 9:51-19:27," *RevExp*, LXIV (1967), 499-512; M. Zerwick, *Leben aus Gottes Wort: Erwägungen zum lukanischen Reisebericht.*

[39]C. F. Evans, "The Central Section," p. 40.

[40]See H. Conzelmann, *Theology*, p. 38. Cf. Luke 6:12-16; 8:1-3; 9:1-2.

[41]Cf. W. C. Robinson, Jr., *Der Weg des Herrn: Studien zur Geschichte und Eschatologie im Lukas-Evangelium: Ein Gespräch mit Hans Conzelmann,* pp. 30-6.

[42]A nagging problem in this whole discussion is why Herod is made to ask the crucial question. Why would Luke assign such an important role to him? In reality, he is not that important, because he acts only as a foil. But aside from the traditional character of the material used by Luke (the story of his reaction to Jesus is already in the Markan source), the Herod episode merely fits the larger problem of the role that Herod plays in the Third Gospel as a whole. If that could be satisfactorily answered, then possibly this nagging problem would also be solved.

[43]See W. Wilkens, "Die Auslassung," p. 194.

teaching and authority of the "Galileans" — those "chosen by God as witnesses" — the recognized of Jesus himself is manifest. This is a distinct Lukan emphasis, and no little part of it is created by the question of Herod and the christological affirmation in the ninth chapter of the Third Gospel.

The Lukan Perspective on the Miracles of Jesus: A Preliminary Sketch

Paul J. Achtemeier

The problem of the way Luke viewed and used the miracles of Jesus is a subject that has remained remarkably innocent of systematic treatment in recent biblical scholarship. H. Conzelmann, in his epoch-making redaction-critical study, devoted only three pages to this problem, and although H. J. Held does on occasion refer to the Lukan miracles, it is only to gain a clearer perspective on the way Matthew employed the traditions about Jesus' miracles, his actual theme.[1] Periodical literature has been equally sparse. The few articles that have been written deal primarily with the way in which miracles function within the narrative of Acts.[2] There is, in short, no serious redaction-critical study of the Lucan miracle-stories of which I am aware, and it is at that point that this preliminary sketch finds its place.

As the title indicates, the emphasis will fall on the miracles of Jesus, and since none are reported in Acts (they are referred to only twice, 2:22 and 10:38), material from that second volume of Luke's "History of Primitive Christianity" will

---

[1] H. Conzelmann, *Die Mitte der Zeit: Studien zur Theologie des Lukas,* pp. 165-7. H.J. Held, "Matthew as Interpreter of the Miracle Stories," *Tradition and Interpretation in Matthew,* eds. G. Bornkamm, G. Barth, H. J. Held; trans. P. Scott.

[2] E.g., J. Fenton, "The Order of the Miracles Performed by Peter and Paul in Acts," *ExpTim,* LXXVII (1966), 381-3; J. Ferguson, "Thoughts on Acts," *CQ,* XXXV (1957), 117-33; J. A. Hardon, S. J., "The Miracle Narratives in the Acts of the Apostles," *CBQ,* XVI (1954), 303-18. There are, of course, remarks on Jesus' miracles in the commentaries on Luke, bu 303-18. There are, of course, remarks on Jesus' miracles in the commentaries on Luke, but not in the context of any systematic attempt at a redaction-critical judgment.

be used only occasionally. We shall consider, first, the methods to be used in this kind of study, and shall then proceed to outline the results of the application of such methods. A brief summary of our conclusions will then be appended.

I

As far as the number of miracles reported of Jesus is concerned, both Luke and Matthew have proportionately fewer than Mark. By my count, Mark has 18 miracle-stories and 4 summaries of miraculous activity, Luke has 20 stories and 3 summaries, and Matthew has 19 stories and 4 summaries. But since Mark is only about 57% of the length of Luke, and 63% the length of Matthew, it is apparent that miracles occupy a larger proportion of the total narrative in Mark than in either of the other two.

Luke has also been selective in his use of Mark's miracle-narratives, having ommitted six of them (Mark 6:45-52; 7:24-30; 7:31-37; 8:1-10; 8:22-26 and 11:12-14, 20) and adding eight of his own (5:1-11; 7:1-10; 7:11-17; 11:14; 17:11-19; 22:50-51; two others, while vaguely reminiscent of Mark 3:1-6, are sufficiently different, in my judgment, to be considered independent stories: 13:10-17; 14:1-6). Five of the six miracles which Luke has omitted occur in the "Great Omission" (Mark 6:45-8:26)[3] and the sixth is the cursing of the fig tree.[4] Luke is thus no more bound to the Markan miracle-traditions than he is to the other Markan materials and is as free in adding miracle-stories as he is in adding parables.

One of the miracles that Luke adds came from "Q" (7:1-10), although, as we shall see, the emphasis is different from that of the story in Matthew. Others may also have come from "Q" but since none are included in Matthew, we have no way of learning which, if any, did. Two of the stories are more concerned with the correct interpretation of the law than with the miracle (13:10-17; 14:1-6), and another wants to contrast the Jews' lack of faith with that of non-Jews (17:11-19; in this case a Samaritan), a point made in other stories in the Gospel (e.g., 10:30-35) and in Acts (13:36; 18:6; 19:8-9; 28:28). The call of Peter is set around a miracle in Luke (5:1-11), perhaps to emphasize that his preeminence came from being first to be called, as well as first to see the risen Lord (24:34), since the story bears similarities to a Johannine story of an appearance of the risen Lord (John 21:4-8). Another miracle is used to introduce the account of a controversy over miracles (11:14), characteristic of Luke, who likes to report miracles performed when miracles are discussed (see 7:21); and still another is so obvious (22:51 — the healing of the ear of the high-priest's servant) that one wonders how the other evangelists could have avoided it. The final story to be mentioned concerns Jesus' raising of a dead youth (7:11-17), an activity known both to Mark (5:35, 42)

---

[3]The reasons for this omission have long puzzled scholars. I have suggested elsewhere that Luke, perhaps aware of the two miracle-catenae that Mark had incorporated into his gospel, simply omitted the second catena, the contents of which roughly parallel Luke's omitted Markan material ("Toward the Isolation of Pre-Marcan Miracle Catenae," *JBL*, LXXXIX [1970], 265-91).

[4]Luke may have thought it unworthy of Jesus, although he is not averse in principle to punitive miracles: cf. Acts 5:1-10; 13:8-12. In that same section, he also omits mention of Jesus leaving Jerusalem after the temple-cleansing (cf. Mark 11:19; Matt 21:17), although he knows that is what Jesus did (Luke 21:37).

and "Q" (Matt. 11:5), and hence not in itself an unusual story.[5]

One way of getting at the Lukan perspective on Jesus' miracles is thus to compare what he includes as miracle stories with those included in one of his sources, viz., Mark. Another method of learning how Luke understood and used miracle-stories of Jesus is to compare what he did with the stories that he took from the source we have, again, Mark. A careful comparison will show, for example, that Luke attempts to remove ambiguities in the Markan narrative. For example, in his treatment of Mark 1:21-28, Luke makes it clear that the adverbial phrase *kat' exousian* is related to *epitassei*, eliminating the alternative possibility in Mark that it is related to *didachē kainē* (Mark 1:27). Again, Luke clears up the question inherent in Mark 1:45 (Who couldn't enter cities? Jesus? The healed leper?), by making it clear that *Jesus* remained in the wilderness (5:16). Again, Luke will smooth out a story by rearranging details (cf. Luke 8:40-42a, 49-55 with Mark 5:22-24, 35-43), or even by omitting them (cf. Luke 9:37-43 with Mark 9:14-29). Again, Luke will change the emphasis in a story, as in 4:31-37 (cf. Mark 1:21-28), where Jesus' mighty act and his teaching are paralleled, rather than having the miracle subordinated to Jesus' "new teaching," as in the Markan form of the story.[6]

Such a comparison also indicates that Luke can adapt a miracle in such a way that interest in pointed away from the recipient of the miracle and toward Jesus, e.g., 18:35-43, where many details about the blind man (Bartimaeus in Mark 10:46-52; Luke does not name him) are omitted, thus lessening our interest in him; or 8:42-48, where details about the woman with the flow of blood are similarly omitted. On the other hand, details about the one who requests the miracle can be added, thus heightening our interest in someone other than Jesus (cf. Luke 7:1-10 with Matt. 8:5-13, and the added details about the kind of man the centurion was).[7]

A third way of approaching the Lukan miracle stories is by way of formal analysis, i.e., to see at what points the stories no longer fit the typical form of a gospel miracle-story, which in turn may give us clues about the point Luke wants to make. To take Luke 7:1-10 again as an example, our analysis of the form will show that the "solution" has, in fact, been omitted. That is, we are never told how, or even that, Jesus healed the boy (that the story once contained such a solution can be seen in Matt. 8:13). The major point has thus become the fact that the

[5]There is a story told of Apollonius of Tyana that has some parallels; for a treatment of them, cf. G. Petzke, "Historizitat und Bedeutsamkeit von Wunderberichten," *Neues Testament und Christliche Existenz: Festschrift für Herbert Braun*, eds. H. D. Betz and L. Schottroff, pp. 367-85.

[6]Such changes are, of course, not unique to the miracles-stories. The fact that Luke exercises the same freedom in shaping the miracle-stories as he does in shaping the other traditions he receives, however, will become important when we consider some changes that Luke might have made in these miracle-traditions, but did not. His reticence there will have nothing to do with an unwillingness to modify such traditions in other ways; it is simply that point that we want to make here.

[7]Luke occasionally adds details that make the story more colorful, e.g., a child healed becomes for Luke an only child (7:12; 8:42; 9:38; the latter two Luke himself has changed from his sources); a sick youth is "valued" (7:2); a man's crippled hand is his right one (6:6). Such details have little apparent theological significance, except perhaps to make the stories more gripping, and thus more memorable.

centurion was worthy to receive the requested miracle (vs. 4), a point confirmed by his own humility (vs. 7; both points are absent in Matthew). Thus, while Matthew's point concerns the power of faith in healing,[8] Luke emphasizes the worthiness of a non-Jew to receive the benefits of Jesus' power. Formal analysis also indicates Luke's predilection for adding a reaction of the crowd, usually to praise God for what they have seen, an emphasis to which we will return in another context.

A fourth way of discerning Luke's intention in his use of miracle-stories told of Jesus is to note their placement in his narrative. Thus, for example, instead of placing the sending out of the twelve after Jesus' rejection in Nazareth (implying that he is now free to turn to others), as in Mark, or instead of introducing it with a statement on the need for harvesters (implying that the leaderless people need to hear Jesus' message), as in Matthew, Luke has it follow immediately on a series of four miracles, thus strengthening the impression that such activity was an important part of their mission. Again, Luke postpones the calling of disciples until after miracles are performed, both implied (4:23b) and discussed (4:25-27), and then presents the call of Peter (and, almost as an afterthought, James and John: 5:10a) in the context of a miracle of which Peter is a witness, hinting at the view that Luke held of the relationship between miracles and discipleship.

In such ways, then, it is possible to gain some insight into Luke's perspective on the significance and meaning of the miracles of Jesus. Let us turn now to consider some of the points that emerge when these ways of examining the miracle-accounts in the Third Gospel are undertaken.

II

A clue to the importance Luke finds in the miraculous activity of Jesus can be seen in the way in which he, in several instances, attempts to balance Jesus' miraculous activity and his teaching in such a way as to give them equal weight. An indication of this balancing can be seen in the fact that Jesus' first sermon (4:23-27) has as its contents a justification of Jesus' activity as miracle-worker (4:23-27) as well as references to his activity as proclaimer (4:18-22). The programmatic nature of that sermon has long been recognized by commentators.

Such balancing is also indicated in the manner in which Luke reproduces the first miracle story in Mark (Mark 1:21-28). In its Markan form, the account clearly brackets the miracle with references to Jesus' teaching.[9] In Luke (4:31-37), on the other hand, the teaching is limited to the opening verses (31-32), after which the healing is recited. In that way, Luke transforms the reaction of the crowd (vss.

---

[8]So H. J. Held, "Matthew as Interpreter," pp. 196, 274.

[9]I am impressed by the evidence that indicates that Mark is responsible for giving the story this framework is vss. 21-22, 27-28, and should argue that such a way of presenting Jesus' first miracle in his Gospel is programmatic for the way he understood Jesus' activity as miracle-worker. Matthew seems to do the same by presenting first (chs. 5-7) an example of Jesus' teaching, and only then (chs. 8-9) an example of his miracle working. Unfortunately, a detailed justification of such assertions is not possible within the limits of this study.

36-37) into a reaction to the miracles alone, and not to Jesus teaching. And both teaching (vs. 32) and miracle-working (vs. 36) are examples of Jesus' activity *en exousia.* In its Lukan form, then, the story tells first of Jesus' teaching, and then of his miracle, thus balancing them, rather than subordinating the one to the other.

In a similar way, when Luke (5:12-16) gives the Markan account of the healing of the leper (Mark 1:40-45), he concludes it by noting that the great crowds who came to Jesus as a result of the news of that healing, came to hear *and* to be healed of their diseases (5:17). Again, *both* characterize the activity of Jesus. Further evidence of such balance is also to be found in the way Luke has arranged his Gospel in chs. 6-7. Luke has followed Mark closely, beginning with the account of the healing at Capernaum (Mark 1:21; Luke 4:31) through the healing of the withered hand on the Sabbath (Mark 3:6; Luke 6:11—Luke's one deviation was to insert 5:1-11). But he then inverts Mark's order (Mark 3:7-19), placing first the choosing of the Twelve, then a summary of mircles (Luke 6:12-19), and then the "Sermon on the Plain." That "Sermon" is then immediately followed by a series of miracles (7:1-17). In this way, Luke has bracketed his long teaching-session of Jesus (6:20-49) with Jesus' activity as miracle-worker (6:17b-19; 7:1-17), being unwilling, apparently, to emphasize the one at the expense of the other.[10]

Within that section of Mark which Luke followed, he has also made some changes in source which further reflect a balancing of proclamation and miracle-working. In the account of the man with the withered hand (Mark 3:1-6), Luke begins by adding specific mention of the fact that Jesus *taught* in the synagogue before the healing occurred (6:6), something Mark did not do. In giving the Markan summary of healings (Mark 3:7-12), Luke makes a subtle change to introduce the element of teaching by changing the Markan reference to the crowds coming because they heard what Jesus *did* (i.e., miracles, Mark 3:8), to an indication that they came "in order to hear him *and* be healed of their diseases" (Luke 6:18). Thus Luke again balances the two activities by introducing (in this case, teaching) into an account of the other (miracles). Again, in Luke's only account of the feeding of the multitudes, he adds to the Markan mention that Jesus taught the crowds (Mark 6:34) reference to the fact that Jesus also healed those who needed it (Luke 9:11).[11] In these ways, then, it would appear, Luke has balanced Jesus' teaching and his miraculous acts, by carefully mentioning the other when his source contained only one.

A second result that emerges from a study of the miracle-stories in Luke centers on the importance of Jesus. Such importance is evident in the fact that Luke will frequently change a detail in a miracle-story to show that Jesus must not be disobeyed. For example, in Mark's account of the cleansing of the leper (1:40-45), although the leper is sternly warned not to speak to anyone of his cure (vs. 43), he does so anyway (vs. 45). In Luke's version (5:12-16), the "report" of the

---

[10]Matthew has the same general order; but, in his arrangement, specific miracle stories come only *after* the long discourse, indicating, I think, their subordinate importance. Note also the inversion of Matt 4:24 (healings) and 4:25 (crowds) in Luke: to 6:17 (crowds) and 6:18-19 (healings).

[11]Luke is obviously drawing on Mark 6:34 at this point, because in the second account of the feeding in Mark (8:1-10), there is no mention in the introduction of any activity of Jesus that would have delayed the crowds. In Matthew's account of the first feeding (14:13-21), he mentions only healing, not teaching (14:14).

event simply "goes out" (vs. 15a), thus lifting responsibility for disobedience from the leper. Again, when Luke (5:17-26) takes over from Mark (2:1-12) the story of the paralytic let down through the roof, he specifically adds the detail that the cured man did, in fact, return to his own home (vs. 25b), as Jesus had commanded him (vs. 24b). Mark may have understood such compliance as implied in his phrasing of 2:12a, but Luke makes it specific. This carries through even to so small a point as the fact that the man with the withered hand, commanded to stand up, does so (Luke 6:8), while in Mark, compliance with Jesus' command to the man to "come here" is never indicated (3:3). Similarly, in the story of the demoniac in the Capernaum synagogue, Luke displaces the detail of the loud cry from the exciting demon (Mark 1:26) to the demon's initial remarks (Luke 4:33), in that way making the demon obedient to Jesus' command to him to be silent (Luke 4:35). In the Markan account, that final cry comes *after* Jesus' command to silence (Mark 1:25-26). In a somewhat similar way, Jesus' importance is indicated in two short notices Luke has placed at the beginning and the end of Jesus' public career. In 4:30, Jesus simply "passes through the midst" of a murderous lynch mob; and in 22:51, the presence of a similar mob does not deter him from an act of compassion: he heals the wounded ear of a member of that mob. In both acts, Jesus, despite the threatening circumstances, shows he is in complete control of the situation, thus pointing to his importance; whatever the situation, he remains in control. The elimination of detail about other characters in two miracle-stories that Luke got from Mark (8:42b-48; 9:37-43) similarly points to the importance of Jesus in the Lukan narrative.

More importantly, however, Luke's treatment of Jesus' miracles shows the importance of Jesus in the fact that miracles have the capacity to validate Jesus. This is most clearly seen precisely in the passage where Jesus is, in fact, asked to validate himself: the question posed to him by John the Baptist (7:18-23; Matt. 11:2-6 "Q"). In Matthew, although the question is raised because John hears about "the deeds" of Jesus, the immediate context is the missionary activity of the disciples, indicating this as the cause of John's question. In Luke, on the other hand, the immediate context is two miracle-stories (7:1-17), indicating that "all the things" John heard about were miracles. Thus, the question of Jesus' validity is posed, in Luke, by miracles. Luke then also understands that they will answer the question. Between the question and Jesus' answer, Luke inserts the information that "in that hour" Jesus performed a variety of miracles and then told John's disciples to report on what they had *seen* and heard (in Matthew, on what they "hear and see!"). Clearly, miracles will answer the question of who Jesus is, and hence they have the power of validating his claims about himself.

That validating power is also indicated in the typically Lukan response to a miracle of Jesus, i.e., praising God, indicating the source of Jesus' power. For example, Mark's ambiguous *kyrios* in Jesus' statement in 5:19 ("tell them how much the *kyrios* has done for you"—Jesus? God?), identified in vs. 20 by the cured demoniac as Jesus, is changed in Luke 8:39 to "God" ("declare how much *ho theos* has done for you"), thus making explicit Jesus' identification of the power by which he performs such acts. This is also very likely the intention of the puzzling phrase at the end of Luke 5:17 ("and the power of the Lord was with him to heal"—the Greek is not entirely clear). It is to identify by what power Jesus performed such acts.

If, then, Luke understood the miracles to have the capacity to validate Jesus, and show the source of his power, two questions immediately follow. If miracles validate Jesus, do they also validate faith in him? And, secondly, if God is the source of Jesus' power, to what extent is Luke influenced in hs understanding of Jesus' miracles by views of magic and magicians that saturated the Hellenistic world? Let us consider them in that order.

First, then, the question of miracles and faith: Can Jesus' miraculous activity serve as the basis of faith? It would be surprising, given the way in which Acts is written, if the answer were to be negative. It is rather clear in Acts that miracles were an effective device for turning people to faith. Peter healed a paralytic, "and all the residents of Lydda and Sharon saw him, and they turned to the Lord" (Acts 9:35). Peter raised Tabitha from the dead, "and it became known throughout all Joppa, and many believed in the Lord" (9:42). When Sergius Paulus saw Elymas the magician blinded by Paul's curse, he "believed" (13:12). The jailer, upon observing the earthquake that broke open the prison for Paul and Silas, asks about faith and is then baptized (16:30, 33). When the seven sons of the Jewish high priest Sceva were routed by demons as they attempted an unbelieving use of Jesus' name, that very name was "extolled" (19:17). J. A. Hardon has shown rather convincingly that in the narrative in Acts, "at every point where the Gospel was first established among a certain people, the foundation was made in a miraculous context, with manifest showing of signs and powers worked by the hands of the Apostles."[12] The many references to "signs and wonders" performed by the apostles (2:43; 5:12; 6:8; 8:6; 14:3; 15:12) make clear Luke's view in this matter. In fact, even a non-Christian could gain a hearing for himself through such acts (Simon, 8:9-11).[13]

Although the evidence for the fact that miracles can be the basis of belief in God is not so massive in Luke's treatment of the miracles of Jesus as it is in Acts, it is nevertheless also present. This can perhaps be most clearly seen in the way Luke characteristically concludes such narratives. For example, there are regular references to the praise of God by those who witness the miracle of Jesus, or by the one who benefitted from it (5:25; 7:16; 9:43; 13:13; 17:15; 18:43), and in one instance, such a reaction is specified by Jesus as the proper response (17:18). While fear is a usual reaction in Luke to manifestations of the divine (e.g., 1:12; 1:65; 2:9; cf. 1:30, where it is implied), Luke also connected it with faith (e.g., Acts 2:43 in its context). Such fear is, then, also a characteristic reaction in Luke's telling of the miracle-stories (5:26; 7:16; 8:35, 37; cf. also 24:5). Thus, in Luke, the reaction to miracles is to see God behind the activity of Jesus, thus acknowledging Jesus to be the one whom God has chosen to do his work. Such an identification of Jesus surely belongs to Luke's understanding of faith (see, e.g., Acts 2:22-23, 36; 1:13; 4:27; 10:38).

The idea that the miracles lead legitimately to faith in Jesus is also shown in some more subtle ways in Luke's narrative. There is, for example, an emphasis on "seeing" which is not found in his sources. For example, in 10:23-24 (Matt 13:16-17 "Q"), Luke does not balance the first sentence ("Blessed are the eyes

---

[12]See "The Miracle Narratives," esp. his discussion beginning on p. 310; the quotation is from p. 311.

[13]This point becomes the basis for the contest of miracles (and, therefore, of faith) in the *Actus Vercellenses*, 32 between Peter and Simon. Peter wins the contest, and therefore the people specifically believe   in Peter and his God, not in Simon and his.

which see what you see") with any reference to "ears" or "hearing," as does Matthew. If that balance was in the "Q" source, Luke chose to alter it; if it was not in the source, Luke did not feel compelled, as did Matthew, to balance "seeing" with "hearing." In either case, the emphasis on "seeing" is clear. Again, in his account of the triumphal entry, Luke gives as the reason for the crowds' praise of Jesus the "mighty works which they had seen" (19:37), an emphasis on "seeing," indeed on the importance of miracles, for the confession of Jesus as the one who comes in the Lord's name, found in neither of the other synoptic gospels. In the account of the response to the Baptist's question, Luke, unlike Matthew (11:4), refers to what John's disciples have first "seen," and then "heard." In the same way, Cleopas' response about Jesus puts "deed" before "word," again giving pride of place to Jesus' mighty acts. Perhaps the same emphasis can be seen in the fact that the content of Jesus' first sermon in Luke (4:16-30) is Jesus' miracles, not the kingdom of God (contrast Mark 1:14-15).

Luke's view that faith legitimately follows miracles also underlies the difficulties in the narrative of the healing of the 10 lepers (17:11-19). The conclusion, "Rise and go your way; your faith has made you well" (vs. 19), spoken to the Samaritan who returned, implies that his return was a manifestation of the faith which healed him. But that does not comport well with the earlier statement that he, along with his nine companions, had already been healed (vs. 14b), or that the nine who showed no such faith were healed despite that fact. But if the order of events in the story is confused, the conclusion is not: Praise of God and gratitude to Jesus (= faith) are the proper response to a miracle of Jesus. That, it appears, is the point Luke wanted to make, and he was so intent on making it that he either wittingly, or unwittingly, distorted the story itself in order to make it. The context confirms that such was Luke's intention: 17:1-19 is organized around the question: "What is faith?" (it forgives, vss. 1-4; it can do all things, vss. 5-6; it is humble, vss. 7-10, and grateful, vss. 11-19). The point of the "miracle-story," therefore, is faith, and the story is reshaped to make that point. That a miracle-story suggested itself to Luke as a vehicle to illustrate the nature of faith is significant for his view of the relationship between the two.

All of this is not to say that Luke had no indication in his sources that miracles could and should lead to a faithful response to Jesus. "Q," for example, holds that those who have not responded correctly to Jesus' miracles (by repentance) are culpable (10:13-14 // Matt 11:21-23). Similarly, the saying about the relationship of miracles and the kingdom of God (11:20 // Matt 12:28) gives the basis for a faithful response to miracles: Jesus' mighty acts are done by God's own power. It acknowledges what is the proper response to the miracles. Such a view of miracles was apparently so widespread in the primitive church that Paul took it for granted when he defended the legitimacy of his apostleship (see I Cor 2:4; Rom 15:18-20). But Luke, more than any other gospel writer, has developed this idea in his two-volume work.[14]

A clear and supportive corollary to this emphasis on faith legitimately growing out of the observation of miracles, rests in the fact that for Luke, miracles are clearly the basis for discipleship. This is most evident in the way Luke has narrated the call of the first disciples, Peter, James, and John. Luke's source,

---

[14]John also knows this kind of tradition (cf. 2:11; 4:53; 6:14; 11:15); but he has included counter-emphases (e.g., 20:29), which I do not find in Luke.

Mark, placed the calling of the first disciples after a summary of Jesus' proclamation (1:14-15) and before there was any hint of Jesus' wondrous power. In Luke, on the other hand, Jesus' ability to perform miracles has been amply demonstrated (4:31-41) and reported (4:23) before there is any mention of calling disciples. Further, the story within which the call of the first disciples is placed (5:1-11) leaves little room for doubt that they followed Jesus because of his wondrous power. Only after Peter, James, and John see the miraculous catch of fish, are they summoned to follow Jesus. In fact, the implication is clear that it was seeing that miracle that prepared Peter to see in Jesus one who ought to be followed. Luke has further altered the Markan order so that even before his call, Peter had seen Jesus heal his mother-in-law. Thus Peter (but not James and John, in Luke) had known of Jesus' wondrous powers some time prior to his call.

Similarly, the second account of the calling of a disciple in Luke (Levi, 5:27) follows immediately after a miracle, identified as such by a technical term (*paradoxos,* vs. 26). Again, Luke has modified his source. In Mark, there is interposed between the healing of the paralytic and the call of Levi the statement that Jesus taught the crowd (Mark 2:13). Luke has omitted this reference, thus clearly implying that, again, a disciple followed Jesus because of a miracle.[15]

Again, Luke is the only evangelist who mentions that the women who followed Jesus were women whom Jesus had cured, specifically Mary Magdalene, from whom Jesus had expelled seven demons (8:2-3). The fact that they are identified both as followers, and as recipients of wondrous acts from Jesus, adds further evidence that Luke understood discipleship as intimately connected to knowledge of Jesus' ability to perform mighty acts. Even the sending out of the Twelve has been arranged in such a way by Luke that it follows immediately on a series of four miracles, showing again the close connection between discipleship and Jesus' mighty power.

Clearly, then, for Luke, knowledge of Jesus' miracles is a legitimate cause for faith in him. This was true not only for the disciples whom Jesus himself called, but also for the followers later won by apostolic activity. In Luke as in Acts, acceptance of the call to follow Jesus, whether as a disciple or in faith, is intimately connected with the miraculous activity of Jesus.

We must turn now to consider the extent to which magical beliefs, so prevalent in the Hellenistic world, influenced the way in which Luke understood and presented the miracles of Jesus. J. Hull, in his recent book, *Hellenistic Magic and the Synoptic Tradition,* has argued strongly that of all the gospels, Luke was most strongly influenced by such magical belief. "Luke wrote about magic because he saw and believed."[16] I find his argument unconvincing, partly

---

[15]It may well be that Luke intends ch. 5 to show correct and incorrect responses to Jesus and his miraculous power. The response of Peter, James, John, and Levi is the correct response. The response of the Pharisees, on the other hand, who also saw Jesus' miraculous power (cf. vs. 17 with vs. 26; Luke has added the information that Pharisees and teachers of the law came from the whole Jewish homeland in vs. 17, thus generalizing their response) is incorrect; they carp at him (vss. 30-33). Vs. 39 is then as explanatory summary of the chapter: the unaccountable refusal of Pharisees to accept Jesus is due to their clinging to the old Law (vs. 39: "And no one, after drinking old wine, desires new; for he says, 'the old is good' "). They are nonetheless culpable, because they have also seen Jesus' wondrous power (cf. 6:11).

[16]P. 86. See the whole of ch. 6. "Luke, the Tradition Penetrated by Magic."

because some evidence cited is speculative, partly because it could be cited of other gospels as well, and partly because some distinctions he makes are without difference.

For example, Hull assumes that "the mature Christ experienced fluctuations in the activity of his power"[17] (an idea long since proposed by S. Eitrem,[18] to whom Hull does not refer), without providing any supportive evidence. In fact, that supposition rests on a view of the historical validity of individual stories and their arrangement in the gospels which form- and redaction-critical studies have simply rendered outmoded.

Again, when Hull argues that to regard objects as an effective means of cure, because they come from the person of the "divine king" (e.g., clothing, spittle), he is referring to a belief that pervades all four gospels, and it can hardly be said to be Luke's special emphasis, Acts 19:11-12 to the contrary notwithstanding (see Mark 5:25-34; 8:22-26; Matt 9:20-22; John 9:1-7). Further, I find pointless Hull's repeated assertion[19] that Luke's addition of the word "power" to the "authority" that Jesus granted the disciples in Matthew and Mark (Luke 9:1; Matt 10:1; Mark 3:15) somehow gives them greater control over the demonic, thus further showing Luke's magical views. It is clear that Matthew and Mark mean as surely as Luke that Jesus' disciples were given power as well as authority over the demonic (cf. Matt 10:1, where "authority" clearly includes power to cast them out). And Mark is just as sure that Jesus cast out the demon when people remarked on his authority (1:27) as is Luke when he has them note Jesus' authority and power (4:36).

All of this is not to say that all such emphasis on "magic" is absent from Luke's accounts of Jesus' miracles. Luke makes explicit why people wanted to touch him: because when they did, power went forth from Jesus to heal them (cf. Luke 6:19 with Mark 3:10 — Mark also knows they sought to touch him, but Luke makes the reason explicit). That "power" is here thought of as objective — to touch Jesus is to contact that power and thus be healed (cf. Acts 5:15; 19:11-12). In the story of the woman with the flow of blood, Luke puts into direct speech the remark that Jesus felt power go forth form him, perhaps showing the same tendency (cf. Luke 8:46 with Mark 5:30). That Luke also thought in such objective terms is shown also in his treatment of the feeding of the multitudes, where he adds *autous* after *eulogēsen* (9:16), thus making bread the object of the blessing, rather than understanding it as the Jewish blessing of God before eating (*bārul* *ᵓattāh* *ᵓ ᵃdonāi* *ᵓᵉlohēnū* . . .). Perhaps Luke thinks that Jesus' blessing on the bread caused it to multiply.

If, however, Luke, does contain some indication of an increasingly magical view of Jesus' miracles, it also contain indications that point in the opposite direction, i.e., that Luke pictures Jesus' miracles in less magical ways than his sources. For example, in the story of the raising of Jairus' daughter (8:40-42a, 49-55), Luke omits the foreign phrase (Mark 5:41), a device that was part of the

---

[17]*Ibid.*, p. 106.

[18]"Some Notes on the Demonology in the NT," *Symbolae Osloenses;* Fasc. Sup. XX.

[19]*Hellenistic Magic*, pp. 107, 115.

repertoire of every magician,[20] and Luke strengthens the impression, by his phrasing of vs. 50 (to "only believe," he adds the phrase "and she shall be saved") that Jairus' faith is an important element in the cure. Again, unlike Hellenistic magicians, Jesus performs his cures openly and allows bystanders to hear what he says in the course of the wondrous act. In raising the young man of Nain (7:11-17), for example, his words to the dead youth are clearly heard. Contrast with that a similar story told of Apollonius of Tyana (Philostratus, *Life* 4. 45) in which he raises a girl by means of a formula whispered "in secret" (*aphanòs*). Luke also omits from the story of the "epileptic" boy (9:37-43) all advice on how to cast out especially difficult demons (cf. Mark 9:29), thus discouraging "do-it-yourself" exorcists from the thought that with some magic formula they could reproduce the act. And, unlike the similarity to sympathetic magic by which Jesus in Mark raises Peter's mother-in-law (he causes her to assume the position of one who is well by pulling her up bodily), in Luke the act is accomplished merely by a word.

Another aspect to which Hull points as evidence of the penetration of magic into Luke's understanding of Jesus is the realm of demons. Arguing that, while magic does not necessarily presume demons, presentation of the demonic almost inevitably includes magic, Hull concludes that Luke has a special emphasis on the demonic. To be sure, Luke does picture the healing of Peter's mother-in-law, contrary to his source, as an exorcism (cf. Luke 4:38-39 with Mark 1:30-31), yet in another instance, Luke omits the words from Mark which imply that the stilling of the storm was an exorcism (cf. Mark 4:39 and 1:25 with Luke 8:24). It is of further interest to note that the one additional story Luke has about demonic possession — the crippled woman, 13:10-13 — is presented in a framework (vss. 14-17) which makes it clear that the interest of that tradition is not in demonic possession, but in the contradiction between Pharisaic belief about the law and their own practices. Jesus' words about the law put his adversaries to shame and caused the people to rejoice, not specifically the exorcism. Similarly in 14:1-6, we have here a miracle-story which has been adapted to make another point altogether, and thus, for all practical purposes, it no longer functions within the tradition as a miracle-story. It now concerns primarily Jesus' dispute about the true intention of the Jewish law.

There can be no question that Luke does understand Jesus' ministry as a successful battle against Satan (cf. 10:18). The way Luke phrases 11:21-22 (cf. Matt 12:29) as the interpretation of vs. 20 makes it clear that with the appearance of Jesus as the stronger one, Satan's "goods," i.e., those he possesses, are in fact being despoiled, a despoliation that continues in the work of the apostles (cf. Acts 16:16-18). But it is also clear that Luke is by no means preoccupied with Jesus' battle with the demonic, and in his telling, the exorcisms have lost the technical vocabulary of Hellenistic demon-exorcism by means of which Mark, for example, has described them.[21] Thus, the adjuration of the demon against Jesus by means

---

[20]Too much weight cannot be put on this point, however, since Luke omits all foreign phrases in his account of Jesus; cf. Luke's record of the last words of Jesus in ch. 23. Yet a "tradition penetrated by magic" would hardly follow such a practice of eliminating recitation of powerful magic formulae.

[21]This point is convincingly made in O. Bauernfeind, *Die Worte der Damonen im Markusevangelium*, pp. 100-1.

of a phrase similar to that used in Hellenistic accounts (Mark 5:7) has become, in Luke 8:28, simply a plea to Jesus.

In sum, there is as much evidence that Luke has toned down the magical aspects of Jesus' miracles, as there is that he presents such stories under the particular influence of the Hellenistic understanding of magic. In fact, the Jesus of Luke appears less influenced by magical practices than the Jesus in Mark. That Luke is writing for people who understood, and perhaps even credited, magical practices could hardly be denied; but he does more, I would argue, to combat such belief than he does, if only inadvertently, to foster it (cf. Acts 13:6-11; 19:18-19). His presentation of the miracles of Jesus, in any case, can hardly be described as "traditions penetrated by magic" (Hull's phrase).

There is, on the other hand, no question that Luke does put a certain emphasis on the wondrous aspects of Jesus' career. Of all the gospels, for example, Luke begins his narrative more massively with the miraculous, not only in the first two chapters, but also in the accounts of Jesus himself. After the programmatic first sermon in ch. 4, whose content, as we have frequently noted, concerns Jesus miracles, Jesus does little preaching (4:31-32; 5:1; 5:17 refer to it), but many miracles. Luke is, to be sure, following Mark's outline. Yet although Mark has miracles in the first three chapters before he gives the content of a session of teaching (ch. 4), Mark places all of Jesus' activities under the rubric of proclamation (1:14-15), and, as we have seen, places his first programmatic miracle within the framework of Jesus' power as teacher (1:21-28). Luke follows this order, but with some significant changes. He omits Mark 1:14-15 altogether, he lessens the stress on teaching in Mark's first miracle, and he displaces until later, and then subordinates to miraculous deeds the call of the disciples.

Again, there are hints in the body of Luke's gospel that, in his understanding, Jesus can summarize his own career in terms of his mighty acts. His reaction to the Baptist's question, a reaction that involves the added performance of the miracles, is an example. Again, when threatened by Herod, Jesus sums up his career with the words: "Behold, I cast out demons and perform cures" (13:32). The implication of the whole passage (vss. 31-33) seems to be that such activity on the part of Jesus ultimately causes his death (vs. 33); nevertheless, Jesus must finish his predestined course. And Luke alone records that in the midst of his fatal crisis, Jesus continues to function as a wondrous healer (22:50-51—this event seems to serve the same function as Matt 26:53: Jesus' power remains intact but he chooses not to use it to save himself).

Along the same line, Luke understands that Jesus' fame is based more on his mighty acts than on his teaching. The spread of Jesus' fame in Luke 4:37, for example, omits the Markan emphasis on Jesus' teaching (Mark 1:28). Similarly, the report in Luke 5:15 is no longer due to the leper's spreading the word, as in Mark 1:45. Rather, the report about Jesus simply goes forth, clearly based on the wondrous act. A third summary (7:17) has been added by Luke, as the condition of Jesus' raising of the youth of Nain. As a result of his view, it is quite in keeping that Luke would understand Herod to have known of Jesus chiefly as a wonder-worker (23:8). The prominence of mighty acts for Luke's understanding of the origins of the faith is also clear in the uniquely Lukan account of the sending out of the Seventy. Given the power to heal (10:9), they single out at their return as the most impressive characteristic of their mission (vs. 17), and vs. 19 confirms the miraculous nature of the power Jesus has given them. The results of such power then are evident in the narrative in Acts, with its regular and frequent mention of the miraculous acts of the disciples, both in general and in specific cases.[22]

III

With the conclusion of our rapid survey of the Lukan perspective on Jesus' miracles, we may underline one or two points that have emerged. Perhaps most important is the impression that of all the gospels, Luke appears to have a more unambiguous reliance on the possibility that miracles, and thus miracle-stories, can serve as the basis for faith in Jesus. They also serve more clearly in Luke to validate Jesus as the one sent by God. To be sure, such conclusions are a matter of degree. Obviously, all gospel authors thought miracle-stories important for faith and for understanding Jesus or they would not have included them in their accounts of his career. The apocryphal gospels show clearly enough that religious tracts about Jesus could be written with no reference to Jesus' miracles at all (e.g., *Coptic Gospel of Thomas, Gospel of Truth,* etc.). Yet of the canonical gospels, Luke seems to view the miracles with a less critical eye,[23] according them, in a number of subtle ways, a more important role in his account of Jesus. A glance at Acts confirms that impression and shows the extent to which Luke understood the miraculous to play an important, if not, indeed, a central role, in the origins of the Christian church.

Luke has done this, I would argue, in full awareness of the magical views and practices which pervaded the Hellenistic world. Indeed, no author of that period, it would seem, could have been unaware of them. Yet Luke has not subordinated his presentation of Jesus to a magical world-view. If he shares to a greater extent than the other gospel authors the importance that his Hellenistic contemporaries accorded to such phenomena, he has not, to the extent Hull has proposed, allowed the traditions of the faith to be penetrated by magic. Perhaps, in the end, the author of the Third Gospel is, of all evangelists, most closely attuned to the Hellenistic world for which he writes, and his perspective on the miracles of Jesus has been shaped accordingly.

In fact, Luke's accounts of the miracles of Jesus are remarkable for the extent

---

[22]The extent of miracles reported or mentioned in Acts is indicated in the following survey; miracles generally mentioned of apostles and disciples: 2:43; 4:30; 5:12, 5:16; miracles attributed to specific people; Jesus: 2:22; 10:38; Peter: 3:2-8; 5:9-11; 5:15; 9:32-34; 9:36-41; Stephen: 6:8; Philip: 8:6; 8:13; 8:39; Paul: 13:9-11; 14:9-10; 16:16-18; 19:11-12; 20:9-10; 28:3-6; 28:8; 28:9; Paul and Barnabas: 14:3; 15:12. In addition, there are three miraculous releases from bondage: 5:19; 12:6-10; 16:25-26.

[23]A good perspective on the more critical use that Matthew makes of the miracle-tradition can be seen in the way he has adapted the miracle-stories to other points; cf. the essay by H. J. Held (see note 1 above). I would urge that the miracle with which Matthew chose to conclude his collection of miracles, 9:32-34, indicates that he saw them as essentially ambiguous in their witness to Jesus, being open to widely differing interpretations. Even the greatest of all wondrous acts, the resurrection, is open to ambiguity; note the second phrase of 28:17. We have already mentioned John 20:26-29 as an indication of the Johannine critique of a faith based on miracles. I have atempted to show the critical handling that the miracle-traditions received in Mark's hands in my article on pre-Markan miracle-catenae ("Toward the Isolation . . .," see note 3 above; "The Origin and Function of the pre-Markan Miracle Catenae," *JBL,* XC [1972], 198-221).

to which they have remained unaffected by any attempt to link them to the thought-world of the OT. In light of some explicit statements to the effect that in Jesus, prophecies are fulfilled (e.g., Luke 24:27, 44; Acts 10:32-33; cf. also 2:25-31; 3:22-26; 13:32-37 — all in speeches in Acts), and in light of the way Luke introduces Jesus' ministry in 4:16-30, one would expect some indication that Jesus' miracles, as narrated in Luke, did in fact perform that function. This is made all the more likely by the fact that in that introduction to Jesus' public ministry, Jesus, immediately after claiming that he is the fulfillment of prophecy (Luke 4:18-20), relates in his own defense two miracles, one of Elijah and one of Elisha. If one is not thus to expect Jesus' miracles to resemble specifically those of Elijah and Elisha, at the least one would expect them to fulfill OT prophetic motifs. Yet strangely, Luke has not shaped the miracle-stories of Jesus in that direction, neither those he got from Mark, nor those from "Q," nor those from his special source. In the one story (Luke 7:11-17) which quotes a phrase from a miracle of Elijah (Luke 17:15b = 1 Kgs [3 Kgdms] 17:23 LXX), the story is so close to a similar one told of Apollonius of Tyana by Philostratus (*Life*, 4.45) that the question of a common source could be raised.[24] While the typically Lukan ending of a miracle of Jesus (glorifying God) may imply fulfillment of prophecy (e.g., 7:16), it need not (e.g., 5:26). That is, in the Lukan ending, "glorifying God" does not equal fulfillment of OT prophecy, or fulfillment of God's prophetic word. That miracles point to God is clear in Luke, but that in itself is not sufficient to affirm that Luke shapes the miracles of Jesus to serve the theological motif of fulfillment of prophecy. That Luke would find precedents for Jesus' miracles in the OT could hardly be denied, but he shares that insight with the entire synoptic tradition. We are concerned here with special Lukan emphases, and fulfillment of prophecy by the miracles of Jesus does not seem to be one of them.

A second possible way Luke could have attempted to link Jesus to the OT may be mentioned, i.e., by designating Jesus as "prophet" in order to tie him to OT traditions. Indeed, the only miracle-workers available for such linking to the OT were prophets (Moses, Elijah, and Elisha). Did Luke identify Jesus as a miracle-worker because such activity was expected of a prophet? The evidence does not appear to support such a suggestion.[25]

Of seven references to Jesus as "prophet" in Luke, two have as their focus the knowledge that Jesus, as a prophet, ought to have (7:39; 22:64), two give identifications of Jesus by the people (9:8, 19), one is a self-designation (13:33), and two, from special Lukan sources, refer to miracles (7:16, crowd reaction; 24:19, identification of Jesus by Cleopas and his companion).[26] One could also

---

[24]For a more detailed exposition of this question, see G. Petzke, "Historizität," pp. 371-8.

[25]While Jesus does seem to refer to himself as prophet in Luke (13:33), the reference has to do more with Jesus' impending death than with his miracles (cf. 11:49-50; 13:34), even though it appears in a context in which miracles are mentioned (13:32). There is another possible such self-designation in 4:24; but, again, although in a context in which miracles are mentioned, the emphasis is this saying on prophet is not on miracles. It is perhaps worth noting that John the Baptist is also called "prophet" in Luke's gospel (1:76; 7:26; 20:6), in one instance by Jesus himself (7:26)!

[26]I remain unpersuaded by the efforts of M. H. Miller (*The Character of Miracles in Luke-Acts*) to demonstrate Luke's attempt to shape miracles in terms of the OT. He has allowed the accounts in Acts to influence excessively what he sees in the Gospel and is able to find

cite the fact that in the programmatic opening-sermon in Nazareth, Jesus compares himself to the miracle-working Elijah (4:25-26) and Elisha (4:27). Such hints are not, however, carried through in any systematic, or even perfunctory, way, when Luke makes use of his miracle traditions. That is to say, while Luke is quite willing to change and adapt the miracle-stories he receives, he does not adapt them to make the point that when Jesus does such things, he is acting as one would expect a prophet to act. The one observable addition to a received tradition, where Luke identifies Jesus as prophet,occurs in the form of a hostile remark on Jesus' lack of appropriate knowledge (7:39; cf. Mark 14:4-5). If Luke did think of Jesus as prophet because he did the things a prophet was to do, Luke did not in any consistent way adapt the miracles-stories of Jesus to make that point.

It is perhaps worth noting, in conclusion, that few if any of the themes normally identified as characteristically Lukan emerge from Luke's telling of the miracles. This is all the more strange in the light of Luke's apparent willingness to adapt the miracle-stories in Acts to such theological motifs. It is clear that Luke is quite willing to adapt and change accounts of the miracles of Jesus. It is not clear why he has not adapted them in ways one would have expected him to, given his theological outlook. The answer to that problem must await further reflection in this particular area of NT scholarship.

---

allusions to the OT where I am not, on occasion even in "unquoted portions" of an OT text (e.g., p. 162). The work also suffers from a lack of clarity in distinguishing between what is characteristic of synoptic miracles in general, and what is uniquely Lukan.

The Prayer Motif in Luke-Acts

Allison A. Trites

Until recent years, the subject of "prayer" in the Bible was frequently overlooked by biblical scholars. This neglect was certainly felt in the area of New Testament studies. In 1965 a German-speaking scholar by the name of Wilhelm Ott addressed himself to this problem. Noting that Luke had often been called "the evangelist of prayer," he drew attention to the fact that the precise significance of this designation had never been properly assessed.[1]

Ott attempted to meet this need by a monograph on Lukan prayer,[2] concentrating on the didactic material of the Third Gospel (notably the Parable of the Unjust Judge, Lk. 18:1-8). In contrast to Matthew, who presents prayer as an expectation of God's coming, Ott understood the Lukan emphasis to be: men "ought always to pray and not lose heart" (Lk. 18:1). Thus he interpreted Jesus' example at prayer as giving strength to this Lukan demand for unceasing petition which was set against the background of: "(1) temptations which began with the

---

[1] P. T. O'Brien, "Prayer in Luke-Acts," *TB*, XXIV (1973), 111. On the general subject one may consult P. R. Baelz, *Prayer and Providence: A Background Study* and F. Heiler, *Prayer: A Study in the History and Psychology of Religion.* On prayer in the Bible see C. W. F. Smith, "Prayer," *The Interpreter's Dictionary of the Bible,* ed. G. A. Buttrick, III, 857-67, who notes that "books on biblical prayer are notoriously lacking, especially in English" (p. 867). Cf. J. Bauer and H. Zimmermann, "Prayer," *Sacramentum Verbi,* pp. 679-86. For two nontechnical studies see Fred L. Fisher, *Prayer in the New Testament,* and Donald Coggan, *The Prayers of the New Testament.*

[2] W. Ott, *Gebet und Heil. Die Bedeutung der Gebetsparänese in der lukanische Theologie.* Cf. O. G. Harris *Prayer in Luke-Acts: A Study in the Theology of Luke,* and, more generally, A. Hamman, *La prière. I. Le Nouveau Testament.* For the purposes of this essay, the author of Luke-Acts is assumed to be Luke.

passion of Jesus and would continue; and (2) the church would remain in the world for an indefinitely long period of time, and its members would not be stifled."[3]

Despite its valuable contributions, especially to an understanding of Lukan paraenetic material on prayer, Ott's study exhibited several weaknesses which scholars have been quick to point out. In the first place, his treatment of prayer in the Acts of the Apostles is altogether too cursory; his thirteen-page survey by no means exhausts the richness of Luke's second volume. In the second place, Ott has largely ignored Luke's frequent mention of the prayer motif at decisive moments in his history of salvation. And finally, Ott has failed to perceive Luke's primary purpose in using the prayer motif. While the Third Evangelist is interested in fostering the cultivation of prayer on the part of his readers (as Ott has demonstrated), this is not his chief concern. Instead Luke's primary interest is to show that prayer is the instrument by which God has directed the course of holy history, both in the life of the Son of Man and in the development of the Christian Church.[4]

The purpose of this brief study is to draw attention to the more important data on prayer in Luke-Acts, to note the general significance of this motif in the two-volume work, and thus to point to avenues for further research. For purposes of convenience, it will be useful to turn our attention first to the Gospel of Luke, and then to the Book of Acts. In this way the distinct contribution of each book may be appreciated. Finally, an attempt will be made to draw some general conclusions which may be applied to the understanding of prayer in Luke-Acts as a whole.

Prayer in the Gospel of Luke

1. The Statistics of Prayer. The crucial significance Luke attaches to prayer becomes clear when one examines the statistics.[5] The verb *proseuchomai*, "to pray, make petition," appears nineteen times in the Third Gospel and sixteen times in Acts, but it is found only ten times in Mark and fifteen in Matthew. The cognate noun *proseuchē*, which is prominent in Paul (fourteen times), is found three times in Luke and nine times in Acts, but only twice each in Matthew and Mark. Taking the noun and the verb together, Luke-Acts uses the principal prayer terms some forty-seven times, contrasted with only seventeen in Matthew, twelve in Mark and none in John. Other words are also used in Luke-Acts which, broadly speaking, are related to prayer. These include *aineō* (six times: 3 in Luke and 3 in Acts), *eulogeō* (fifteen times: 13 and 2), *doxaxō* (fourteen times: 9 and 5), *eucharisteō* (six times: 4 and 2), *deomai* (fifteen times: 8 and 7), *deēsis* (three times in Luke), and *agalliaō* (four times: 2 and 2). It is true that thanksgiving does

---

[3]O'Brien, "Prayer in Luke-Acts," who summarizes Ott's case. In his stress on the theological importance of the delay of the parousia Ott reveals his real indebtedness to Hans Conzelmann, *Die Mitte der Zeit*, translated into English as *The Theology of St. Luke* by Geoffrey Buswell.

[4]O'Brien, "Prayer in Luke-Acts," p. 112.

[5]The statistics are taken from R. Morgenthaler, *Statistik des neutestamentlichen Wortschatzes*. Acts also uses *krazo* (twice) and *proskartereō* (three times) in prayer contexts, and even the adverb *homothumadon* is used to express unity in prayer in Acts 1:14 and 4:24. The church gathers for prayer *epi to auto* in Acts 1:15 and 2:1; cf. 1 Cor. 11:20; 14:23.

not occupy the major place in Luke-Acts that it does in Paul's thought, where *eucharisteo* is used some twenty-four times. Nevertheless a survey of the prayer terminology of Luke-Acts strongly suggests that prayer—especially petitionary prayer—is a theme of considerable significance in the Lukan writings.

2. The Importance of Prayer. This impression is strengthened by a comparative study of the actual contents of the Four Gospels. This is not the place to undertake a full scale investigation of the topic, so a few cursory remarks must suffice.

Mark's Gospel only occasionally speaks of prayer.[6] In one case Mark attributes the failure of the disciples to their unfaithfulness in prayer (Mk. 9:29; some MSS add: "and fasting"). The disciples are taught to meet a great crisis by prayer and watchfulness (Mk. 14:38; cf. Mt. 26:41), and prayer is enjoined in an eschatological context (Mk. 13:18; cf. Mt. 24:20). In the cursing of the fig tree instruction in prayer is given in connection with the explanation of a dramatic action (Mk. 11:24; cf. Mt. 21:22). To this teaching a warning is added stressing the importance of forgiving others (Mk. 11:25; cf. Mt. 6:14, where the warning appears in a different context). Mark, followed by Luke, calls attention to the danger of self-deception and hypocrisy in prayer; for this reason lengthy prayers used as a smoke screen to hide social sins are roundly rebuked (Mk. 12:38-40; Lk. 20:45-47; cf. Mt. 23:1-7). Like Matthew and Luke, Mark speaks of the cleansing of the temple in terms of Isaiah 56:7, but underscores the fact that God's house was intended as a house of prayer "for all the nations" (Mk. 11:17; cf. Mt. 21:13; Lk. 19:46). In summary, Mark's Gospel shows little interest in prayer. The Model Prayer is not recorded, and in several cases where prayer terms are used, Mark's chief concern is focused elsewhere on faith, willingness to forgive, the danger of hypocrisy, etc.[7] Mark wrote to the Romans, who were more impressed by deeds than discourses. Everywhere in his Gospel Jesus is presented as the mighty Son of Man. Hence it is understandable that prayer is not stressed unduly. This is preeminently the "Gospel of Action."

Turning to Matthew's Gospel, we strike a richer vein. Obviously worship plays a prominent part in Matthew's thinking (note the use of *proskunein* in 2:2, 8, 11; 14:33; 28: 9, 17), so it is not surprising that prayer should loom larger on this Evangelist's horizon than is true of Mark. Here it is appropriate to recognize the fact that much of the teaching on prayer in the Gospels is preserved in the subject matter which Matthew and Luke share together. This "Q" material contains "the Great Thanksgiving" (Mt. 11:25-27; Lk. 10:21-22), the instruction on Asking and Receiving (Mt. 7:7-11; Lk. 11:9-13), the famous Mission Charge (Mt. 9:37-38; Lk.

---

[6]There are, however, at least eight times when Mark draws attention to the prayer life of Christ (Mark 1:35; 6:41,46; 7:34; 8:6f.; 14:22f.,32-39; 15:34).

[7]O'Brien, "Prayer in Luke-Acts," p. 116. However, Mark "alone of the Evangelists," as F. W. Farrar has pointed out, *The Message of the Books*, p. 65, "tells us of no less than eleven occasions amid his work on which Christ retired, either to escape from his enemies, or in solitude — that best 'audience-chamber of God' — to refresh with prayer his wearied soul." The passages are: Mark 1:12; 3:7; 6:31; 7:24,31; 9:2; 10:1,34. The explicit references to Jesus at prayer are 1:35; 6:46; 14:32,35,39.

10:2), the Teaching on Trust in God (Mt. 6:25-33; Lk. 12:22-31), the Counsel on Loving and Praying for Enemies (Mt. 5:44; Lk. 6:27, 28) and possibly, the Rejection of Superficial Piety (Lk. 6:46; cf. Mt. 7:21). Both Matthew and Luke have a version of the Lord's Prayer. Without examining here the Model Prayer in detail,[8] it may be noted that the prayer begins with God and moves on to man. After a right emphasis has been placed upon the hallowing of God's name, the coming of his kingdom and the doing of his will, the Father may be entreated for daily needs, the forgiveness of sins and victory over temptation and evil (Mt. 6:9-13; cf. Lk. 11:2-4, whose version is slightly more condensed). In other words, the Matthean evidence is considerably more extensive than Mark and includes some prayer material not found in Luke (e.g. Mt. 6:5-8, 14f; 18:19f; 21:22; 24:20). Matthew, however, does not have the same thematic interest in prayer that characterizes Luke. In Mt. 6:5-15, for instance, references to prayer occur in a section devoted to "True Piety" where prayer is one element, standing alongside of other elements such as almsgiving and fasting. In Mt. 18:19f, mention is made of answered prayer, but it is placed in a context which stresses the blessings which come from Christian unity. In Mt. 21:21f, it is faith rather than prayer which stands out as the central issue in the reference to the casting of a mountain into the sea. Similarly, in Mt. 24:20 and 26:41 the references to prayer spring out of particular situations, and are not offered as general instruction in the art of prayer. In other words, while Matthew's Gospel frequently mentions prayer obliquely or incidentally, it does not develop the theme with the same degree of sustained concentration observable in the Third Evangelist. The fact that there are no special Matthean prayer parables offers further support for this conviction.[9]

In the Fourth Gospel prayer is not prominent, though the Gospel itself is the Evangelist's gift to the world of his "thought, prayers and meditations about the Life which is Light of men."[10] The intimate and unending fellowship of Jesus with the Father is everywhere assumed (1:18; 3:35; 5:19-23; 6:37-40; 10:29, 30), but only once in a while does it surface in the form of actual prayer (e.g., 11:41, 42; 12:27, 28). For John the source of Jesus' strength and power is found in his abiding fellowship with the Father (5:17; 10:32, 38; 12:49). The longest prayer is the magisterial high priestly prayer of John 17, which embodies not only Jesus' personal communion with the Father (17:1-5) but also his intercession for his disciples, both present and future (17:6-26). For the Fourth Evangelist the whole Christian life is one of personal fellowship with God in and through Christ (14:6ff.; 17:3). Though John does not specifically say so, prayer is surely a *sine qua non* for such a life of fellowship with God (15:1-11). To those who abide in Christ, large promises are given to encourage the development of an active prayer life (14:13, 14).

---

[8] On the Lord's Prayer see J. Jeremias, *The Lord's Prayer,* trans. J. Reumann; E. Lohmeyer, *The Lord's Prayer,* trans. J. Bowden; and H. Thielicke, *The Prayer that Spans the World,* trans. J. W. Doberstein. Cf. also Jeremias, *New Testament Theology: The Proclamation of Jesus,* pp. 36,56-68,178-203.

[9] O'Brien, "Prayer in Luke-Acts," pp. 116-7.

[10] J. B. Phillips, *The Gospels in Modern English. While proseuchomai* and *proseuchē* are absent from John, the verb *erotaō* is prominent. Though it can be used in asking a question (e.g., 1:19,21,25; 5:12; 9:2; 12:21; 16:19), it is frequently employed in the Fourth Gospel in asking a person to do something, often in the context of prayer (cf. 4:40,47; 14:16; 16:26; 17:9,15,20).

In other words, while we can be grateful for the various contributions of the other Gospels, Luke's Gospel stands out as the primary source for an understanding of the prayer motif in the Gospels and for instruction in the art of prayer.[11]

In the Third Gospel the emphasis clearly falls on the prayers of Jesus, not his people (unlike the Acts, where quite naturally it is the other way around). Of the fourteen probable instances of prayer on the part of Jesus in the canonical Gospels, two appear in all three Synoptic Gospels, "one in Matthew and Mark, two in Mark alone, two in John alone, and seven in Luke alone."[12] The majority of cases are recorded by Luke, whose Gospel for that reason has sometimes been termed "the Gospel of Prayer." Luke alone calls his readers' attention to the fact that prayer was associated with a great many of the "red letter days" in the life of Christ. The Son of Man was divinely guided step by step throughout his brief earthly career.

Harvie Conn, following Alfred Plummer and other scholars, has reminded us of the uniqueness of Luke's account of the prayer life of Jesus. Luke mentions nine prayers of Jesus. Seven of these prayers are recorded by him alone, and not by the other evangelists. Luke is the only gospel writer to tell us that Jesus was praying at his baptism when the heavens opened (3:21). Only Luke speaks of Jesus praying alone at Caesarea Philippi, when he asked his disciples the searching question, "Who do the multitudes say that I am?" (9:18). Only Luke tells us that Jesus took Peter and James and John up to the mountain "to pray" (9:28); it was "while he was praying," Luke notes, that "the appearance of his face became different, and his clothing became white and gleaming" (9:29). Only Luke draws attention to the request of Christ's disciples: "Lord, teach us to pray just as John also taught his disciples" (11:1). Only Luke describes the prayer parables of the friend at midnight who begs for bread (11:5-8) and the persistent widow who troubles the judge (18:1-8). Only Luke records Jesus' intercession for Peter that Satan would not "sift" him (22:31, 32), and his instruction to the disciples to pray on their arrival at Gethsemane (22:40).[13] In addition, Luke alone tells us that Jesus prayed before his first clash with the scribes and Pharisees (5:16), and Luke alone preserves the "Father" prayers uttered on the Cross (23:34, 46). These last two instances are sometimes not counted, for the incidents

---

[11]Cf. A. Plummer, *A Critical and Exegetical Commentary on the Gospel According to St. Luke,* p. xlv.

[12]A. Plummer, "Prayer," *A Dictionary of Christ and the Gospels,* ed. J. Hastings, II, 390-3. Perhaps because of its stylized character Plummer omits John 17 from the prayers of Jesus. See Ernest Käsemann, *The Testament of Jesus According to John 17,* trans, G. Krodel. Some might wish to add the blessing of the children to the list of Christ's prayers, for Matthew sees prayer as a motive for the disciples' action (*hina . . . proseuxetai,* Matthew 19:18) and Mark records the actual blessing (*kateulogei,* Mark 10:16). L. E. Keck, "Jesus' Entrance Upon His Mission," *RevExp,* LXIV (1967), 473, n. 31, recognizes that "Luke regularly reports prayer at pivotal occasions," but dismisses the historical significance of this insight for the prayer life of Jesus in the light of "Luke's stylized interest in prayers." G. A. Buttrick is much less skeptical, and speaks of the "ungainsayable testimony" of Christ's prayers in his well-known book, *Prayer,* p. 36.

[13]H. M. Conn, "Luke's Theology of Prayer," *CT,* XVII (1972), 6-8. Cf. M. Tolbert, "Leading Ideas of the Gospel of Luke," *RevExp,* LXIV (1967), 441-51, who lists prayer as a "subsidiary emphasis." For a helpful recent study see Lindell O. Harris, "Prayer in the Gospel of Luke," *SwTJ,* X (1967), 59-69.

with which they are associated are mentioned in the other Synoptists (namely, the healing of a leper and the words spoken from the Cross), but the specific reference to prayer in the former and the actual prayer in the latter are peculiar to Luke and should therefore be included, if Lk. 23:34 is accepted as genuine.[14] Moreover, the earnestness of Jesus' last prayer is especially mentioned by Luke, who notes that Jesus "cried out with a loud voice" (phonēsas phonē megalē, Lk. 23:46). This prayer is especially poignant, as it was the traditional "evening prayer" of Judaism (Ps. 31:5). It seems that, among other things, Luke was concerned to underscore the monotheistic credentials of the Christian faith. God is the main agent in what happens.

3. The Elements of Prayer. Since Luke wishes to teach Christians how to pray and to show them how God has guided his people through every phase of holy history, it is worthwhile studying the different elements of prayer as he presents them. The Third Gospel, for instance, is truly rich in suggestiveness regarding the elements of prayer. Communion with God is plainly a feature of the prayers of Jesus. It is implied in the descent of the Spirit at the Baptism (3:21), in the withdrawal from the multitudes into the solitude of the wilderness (5:16), and in the all night prayer vigil in the hills (6:12). It was central in the Transfiguration, where Jesus was transfigured "while he was praying" (9:29). After one such experience of fellowship the presence of God was so real that the disciples requested instruction of Jesus in the method of prayer (11:1). Beyond any need or request was the simple, instinctive drawing near to the "Father" (2:49; 22:42; 23:(34), 46).[15]

Thanksgiving sprang quite naturally from the lips of one so steeped in fellowship with his Father. On one occasion Luke observes that Jesus "rejoiced in the Holy Spirit and said, 'I thank thee, Father, Lord of heaven and earth, that thou has hidden these things from the wise and understanding and revealed them to babes; yea, Father, for such was thy gracious will . . .'" (Lk. 10:21, 22; cf. Mt. 11:25-27, where no mention is made of rejoicing in the Spirit).[16] Here thanksgiving and praise are the perfect vehicles to express the loving relationship and intimate communion which Jesus enjoys with his Father. Against

---

[14]There is a serious textual problem in Luke 23:34, so any argument on the first "Father" prayer from the cross is highly precarious. The prayer is not found in such early and varied witnesses as: p^{75} BD*Wθit^{a,d} syr^s cop^{sa,bo} .
However B. M. Metzger, A Textual Commentary on the Greek Testament, p. 180, suggests that the logion "bears self-evident tokens of its dominical origin." John Navone, Themes of St. Luke, pp. 118-131, whose treatment of Lukan prayer is otherwise most suggestive, completely ignores the problem.

[15]Cf. Adrian Hastings, Prophet and Witness in Jerusalem, p. 88. On the significance of "abba" in prayer see J. Jeremias, The Central Message of the New Testament, pp. 9-30. On the prayers of Jesus see J. Jeremias, The Prayers of Jesus, and E. Trueblood, The Lord's Prayers. Pater is very prominent in John's Gospel (137 times).

[16]Five references to God as "Father" occur in this prayer. On the filial dimension in prayer see John Navone, Themes, pp. 120-2, who comments: "The prayer not only reveals Jesus' unique filial relationship with God, but also his capacity for extending that relationship to his disciples." On the Lukan version he adds: "This is the only text in the Gospel where we read of Jesus' rejoicing. His joy is analogous to that of Mary and Elizabeth who rejoice because of their insight into and participation in God's effective plan of salvation (1:14,47). In both cases joy is associated with the Holy Spirit."

such a background it would have been strange indeed if Jesus had not given thanks as he celebrated the Passover with his disciples or broke bread with them after his resurrection (Lk. 22:17, 19; cf. 24:30; Matthew and Mark speak of "blessing" the eucharist bread, Mt. 26:26; Mk. 14:22). Nor is Jesus alone in worshipping and thanking God, for that has always been true of the people of God and will continue to be true until the parousia (Lk. 21:36). So in the opening chapters Luke speaks of Anna as one who worshipped "with fasting and prayer" and "gave thanks to God" (Lk. 2:37, 38), and later in the ministry of Jesus mentions a healed Samaritan who "fell on his face at Jesus' feet, giving him thanks" (17:16), which is interpreted as "giving praise to God" (17:18; cf. 13:17). Here thanksgiving and praise are obviously closely related.

Luke's Gospel is full of praise, a dimension not sufficiently recognized by Ott and O'Brien. Only the Lukan nativity story includes the beautiful *Gloria in Excelsis*, and speaks of a "multitude of the heavenly host praising God" (2:13, 14). Only the Lukan narrative mentions the shepherds returning, "*glorifying* and praising God for all that they had heard and seen" (2:20; cf. 5:25, 26; 7:16; 13:13; 17:15). Only the Lukan version of the healing of blind Bartimaeus records his response in terms of "glorifying God," and notes the reaction of the people, who "gave praise to God" (Lk. 18:43, where *ainos* is used). Only the Lukan account describes the disciples at the descent of the Mount of Olives as beginning "to rejoice and praise God with a loud voice for all the mighty works that they had seen" (19:37; cf. 13:17; but note Mt. 21:16, which quotes Ps. 8:2 LXX and mentions "praise").[17] Only the Lukan passion story tells of the centurion who witnessed the death of Christ and "glorified God" (23:47), and only Luke's Gospel opens with God's people in prayer and closes with them joyfully blessing God (1:10; 24:52, 53). It is no accident that the lovely Songs of Mary (1:46-55), Zechariah (1:67-79) and Simeon (2:29-32) are all found in the Third Gospel. Mary "magnifies" the Lord and "rejoices" in God her Saviour (*megalunei*, 1:46; *ēgalliasen*, 1:47). Zechariah, "filled with the Holy Spirit," "praises" the Lord God of Israel who has accomplished salvation for his people (1:67, 64, 68). Simeon "blesses" God (2:28), and Anna begins to "praise God aloud" (*anthomologeito, tō theō*, 2:38). This atmosphere of worship, praise and thanksgiving is carried over into Acts (4:24; 11:18; 13:48; 16:25; 21:20), and surely comes very close to the heart of prayer.

But prayer is not all praise and thanksgiving; there must also be a place for petition and intercession. The people of God live in an eschatological tension between "the now" and "the not yet." While God in Christ has "visited and redeemed his people" (1:68; cf. 1:78; 7:16; 19:44), they still live "between the times," that is, between the first advent of Christ in lowliness and obscurity and his final advent in power and great glory. In the interval the Church is to pray in order to escape temptation (Luke 22:40, 46; cf. Acts 2:42, 46), and has Christ himself as the great model set before her (Luke 22:41ff.; cf. John 13:15; Even the Model Prayer which recognizes the priority of God and his kingdom moves on to consider man and his needs (Lk. 11:2-4; cf. Mt. 6:9-13). The role of petition is recognized early in Luke's Gospel, where an angel appears on the right

---

[17] Luke seems to make a deliberate link between Palm Sunday and the Nativity, for he uses *doxa en hupsistois* in both Luke 2:14 and 19:38. Cf. I. H. Marshall, *Luke: Historian and Theologian*, pp. 202-7, who writes helpfully on the relation between praise and prayer, and Navone, *Themes*, pp. 125-9, who discusses praise and blessing.

side of the altar of incense and says: "Do not be afraid, Zechariah, for your petition has been heard, and your wife Elizabeth will bear a son, and you will call his name John" (1:13). It reappears again in the next chapter in Anna's "prayers" which are more accurately described as "petitions" or "requests" (2:37); for this reason the Revised Version always translates *deēsis* as "supplication" (e.g. Lk. 5:33, "The disciples of John fast often, and make supplications"). Certainly Jesus prayed for himself in his hour of need, humbly kneeling in Gethsemane (22:41f.). Indeed, according to one textual tradition, Luke lays great stress on the intense earnestness and costliness of this petitionary prayer: "And being in an agony he prayed more earnestly; and his sweat became like great drops of blood falling on the ground" (22:44).[18] This tradition at least is in full agreement with the Epistle to the Hebrews, which speaks of Jesus offering up "prayers and supplications, with loud cries and tears" (Heb. 5:7).

Prayers are also offered in Luke's Gospel for others. Two examples of such prayers may be mentioned on the part of Christ. One is the confession made by Peter at Caesarea Philippi, which only Luke introduces by the explanation, "Now it happened that as he was praying alone the disciples were with him" (Lk. 9:18ff.; cf. Mt. 16:13-23; Mk. 8:27-33). "By his introductory words the Third Evangelist wishes us to understand that the petition of Jesus had been effective since the Father has revealed to Peter the secret of his Messianic person and dignity."[19] Another instance occurs in the prophecy of Peter's denial (Lk. 22:31-34), where one of the few objects of Christ's prayers is singled out: "I have prayed for you that your faith fail not." Here in view of his impending treachery Satan has demanded to have Peter as well as Judas. While "Satan thus acts as the cunning adversary, Jesus acts as the intercessor, the advocate of his disciples and especially of that particular one whom he had previously pointed out as a leader amongst them."[20] Luke also records his version of the intercessory prayer commanded on behalf of the Church's missionary enterprise, which he relates to the sending forth of the seventy or seventy-two (Lk. 10:1, 2).[21]

The one element conspicuous by its absence in the Lukan prayers of Jesus is confession of sin. While it is true that the disciples are taught to pray, "forgive us our sins" (11:4), there is no suggestion that Jesus himself ever did so; perhaps this is the Evangelist's indirect way of teaching the sinlessness of the Son of Man (cf. 23:41, 47). Elsewhere in the Gospel the general need to confess sin is affirmed, particularly in the Parable of the Pharisee and the Publican (18:9-14); there the tax collector beats his breast saying, "God, be merciful to me a sinner!" Another illustration of true confession is furnished by Zacchaeus who declares, "Behold, Lord, the half of my goods I give to the poor, and if I have defrauded any one of anything, I restore it fourfold" (Lk. 19:8). Here confession and restitution are closely linked together, as indeed is the case in the Old Testament (Ex. 22:1; Lev. 6:5; Num. 5:7; 2 Sam. 12:6). Notice must also be taken of Peter's confession of sinfulness after the great catch of fish (Luke 5:8).

---

[18]On the textual evidence see B. M. Metzger, *A Textual Commentary on the Greek New Testament*, p. 177.

[19]O'Brien, "Prayer in Luke-Acts," p. 115.

[20]Norval Geldenhuys, *Commentary on the Gospel of Luke*, p. 567.

[21]On the textual problem see B. M. Metzger, "Seventy or Seventy-two Disciples," *NTS*, V (1958-59), 299-306.

4. The Parables of Prayer. Luke's teaching on prayer is clearly displayed in his three distinctive prayer parables. Both the Friend at Midnight (11:5-8) and the Unjust Judge (18:1-8) teach the need for importunity and persistence in prayer. "So far as the two parables differ, the former teaches that prayer is never out of season, the latter that it is sure to bring a blessing and not a curse."[22] The argument in each case is an *a fortiori* one, and is especially clear in the second parable. If an unjust judge would yield to the repeated appeals of an unknown widow for such a selfish reason, how much more will a loving God, the helper of widows and of all in distress, reward the unremitting cries of his own people? (Luke 18:7).

It seems that Luke is addressing himself to a critical situation in which Christian people are experiencing real persecution and are in danger of denying or repudiating their faith. In this connection verse 18b (whether it is an autonomous logion of Jesus or a Lukan comment) suggests a terrifying crisis:

> God will assuredly vindicate his servants soon. The parousia may be near, but the saints are to remember (and this is the point of verse 8b) that when it comes the parousia will mean judgment for them as well as for their persecutors. Will they themselves be found faithful when the Lord returns?[23]

The Parable of the Pharisee and the Publican (18:9-14) has its central concern righteousness, not prayer (note the use of *dikaioi* in 18:9 and *dedikaiōmenos* in 18:14). The two characters of the parable present sharply contrasting attitudes, prayers and results. Both go up to the temple ostensibly to commune with God (*proseuxasthai* is an aorist infinitive expressing purpose in 18:10), but only one really prays and gets results; the other is only practicing egotistical self-deception (18:11). As a recent commentator has said:

> If the parable furnishes any guidance concerning the right way to pray it is that prayer should be humble, and that the person praying should have a true dependence on God. In the two preceding episodes Luke is dealing with a pending judgment (17:20-37) in which strict justice will be meted out (18:1-8). Who then will be found just? This parable gives the answer.[24]

5. The Paradigm of Prayer. Already we have observed much of Luke's teaching on prayer. But any study of the subject would be woefully incomplete if it did not consider the "paradigm of prayer" which Jesus gave to his disciples (Lk. 11:2-4).

Luke's setting for the Model Prayer makes the exemplary character of Jesus' own prayer life unmistakably plain: "And it came about that while he was praying in a certain place, after he had finished, one of his disciples said to him, 'Lord, teach us to pray, just as John also taught his disciples.'" (Luke 11:1). There was, Luke suggests, a radiant vitality to the prayer life of Jesus which made a profound impression upon his friends and associates. Above and beyond any formal

---

[22]Plummer, "Prayer," p. 392.

[23]O'Brien, "Prayer in Luke-Acts," pp. 117-8.

[24]*Ibid.*, p. 118.

teaching, the disciples were confronted with a glowing example of genuine communion with God which made an indelible impression upon them. Clearly the paraenetic aspect of prayer to which Ott has directed attention is in evidence here. In Luke's view prayer was indispensable for both Jesus and his followers.

When we turn to the prayer itself, we are struck at once by its simplicity and profundity. The Lukan version, which interests us particularly here, is shorter and probably more primitive than its counterpart in Matthew (Mt. 6:9-13). Certainly the beautiful doxology with which the Matthean version finishes is a secondary addition (Mt. 6:13b), probably representing an adaptation of the prayer to the liturgical needs of the early church (cf. Didache and the liturgy ascribed to John Chrysostom).[25]

The family prayer begins simply by addressing God as "Father"; Matthew's use of the collective "our Father" is plainly a modification of the prayer for use in corporate worship (Mt. 6:9). This "Abba" designation, as Jeremias has powerfully reminded us, can be traced back to Jesus himself, who was probably the source of the early church's use of the title (Gal. 4:6; Rom. 8:15).[26]

While the vocative *pater* suggests access and intimacy, the first petition demands reverence. There seems to be a perfect balance in this prayer between imminence and transcendence. God is recognized as both near and yet infinitely holy (cf. Ezek. 36:23). The "name" represents the character of the one mentioned. In the Old Testament it was considered a serious sin to take God's "name" falsely in an oath; indeed, one of the Ten Commandments insisted that "the Lord will not hold him guiltless who takes his name in vain" (Ex. 20:7; Deut. 5:11; cf. Zech. 5:3f.; Wis. 14:29-31).

> The name of God means both the mystery of the being of God and all that he has shown himself to be in history and experience. For Jesus hallowing this name was the duty of every man . . . . The disciple will pray that he may follow Jesus in this profound reverence for the Father.[27]

The second petition teaches us to pray for the coming of God's kingdom, that is, the long-awaited realization of God's righteous rule in the affairs of men.[28] John the Baptist has heralded the imminence of such a divine intervention, Simeon had longed for it, and Anna had fervently prayed for it (Lk. 1:17, 76; 2:25, 37, 38; 3:4-17). Now in the ministry of Jesus there was the startling announcement that the sovereign reign of God was entering history and actualizing itself (Lk. 4:16-21;

---

[25]Metzger, *A Textual Commentary*, p. 17. E. F. Scott, *The Lord's Prayer*, p. 100, however, argues for the originality of the Matthean version, particularly with respect to the fourth petition.

[26]J. Jeremias, "Abba," *The Prayers of Jesus*, pp. 11-65.

[27]E. J. Tinsley, *The Gospel According to Luke*, pp. 124-5. Cf. S. MacLean Gilmour, "Luke," *The Interpreter's Bible*, ed. G. A. Buttrick, VIII, 201.

[28]There is no mention in Luke of the Matthean phrase "thy will be done, on earth as it is in heaven" (Matthew 6:10b,c). Some later manuscripts substitute the phrase, "thy Holy Spirit come upon us and cleanse us." See Metzger, *Textual Commentary*, pp. 154-6, who sees the variant reading as a "liturgical adaptation of the original form of the Lord's Prayer, used perhaps when celebrating the rite of baptism or the laying on of hands."

cf. Mk. 1:15; Mt. 4:17).[29] The disciples gradually came to understand that the kingdom had been inaugurated in Jesus, and that the kingdom would be consummated in him (Lk. 17:20, 21; Acts 1:6, 11; 3:20, 21; cf. Mk. 14:61, 62). They were taught to pray for the glorious fulfillment of the kingly reign of God, which entailed their faith, dedication and obedience. Prayer then, according to Luke, has a direct bearing on the out-working of God's purposes and the bringing of his sovereignty to its final and ultimate expression. It has an indispensable role to play in *Heilsgeschichte*.

The third petition turns the focus from God to man, and this movement indicates the true priorities in prayer. Elsewhere Jesus had commanded his disciples to seek first the kingdom of God and his righteousness, and had promised them that all needful things would be added (Mt. 6:33; cf. Lk. 12:31). Now, in harmony with that promise, the disciples are instructed to ask God for the needed material things of life, symbolized by bread, "the staff of life." The qualifying adjective *epiousios* is difficult to pin down. It may refer to bread (1) necessary for existence, (2) for the current day, (3) for the following day, or (4) for the future.[30] The exact nuance is hard to detect with certainty,[31] but the general thrust of the petition is clear—it is legitimate and fitting for man to look to God to meet his basic earthly needs in an attitude of loving trust and expectancy.

The fourth petition concern the forgiveness of sins. The basic presupposition behind this request is stated elsewhere in the Gospels: "Who can forgive sin but God alone?" (Mk. 2:7; Lk 5:21). Man's acknowledgment and confession of his own sinfulness before God is predicated upon God's ability and willingness to forgive sin. To experience this divine forgiveness in sincerity and integrity, one must exercise the same attitude of compassionate forgiveness towards his fellows (Lk. 6:37; cf. Mt. 18:34, 35; Eph. 4:32; Col. 3:13). While Matthew refers to "debts," Luke speaks of "sins." The juridical aspect of forgiveness is not forgotten in Luke, however, "for we ourselves also forgive everyone who is indebted to us" (Lk. 11:4b).

The final petition asks for help in facing temptation. Anyone who has honestly prayed for the forgiveness of sin must be concerned to avoid moral failure in the future. The word *peirasmos* can mean "testing" as well as "temptation." As in the case of Christ himself (Mt. 4:1-11; Mk. 1:12-13; Lk. 4:1-13; cf. Heb. 4:15), God allows us to be tempted (cf. Jn. 17:15; Rev. 3:10) to test and purify us (*peirazein* has this meaning in Gen. 22:1 and Jn. 6:6). We only succumb to our temptations when we are "drawn away by our own lust and enticed" (Jas. 1:14). While temptation is common to man (*anthropinos*), God has promised not to permit his servants to be tempted beyond the point of endurance, but rather to provide for them the way of escape (*kai tēn ekbasin*, 1 Cor. 10:13).

---

[29]On the kingdom theme see H. Ridderbos, *The Coming of the Kingdom,* and John Bright, *The Kingdom of God,* which is especially useful on the Old Testament background.

[30]W. F. Arndt and F. W. Gingrich, eds., *A Greek-English Lexicon of the New Testament and Other Early Christian Literature,* pp. 296-7.

[31]Probably (2) or (3) are the most likely. See Sherman E. Johnson, "Matthew," *The Interpreter's Bible,* ed. G. A. Buttrick, VII, 312-3 and Scott, *Lord's Prayer,* pp. 98-9. Cf. the use of the feminine participle *epiousa* in Acts 7:26; 16:11; 20:15 and 21:18 to mean "next."

We pray, therefore, that we may not be tried above what we are able, and this is defined by the following words: Our prayer is, Let not the tempting opportunity meet the too susceptible disposition. If the temptation comes, quench the desire, if the desire, spare the temptation.[32]

In brief, the Model Prayer summarizes the central features of Jesus' teaching on prayer and sets them forth for emulation by disciples in one glorious paradigm. It is remarkable for its tone of holy confidence (cf. Rom. 8.15), its absolute unselfishness, its entire spirituality, its brevity (cf. Eccles. 5:2) and its simplicity. "For these reasons the Fathers called it 'the Epitome of the Gospel' and 'the pearl of pearls.' "[33]

Prayer in the Book of Acts

Having surveyed the Third Gospel, we are now ready to review the teaching on prayer in the Book of Acts. Since we have already outlined the statistics on prayer, we can move directly into the importance of prayer.

1. The Importance of Prayer. The Acts of the Apostles contains approximately twenty-five significant instances of prayer. The birth of the church was the result of prayer. The disciples had been specifically instructed to remain in Jerusalem until they were "clothed with power from on high" (Lk. 24:49; Acts 1:4, 5). They obeyed this injunction, waiting for the promised coming of the Spirit and devoting themselves to prayer, together with the women, Mary the mother of Jesus, and his brothers (Acts 1:8, 13, 14). One of their real concerns at this time was the finding of a suitable replacement for Judas; while they used the time-honored method of casting lots as in 1 Sam. 14:41, they did so in an earnest desire to discover the will of God (Acts 1:24-26, where God is addressed as *kardiognōsta pantōn*).

The answer to the ten day period of prayerful preparation came on the day of Pentecost with the gift of the Holy Spirit (2:1-13). Those who received Peter's message were baptized, and three thousand converts were added to the infant church (2:41). The new believers "devoted themselves to the apostles' teaching and fellowship, to the breaking of bread and the prayers" (2:42). Prayer was thus an integral part of the Christian movement from the start, and its vitality was closely related in Luke's eyes to the growth of the church (2:47).

The mettle of the early Christian community was soon tested by persecution. When Peter and John were arrested by the leaders of the Sanhedrin, the believers "lifted up their voices together to God" in earnest united prayer (4:24-30). The result of their intercession was a powerful demonstration of the power of God (4:31).

This communal *esprit de corps*, developed in unselfish prayer, was expressed also in the sharing of goods (2:44f.; 4:34-37), a practice similar to that of the Essenes. While this custom was voluntary and temporary, it could become a source of temptation,and possibly a lack of prayerfulness was responsible for the duplicity of Ananias and Sapphira (Acts 5:1-11; cf. Lk. 11:4; 21:36; 22:40, 46). In any case, this incident served to solemnize the new community, for "great fear

[32]F. W. Farrar, The Gospel According to St. Luke, pp. 210-1.
[33]Ibid., p. 209.

came upon the whole church, and upon all who heard of these things" (Acts 5:11).

The story continues with the apostles working great miracles, the number of converts increasing (5:12-16), and the apostles suffering arrest for the second time (5:17, 18). But even in prison the prayerful apostles are encouraged by the message: "Go and stand in the temple and speak to the people all the words of this life" (5:20; cf. 12:7-9).

The choice of the Seven was made to allow the maximum opportunity for the Twelve to devote themselves "to prayer and to the ministry of the word" (6:4). After suitable candidates for administrative office had been selected, they were set before the apostles, who "prayed and laid their hands upon them" (6:6). Luke adds a footnote to indicate that the growth of the church continued (6:7); the Christian community had evidently been guided in the disposition of its own affairs so that its witness to "those outside" remained vibrant and attractive (cf. 1 Thess. 4:12). This is clearly the case when one of these very appointees prays as he is martyred, "Lord Jesus, receive my spirit" (Acts 7:59; cf. Lk. 23:46), and "Lord, do not hold this sin against them: (Acts 7:60; cf. Lk. 23:34). The fact that the dying Stephen acts like his prayerful Lord is apparent in the deliberate parallels which Luke has drawn between the two incidents. As Augustine once remarked, if Stephen had not prayed, the Church would not have had Paul.

According to Acts 1:8, the next stage of the church's expansion was from Jerusalem and Judea into Samaria. For the early church to evangelize the Samaritans was definitely to take a step in the direction of a world-wide mission. For this reason it was essential to know that this move was in keeping with the divine purpose; this was confirmed when Peter and John visited the Samaritans on a goodwill mission and prayer for them. When the apostles laid hands on the Samaritan converts, they received the Holy Spirit (8:14-17), thereby giving tangible evidence of the solidarity of the Samaritan community with the Jerusalem one.

Nowhere does the importance of prayer in the development of the Christian mission loom larger than in the case of Paul. Luke seems to go out of his way to stress the guidance of God at every stage of the apostle's career. The arch persecutor of Christians falls to the ground when he hears the haunting divine voice, "Saul, Saul, why are you persecuting me?" (9:4-6). Later Ananias is told that Paul is praying at the house of Judas on Straight Street, Damascus (9:10-15). Paul's prayer is answered when Ananias lays hands on him, prays for his sight and infilling by the Spirit, and Paul receives Christian baptism (9:17, 18).

After his conversion Paul prays in the temple in Jerusalem and in a trance is told of his mission to take the gospel to the Gentiles (22:17-21). Paul and Barnabas pray when they appoint elders for the churches of South Galatia (14:23). At Philippi Paul shares in a prayer meeting and prays with Silas while his feet are fastened in the prison stocks (16:16, 25). On the shore at Miletus he prays in a touching scene with the Ephesian elders (20:36), and similarly kneels on the beach with the disciples at Tyre (21:5). Even in the midst of a violent Mediterranean storm Paul prays, encouraging the crew and passengers as he takes bread and gives thanks "in the presence of all" (27:35). Finally, Paul is found in Malta praying and laying hands on a man suffering from recurrent fever and dysentery (28:8). Here too, as in similar cases in Peter's ministry, "the prayer offered in faith restores the one who is sick" (cf. Acts 5:12-16; Jas. 5:15).

Prayer, then, is as decisive for the Book of Acts as it is for the Third Gospel. For Luke holy history continues. Prayer marks not only the ministry of Jesus and his first disciples, but also every stage in the outreach of the gospel to the Gentile world. It is one of the principal methods by which God has taught and strengthened his people, enpowering them by his Spirit for service and ministry in the world.

2. The Elements of Prayer. The salient features of true prayer are well represented in the Acts. Here prayer is set in the midst of Luke's general interest in the importance of worship, an interest we have already observed in the Third Gospel (e.g., Lk. 1, 2; 4:16). The worship motif is indicated several times in Stephen's speech in Acts 7 (note the use of *latreuo* in 7:7 (quoting Amos 5:26). The tragedy of Jewish history in Luke's eyes was its departure from God-appointed worship into idolatry and apostasy. So central a concern was worship that a cabinet minister would leave the affairs of state for a religious pilgrimage to Jerusalem (8:27). Worship could be practiced in ignorance, as Paul reminded the Athenians (17:23, where note the use of *eusebeo*). Worship, defined as "reverent honor and homage paid to God" is certainly important in the Acts of the Apostles (cf., e.g., 26:7; 27:23). This is especially clear when the Apostle Paul journeys to Jerusalem "to worship" (24:11). In Luke's view, "ministering to the Lord" was a matter of the utmost importance, as he observes in the case of the leaders of the church at Antioch (13:1-3).[34] Here we see that "the normal preparation of the Church for receiving the Spirit is regular worship and self-discipline."[35]

Adoration was involved in early Christian prayer. This doxological note is obvious in their confident appeal to God as the great Creator, the "Sovereign Lord" of heaven, earth and sea (4:24; 17:24). Sometimes this adoration bursts forth spontaneously, as in the case of the lame man healed at Solomon's portico (3:8, 9); here his praise serves as evidence of his cure and witness to his faith. Sometimes it breaks out at unorthodox times and places, as in the midnight praises of Paul and Silas in prison (*proseuchomenoi hymnoun ton theon*, 16:25).

Worship and adoration are related to rejoicing, which is certainly a characteristic of the Lukan writings.[36] In the Book of Acts the apostles "rejoice" that they have been considered worthy to suffer shame for Christ's name (5:41). Philip, the human instrument in the conversion of the Ethiopian eunuch, baptizes him and goes on his way "rejoicing" (8:39). When Barnabas reaches Syrian Antioch and witnesses the grace of God at work, he "rejoices" and encourages believers to remain steadfast in their Christian commitment (11:23). In Pisidian Antioch Paul turns to the Gentiles when the Jews of the synagogue oppose his message, and they commence "rejoicing and glorifying the word of the Lord" (13:48). And the Philippian jailor, who a short time before would have killed himself, "rejoiced greatly, having believed in God with his whole household" (16:34). Formally and informally, in season and out, the early Christians were

---

[34]On the classical background of *leitourgeo* (Acts 13:2) see F. J. Foakes-Jackson and Kirsopp Lake, eds., *The Beginnings of Christianity, IV, 110.*

[35]C. J. Barker, *The Acts of the Apostles,* p. 104.

[36]On "joy" in Luke see John Navone, *Themes,* pp. 71-87.

apparently learning to "rejoice always, pray constantly, give thanks in all circumstances" (cf. 1 Thess. 5:16-18). In doing so, they were following the teaching and example of their Lord.

Thanksgiving was also a feature in their prayers. We have already observed Paul giving thanks as he takes food at sea (Acts 27:35). When the Italian Christians come out to meet him, Paul again thanks God and takes courage (28:15). While the element of thanksgiving achieves greater prominence in Paul's epistles, it is not absent in the Acts.

Prayer occasionally takes the form of confessing one's sins (19:18), and in at least one case confession is clearly demanded (8:18-24); in this instance Simon the sorcerer, rebuked for his blatant sinfulness, is both commanded to pray and requests Peter's help in prayer.

Supplication, as we have seen, is one of the major elements in the prayers recorded in Acts. So the pre-Pentecostal prayer of the 120 prepares the way for the promised coming of the Spirit (Acts 1:8, 14; 2:1-4). Prayer is invoked in the appointment of Matthias (1:24-26), and again in meeting a threatening situation with the Jewish authorities (4:24-31). When Peter finds himself in prison, the church engages in "earnest" prayer for him (ektenōs, 12:5; cf. 12:12). Peter kneels at the bier of Dorcas, prays for her resuscitation, and raises her up (9:40-42). Later Paul prays for his fellow travellers and for the father of Publius (27:23-25; 28:8).

Most of the above prayers are intercessions offered on behalf of other individuals or the community at large, but there is a place in Acts for personal petitions. Cornelius, for instance, is told that his prayer has been heard (10:31). The context makes it obvious that he is praying for himself and his household (10:33: "we are all here present before God"). Paul prays for personal illumination as he asks: "Lord, what shall I do?" (22:10). Peter prays concerning the meaning of a perplexing vision (10:19, 20). Ananias prays for himself as he argues with God concerning the wisdom of approaching Saul of Tarsus, the known opponent of the Christian movement (9:13-16). Even rough and ready sailors pray for daybreak in the midst of a storm at sea (27:29).

Fellowship was evident in prayer. As believers engaged both in corporate worship in the temple and in private worship in their homes, there was a spirit of generosity and gladness, coupled with a genuine note of praise to God (2:45-47). "The first Christians were men controlled and inspired by the Holy Spirit, welded by that indwelling power into a compact and loyal community which was able to confront its crises with confidence and decisiveness."[37]

But such radiant fellowship was possible only when the decks had been cleared of sin and selfishness. Conviction of sin, followed by sincere confession and repentance, was an indispensable condition for the creation and maintenance of such a vibrant common life (Acts 2:37-42; 3:19; 5:31; 20:21; cf. 2 Chron. 7:14; Dan. 9:4-19; Lk. 19:8).[38]

3. The Special Features of Prayer. Before completing our survey, several features of prayer in Acts call for notice. One is the fact that visions are quite

---

[37]Barker, *Acts*, p. 14. Cf. Frank Stagg, *The Book of Acts*, p. 67.

[38]Cf. Karl Barth, *The Epistle to the Romans,* trans. C. Hoskyns, pp. 88-9.

prominent, and they are generally related to prayer (9:11, 12; 10:2-6, 9-17; 18:9, 10; 22:17-21; 23:11; cf. 16:9, 10; 26:13-19; Lk. 1:8-20). For example, Cornelius is told in a vision: "Your prayers and your alms have ascended in a memorial before God" (Acts 10:4; cf. 10:30f.). The next day Peter has a vision as he prays on the housetop of Simon the tanner in Joppa (10:9; cf. 11:5-9). As

> ... in the visions of Paul and Ananias in the previous chapter, the main point Luke wishes to emphasize is that the hand of God is in the affair; it is not a chance whim that induces Cornelius to send for Peter as it was no coincidence that sent Ananias to Paul.[39]

Similarly, a message from God is described by Luke as from an "angel of God" in 8:26; 10:3 and 27:23. God is faithful in answering the needs of his people (cf. Lk. 11:10; 18:7).

In the second place, a point of similarity with the Synoptics may be noted. This is the fact that sometimes fasting and prayer are linked together in Acts (*nesteia* is used in 14:23; *nesteuō* in 13:2, 3). This association is observable in the practice of the prophets and teachers of Antioch (13:1-3) and in the selection of elders for the Pauline churches (14:23). Fasting was well known in Jewish tradition (Isa. 58:3-6; Zech. 7:5, 6; Dan. 9:3; cf. Mt. 6:16-18; Lk. 2:37; 18:12), and Jesus himself had predicted the time would come when his disciples would fast (Mt. 9:14, 15; Lk. 5:33-35). Luke in the Acts records the fulfillment of Jesus' expectation. "The moral significance of fasting is that it is a denial of self-satisfaction as the ideal of life."[40]

In the third place, the earliest Christian community did not abandon the observance of Jewish worship patterns.[41] They maintained a lively interest in the temple and kept up attendance at Jewish hours of prayer (Lk. 24:53; Acts 3:1; 22:17; cf. 10:3, 30). Their Lord had been faithful in worship at the synagogue (Lk. 4:16), and had used it as a center for spreading his teaching (Lk. 13:10; cf. Mt. 12:9). So too Paul and his colleagues were to employ the synagogues as the launching pad for their evangelistic endeavors (Acts 9:20; 13:5, 14ff.; 14:1; 17:1ff.; 18:4; 19:8).

Fourth, several times the practice of kneeling in prayer is mentioned (7:60; 9:40; 20:36; 21:5; cf. Lk. 22:41; Dan. 6:10); this is in contrast to the customary Jewish posture of standing (Mt. 6:5; Lk. 18:11, 13; Mk. 11:25). Kneeling, however, was well known (Ps. 95:6; 1 Kgs. 8:54; 2 Chron. 6:13; Ezra 9:5; cf. Eph. 3:14; Phil. 2:10).

Fifth, prayer is sometimes associated with the laying on of hands, either in an official appointment to office (Acts 6:6; 13:3; 14:23; cf. 1 Tim. 4:14; 5:22; 2 Tim. 1:6) or in connection with healing (Acts 28:8; cf. 19:11f.).

> This laying on of hands was an act reminiscent of Jesus; he had laid his hands upon the sick that they might recover (e.g., Mk. 5:23; 6:5; Lk. 4:40; Mt. 9:18),

---

[39]William Neil, *The Acts of the Apostles*, p. 138. Cf. David L. Edwards, *Good News in Acts*, pp. 30-56.

[40]Barker, *Acts*, p. 103.

[41]See J. J. von Allmen, "The Theological Meaning of Common Prayer," *SL*, X (1974), 125-36 and G. J. Cuming, "The New Testament Foundation for Common Prayer," *SL*, X (1974), 88-105. On the frequency of Prayer (suggested in Acts 1:14; 2:41f., 47; 6:4) see O'Brien, "Prayer in Luke-Acts," p. 122.

communicating by bodily contact the vital power of God. Just as Jesus had received a body that he might be able to touch as well as be seen and handled, so those in whom he lived by the Spirit would by their touch make others sure of God's presence, care and vital power.[42]

Sixth, prayer is occasionally invoked in cases of exorcism, witness the hysterical girl at Philippi (Acts 16:16-18; cf. Mk. 16:17); when exorcism is practiced purely mechanically without Christian faith and prayer, it fails disastrously (Acts 19:13-16). Exorcisms had been performed in the ministry of Jesus (Mk. 9:25-27; Mt. 12:22-28; Lk. 11:14-20) and his disciples (Mk. 6:7; Lk. 9:1; 10:17; Mt. 10:8), and they continue in the apostolic period.

Seventh, prayer was so characteristic of Christian discipleship that "calling upon his name" was often used as a synonymn to describe what is meant to be a Christian (2:21; 7:59; 9:14, 21; 22:16).

Finally, the Spirit in both Luke and Acts is related to prayer on the one hand and to the kingdom of God on the other. In the Third Gospel the triadic relationship between the Spirit, prayer and the kingdom is evident in Christ's birth (Lk. 1:30-35, 46-55), baptism (3:21, 22), transfiguration (9:28-36) and ascension (24:44-51), to mention but a few of the decisive points for *Heilsgeschichte*. In Luke's view the Holy Spirit is given to believers in answer to prayer (Lk. 11:13, where Matthew has "good things," Mt. 7:11).[43] The same triadic relationship is evident in Acts in the election of Matthias (1:24-26), in the inception of the church at Pentecost (2:1-4), in the early church's intercessions (4:24-31), in the appointment of the Seven (6:3-6), and in the confirmation of the Hellenistic mission to Samaria (8:4-25). All this has been convincingly demonstrated by Stephen Smalley, who sums up the significance of this triadic relationship as follows:

> Luke . . . regards petitionary prayer as the means by which the dynamic power of God's Spirit is historically realized for purposes of salvation. Luke's theological understanding, moreover, is such that he also views the activity of the Spirit among men and the arrival of the kingdom of God as aligned if not synonymous. Where the Spirit is, there is the kingdom.[44]

The Theology of Prayer in Luke-Acts

It is now time to evaluate the various strains in Luke's theology of prayer. A number of points can be made about the general significance of this motif:

1. Prayer is an important element in the Lukan writings as both the terminology and the contexts make clear. Luke lays special stress on prayer, particularly during moments of divine revelation (Lk. 3:21; 9:28f.; cf. 22:43; Acts 9:40; 10:9f., 30f.; 13:2; 22:17).

2. "The prayer of praise occurs more frequently in Lukan writings than in the

---

[42]Barker, *Acts*, p. 103. On the terms for ordination and laying on of hands see M. R. Cherry, *Toward a Theology of Ministry*, pp. 13-25.

[43]On the textual problem in Luke 11:13 see Metzger, *Textual Commentary*, p. 158.

[44]Stephen Smalley, "Spirit, Kingdom and Prayer in Luke-Acts," *NovT*, XV (1973), 59-71, esp. 66-8. On the teaching about the Spirit in Luke-Acts see Marshall, *Luke*; Navone, *Themes*, pp. 151-69, and especially G. W. H. Lampe, "The Holy Spirit in the Writings of St. Luke," *Studies in the Gospels*, ed. D. E. Nineham, pp. 159-200.

rest of the New Testament together."[45]

3. Luke presents a far fuller picture of Jesus at prayer than either of the other Synoptists or John. He does so not only because of a theological or christological interest, but also because of a didactic purpose. The distinctively Lukan teaching in the Gospel and the Third Evangelist's handling of the material common to Matthew and himself both underscore this point. Regular and consistent prayer is inculcated upon the disciples, particularly as a means of overcoming temptation. This exemplary character of Jesus' prayer is particularly clear in the scene on the Mount of Olives (Lk. 22:39-46), where Luke "emphasizes the meaning of the event more for the faith of the church than for the experience of Jesus."[46] Similarly in the Lukan account of the transfiguration Jesus was changed as he prayed (9:28, 29) and Luke wishes to remind his readers that for them too, prayer can change things.

4. The Lukan teaching on prayer emphasizes the need to engage in this activity continuously and that for spiritual ends, e.g., for the coming of the Lord (21:36), the Holy Spirit (11:13), not to enter temptation (22:40, 46), and so on.

5. The evidence of Acts, particularly the summary statements, shows that the early church and its members heeded this injunction to unremitting faithfulness in prayer (1:14, 24; 2:42, 46, 47; 4:24-31; 12:5, 12; 20:36; 21:5).

6. Prayer is a prominent characteristic in the spiritual leadership of the early church, as a study of Acts makes clear (1:14; 6:4, 6; 7:60; 8:15; 10:9; 13:3; 16:25; 21:5; 28:8). "For Luke-Acts the *ephapax* of Jesus' historical ministry can be shared and is 'transmittable' precisely because the same Spirit that originated and empowered the life and acts and teaching of the historical Jesus continued to originate and empower the lives and acts and teaching of his brethren."[47]

7. But perhaps Luke's central concern in his presentation of this theme is to show that it had an important supporting role in his account of redemptive history, for by it God had guided his people.[48] In view of the delay of the parousia, prayer is of vital importance in preparing the people of God to function effectively in the period of the Church's mission.

In conclusion, it is fair to say that Luke relates prayer to his understanding of redemptive history. He sees Jesus as inaugurating a new phase in God's relations with men. Jesus, the Anointed of the Spirit, enters into the age of the Spirit as a Forerunner and Pioneer.

> Acts provides the link between Jesus and his covenant people, the prayer-sign for the people who live in the between times .... The Messianic kingdom ministry

---

[45]Navone, *Themes,* p. 125.

[46]William Baird, "Luke," *The Interpreter's One-Volume Commentary on the Bible,* ed. C. M. Laymon, p. 702.

[47]J. D. Quinn, "Apostolic Ministry and Apostolic Prayer," *CBQ,* XXXIII (1971), 485, who grounds the Church's concern for prayer in her Lord's concern, and his concern in turn in the monotheistic worship of Israel (pp. 479-91). He welcomes the "renewal of the Church's primary ministry of prayer," and stresses "the role of the ordained ministry" in teaching, guiding and enriching the prayer of the Church (p. 479). Cf. Ernst Haenchen, *The Acts of the Apostles,* trans. R. McL. Wilson *et al.,* p. 263.

[48]O'Brien, "Prayer in Luke-Acts," p. 120-1, 126-7. Cf. also O'Brien's recent monograph on Pauline prayer, *Introductory Thanksgiving in the Letters of Paul.*

now becomes the Messianic kingdom ministry of Jesus' people. And with both Jesus and his people, it is a ministry related to prayer.[49]

As Stephen Smalley has finely expressed it:

> If it is true that the critical moments in the progress of the *Heilsgeschichte* are associated with petitionary prayer, as a response to the petition, it is also true that prayer is the means by which the dynamic power of the Spirit of God is realized and apprehended for purposes of salvation in history.[50]

---

[49]Smalley, "Spirit, Kingdom and Prayer in Luke-Acts," p. 62.

[50]*Ibid.* J. Burnaby, "Christian Prayer," *Soundings,* ed. A. R. Vidler, pp. 220-37, thinks that the naive belief in the effectiveness of prayer raises difficulties for thought: "These are due to varying assumptions in regard, for example, to divine providence, natural law, and human freedom" (p. 220). However, his essay betrays a woefully inadequate understanding of prayer on the part of both Jesus and the apostolic church (to which he devotes merely 1½ pages!) when he suggests that prayer means primarily asking God for what we need. In the case of Luke-Acts, this is a gross oversimplification which completely overlooks the importance which Luke attaches to worship, adoration, rejoicing, thanksgiving, and praise.

The Role of Commissioning Accounts in Acts

Benjamin J. Hubbard

In an earlier essay[1] I concentrated on the literary form of commissioning narratives in Luke-Acts and sought to trace the antecedants of the form both in the Hebrew Bible and in other ancient near eastern literature. In the present study, I plan to limit my attention to commissioning stories in Acts and to study the role which they play in the overall plan of the book. Brief mention will be made of the commissioning material in the Lukan Gospel so as to highlight the importance of the commissionings in Acts.

Central to my previous article was the conviction that the commissioning narratives were structured along definite lines. These included all or several of the following elements: an *introduction* (INT) describing the circumstances surrounding the commissioning; a *confrontation* (CONFR) between the commissioner (usually God or his messenger) and the individual to be commissioned; a *reaction* (REACT) of fear, amazement or unworthiness to the presence of the august commissioner; the *commission* (COMM) itself in which the recipient is told to undertake a specific task in the service of the commissioner; a *protest* (PROT) in which the commissioned person questions in some way the word of the commissioner; a *reassurance* (REASS) to the individual by way of a statement from the commissioner providing confidence and allaying misgivings, e.g., "fear not", "I am (will be) with you", etc.; a *conclusion* (CONCL) to the narrative usually consisting of a statement that the one commissioned starts to carry out his task.

---

[1]"Commissioning Stories in Luke-Acts: A Study of Their Antecedants, Form and Content," *Semeia*, VIII (1977), 103-26.

While my study of commissionings in Luke-Acts was in press, T. Mullins published a similar article[2] in which, with a few reservations, he draws upon findings from a book[3] in which I first proposed the theory of a commissioning form in the biblical tradition. His conclusions are quite similar to those in my article on Luke-Acts.

Mullins' principal observations in terms of the present essay are threefold: 1) confrontation, commission and reassurance appear to be the really indispensable elements in biblical commissions;[4] 2) the function of each element in the commission form needs to be clearly described if the individual usages of the form are to be understood accurately;[5] 3) certain themes tend to reoccur in the commissioning narratives of Luke-Acts which further define the nature of the commission. These are: identification of a commission by time or place, command to rise or reference to standing, reference to a voice or a vision, reference to an angel, reference to the commissioned person's fear[6]. I shall respond to Mullins' observations in the course of the article. Generally, I feel that he has clarified many points and moved forward the discussion of the commission form.

However, the purpose of the present article, as already stated, is to examine how commissions are used by the author of Acts to carry forward the total narrative of the book. I intend to show that the commission accounts are situated by Luke at key points in his story of the Church's origins and indicate continual divine guidance and protection.

The Form of a Commission

I shall begin with a detailed, formal analysis of one pericope from Acts, Peter's vision of unclean animals (l0:9-23), to indicate concretely the elements in a commission. It happens to be the only commissioning account in Acts where all seven elements appear (there are three instances in the Gospel of Luke). The form was used by Luke, and the biblical authors generally, with considerable flexibility.

INT: (9-10a). At noon Peter goes up on the housetop to pray, but gets hungry and requests some food.

CONFR: (10b-12). Falling into a trance, he sees a great sheet full of various animals, reptiles and birds.

COMM: (13). A voice tells him to rise, kill and eat.

PROT: (14). Peter objects that this would be contrary to Jewish dietary laws.

COMM: (15-16). The command to eat is repeated three times before the great

---

[2]"New Testament Commission Forms, Especially in Luke-Acts," *JBL*, XCV (1976), 603-14.

[3]*The Matthean Redaction of a Primitive Apostolic Commissioning: An Exegesis of Matthew 28:16-20.* See esp. pp. 25-33, 62-7, 69-72 and 102-4.

[4]Mullins, "New Testament Commission Forms," 603.

[5]*Ibid.*, 606-9.

[5]*Ibid.*, 606-9.

[6]*Ibid.*, 610.

sheet is taken up to heaven.

REACT: (17a). Peter is perplexed about the visions's meaning. (In vss. 17b-18 the three men sent by the Roman centurion, Cornelius, to get Peter arrive at his house.)

COMM: (19-20). The Spirit instructs Peter to go with the men. This complements the earlier command (vs.13) to eat the unclean animals since the conversion of Cornelius will mean the beginning of table fellowship with Gentiles by Peter (cf. Acts 10:48).

REASS: (20). "...accompany them without hesitation; for I have sent them". The Spirit reassures Peter that God is behind both the strange vision and the arrival of the three men sent by Cornelius.

CONCL: (21-3). Peter welcomes the men and accompanies them to Caesarea the following day.

Not only is the formal structure of the pericope typical of commissioning narratives in Luke-Acts, but also the role of the story is highly significant: it enables Peter to shake off his scruples regarding table fellowship with Gentiles and thus overcome a major barrier to the Gentile mission. It is notable that several of the "themes" associated with commissions appear: reference to prayer (vs.9), command to rise (vss.13 and 20) and reference to a vision (vss. 17, 19) and a voice (vss. 13, 15). These will be elaborated upon in the following section.

Before proceeding to analyze the role of each commissioning account in Acts, it will be useful to schematize the formal elements in the twenty-five commissioning accounts in Luke-Acts. A parallel schematization will then be done with the thematic elements.

It can be seen from the chart (p. 190) that four elements appear in all of the commissions (INT, CONFR, COMM, REASS),[7] a fifth (CONCL) is missing only twice. In one of the two cases (Acts 22:17-21), Paul is narrating the commission in a speech and is interrupted by his audience at the point where he would have been expected to say that he did, in fact, go "far away to the Gentiles" (22:21). The remaining two elements (REACT and PROT) appear less frequently. However, one or the other or both appear fifteen times (60%). This indicates a general tendency for the individual to elicit some sort of response: either fear, amazement, etc. in the presence of the commissioner (REACT) or some kind of questioning of the commission itself (PROT).

The chart also makes clear the frequent use of the commissioning form in the Lukan infancy gospel (three times) the resurrection account (twice) and at strategic points throughout Acts. It appears that divine interventions in the form of commissions were needed both before and after Jesus' earthly ministry. The only exception is Lk. 5:1-11, a pericope without parallel in Mark and Matthew which corresponds in some respects to Jn. 21:1-11, the post-Easter apostolic

---

[7]In five instances parentheses have been placed around the verse(s) in which the REASS is found to indicate that it is present only implicitly. For example, in the second account of Paul's call (Acts 22:6-11) the REASS consists in the risen Jesus' statement that after Paul goes into Damascus he will be told what he is appointed to do (22:10). This certainly reassures the stunned and blinded Paul.

	INT	CONFR	REACT	COMM	PROT	REASS	CONCL
Luke 1:5-25	5-10	11	12	13b-17	18	13a,19-20	21-5
Luke 1:26-38	26-7	28	29	31-3,35	34	30,36-7	38
Luke 2:8-20	8	9a-b,13-14	9c	11-12	--	10	15-20
Luke 5:1-11	1-2	3	8-10a	4,10c	5	10b	11
Luke 24:1-9	1-3	4	5a	6-7	--	5b	8-9
Luke 24:36-53	36a	36b	37,41	44-48	--	49	50-53
Acts 1:1-14	1-2,9	3-5,10	6	7-8	--	11	12-14
Acts 5:17-21a	17-18	19	--	20	--	(19-20)	21a
Acts 8:26-30	(4-13), 27b-28	26a,29a	--	26b,29b	--	(39)	27a,30
Acts 9:1-9	1-3a	3b,4b-5	4a,7	6a	--	6b	8-9
Acts 9:10-19	10a	10b	--	11-12	13-14	15-16	17-19
Acts 10:1-8	1-2	3	4a	5-6	--	4b	7-8
Acts 10:9-23	9-10a	10b-12	17	13,15-16, 19-20a	14	20b	21-3
Acts 10:30-33	30a	30b	--	32	--	31	33
Acts 11:4-12	4-5a	5b-6	--	7	8	9	10-12
Acts 12:6-12	6	7a	--	7b-8	9	11	12
Acts 13:1-3	1-2a	2a	--	2b	--	(2c)	3
Acts 16:8-10	8	9a	--	9b	--	(10b)	10a
Acts 18:7-11	7-8	9a	--	9b	--	10	11
Acts 22:6-11	6a	6b,7b-9	7a	10a-b	--	(10c)	11
Acts 22:12-16	12	13	--	14-15	--	(15)	11
Acts 22:17-21	17	18a	--	18b,21	19-20	21	16
Acts 23:11	11a	11b	--	11a	--	11c	--
Acts 26:12-20	12	13,14b-15	14a	15-18	--	(17a)	19-20
Acts 27:21-26	21-23a	23b	--	24b	--	24a	25-6
Overall %	100%	100%	48%	100%	32%	100%	92%
% in Acts	100%	100%	32%	100%	26%	100%	89%

commission of Peter. Mullins[8] identifies five other pericopes in Luke's Gospel as examples of the commission form: 7:20-8, 10:1-17, 15:11-31, 22:7-13 and 22:14, 35-38. The first (7:20-8) seems merely to be a response by Jesus to the question asked by John the Baptist through two of his disciples about Jesus' mission. The second (10:1-17) might qualify but is more of a set of instructions[9] about missionary work than the kind of brief and direct commission typical in the Hebrew Bible and generally elsewhere in the New Testament. The third (15:11-31) is difficult to justify since the CONFR is between the prodigal son and his father (v. 20b), the COMM is given to the servants (vv. 22-4) and the PROT is made by the older son (vv. 25-30) who then is given a REASS by his father (v. 31). The fourth (22:7-13) might qualify, though it seems to hinge on the secrecy surrounding the location where Jesus would celebrate Passover rather than on the significance of the task for Peter and John themselves. The fifth (22:13,35-8) is an instruction to be prepared for the period after Jesus' return to the Father when missionaries will face various perils. But there is no real commission to a new task.

In Acts there is greater correspondence between my findings and Mullins'. I have identified as commissioning narratives four pericopes not mentioned by him: 5:17-21, 8:26-30, 16:8-10, 18:7-11. I have omitted only two from his list: 7:30-6 and 16:24-34. The first is certainly a commissioning account, that of Moses at the burning bush. However, it closely resembles LXX Ex. 3:1-10 and is part of Stephen's speech recounting Israel's history, particularly her infidelity and stubbornness (e.g., 7:35, "This Moses whom they refused, saying, 'Who made you a ruler and judge?'. . ."). Its function is related, therefore, to Stephen's general indictment of Judaism[10] rather than to the commissioning of someone in the early Church who would further its work. The second (16:24-34) is less a commission than an exhortation to the Philippian jailer, amazed by the earthquake and the miraculous opening of the prison doors and the prisoners' chains, to believe in Jesus.

Themes in a Commission

As mentioned in the Introduction, Mullins identifies several themes which appear frequently in commissions. Each of them will now be critically examined.

1. Time/Place. According to Mullins, the identification of a commission by time or place fixes "the temporal or spatial relevance of the commission."[11] E.g., Ananias' commission to find and heal the blinded Saul (Acts 9:10ff) is fixed at a specific time in the history of Christian origins: after Stephen's martyrdom and before the beginning of the Gentile mission. Although the commission does occur at this point, the INT to the commissioning of Ananias is actually more modest: "Now there was a disciple at Damascus named Ananias" (10:1). The commissions occur at strategic points in the story of Acts, but the INT almost never indicates this by itself. One has to look at the whole narrative framework. I do not, therefore, consider time/place to be a theme as such. It is, as explained,

---

[8]"New Testament Commission Forms," 605-6.

[9]Note that Mullins' COMM in this pericope is fourteen verses long.

[10]Cf. E. Haenchen, *The Acts of the Apostles, A Commentary*, pp. 288-9.

[11]"New Testament Commission Forms," 611.

the first element in the commission form which describes the *immediate* circumstances of the event.

2. Voice/Vision. The specific reference to a voice and/or a vision indicates that the experience is subjective. The two modes of communication share a common separation from ordinary experience and sometimes are intechangeable. In Acts 22:17-18, e.g., Paul describes his temple Christophany with the expression, ". . . I *saw* him *saying* to me . . ."[12] I would add that five of the commissions occur in dreams,[13] which further specify subjectivity.

3. Angel. Mullins contends that the mention of an angel functions in an opposite fashion to that of voice or vision, i.e. to interpret the experience as objective. He illustrates this through Acts 12:6-12 where an angel releases Peter from prison. In 12:9 we are told that Peter ". . . did not know what was done by the angel was real, but thought he was seeing a vision." Then in vs. 11, when the escape is complete and the angel has departed, Peter exclaims that now he is sure the Lord has sent his angel to rescue him. There is, however, a better way of explaining this contrast than that supplied by Mullins. According to Haenchen,[14] 12:6-10 did not originate with Luke. His descriptions of angels[15] are more dignified than this scene in which Peter is prodded from sleep and directed to get dressed step by step. Vs. 11, however, is Lukan in its clear proclamation of the divine rescue. The role of the angel as lending objectivity in contrast to the subjectivity indicated by a voice/vision reference is also questionable in view of Acts 10:3 where Cornelius "saw clearly in a *vision* an *angel* of God . . ." Moreover, in Acts 27:23 Paul describes a dream in which an angel appeared and assured him that all those on the ship would be saved. It seems, therefore, that Mullins has not made a convincing case for the angelic function of objectification.

4. Command to Rise. The function of the command to rise or stand is to show that the person who stands is accepted as the representative of the commissioner.[16] The apostles are to "go and stand in the temple and speak to the people . . ." (Acts 5:20). Philip is to "rise and go toward the south" to meet and convert the Ethiopian eunuch (8:26). Peter overcomes his doubts regarding the command to eat unclean food when he hears the Spirit telling him to "rise and go down and accompany" the men sent by Cornelius (10:20). Paul is told by the risen Jesus to "rise and stand upon your feet" so that he may be a witness to what he has seen and heard (26:16). Sometimes, rather than a command to rise or stand, the commissioner himself is described as standing.[17] Mullins sees this as

---

[12]*Ibid.*, 611-2.

[13]Acts 12:6-7, 16:9, 18:9, 23:11, 27:23.

[14]*Acts*, p. 390.

[15]See, e.g., Luke 1:11-20, 26-38; Acts 5:19-20; 10:3-6; 27:24.

[16]Mullins, "New Testament Commission Forms," 612.

[17]Acts 10:30, 16:9, 22:13, 23:11 (Cf. 22:10 where Paul notes that he was "standing by and approving" when Stephen was martyred.) A. Leo Oppenheim, *The Interpretation of Dreams in the Ancient Near East* notes the use in Sumerian, Akkadian, Hebrew and Greek dream reports of a phrase (in the CONFR) indicating that the deity or his messenger stood (suddenly) at the head of the sleeper. In Greek literature see, e.g., Iliad, II, 11. 20-1 where the dream "stood" (*stê*) over Agamemnon's head in the likeness of Nestor. Other examples: Herodotus' History, VII , 12, 14, 17. (See further examples in Hubbard,

equivalent to the command to rise/stand.[18] Though disagreeing that it is equivalent, I see a similarity in that the one who commissions is thus pictured in an authoritative role: he "stands before" the individual to be commissioned.

5. Fear. References to the fear of the person being commissioned are not at all frequent in Acts (only one occurrence, 27:24, in the pericopes under consideration). This feature falls under the general heading of the REACT and has been discussed already in that connection.

6. Prayer. There is, however, a final theme found in some of the commissioning narratives: the fact that the recipient of the epiphanic commissioning is sometimes engaged in prayer. Prayer is an important aspect of Lukan theology, as the article in this volume by A. Trites, "The Prayer Motif in Luke-Acts," makes clear. Its function in the present context is to indicate that the individual is in an ideal position to receive a commission from God or his messenger. Both Cornelius (Acts 10:2, 30) and Peter (10:9, 11:5) are described as praying when their interlocking commissions occur. Paul is praying in the temple at Jerusalem when Jesus tells him to leave the city and go to the Gentiles (22:17).[19]

We are left, then, with three themes (voice/vision, command to rise/reference to standing, and prayer) which add anything substantial to our earlier form critical observations. If we treat voice/vision and command to rise/reference to standing as two pairs of distinct but related phenomena, the following schematic summary of Acts results.

	Voice	Vision	Command to Rise	Reference to Standing	Prayer
Acts 1:1-14	--	--	--	(10)	--
Acts 5:17-21a	--	--	20	--	--
Acts 8:26-30	--	--	26	--	--
Acts 9:1-9	4	3	6	--	--
Acts 9:10-19	--	10	11	--	11
Acts 10:1-8	--	3	--	--	2
Acts 10:9-23	13	17,19	13,20	--	9
Acts 10:30-33	--	--	--	30	30
Acts 11:4-12	7,9	5	7	--	5
Acts 12:6-12	--	9	7	--	(12)
Acts 13:1-3	--	--	--	--	2
Acts 16:8-10	--	9,10	--	9	--
Acts 18:7-11	--	9	--	--	--
Acts 22:6-11	7	6	10	--	--
Acts 22:12-16	14	--	16	13	--
Acts 22:17-21	--	17	--	--	17
Acts 23:11	--	--	--	11	--
Acts 26:12-20	14	13,19	16	--	--
Acts 27:21-26	--	--	24	23	--

"Comissioning Stories in Luke-Acts," 110,112.) Three of the six references to standing in Acts occur in dreams (16:9, 23:11, 27:23).

[18]*Ibid.*, 612.

[19]See also Acts 9:11, 12:12, 13:2, 16:25 and Luke 1:10.

Although the themes do not occur as frequently as the elements in the commissioning form, *voice/vision* are found twelve times (63%), the *command to rise/reference to standing* fifteen times (79%), and prayer eight times (42%).

The Quotation from Joel (Acts 2:17-21)

Peter's Pentecost discourse is widely accepted as a sort of inaugural address for the missionary work which comprises the Acts of the Apostles.[20] One feature of the speech, however, has not received adequate attention, the citation by Peter of Joel 2:28-32 (LXX 3:1-5). Since one element in the Joel passage bears directly on what is to follow in this essay regarding the role of commissions in Acts, some comments on the prophetic quote are necessary. The Joel quote was seen in the rabbinic tradition as referring to God's final intervention in history.[21] Luke has helped along this interpretation by adding the words "in the last days" (Acts 2:17) to the citation. The Joel text then mentions the pouring out of the Spirit upon all flesh. Not only is the Holy Spirit expressly involved in four of the commission accounts (Acts 9:29, 10:19, 11:12, 13:2)[22]; but also he is the constant source of apostolic activity throughout the book, beginning with the experience of Pentecost day.[23]

The next ingredient in the text of Joel is the promise that "your sons and your daughters shall prophesy." Prophetic activity is expressly mentioned in 11:28 (Agabus foretells[24] by the Spirit that there would be a world-wide famine); 13:1-3 (the "prophets and teachers" in the church at Antioch are directed by the Spirit to select Paul and Barnabas for missionary work); 15:32 (the prophets, Judas and Silas, exhort the congregation at Antioch); 21:9 (mention is made of the four unmarried daughters of Philip who prophesied); 21:10-11 (Agabus foretells Paul's arrest at Jerusalem by a symbolic act resembling that of an Israelite prophet). In a more general sense, the entire book of Acts can be viewed as the record of prophetic activity inspired by the Holy Spirit.

The text of Joel goes on the predict that "your young men shall see visions and your old men shall dream dreams" (2:17). The contention of the present essay is that the nineteen commissions in Acts occur, with one possible exception,[25] in visions, five of which are further described as occuring at night, i.e. in dreams.[26] The word "vision" (*horama*) is used in several of the epiphanies, as

---

[20]R. Zehnle, *Peter's Pentecost Discourse (Tradition and Lukan Reinterpretation in Peter's Speeches of Acts 2 and 3),* pp. 123-31.

[21]*Ibid.,* pp. 29-30.

[22]Note also the Spirit's role in 11:28; 16:6-7; 19:21; 20:23; 21:4, 11.

[23]Haenchen, *Acts,* p. 187, summarizes the Spirit's activity throughout Acts and notes 62 occurrences of the word *pneuma.*

[24]See Haenchen, *Acts,* p. 373, on the tendency evident here to identify prophecy with uncovering the future.

[25]The exception is 22:12-16 where Ananias commissions Paul to "be a witness for him [God] to all men of what you have seen and heard" (vs. 15). We know from Acts 9:10-17, however, that a commission by the risen Christ was behind Ananias' subsequent assistance to Paul.

[26]See above, p. 192.

already noted.[27]

The quotation from Joel then repeats the promise of the Spirit's outpouring (Acts 2:17); and Luke may have added the words, *kai prophētousousin,* "and they shall prophesy," missing in the Hebrew and LXX.[28] In any case, this second mention of the outpouring of the Spirit is also linked to the gift of prophecy. The next element in the quotation is the "wonders in the heaven *above* and *signs* on the earth *beneath*" (2:19)[29] which will accompany the last days. The expressions, "wonders and signs" (*terata kai sēmeia*) or simply "signs," are used eleven times[30] in Acts to describe the divinely-aided activity of the apostles. With respect to the apocalyptic "wonders" described in the Joel quotation, "blood and fire and vapor of smoke; the sun ... turned into darkness and the moon into blood" (Acts 2:19-20), there was no way for Luke to make a direct link to the events chronicled in Acts. An interval still remained before those specific heavenly signs would happen. In the meantime the signs and wonders that *are* mentioned signify a foretaste of the end. Furthermore, these cosmic events can only be ultimately averted by whomever "calls upon the name of the Lord" (2:21). The "Lord" in question is now Jesus,[31] and the importance of belief and baptism in his name is the final link made by Luke between the passage in Joel and the event of Pentecost being interpreted by Peter.[32]

Thus the quotation by Peter of Joel 3:1-5 (LXX) in his keynote address at Pentecost provides the author of Acts with a program within a program, a text from the prophets which he can link to much of the subsequent narrative of Acts in a promise-and-fulfillment sense. This is certainly true of visions and dreams which provide a crucial means of describing the divine guidance given to the leading figures in Acts. We can now turn directly to the commissioning narratives to study in detail the role which they play in Luke's overall plan.

Commissioning Texts and the Structure of Acts

1. 1:1-14. the Christophany at the beginning of Acts consists of the command to remain in Jerusalem and await the baptism of the Holy Spirit (1:4-5) and the formal commission to "be my witnesses in Jerusalem and in all Judea and Samaria and to the end of the earth" (1:8). The specification of these three geographical stages corresponds roughly to the general plan of Acts: 1-7 (Jerusalem and Judea), 8-9 (Samaria) and 10-28 (the end of the earth,

---

[27]See above, pp. 192-4. The quote from Joel uses a variant word for visions, *horasis;* but both it and *horama* are derived from the verb for "see" *horaó.*

[28]This is the cautious opinion of Zehnle, *Peter's Pentecost Discourse,* p. 33; though see Haenchen, *Acts,* p. 179, n. 4.

[29]The italicized words are probably Lukan additions according to Zehnle, *Peter's Pentecost Discourse,* p. 33.

[30]Acts 4:16,22; 8:6 (*sēmeia* alone); 8:13 (*semeia kai dynameis megalas*) 2:22,43; 4:30; 5:12; 6:8; 14:3; 15:12 (*terata kai sēmeia* or vice-versa). "Signs and wonders" is also used by Stephen in 7:36 to describe how Moses led the Israelites out of Egypt.

[31]Haenchen, *Acts,* p. 186.

[32]Express mention of calling upon Jesus' name is made in Acts 2:21; 9:14, 21; 22:16. In addition, his name is described as the active source of the apostles' work or as the object of belief in 3:16; 4:10,12,30; 8:12; 9:16,27; 10:43; 19:13; 21:13.

culminating with Paul's presence in Rome).[33] So the commission is the charter of the apostles for the entire missionary activity to follow.

2. 5:17-21a. Arrested by the high priest and the Sadducees for their preaching and healing in Jerusalem, the apostles are released by an angel who tells them to "go[34] and stand in the temple and speak to the people all the words of this life." The apostles thereby receive a divine mandate to continue their activity in Jerusalem, the city from which the saving work must begin (Luke 24:47, Acts 1:8).

3. 8:26-30. After Stephen's martyrdom, a persecution arose against the Church, and its members were scattered throughout Judea and Samaria. Philip undertook missionary work in the latter area and was later joined by Peter and John (8:14-25). Philip was then told by an angel of the Lord to "arise and go" (anastēthi kai poreuou, 8:26) toward the south (i.e. towards Gaza). He encountered an Ethiopian eunuch whose religious affiliation (Jew or "God-fearer") is deliberately left vague by Luke so that the formal beginning of the Gentile mission with Cornelius' conversion would not be preempted. Nonetheless, the reader gets the impression that the missionary work has moved beyond Judea and Samaria with the conversion of Queen Candace's finance minister.[35] So the directive of the angel (8:26), made more explicit by that of the Spirit (8:29), carries the program of Acts a step closer to completion.

4. 9:1-9. Saul's confrontation with the risen Jesus on the Damascus road begins the series of events that will project the former persecutor into the starring role in the book as missionary to the Gentiles. The commission itself is intermediate in nature: "to rise and enter (anastēthi kai eiselthe) the city" (9:6) and there receive further instructions.

5. 9:10-19. the commissioning of Paul for the Gentile mission is completed via the Christophany to Ananias who, despite his protests, is told to "go (poreuou), for he [Saul] is a chosen instrument of mine to carry my name before the Gentiles and kings and the sons of Israel" (9:15).

6. 10:1-8. The first step in Cornelius' conversion, which inaugurates the Gentile mission in the person of this Roman military commander, is the angelophany instructing him to send for Peter.

7. 10:9-23.[36] Peter's vision of the great sheet containing various animals, reptiles and birds which he told to "kill and eat" complements Cornelius' angelophany. As he ponders the vision, the Spirit completes the commission by telling him to "rise and go down and accompany (anastas katabethi; kai poreuou)" the three men sent by Cornelius (10:20).

---

[33]R. Dillon, "Acts of the Apostles," Jerome Biblical Commentary, ed. R. E. Brown et al., II, 169.

[34]On the frequency of "go" (usually a form of poreuomai) in the LXX in connection with commissioning accounts, see Hubbard, Matthean Redaction, p. 67.

[35]Haenchen, Acts, p. 314. He goes on (pp. 314-5) to explain that the source of Luke's account was the Hellenistic tradition of the first gentile conversion by Philip skillfully incorporated by the author so that it does not upstage the Palestinian Jewish tradition of the first Gentile coversion by Peter (Acts 10).

[36]See earlier comments, pp. 188-9 above.

8. 10:30-3. Here Cornelius recounts his angelophany in the first person. The retelling of the experience in a speech heightens the drama of this pivotal episode.

9. 11:4-12. Peter's speech recounts his visionary experience and thus parallels Cornelius' in terms of its dramatic function.

10. 12:6-12. A new episode begins in Chapter 12 with Herod Agrippa I's execution of James, John's brother, and with the arrest of Peter. Just as an angelophany made possible the miraculous release of "the apostles" (5:10), so Peter is now ordered to get dressed and follow the angel and so is rescued. His deliverance strengthens the Church (12:24) while Herod's actions lead to his undoing (12:20-3).

11. 13:1-3. Paul's first missionary journey is the work of a commission by the Holy Spirit to five "prophets and teachers" at Antioch. They are told to set apart two of their number, Barnabas and Paul, "for the work to which I have called them" (12:2) sc., the real start of the mission to the Gentiles and "to the end of the earth" (1:8).

12. 16:8-10. Paul sees in a dream a Macedonian "standing" beseeching him to come to Macedonia "and help us" (16:9). This vision of a man who represents his country and his people[37] facilitates Paul's decision to extend his missionary work into Europe. Another step has been taken in the programmatic spread of the gospel.

13. 18:7-11. In a terse, Genesis-like epiphany,[38] Paul is commissioned and encouraged to continue his work at Corinth despite resistance from Corinthian Jews (18:6, 12-17). The commission thus explains Paul's eighteen month stay which contrasts with the general Lukan view that he moved quickly from country to country.

14. 22:6-11. The second account of Paul's apostolic commissioning is narrated by him in his speech before the Jerusalem crowd. Though similar to the account in 9:1-9, the commission is preceded by Paul's description of his past devotion to Judaism and explains why he stopped persecuting the "way" (22:4) and began to preach to the Gentiles.[39] For Luke, in light of the debate in his own day between Judaism and Christianity, this first person account of Paul's call adds support to the Christian interpretation of history in Acts.

15. 22:12-16. As in 9:10-19, Ananias' role is described. The actual COMM consists of his statement that God has appointed Paul to be a witness of what he has seen and heard (22:14-15). Ananias further assists Paul by telling him to "rise (*anastas*) and be baptized . . ." (22:16). Since Ananias is a devout Jewish Christian who observes the law (22:12), his commissioning of Paul stresses Paul's connections with Judaism and temporarily (see 22:21) mutes the problem of the mission to the Gentiles.

16. 22:17-21. In the same speech at Jerusalem, Paul describes his temple Christophany. While praying there after his return to the city, Paul is told to leave

---

[37]Haenchen, *Acts*, p. 488.

[38]E.g., Gen 26:24.

[39]Notice again the expression "rise and go" (*Anastas poreuou*) (22:10).

because his testimony about Jesus would not be accepted in Jerusalem. He objects on the basis of his past record of persecuting Christians. Nonetheless he is told to "depart" (*poreuou*) for the mission to the Gentiles (22:21). So this commissioning account provided additional authentication for Paul's mission (as well as for the shape of Christianity in Luke's time).

17. 23:11. Now under arrest at Jerusalem, Paul receives another Christophany (succinctly narrated as in 18:9-10.) The reader is assured that Paul will bear witness at Rome, just as he had done at Jerusalem. Luke's panorama — the mission from Jerusalem to Rome — is recapitulated by the commissioning.

18. 26:12-20. Again in a speech, his defense before Herod Agrippa II at Caesarea, Paul narrates his call.[40] It most closely resembles his own autobiographical version in Gal. 1:11-17 by stressing the Gentile mission[41] and making clear that he knew about it from the beginning directly from Jesus (Ananias' role is not mentioned). The speech as a whole establishes Paul's innocence and the reasonableness of his position vis-a-vis Rome. It thereby assists the Christians of Luke's day to pursue a similar course. Thus the third narration of the Pauline call fits into the larger framework and purpose of Acts in a supporting role.

19. 27:21-26. While under arrest and journeying to Rome, Paul and the ship's crew encounter a terrible storm (27:13-20). He eventually speaks to the crew who have abandoned all hope of being saved. In the speech, Paul describes an angelophany[42] assuring him that all would be spared and commissioning him to "stand (*parastenai*) before Caesar" (27:24). We are thus told indirectly that Paul witnessed to Christ before Nero.[43] This final commissioning brings Luke, at least in anticipation, to the goal of his narrative: the spread of the gospel to Rome.

Conclusions

Haenchen has stated that the speeches in Acts "give the book its intellectual and spiritual weight."[44] I would parallel this by maintaining that the epiphanic commissioning accounts in Luke's second volume give it its theological authentication. They occur at decisive places throughout the narrative in such a way that God's hand is continually seen as making possible each new step in the missionary program of the book. Acts is a success story made possible by divine intervention. Moreover, the commissioning accounts, as has been demonstrated, follow a consistent literary pattern and express recurring themes which heighten the theological significance of the accounts. Finally, it is remarkable how the quotation of Joel 2:28-32 by Peter in his Pentecost speech alludes to so many of the phenomena (including dreams and visions) which characterize the Lukan version of Christian origins.

---

[40]Notice again the stereotyped formula, "rise and stand" (*anastethi kai stethi*) upon your feet (26:16).

[41]Cf. Acts 26:17 to LXX Jer. 1:5, 7-8.

[42]"This very night there stood (*pareste*) by me an angel . . ." (27:23).

[43]Haenchen, *Acts*, p. 705.

[44]*Ibid.*, p. 212.

The Missionary Journeys Narrative: Patterns and Implications

Donald R. Miesner

The burden of this essay will be to suggest a chiastic structure for the Pauline missionary journeys account in Acts, and then to posit some implications which may be drawn from that structure. In order to lay the groundwork for the consideration of such a pattern, a brief overview of what Luke has done with the journey account in the Third Gospel will be offered.

The Pattern of the Lukan Journey

Luke highlighted Jesus' journey to Jerusalem by devoting nearly forty percent of the space of his Gospel to the travel section, which extends from 9:51 to 19:44.[1] Mark devoted only one chapter to the journey, and Matthew gave two chapters' space to it; that makes Luke's expansion of the same to ten chapters rather striking.

Scholars have generally agreed that the travel notices within the journey

---

[1] That is the extent of the journey posited by John J. Navone, "The Journey Theme in Luke-Acts," *BibT*, LVIII (1972), 617; and basically also by Kenneth Bailey (*Poet and Peasant*, pp. 79-83). Hans Conzelmann (*The Theology of St. Luke*, p. 73) has indicated its extent to be from Luke 9:51 to 19:27; Michael Goulder has abbreviated the extent of the journey structure to Luke 10:23-18:30. Cf. his "The Chiastic Structure of the Lucan Journey," *Studia Evangelica*, F. L. Cross, II, 195-202. Cf. also Charles Talbert (*Literary Patterns, Theological Themes and the Genre of Luke-Acts*, pp. 51-6) who exposits on a framework similar to that of Goulder.

narrative are not found within the traditional units themselves, but are a part of the Lukan frame which houses the units. Conzelmann sees the journey as a pattern imposed by the editor to express his view of Jesus' ministry. He cites the observation of K. L. Schmidt, that "although Jesus is travelling to Jerusalem all the time, he never really makes any progress."[2] A brief look at the content of the extensive travel narrative in Luke will quickly convince the reader that the accent on this section, with its scant geographical notes, is one of more than mere historical or geographical interest. The geographical hints promote the theology of the work.

Some writers have observed that Luke's use of chiasm stresses the geographic frame and is another way to elucidate the theological intention of his Gospel. Bailey, building upon Goulder's work, has observed a pattern for the Lukan journey with ten parallel points, indicating the prominence of Jerusalem. The following is the skeletal outline for his "Structure of the Jerusalem Document (Luke 9:51-19:48)."[3]

1. Jerusalem: Eschatological Events 9:51-56

  2. Follow Me 9:57-10:12

   3. What Shall I Do to Inherit Eternal Life? 10:25-41

    4. Prayer 11:1-13

     5. Signs and the Present Kingdom 11:14-32

      6. Conflict with the Pharisees: Money 11:37-12:34

       7. The Kingdom is Not Yet and is Now 12:35-39

        8. The Call of the Kingdom to Israel 13:1-9

         9. The Nature of the Kingdom 13:10-20

          10. Jerusalem: Eschatological Events 13:22-35

         9^1 The Nature of the Kingdom 14:1-11

        8^1 The Call of the Kingdom to Israel and to the Outcasts 14:12-15:32

       7^1 The Kingdom is Not Yet and is Now 16:1-8, 16

      6^1 Conflict with the Pharisees: Money 16:9-31

     5^1 Signs and the Coming Kingdom 17:11-37

    4^1 Prayer 18:1-14

   3^1 What Shall I Do to Inherit Eternal Life? 18:18-30

  2^1 Follow Me 18:35-19:9

 1^1 Jerusalem: Eschatological Events 19:10, 28-48

The three-fold repetition of Jerusalem at the extremities and at the center of the structure gives it an emphasis which fits well with the general theological use of the geographic pattern of Luke. Goulder has made the point that the Gospel

---

[2]Conzelmann, *Luke*, p. 61, quoted from K. L. Schmidt's *Der Rahmann der Geschichte Jesu*, p. 269.

[3]Bailey, *Poet and Peasant*, pp. 80-2.

shows the pattern of invitation moving inward, from Galilee through Samaria to Judea and Jerusalem, and then from Jerusalem outward, through Judea and Samaria to the uttermost part of the earth.[4] As Israel's rejection in Jerusalem led to opportunity for the outcasts in Luke, so also in Acts, the Jews' rejection resulted in the preaching to the gentiles.

Goulder has suggested that the first half of the Lukan journey presents the darker picture of rejection, while the second half of the journey gives the brighter slant, the extension of the gospel to the outcasts.[5] In this essay the writer hopes to demonstrate that the important theme of outreach, observable from the Lukan journey account, is also placed into a chiastic structure in Acts. The structure will show Athens to be the center of the missionary journeys stage of the gospel outreach. In Acts, also, the first part of the journey account highlights the theme of rejection; Paul's stays at the various cities are repeatedly cut short by persecution. In second half of the journey account, after he arrived at Athens, the spiritual hub of the gentile world and the citadel of classical culture, Paul has longer ministries; he serves for months and even years at the cities of Corinth and Ephesus. There the gospel received a widespread hearing.

There are two major precedents which have led the writer to the cautious conclusion that Luke may have structured the Pauline missionary journeys account in Acts in the form of a chiastic framework. As has been pointed out, the Lukan presentation of Jesus' journey to Jerusalem is viewed by some as a chiastically arranged account. If this is a viable observation, it would seem very possible that Luke used a similar structure in his second volume to serve corresponding thematic purposes.

The second precedent can be found in contemporary first century classical literature. Duckworth has made a strong case for the chiastic structure of Vergil's *Eclogues* by showing the inverse correspondence of content, by poems,[6] and for extensive and detailed serial parallelism of the two halves of the *Aeneid*.[7] It is this careful symmetry of the books of the *Aeneid* that is the most useful contribution of Duckworth's studies for the purposes of this essay. His parallel columns show the many striking likenesses and contrasts between Books I and VII, between II and VIII, and so on, consecutively, until Book VI is paralleled with the final Book, XII. This study will propose to show that the itinerary accounts of Acts 12:25-21:16 can be seen to have the same kind of patterning between blocks of material, in addition to having a chiastic order of progression (as is the case with the *Eclogues*). It is this high degree of conscious art with which Duckworth credits Vergil and for which he has widespread agreement from his reviewers,[8] which this essay will posit for Luke's presentation of the missionary journeys narrative. Given these precedents, it would not be surprising, then, that Luke, who set out "to write an orderly account for . . . Theophilus," would employ such

---

[4]Goulder, "Chiastic Structure of the Lucan Journey," pp. 195-6.

[5]*Type and History in Acts*, p. 60.

[6]George E. Duckworth, *Structural Patterns and Proportions in Vergil's Aeneid: A Study in Mathematical Composition*, p. 3.

[7]*Ibid.*, pp. 8-10.

[8]Cf. Donald R. Miesner, *Chiasm and the Composition and Message of Paul's Missionary Sermons*, pp. 65-6.

known and revered orderly devices of communication.

The Pattern of the Missionary Journeys

Luke has employed the "journeys" theme[9] not only in his Gospel, but also in Acts. Cadbury stressed that the itineraries and the speeches in Acts are the two elements which require special classification. He suggested that the itinerary in Acts is an editorial framework for events which are strung onto it as beads are put on a string.[10] Harnack, too, has noted the importance of the travel theme; he has asserted that in both Luke and Acts the journey motif *"liefert den Faden der Erzählung."*[11] Beginning with Acts 21:17 this "guiding thread" disappears, according to Dibelius.[12] Selby has drawn an analogy between the Gospel and Acts when he states that "Jesus' journey to Jerusalem prepares the reader for the corresponding journeys of Paul." Thus, he considers the accounts beginning at Luke 9:51 and at Acts 13:1 to be literary parallels.[13]

The missionary journeys narrative is a well defined unit within the structure of Acts. Dibelius has identified it as the central part of the message of Acts; it is the third of four divisions into which he has structured the book. In his view, the section extends from 13:1 to 21:16. Fittingly, he has remarked that after Caesarea is the caesura.[14] Goulder has described the ministry of Paul as a series of four recurring cycles; Acts 12:25-21:17 accounts for the first three of these cycles. According to him, these cycles represent the outreach that extends first to Cyprus and Galatia, next to Greece, and then to Asia, before finally extending to Rome in the narrative following the missionary journeys. Goulder's three cycles for the Pauline missionary journeys run respectively from 12:25-16:5; from 15:30-18:22, with Athens as the climactic point; and from 18:24-21:17.[15] Goulder's cycles correspond very neatly with the writer's proposed chiastic structure in that his first and third Pauline cycles each cover nearly five full panels on the extremes of the proposed chiastic pattern for the journeys account; his second cycle corresponds to the center of the structure, which also accentuates the importance of Athens. The writer's inclusion points (12:25 and 21:16) correspond with the division points of Dibelius and Goulder, noted above.

The following skeletal outline for the missionary journeys' chiastic structure should enable the reader to observe correspondences in inverse order at a glance.[16] Immediately apparent is the paralleled position of Paul's initial address

[9]Navone, "The Journey Theme in Luke-Acts," p. 616, has urged that the journey motif is a dominant biblical literary pattern; he has cited the journeys of the patriarchs, of the exodus, of Joshua, of the judges, and of the exile, in support of his contention.

[10]Henry J. Cadbury, *The Making of Luke-Acts*, pp. 60-1.

[11]A. Harnack, *Ist die Rede des Paulus in Athen ein ursprunglicher Bestandteil der Apostelgeschichte?*, p. 5.

[12]Martin Dibelius, *Studies in the Acts of the Apostles,* ed. H. Greeven, trans. M. Ling, p. 8.

[13]Donald J. Selby, *Introduction to the New Testament*, p. 160.

[14]Dibelius, *Acts*, pp. 10, 193, 209.

[15]Goulder, *Type*, pp. 26-9.

[16]Of interest at this point is the fact that Charles H. Talbert, working independently of this writer, also has posited a chiastic structure for much of the Acts journey narrative. His analysis, covering Acts 15:1-21:26, in *Literary Patterns*, pp. 56-8, deserves attention.

at Antioch and his farewell address at Miletus, near the opposite ends of the structure; the Areopagus address appropriately forms the center and climax of the longer construction. The paralleling takes place both by the correspondence of events as well as by the repetitive use of distinctive vocabulary. The abbreviated outline, given on the next page, presents the more striking events which are repeated in parallel fashion in corresponding sections of the missionary journeys narrative. Of considerable significance are the great numbers of parallels observable within all of the corresponding sections. Additionally, alternate sections include clusters of travel notes, while the intervening sections concentrate upon the missionaries' ministry within a given city; the latter contrapuntal arrangement has been documented and discussed elsewhere;[17] space considerations prohibit its inclusion here.

In an extended section covering nearly nine biblical chapters, one would not expect that the individual events recounted within the given corresponding sections would always fall precisely in order; the fact that such disarrangement does exist within most of the parallel sections may be attributed to Luke's fidelity to the traditional materials. Yet, Luke has showed considerable artistry also in the area of selection and arrangement of materials; sections CC' and DD' are strikingly close to each other in their sequence for the paralleled events. In the more detailed accompanying chiastic structure of the missionary journeys narrative the reader can spot the correspondences of the sections paralleled by matching up the lowercase letters which precede the given sentences.

A Chiastic Structure for the Missionary Journeys Narrative

A ACTS 12:25-13:14a	*A' ACTS 21:1-16*
a Barnabas and Saul returned from Jerusalem bringing John Mark.	i "We" returned from Asia Minor, enroute to Jerusalem.
b There are five prophets at Antioch.	j Various itinerary points are named.
c Through the Spirit Barnabas and Saul are called (to the work) at Antioch.	e Cyprus is sighted near the end of the journey.
d Fasting and praying lead to sending.	c Through the Spirit Paul is warned not to go (to Jerusalem) at Tyre.
e Cyprus is the scene of work early in the journey.	d Kneeling and praying lead to farewells and departure.
f The false prophet (Elymas) opposes the Spirit's work on the gentile proconsul.	b There are five prophets at Caesarea (including four unmarried women).

(continued on p. 205)

Contrapuntal patterns are common to high literary artistry, as Talbert has cogently argued elsewhere ("Artistry and Theology: An Analysis of the Architecture of John 1: 19-5: 47," *CBQ*, XXXII [1970], 362-3).

[17]Cf. Miesner, *Chiasm and Composition*, pp. 301-22, for the pattern of alternation of travels and cities and for its relation to Luke's "theology of the way."

Skeletal Outline For The Missionary Journeys' Chiastic Structure

A (12:25-13:14a) From Jerusalem to Syrian Antioch, Cyprus to Asia Minor; five prophets at Antioch; the false prophet Elymas opposes the gentile proconsul's conversion; Paul rebukes the false prophet's opposition to the paths of the Lord.

B (13:14b-52) PAUL'S INITIAL ADDRESS AT ANTIOCH, TO JEWS

C (14:1-28) Paul, persecuted at Iconium, has a short speech at Lystra following the healing of a cripple; Paul, who was stoned at Lystra and supposed dead, rises; he returns to Antioch after appointing elders.

D (15:1-29) Paul and Barnabas travel to Jerusalem because there was "no small dissension and debate," as the Pharisees defend Moses' law; between Peter and James' speeches mention is made of Barnabas and Paul's unrecorded speeches; all listen attentively; there is a decree for the restoration of order.

E (15:30-16:19) Paul travels to Antioch; Mark's work was deficient; he ministers, separated from Paul; Paul strengthens the churches; Timothy becomes co-worker; the Spirit prevents Paul from preaching in Asia; Paul has a vision to preach in Macedonia (Europe is opened!); the spirit of divination is driven from a slave girl who had misused God's name.

F (16:20-40) Paul and Silas are charged as breakers of Roman law; there is an earthquake at midnight; the jailer believes and is baptized with all his household; the magistrates respect the Roman citizenship of Paul and exonerate him.

G (17:1-15) Paul argued in the synagogue and said, "This Jesus . . . is the Christ"; Jews and Greeks were persuaded; Paul stayed with Jason, who was accused before civil authority of harboring opponents of Caesar and proponents of King Jesus; Jewish opposition leads to Paul's withdrawal to more receptive Berea; Silas and Timothy stayed behind while Paul went to Athens.

H (17:16-34) THE AREOPAGUS ADDRESS, TO GENTILES

G' (18:1-7) Paul stayed with Aquila and Priscilla, who had been exiled from Rome by (Emperor) Claudius; Paul argued in the synagogue and said that Christ was Jesus; he persuaded Jews and Greeks; Silas and Timothy rejoin Paul after he came from Athens; Jewish opposition leads to Paul's withdrawal to the more receptive gentiles.

F' (18:8-18a) Paul and Silas are charged as breakers of Jewish law; Paul has a night vision; Crispus, synagogue ruler, and all his household believed; many Corinthians are baptized; Gallio dismissed the religious charge, as he deals only with Roman law.

E' (18:18b-19:20) Paul travels toward Syria; he strengthens the disciples; Apollos becomes a co-worker; his knowledge was deficient; he ministers, separated from Paul; the Spirit comes on about twelve at Ephesus (a new Pentecost!); all Asia heard the word; the expelled evil spirit overcomes the seven exorcists who had misused the Lord's name.

D' (19:21-41) Paul plans to travel to Jerusalem and to Rome; at about that time there was "no little stir" because the silversmiths defended their business; between Demetrius and the town clerk's speeches a mention is made of Paul and Alexander's being kept from speaking; the assembly is in utter confusion; order is restored by the reminder of "due process" of law.

C' (20:1-17) Paul, plotted against in Greece, has a long speech at Troas as Eutychus falls asleep and falls three stories; Paul takes him, supposed dead, up alive; Paul decides to return to Jerusalem and convokes the Ephesian elders.

B'(20:18-38) PAUL'S FAREWELL ADDRESS AT MILETUS, TO THE ELDERS OF THE CHURCH

A'(21:1-16) From Asia Minor past Cyprus, (Syrian) Tyre to Caesarea, to Jerusalem; five prophets at Caesarea; the Jewish prophet Agabus predicts Paul's delivery to the gentiles; Paul rejects the people's plea, which opposes the will of the Lord.

g Paul rebukes the false prophet's opposition to the paths of the Lord.

h Sergius Paulus, proconsul of Cyprus, is the first convert mentioned on the journey.

i Paul and his company go to Asia Minor, Mark to Jerusalem.

j Various itinerary points are named.

f The Jewish prophet (Agabus) symbolically shows by the Spirit Paul's future deliverance to the gentiles.

g Paul rejects the people's pleas which oppose the will of the Lord.

a "We" and some disciples from Caesarea went to Jerusalem.

h Mnason, of Cyprus, an early disciple, is the last person named on the journey.

B ACTS 13:14b-52

Paul's Initial Address, at Antioch
- He speaks to the Jews first, who reject; then to the gentiles.

- He preaches resurrection and forgiveness.

- Departure follows shaking off dust.

B' ACTS 20:18-38

Paul's Farewell Address, at Miletus
- He speaks to the elders of the church.

- He gives pastoral admonitions, apologetic notes.

- Departure is amid weeping, kissing, embracing, and sorrowing.

C ACTS 14:1-28

a Paul worked at Iconium where the gentiles' minds had been poisoned.

b They remained a long time, speaking boldly for the Lord.

c A persecution attempt leads to flight from Lystra and Derbe.

d The priest of Zeus and the people wanted to offer sacrifice (pagan worship).

e Paul's short speech follows the uproar caused by the healing of a cripple from birth.

f Paul, who was supposed dead, rose.

C' ACTS 20:1-17

a Paul left Ephesus, where the gentiles had been stirred up.

b They gave much encouragement in Macedonia; then stayed three months in Greece.

c A plot by the Jews changed travel plans to a land route; Paul joined with companions from Derbe and Lystra (Timothy).

d After the days of Unleavened Bread, "we" gathered on the first day of the week to break bread (Christian worship).

e Paul's long speech leads to a deadly fall.

f Eutychus, who was supposed dead, is pronounced alive by Paul.

g Itinerary points on the return trip are clustered.

h Elders are appointed and committed to the work of the church.

i They returned to Antioch, mission base, and told the church about the gentiles' faith; there they stayed "no little time."

D ACTS 15:1-29

a There is "no small dissension" and debate with the Jews over circumcision.

b Paul, Barnabas, and others go to Jerusalem, passing through Phoenicia and Samaria,

c reporting gentile conversions.

d Believers among the Pharisees are quoted as requiring circumcision and Moses' law.

e Apostles and elders were gathered together.

f Peter's speech shows God's grace is for all,

g but this grace is endangered.

h Silence and attentiveness exists in the assembly after Peter's speech.

i Barnabas and Paul's speech to the respectful assembly is unrecorded.

j James refers to the speech of "Symeon" (Jewish name, unique).

k The prophets give authority to Peter's speech as the Lord's word.

l Judas and Silas are sent to Antioch.

m A letter conveys the message which settles the issue.

n The cause of Paul's people is defended.

g Itinerary points on the return trip are clustered.

i They decided to return to Jerusalem before Pentecost (where they would stay "no little time").

h From Miletus he called for the elders of the church of Ephesus.

D' ACTS 19:21-41

b Paul resolved in Spirit to go through Macedonia and Achaia to Jerusalem,

c and then to Rome (gentile capital).

l Timothy and Erastus are sent to Macedonia.

a There arose "no little stir" from the gentiles concerning the Way.

e Craftsmen and workmen of like occupation were gathered together.

d Demetrius, the silversmith, is quoted in defense of his business.

f Demetrius' speech shows Artemis as worshiped by all,

g but her worship was endangered.

h Rage, clamor, and confusion fill the city after Demetrius' speech.

i Paul was not allowed to go to the violent crowd (to speak).

j Alexander, a Jew, is put forward for a speech.

k The crowds cite the authority of Artemis in repulsing Alexander.

m The town clerk speaks the words which restore order.

n The conduct of Paul's people is defended.

o The gentiles are asked to follow the prescribed rules.

o The Ephesians are reminded of
their "due process" under law.

E ACTS 15:30-16:19

a They (Judas and Silas, with Paul
and Barnabas) went to Antioch,
taking the decree.

b Judas and Silas returned to
those who sent them.

c Paul decided to return to visit
the brethren in the cities
where he had preached the
Word.

d The work of Mark had been deficient.

e Barnabas took Mark along to
Cyprus.

f He (Paul) went through Syria and
Cilicia, strengthening the
churches.

g Timothy, part Jew (circumcized)
well spoken of, becomes a
co-worker in the mission.

h They went through Phrygia and
Galatia, forbidden by the
Spirit to speak in Asia.

i A vision to Paul at Troas is God's
call to him to preach the gospel
in Macedonia. (Europe is
opened!)

j Lydia and her household were
baptized.

k In the name of Jesus Christ,
the spirit of divination
was driven out from the
slave girl, who had misused
the name of the Most High
God; this brought economic
loss (involuntary).

E' ACTS 18:18b-19:20

a Paul (with Priscillan and Aquila)
left to sail for Syria; Paul
fulfilled his vow.

c Paul promised he would return to
Ephesus, where he had argued
briefly.

b He returned (by way of Jerusalem?) to Antioch (his sending church).

f He went through Galatia and
Phrygia, strengthening the
disciples.

g Apollos, a Jew, eloquent and
versed in the Scriptures, becomes a co-worker in the mission.

d The knowledge of Appollos had
been deficient.

e Priscilla, Aquila, and others
taught and helped transfer
Apollos to Corinth.

j The Ephesians were baptized in
the name of the Lord Jesus.

i When Paul laid his hands on the
Ephesians, the Holy Spirit
came on them, they spoke in
tongues, and prophesied. There
were about twelve. (A new
Pentecost!)

h Paul argued daily in the hall of
Tyrannus for two years so that
all of Asia heard the Word of
the Lord.

k The evil spirit came out of the
man and mastered the exorcists,
seven sons of the Jewish high
priest Sceva, who had misused
the name of the Lord Jesus;
the name was then extolled;
this brought economic loss
(voluntary).

F ACTS 16:20-40

a Paul and Silas are charged as advocates of practices against Roman law.

b Paul and Silas are attacked (by gentiles), beaten by the crowds and the magistrates, and are put into prison.

c At midnight Paul and Silas pray and sing; the prisoners listen; and, there is an earthquake.

d The jailer believes in the Lord Jesus, and is baptized with all his household.

e The magistrates respect Roman citizenship and publicly exonerate Paul and Silas.

f They visited Lydia and the brethren briefly before they left.

G ACTS 17:1-15

a Paul argued in the synagogue at Thessalonica, as was his custom, for three weeks.

b Paul said, "This Jesus . . .is the Christ."

c Some Jews were persuaded, as were devout Greeks.

d The jealous Jews of Thessalonica gathered a crowd and started an uproar.

e At Thessalonica Paul stayed with Jason, who was dragged before the city authorities and accused of harboring opponents of Caesar's decrees and proponents of another king, Jesus.

f Paul and Silas left the Thessalonians, fleeing by night, for the more receptive Bereans, both Jews and Greeks.

g Silas and Timothy remained while Paul went to Athens.

F' ACTS 18:8-18a

d Crispus, the synagog ruler, believes in the Lord with all his household; many Corinthians believe and are baptized.

c Paul has a night vision, is told to speak, not to be silent, that there will be no harm, and that God has many people here.

a Paul and Silas are charged as advocates of practices against Jewish law.

e Gallio deals only with Roman law, refusing to entertain the petty Jewish charges against Paul and Silas.

b Sosthenes is seized and beaten by the Jews before the tribunal; Gallio, the proconsul, paid no attention.

f Paul stayed many days longer before leaving the brethren.

G' ACTS 18:1-7

e At Corinth Paul stayed with Aquila and Priscilla, who had been exiled from Rome by (Emperor) Claudius.

a Paul argued in the synagog at Corinth every sabbath.

c He persuaded Jews and Greeks.

g Silas and Timothy came from Macedonia to Corinth.

b Paul testified that the Christ was Jesus.

d The Jews oppose and revile Paul.

f Paul left the synagog, openly declaring the Jews' guilt, for the more receptive gentiles.

H ACTS 17:16-34

17:16-22a The setting shows Paul disturbed
by idolatry; he is invited to
address the Areopagus.

17:22b-31 THE AREOPAGUS SPEECH declares
the unknown God.

17:32-34 The result shows that Paul's teaching disturbs some while Dionysius,
the Areopagite, and others believed.

Implications of the Structure

Since Luke's historiography is governed primarily by the theological purpose of showing the advance of the gospel to "the end of the earth," Dibelius has noted that the omission of other materials which do not serve that immediate purpose would be expected.[18] The extensive structure of the missionary journeys account, outlined above, suggests that Luke also drew heavily upon artistic devices in order to serve his theological purpose. Apparently, Thiering is correct in her observation that there is a vital connection between artistry and "the details of people, places, and times."[19]

1. Selection of Materials. The parallelism which Luke has built into the missionary journeys narrative may account for the inclusion and shaping of the story of certain events. At this point the writer does not propose to reflect on the many striking parallels that are observable in the corresponding sections of the above outlined structure; the reader may quickly spot these by a rapid overview of the skeletal outline presented for the missionary journeys. Instead, the study will deal briefly only with such events or notes in the narrative which seem somewhat strange by their inclusion or exclusion, or by the amount of space devoted to them.[20] Comment will be offered on the sections, in order, beginning with AA' and progressing toward the center of the structure. There will be no discussion of BB' at this point since these sermon sections are dealt with in parallel separately later.

Dibelius has found the list of names in Ab (13:1) troublesome.[21] The five men there named were "prophets and teachers" in the church at Antioch. It is possible that the three prophets who are listed in addition to Barnabas and Saul, and who do not figure in the Acts narrative, are named to provide balance for the mention of the five prophets (and prophetesses) who are listed in the corresponding section, A'b (21:9-10). This could be one of the elements of "inclusion" for the

---

[18]Dibelius, *Acts*, p. 209.

[19]Barbra Thiering, "The Acts of the Apostles as Early Christian Art," *Essays in Honor of G. W. Thatcher,* ed. by E. C. B. MacLaurin, pp. 140-1.

[20]Future studies might make additional observations regarding the same or other events paralleled within the given sections; these comments are no attempt at comprehensiveness; they are simply illustrative of the type of values such a structure may have for interpretation.

[21]Dibelius, *Acts*, pp. 10-1.

entire structure, as the journeys begin with the mention of prophets and their work and conclude similarly; fittingly, this may alert the reader to the prophetic task of declaring the whole counsel of God, which is developed throughout the journey narrative. The mention of Cyprus, which was sighted to the left in A'e (21:3), seems unnecessary until one remembers the important place of this island in the first missionary journey, described in the corresponding section. This type of logic receives some support by the mention of Mnason of Cyprus, an early disciple, with whom the itinerants lodged at the very end of their missionary journeys, A'h (21:16). A glance at the corresponding section. Ah (13:12). indicates that another Cypriote of great importance, the proconsul, is the first convert mentioned on the journeys. No longer does the detail regarding Mnason seem unimportant. Further, the clustering of itinerary notes at 21:1-3 (A'j) seems more explicit than necessary. A glance at the corresponding cluster in section Aj (13:13-14a) indicates itinerary points of great importance for the total work of the mission. Thus, the details of 21:1-3 provide a worthy artistic flourish in addition to giving geographic detail of possible interest to the Near Eastern or European reader.

Morgenthaler has noted that Acts records a one-minute sermon (at Lystra) but in chapter 20 does not record a single word of the address which Paul made that extended for hours.[22] It is not only fitting that the mention of the very long speech at Troas in C'e (20:7) is balanced by the inclusion of a brief one at Lystra; but the Lystra speech also has a vital introductory function in relation to another address, the Athens sermon.[23] The mention of the appointment of elders in Galatia, Ch (14:23), is a detail which might be omitted in the interest of including other worthy events; however, the corresponding recital of Paul's summons of the Ephesians elders, C'h (20:17), explains the important role for the ongoing work of the church that these leaders were to exercise. In respect to C'f (20:9-10), Dibelius has observed that there is a conscious ambiguity regarding whether Eutychus is dead or alive.[24] A glance at the corresponding "resurrection" note in Cf (14:19-20) suggests that the latter "ambiguity" may be intentional; certainly, Paul was considered dead by some; but, as the account indicates, he still was very much alive. Luke seems to be cultivating a literary parallelism here.

The silence and attentiveness indicated in Dh (15:12) seems to be superfluous detail. A glance at the parallel note in 19:28-29 shows the utter contrast between the tranquility and sublimity of the Apostolic Council as compared to the confusion, clamor, and rage that characterized the public assembly led by the silversmiths at Ephesus. The contrast illustrates another Lukan idealization of the interpersonal relationships of the apostles and the elders in the interest of the promotion of the gospel. Another matter of interest is the fact that the speeches of Barnabas and Paul in Di (15:12-13) are not recorded, even though those of Peter and James are recounted. A glance at the corresponding section (19:30-34) reveals that there also Paul and another speaker do not have speeches recorded; even more, they were prevented from speaking. Perhaps, in the interest of artistic parallelism, Luke found it desirable to

---

[22]Robert Morgenthaler, *Die lukanische Geschichtsschreibung als Zeugnis*, II, 73.

[23]Cf. Miesner, *Chiasm and Composition*, pp. 215-45, for the development of this point, including the architectonic structure of the speeches.

[24]Dibelius, *Acts*, p. 18.

omit the speeches of Barnabas and Paul in Acts 15 and to make his point through the means of the two speeches that are presented. In respect to D'b (19:21), which announces Paul's intention to go to Jerusalem after passing through Macedonia and Achaia, Selby has observed that the insertion of the travel plans at this point make the Ephesus riot seem awkard since there is another departure notice at 20:1-2.[25] Not only is this travel notice, which goes on to tell of Paul's plan to go to Rome, a foreshadowing of Luke's stated motif of having the gospel extend to the end of the earth; but, coming where it does, it may be an artistic device in addition. There is a corresponding note in regard to Paul and Barnabas in Db (15:3) which also describes them as going to Jerusalem after passing through two other territories.

The report in Eh (16:6), that they were forbidden by the Spirit to speak the word in Asia, not only is a dramatic build-up for the vision to "come over to Macedonia and help us," which signaled the opening of Europe for the gospel; it also points ahead to E'h (19:10); there the Holy Spirit was clearly with the preaching of the word to the extent that "all the residents of Asia heard the word of the Lord." The bringing of the word to Asia was part of God's plan; but, it would be done in His way and time! Thiering has observed that the narrator is presenting more than mere historical chronicling when he omits what might be an interesting recital of events from Paul's second trip to Galatia and Phrygia E'f (18:23).[26] Ef (15:41) reflects a similar Pauline passage through two territories in which previous converts were strengthened. In both cases Luke apparently has something more dramatic in mind in shortening the account of the events; he is building up toward a narration of the break-through of the gospel into new territory, in the one case to Europe, in the other case "to all of Asia." In respect to E'i, one is led to ask why the narrator sees fit to mention that there were about twelve of those upon whom the Holy Spirit came (19:6-7). The entry of the Spirit with the accompanying signs of tongues and prophecy are elements which remind the reader of the dramatic outpouring of power at Pentecost. Is Luke suggesting that a new Pentecost is taking place here in Ephesus, among the very people to whom Paul would leave his "testament" for the church (Acts 20:17-35)? A glance at the corresponding note, Ei (16:9-10), suggests another dramatic Spirit-motivated advance of the gospel to a new territory "among the nations," as Paul receives a vision and a call to come into Europe to preach there.

Why was Sosthenes beaten in F'b (18:17)? Luke does not say; however, the event does heighten the effect of official indifference to the petty charges leveled against Paul. Further, it strikes a literary connection with Fb (16:22-23) where Paul and Silas were beaten through the agency of the magistrates and the crowds and were imprisoned, before being eventually exonerated in public. Thus, both by itself and in parallel with the missionary maltreatment at Philippi, the beating of Sosthenes helps to paint the picture of Pauline innocence before the bar of justice. In F'c (18:9) Paul is described as having a night vision at Corinth. Goulder has pointed out that the Pauline section of Acts is one of darkness, that there is no reference to daylight throughout its duration; thus, Goulder suggests that for Luke the gentiles are the people of the night. They are brought in in the additional twelve hours beyond the daylight hours, which are dedicated to the

[25]Selby, *Introduction*, p. 303.

[26]Thiering, "Acts as Early Christian Art," p. 140.

salvation of the Jews. Only as the gentiles enter is the true Israel complete; the twenty-four hours of the day are filled.[27] Beyond the possible explanation given by Goulder, it seems that Luke is drawing a literary parallel to another night reference Fc (16:25-26), in the corresponding section of the itinerary account. As God assured Paul through a night vision that he would be with him and that he had many people for him to gain in Corinth, so through a midnight "act of God," an earthquake, the way was prepared for the conversion of the jailer of Philippi and his whole family.

It is of interest that Ehrhardt has seen a parallel between 17:6-7 and 18:2; he sees the accusation of the mob at Thessalonica that Paul and his companions had "turned the world upside down" as reflective of the very words of the decree of Claudius by which Aquila and Priscilla were driven out of Rome.[28] His suggestion receives formal support by the mention of Caesar in Ge (17:7) and the name of the emperor, Claudius, in G'e (18:2). Apparently, Claudius viewed the group to which Aquila and Priscilla belonged as insurgents much in the same way that the Thessalonians saw Paul and Silas as a threat to the imperial throne. Furthermore, there seems to be an undue amount of emphasis on the fact that Silas and Timothy do not accompany Paul to Athens in Gg (17:14-15). In the corresponding note, G'g (18:5), Silas and Timothy are described as coming to Corinth from Macedonia to join Paul there after he himself had arrived from Athens. The paralleling of these seemingly unimportant travel notes has the dramatic effect of presenting Paul as all alone in Athens. There he looms large as a man of epic proportion. He is the "conquering hero" of the Greek-Christian world; he alone entered the lion's den that is the Areopagus, and emerged, so the speak, "having eaten the lion." The conversion of the Areopagite vividly dramatized the power of the gospel which Paul preached.[29]

2. *Placement of sermons.* Brief comment needs to be made yet regarding the missionary sermons of the journey narrative. Myres has pointed out the importance of speeches in the classical epic for punctuating the narrative and for emphasizing turning points in the story.[30] Duckworth has amply illustrated from the Vergilian epic of Rome that the focal point of the story is often a significant speech.[31] Thus, in the middle section of the triadic structure of the *Aeneid*, where the national and patriotic theme comes through most strongly, the speech of Anchises with its stress on Roman heroes, the greatness of Augustus, and the Romans' task is centrally placed.[32] Also Luke, in the concluding section of Acts, which deals with the bringing of the gospel to Rome, uses the speeches of chapter 28 in a vital way to signal the passage of the gospel from the hardened

---

[27]Goulder, *Type*, pp. 221-5.

[28]Arnold Ehrhardt, "The Construction and Purpose of Acts," *ST*, XII (1958), 74.

[29]Ernst Haenchen (*The Acts of the Apostles*, pp. 518-28) noted the numerous literary parallels between Paul and Socrates at Athens. Both speak in the market place to every man; both were suspected of introducing new gods, and therefore were brought before the council. However, while Socrates was sentenced to death and drank the hemlock, Luke showed Paul and his cause in triumph. The gospel had reaped a harvest even from this rocky ground.

[30]John L. Myres, *Herodotus: Father of History*, p. 80.

[31]Duckworth, *Structural Patterns*, pp. 23-4.

[32]*Ibid.*, p. 12.

Jews to the receptive gentiles.[33]

In respect to the missionary journeys narrative, the symmetrical and climactic placement of the three larger Pauline sermons suggests a careful Lukan design in keeping with the theme of Acts. The placement of two of Paul's three major journey sermons at the first and last itinerary points to which Luke devoted considerable space in his story and the positioning of the Athens sermon at the center of the entire structure do not appear to be literary accidents or coincidences. The architectonic patterns discovered for the other speeches in Acts[34] add substance to the suggestion of Dibelius that "the selecting of the occasion and the elaboration of the speech is in each case the work of the author."[35] Why, for example, should the single model Pauline sermon to the gentiles be placed at Athens? From Acts it is apparent that Paul's success in missionizing was much greater at Corinth; from the epistles it is apparent that a lively Christian congregation was established at Philippi; only a few converts are recorded for Athens. Even so, there are clues that Luke was purposeful in selecting Athens for the only recorded sermon of Paul on Greek soil. The piety and the philosophy of Athens were "the heart of the spiritual life of Greece."[36] The Athens speech symbolizes Paul's penetration to the center of the Hellenistic cultural world. Luke's placement of a sermon at this spot is suggestive of the outreach of the gospel.

The three major Pauline sermons within the missionary journeys structure exhibit great variety, as well as progression. One of the speeches is in a Jewish synagogue, given to Paul's countrymen; the second address is before the gentiles; and, Paul's pastoral farewell is delivered to the elders of a Christian congregation. The sermons are placed symmetrically within the missionary journeys structure. The Antioch sermon is given near the start of Paul's first of three missionary journeys; the Athens sermon is dramatically placed near the center of Paul's second missionary journey; the Miletus address fittingly comes near the end of the third missionary journey. The Antioch sermon shows that the gospel was given first to the Jews, who rejected it; then it was delivered through the Athens sermon to the gentile world; finally, it was entrusted to the church, comprised of both Jews and Greeks, through the testament offered to the elders at Miletus. The parallel placement of the Antioch and Miletus sermons in the chiastic structure suggests that the church has received what the Israel after the flesh had refused. The church (as symbolized by the Ephesian elders) has become the repository of the testament of the word of salvation, first delivered to the Jews (as indicated in the Antioch sermon). Although the Jews rejected the ministry of Paul and Barnabas who left shaking the Antiochene dust off of their feet, the Christian church, made up of all nations, openly embraced and lovingly wept over the departing Paul at Miletus. Both in the chiastic structure as well as in the literary plan of Luke, the Athens speech forms an important climax of the missionary outreach, as indicated above. The communication bridges to the classical literature and life that are built into the Athens sermon indicate that the

[33]Miesner, *Chiasm and Composition*, pp. 119-29.

[34]*Ibid., passim.*

[35]Dibelius, *Acts*, p. 165.

[36]*Ibid.*, p. 152.

attempt to reach the gentiles is a serious and all-our effort. Having reached the capital and pinnacle of the Greek spirit at Athens, Luke may now turn to the conquests of the gospel within the imperial capital, at "the end of the earth," where Paul's final speech and the Lukan summary point to the unhindered gentile mission (Acts 28:23-31).

By Land and By Sea:
The We-Passages
and Ancient Sea Voyages

Vernon K. Robbins

The accounts of Paul's travels throughout the Mediterranean world begin in Acts 13. Prior to this chapter Paul (Saul) was present at Stephen's death (8:1), temporarily blinded and permanently converted on the road to Damascus (9:1-9), blessed and baptized by Ananias (9:17-19), and transported by night out of Damascus so the Jewish residents could not kill him (9:20-30). After some time Barnabas took Paul to Antioch where they spent a year together with the Christian community (11:25-26). When Barnabas and Paul were selected to take relief offerings to Jerusalem (11:29-30), they brought John Mark with them on their return (12:25).

Throughout all of this, Paul travels on land. In fact, in all of Luke and Acts 1-12 no one travels on the sea. In contrast to Mark and Matthew where Jesus frequently travels on the Sea of Galilee, in Luke Jesus never even goes alongside the sea (*para tēn thalassan*).[1] On two occasions Jesus gets into a boat and goes onto or across "the lake" (*hē limnē*: 5:1, 2; 8:22, 23, 33). This "lake" is called Gennesaret in 5:1; never in Luke does Jesus go to or across "the Sea of Galilee." The author's choice of vocabulary indicates that he distinguishes between "the lake" and "the sea." "The lake" is a body of inland water on the eastern edge of Galilee. A person can sail across this lake (or "down" it, *katapleuō:* 8:26) to the land of the Gergesenes (or Gerasenes or Gadarenes) that lies opposite Galilee

---

[1]*Thalassa* occurs 18 times in Mark, 17 times in Matthew, and 3 times in Luke. Each of the occurrences in Luke is in a saying rather than narration: Luke 17:2,6; 21:25.

(*antipera tēs Galilaias*: 8:26). In contrast, "the sea" is that expanse of water which can take you to Cyprus, Macedonia, Achaia, Crete, or Italy. Jesus sets a precedent for sea travel on the lake, but Jesus himself never travels or voyages on the sea. Even Peter and John never travel on the sea. Only Paul and his associates face the challenge, adventure, and destiny of voyaging across the sea.

Sea travel appears for the first time in Acts 13. Paul and his company sail from Seleucia to the island of Cyprus, then from Cyprus to Pamphylia (13:4, 13). This sea travel holds little adventure or danger. Only two short clauses relate the means of travel; all the narrated episodes occur on land. Two more short clauses recount sea transportation in this section of Acts. Paul and Barnabas are taken back to Syrian Antioch in a boat (14:26), and Barnabas and John Mark go to Cyprus in a boat after the disagreement with Paul (15:39). Still, however, no detailed sea voyage occurs. Only in chapter 15 do extended sea voyages begin, and when they occur, the narration moves into first person plural "we."

The coincidence of sea voyages and first person plural narration in Acts is striking. There are four we-sections in Acts: 16:10-17; 20:5-15; 21:1-18; 27:1-28:16. In each instance, a sea voyage begins as the first person plural narration emerges. While this observation can lead the interpreter in various directions, it points vividly to accounts of sea voyages in antiquity. Sea voyages are often couched in first person narration. Either the author narrates it as a participant (I sailed to Byblos . . . .) or the author stages a participant recounting the voyage (he then said, "As I was sailing to Byblos . . . ."). Sea voyage narratives in Greek and Roman literature, however, become a distinct genre. One of the features of this genre is the presence of first person *plural* narration. Undoubtedly the impetus for this is sociological: on a sea voyage a person has accepted a setting with other people, and cooperation among all the members is essential for a successful voyage. Therefore, at the point where the voyage begins, the narration moves to first person plural.

The author of Luke-Acts employs the sea voyage genre with great skill. His narrative builds toward a conclusion that is reached through a dramatic sea voyage., First plural narration emerges in the sections that present "mission by sea." There is evidence to suggest that Paul's voyages across the sea were in view during the composition of the first volume of the work. To explain the role of the we-passages in Acts, we will undertake six steps of analysis. (1) Since the we-passages in Acts present sea voyages, a survey is made of narrative style that accompanies sea voyages in Greek and Roman literature; (2) since third person narrative style surrounds the we-passages in Acts, an investigation follows concerning historiographical literature that is pervaded by third person narrative; (3) since there are other texts that alternate between third person and first person plural narration, Greek literature that reflects the same style of narration as Acts is presented; (4) on the basis of the survey, the primary features of the sea voyage genre are explored, and the we-passages are examined for the presence of these features; (5) the position of the we-passages in the structure of Acts is investigated; and (6) we posit a conclusion regarding the function of the we-passages in the purpose of Luke-Acts. These explorations are intended to suggest that the author of Luke-Acts is a versatile Hellenistic writer who is an intelligent participant in the literary arena of Mediterranean culture. The author has employed first person plural narration for the sea voyages, because it was conventional generic style within Hellenistic literature. This style contributes directly to the author's scheme of participation in history through narration of its dramatic episodes.

Narrative Style in Ancient Sea Voyages

There is a natural propensity for portraying sea voyages through the medium of first person narration. This style for narrating voyages extends as far back as the most ancient Mediterranean literature known to us. Two Egyptian tales, *The Story of Sinuhe* (1800 B.C.) and *The Journey of Wen-Amon to Phoenicia* (11 cent. B.C.), recount sea voyages through first person *singular* narration.[2]   Also Utnapishtim, in the Akkadian *Epic of Gilgamesh,* recounts his voyage upon the waters in first person *singular.*[3]   In the Egyptian and Mesopotamian accounts the narrator uses first person singular "I," even when others are present with him on the voyage.[4] Homer's *Odyssey,* in contrast, contains the earliest example among Mediterranean literature of a sea voyage that employs first person *plural* narration.

In books 9-12 of the *Odyssey,* the travels and adventures of Odysseus are recounted to the Phaeacians at a banquet. The reader therefore hears about the breath-taking episodes from the lips of Odysseus himself.   This narrative technique allows the dynamics of traveling on the sea and encountering strange, new peoples to emerge directly through personal narration. When Alcinous, king of the Phaeacians, asks Odysseus to recount his adventures, he begins, after the initial formalities, with:

> From Ilios the wind bore me and brought me to the Cicones, to Ismarus. There I sacked the city and slew the men . . . . (9.39-41).[5]

Here, first person *singular* narration begins the account, and first person *singular* narration occurs frequently throughout these four books of the *Odyssey.* However, first person *plural* narration becomes a formulaic means for launching the ship, sailing for a number of days, and beaching the ship at the end of a voyage.   Therefore, first person *plural* formulaic clauses unify the sailing accounts. Five times, voyages begin with all or part of the following first person *plural* formula:

> From there we sailed on, grieved at heart, glad to have escaped death, though we had lost our dear comrades . . . .[6]

Twice, the length of a voyage is recounted in another first person plural pattern:

> For nine (six) days we sailed, night and day alike . . . .[7]

---

[2]James B. Pritchard, ed., *Ancient Near Eastern Texts,* pp. 18-22, 25-9.

[3]Tablet XI; *ibid.,* pp. 92-7.

[4]See *Wen-Amon* 10, where he refers to "a man of my ship," and *Gilgamesh* XI:84, where he recounts that he made all his family and kin go aboard the ship.

[5]The quotations from the NT are taken from the Revised Standard Version; unless otherwise indicated, the quotations from Greek and Latin literature are from the Loeb Classical Library edition of the work.

[6]*Enthen de proterō pleomen akachēmenoi ētor, asmenoi ek thanatoio philous olesantes hetairous.* These two lines occur at 9.62-63; 9.565-566; 10.133-134. The first line occurs further at 9.105; 10.77. The variant *entha katepleomen* occurs at 9.142.

[7]10.28; 10.80: *Ennēmar (Hexēmar) men homōs pleomen nuktas te kai ēmar.*

The voyage ending is captured in first person plural clauses that depict the beaching of the ship:

> Then, on coming thither, we beached our ship on the sands, and ourselves went forth upon the shore of the sea.[8]

In Homeric literature, therefore, first person narration transfers the excitement and anxiety of a sea voyage in the most vivid narrative technique available to the pen. Homeric couplets perpetuate the dynamics in poetic form, and first person plural narration becomes as familiar as the *Odyssey* itself:

> From there we sailed on, grieved at heart, glad to have escaped death, though we had lost our dear comrades . . . .[9]

The same technique is used by Vergil (70-19 B.C.) in books 2-3 of the *Aeneid.* Since the structure of the *Aeneid* imitates the *Odyssey,* Vergil's use of first person narration results directly from Homeric influence.[10] Aeneas himself recounts the destruction of Troy and the voyage that ends in a shipwreck offshore Carthage. In book 3, his first person account to Dido turns from the sack of Troy (book 2) to his subsequent travels that have brought him to Carthage. With the launching of the boat, first person *plural* narration becomes commonplace:

> With Asian power and Priam's tribe uprooted,
> though blameless, by heaven's decree; with Ilium's pride
> fallen, and Neptune's Troy all smoke and ash,
> God's oracles drove us on to exile, on
> to distant, lonely lands. We built a fleet
> down to Antander and Ida's Phrygian peaks,
> uncertain which way Fate led or where to stop.
> We marshaled our men. When summer first came on,
> Anchises bade us trust our sails to fate (3.1-9).[11]

These two examples come from the prestigious epic literature of Greek and Roman culture. Their influence was pervasive in the literature of the Mediterranean world. Sea voyages are not only adventurous but lead to the founding of new cities and the establishment of new leaders. Shipwrecks create the setting for man's display of strength and take the passengers, unplanned, to famous islands and cities of the Mediterranean world. Through these voyages, destiny unfolds and the ways of the gods with men are displayed.

From the seventh century B.C. onwards, Greek poetry contained sea voyage imagery, and it is not unusual for the lines that contain this imagery to be formulated in first person plural style. Two poems by the lyric poet Alcaeus (b. ca. 620 B.C.) reflect this style. Both poems were cited by Heraclitus (1 cent. A.D.) as

---

[8] 9.546-547; 12.5-7: *nēa men enth' elthontes eleísamen en psamathoisin, ek de kai autoi bēmen epi hrēgmini thalassēs.* Variations of this pattern occur at 9.149-151; 9.169. Cf. 9.85; 10.56; 11.20.

[9] Cf. Werner Suerbaum, "Die Ich-Erzahlungen des Odysseus," *Poetica,* II (1968), 176-7, n. 58. Also W. J. Woodhouse, *The Composition of Homer's Odyssey,* p. 44: "The sea-stories proper constitute the content of a comparatively short portion of the life of the hero... in the string of adventures supposed to be narrated by Odysseus himself at the court of king Alkinoos, Homer has raised these age-old stories to a power of illusive reality, to an artistic and ethical level, that together give this portion of the Odyssey its own special undying quality."

[10] Cf. Brooks Otis, *Virgil: A Study in Civilized Poetry,* pp. 215-312.

[11] Vergil, *The Aeneid,* trans. by Frank O. Copley, p. 49.

allegories of political trouble in the state.[12] Alcaeus 6 maintains first person plural throughout the scene of sailing on dangerous waters:

> This wave again comes [like?] the one before:
> it will give us much labour to bale out,
> when it enters the vessel's [...]
> [...] let us fortify the [...] with all speed,
> and run into a secure harbour.
>
> And let not unmanly hesitance take hold of any one [of us]:
> a great [...] is clear before us.
> Remember our [toils] of yesterday:
> now let each prove himself a steadfast man.
>
> And let us not disgrace [by cowardice]
> our noble fathers lying under the earth . . . .[13]

Alcaeus 326 alternates between first person singular and plural as the poet captures the anxiety that attends the injury inflicted on a ship in a storm:

> I cannot tell where the wind lies;
> one wave rolls from this side,
> one from that, and we in their midst
> are borne along with our black vessel
>
> Toiling in a tempest passing great.
> The bilge is up over the masthold,
> all the sail lets the daylight through already,
> and there are great rents along it,
>
> And the wooldings are slackening,
> the rudders . . . both feet stay [entangled]
> In the sheets: that alone it is that [saves] me;
> the cargo . . . is carried away above . . . .[14]

Theognis (fl. 544-541 B.C.) continues this imagery and style of narration in the section of his lyric poetry that treats the city-state metaphorically as a ship on a turbulent sea:

> Now we are borne along with white sails, casting about on the open sea near Melos through the dark night; The crew does not want to bale; and the sea casts over us on both sides of the ship . . . (671-674).[15]

The metaphor of the city-state as a ship on the sea also appears in tragic poetry. In *Seven Against Thebes,* Aeschylus (525/4-456 B.C.) has a messenger announce the successful defense of the city against its aggressors in these

---

[12]*Allegories of Homer* 5; available in Felix Buffiere, *Heraclite: Allegories d'Homere*, pp. 4-5.

[13]Alcaeus 6 (Diehle)/A6 (Lobel and Page); this translation is from Denys L. Page, *Sappho and Alcaeus*, p. 183.

[14]Alcaeus 326 (Diehle)/Z2 (Lobel and Page); translation from *ibid.*, p. 186.

[15]Author's translation; for the text with commentary, see David A. Campbell, *Greek Lyric Poetry*, pp. 85-6, 368-70. Pindar (518-438 B.C.) used sea voyage imagery metaphorically to describe the process of writing an ode; see Gogo Lieberg, "Seefahrt und Werk," *GIF*, XXI (1969), 209-13. Nemea 4.36-8 is especially interesting for its use of first person plural; for analysis of this passage, see Jacques Peron, *Les Images maritimes de Pindare*, pp. 90-100. For a detailed study of first person in Pindar, see Mary R. Lefkowitz, *"TŌ KAI EGŌ" The First Person in Pindar*," *HSCP*, LXVII (1963), 177-253.

words:

> Both in fair weather and in the many blows of the surging
> sea the city has not shipped water.
> The bastion is water-tight
> and we have bulwarked her ports with champions
> who in single-handed fight have redeemed their pledge
> (795-798).[16]

The attack on the city is like a storm that threatens to destroy a ship at sea. With disciplined effort and gradual abatement of the storm, the ship is successfully kept afloat. Aeschylus also uses sea voyage imagery in a speech by Electra in *The Libation-Bearers:*

> But the gods whom we invoke, know
> by what storms we are tossed like sailors.
> Yet, if it is our fate to win safety,
> from a little seed may spring a mighty stock (201-203).

The difficult situation faced by Electra and her companions calls forth the danger of sailing on the sea. Mortals have little choice but to turn their petitions to heaven and hope for a successful outcome. First person plural narration attends this imagery in epic, lyric, and tragic poetry. During later centuries, this literature is copied, quoted, and read, and its influence is found in widespread sectors of Hellenistic and Roman civilization.

In his *Menippean Satires,* Varro (116-27 B.C.) provides evidence that first person style persists in voyage imagery during the first century B.C.[17] Fragments 276 and 473, preserved by Nonius Marcellus (early 4th cent. A.D.), read respectively:

276:

> Here at the crossroads we boarded a swampboat,
> which the barge boys pulled along through the
> sedge with a rope.

473:

> Wherever we wanted to go, the wind blew against us.[18]

Nonius also recounts that Varro knew a two-book satire entitled *Periplous* (Voyage),[19] and fragment 418, from book 2, contains first person plural narration.[20]

---

[16]See the translation and commentary in Howard D. Cameron, *Studies on the Seven Against Thebes of Aeschylus,* p. 63.

[17]See Eduard Norden, *Agnostos Theos,* p. 313. I have been informed at many places in this paper by his appendix, *"Zur Komposition der Acta Apostolorum,"* pp. 311-32.

[18]These fragments are most readily available in *Petronii Sarturae,* ed. by F. Buecheler, pp. 193, 214:

> 276: *hic in ambivio naven conscendimus palustrem, quam nautici equisones per ulvam ducerent loro.*

> 473: *quocumque ire vellemus, obvius flare.*

I am indebted to my colleague, Professor David F. Bright, for the translations of the material from Buecheler.

[19]See M. Terenti Varronis, *Saturarum Menippearum,* ed. by Alexander Riese, pp. 197-8.

[20]Buecheler, *Petronii Sarturae,* p. 208: ". . . lest we wander, that there were many bypaths, and that the way was quite safe but slow going." *et ne erraremus, ectropas esse multas, omnino tutum, esse sed spissum iter.*

By the first century A.D., sea voyages, interrupted by storms, were an established part of Mediterranean literature outside of epic. And first person narration of voyages appears to be not only fashionable but preferred. Dio Chrysostom (A.D. 40-after 112), from whom portions of 78 discourses are extant, most frequently recounts tales in third person narration. But in the seventh discourse, when a sea voyage, which ends in a shipwreck and a journey, is recounted, he uses first person narration:

> . . . at the close of the summer season I was crossing from Chios with some fisherman in a very small boat, when such a storm arose that we had great difficulty in reaching the Hollows of Euboea in safety (7.2).

After a short while on shore, a hunter invites him to travel with him. The narrative thus continues:

> As we proceeded on our way, he told me of his circumstances and how he lived with his wife and children . . . (7.10).

Dio's use of first person narration for this tale of voyage and adventure suggests that he was responding to the genre itself. This style had established itself within the cultural milieu, and writers found it natural to respond to this convention.

Within sea voyage accounts, the shipwreck became an increasingly attractive feature. Petronius (1st cent. A.D.) exhibits this interest in shipwreck accounts and also shows the natural propensity for first person narration in them. It only seemed proper to recount the dangerous episode with first person plural:

> While we talked over this matter and others, the sea rose, clouds gathered from every quarter, and overwhelmed the day in darkness . . . . One moment the wind set towards Sicily, very often the north wind blew off the Italian coast, mastered the ship and twisted her in every direction; and what was more dangerous than any squall, such thick darkness had suddenly blotted out the light that the steersman could not even see the whole prow . . . (chap. 114).

Even the Jewish historian Josephus mentions a sea voyage and a shipwreck in his biography. And little surprise it is that he shifts from first person singular to first person plural as he recounts it:

> I reached Rome after being in great jeopardy at sea. For our ship foundered in the midst of the sea of Adria, and our company of some six hundred souls had to swim all that night. About daybreak, through God's good providence, we sighted a ship of Cyrene, and I and certain others, about eighty in all, outstripped the others and were taken on board (3; sections 14-16).

By the first century A.D. the sea voyage, threatened by shipwreck, had established itself as a distinct genre. An essential feature of this genre was first person narration. The status of the genre provided the possibility for authors to employ the situation of a sea voyage to interpret many situations in life. Thus Ovid, in *Tristia* 1.2.31-34 (composed A.D. 8-9), compares his life in exile to a sea voyage threatened by shipwreck:

> The helmsman is confused nor can he find what to avoid or what to seek; his very skill is numbed by the baffling perils. We are surely lost, there is no hope of safety . . . .

Being in exile is like being thrown on a ship that starts on a voyage. One is dependent upon the crew for the outcome, but even the crew cannot predict the fortune of the journey. Together they face the peril of the sea, and when the wind becomes a storm and the waves begin to threaten, every occupant of the ship faces the same jeopardy. Together they experience the confusion, the fear, and the hope that all is not lost. As Ovid uses this situation on the sea to explain his experience in exile, he expresses the anguish in first person plural: "We are surely lost, there is no hope of safety . . . ."

In the second century A.D., Lucian (A.D. 125-180) wrote a sea voyage parody entitled *A True Story.* If Ovid's use of a sea voyage to interpret his exile leaves any doubt with regard to the status of this genre, Lucian's parody gives even firmer evidence. In his work Lucian recounts a fantastic voyage with tongue in cheek. His parody reveals the essential features of the sea voyage genre. He narrates the voyage as Odysseus, Aeneas, Dio Chrysostom and Josephus narrate theirs. He begins in first person singular and shifts to first person plural at the embarkation.

> Once upon a time, setting out from the Pillars of Hercules and heading for the western ocean with a fair wind, I went a-voyaging . . . . For a day and a night we sailed before the wind making very little offing, as land was still dimly in sight; but at sunrise on the second day the wind freshened, the sea rose, darkness came on, and before we knew it we could no longer even get our canvas in . . . . On the eightieth day the sun came out suddenly and at no great distance we saw a high, wooded island . . . . Putting in and going ashore, we lay on the ground for some time in consequence of our long misery . . . (1.5-6).

Even though Lucian made light of sea voyage accounts by presenting one of the most fantastic voyages imaginable, the sea voyage genre had a firm place within the literature of the culture. Thus Achilles Tatius (A.D. second century) includes a sea voyage in the *Adventures of Leucippe and Clitophon,* and the appeal of the account is strengthened by first person narration:

> . . . as we arrived at the harbour of Berytus, we found a ship just sailing, on the very point of casting loose; so we asked no questions as to her destination, but embarked all our belongings aboard . . . (2.31.6).

> On the third day of our voyage, the perfect calm we had hitherto experienced was suddenly overcast by dark clouds and the daylight disappeared, a wind blew upwards from the sea full in the ship's face, and the helmsman bade the sailyard be slewed around . . . (3.1.1).

In 4.9.6. these adventures are summarized in first person plural:

> We escaped the terrors that awaited us at home, only to suffer shipwreck; we were saved from the sea, . . . [lacuna]; we were rescued from the robbers, only to find madness waiting for us.

This style continues in the third century (A.D. 220-250) in Heliodorus' *Ethiopian Story* about Theagenes and Chariclea. The author has established third person style of narration up to this point, so he leads into the voyage with this style:

> When they got on board the Phoenician vessel, he said, in their flight from Delphi, the beginning of their voyage was quite agreeable, as they were borne along by a following wind of moderate strength . . . (5.17).

But after only a few lines, Heliodorus turns the narrative over to Calasiris for a personal account of the voyage.

> Calasiris then pursued his narrative thus: "We made our way through the strait," he said, "and when we had lost sight of the Pointed Isles, we fancied that we could distinguish the headland of Zacynthus creeping into our view like a dark

cloud . . ." (5.17).[21]

Since first person narration emerged naturally in relation to sea voyage literature, there could be no complete reversal of the trend. The dynamic of voyaging on the sea brings with it the experience of working with others to achieve a safe voyage and of sharing with others the fear and desparation when storm threatens to end the voyage in shipwreck. The social setting that emerges through a voyage on the sea gave rise to the sea voyage genre recounted with the personal plural dynamic: "We thought we were lost, we did what we could, and we made it through."

Third Person Narration in Greek Literature

But now it is necessary to look at the genre where third person narration dominates. If the examples given thus far suggest a natural affinity between first person narration and sea voyages, they do not reveal the strong bias toward third person narration in Greek and Latin prose literature. At least as early as Thucydides (ca. 460-400 B.C.) a standard had been set for narrative historiography that included third person narrative style. Thucydides carried this style through with remarkable candor, so that, beginning with book 4 of the *History of the Peloponnesian War*, he recounted his own activities in the army in third person narration. Thus he introduces himself into the narrative with these words:

> . . . the opponents of the traitors . . . acting in concert with Eucles the general . . . sent to the other commander of the Thracian district, Thucydides son of Olorus, the author of this history, who was at Thasos, a Parian colony, about a half-day's sail from Amphipolis, and urged him to come to their aid. And he, on hearing this, sailed in haste with seven ships which happened to be at hand . . . (4.104.4ff).

Thucydides, the objective, truthful narrator features himself in the narrative for a number of pages, never using first person narration. By this means Thucydides hopes to persuade his readers that his account is based on the finest evidence and presented in the most accurate manner (1.1.1-2).

Xenophon (428/7-354 B.C.) used this same style for the *Anabasis* and the *Hellenica*. Therefore he introduces himself into the narrative in book 3 of the *Anabasis* in the following way:

> There was a young man in the army named Xenophon, an Athenian, who was neither general nor captain nor private, but had accompanied the expedition because Proxenus, an old friend of his, had sent him at his home an invitation to go with him; Proxenus had also promised him that if he should go, he would make him a friend of Cyrus . . . (3.1.4). Xenophon . . . after offering the sacrifices to the gods that Apollo's oracle prescribed, set sail, overtook Proxenus and Cyrus at Sardis as they were on the point of beginning the upward march, and was introduced to Cyrus . . . . It was in this way, then, that Xenophon came to go on the expedition . . . (3.1.8).

From this point on Xenophon becomes a participant in the action and the dialogue. Never, however, does the author use first person narration for his own participation.[22] Both Thucydides and Xenophon consider third person narration

---

[21]Heliodorus, *Ethiopian Story*, trans. by Walter Lamb, pp. 123-4.

[22]Xenophon, in contrast with Thucydides, does not even claim authorship of the

to be the proper historiographical style. They even recount sea voyages in this style.

From the same century as Xenophon's works, a sailing manual for mariners has been preserved.[23] This *Periplus of the Mediterranean Sea*, as it is entitled, is attributed to Scylax the Younger. The author starts the manual with first person singular: "I will begin [my description] from the Pillars of Hercules . . . ." After this, the journalistic description of cities, people and distances is given in third person, except for fourteen interjections where he says, "Now I will return to the coast, from which I turned away [in my description]."[24] This document is too non-literary to be influenced by the historiographical tradition. Yet it does represent sea voyage information in a third person informational style.

A similar manual tradition emerges in the *Periplus of the Erythraean Sea* (A.D. 50-95).[25] This document is a third person description of the harbors, cities and peoples along the coastline of the Indian Ocean. Even in this account, however, the propensity for first person plural is exhibited. When the author is describing a dangerous section of the coastline, he automatically slips into first person plural style.

> Navigation is dangerous along this whole coast of Arabia, which is without harbors, with bad anchorages, foul, inaccessible because of breakers and rocks, and terrible in every way. Therefore we hold our course down the middle of the gulf and pass on as fast as possible by the country of Arabia untl we come to the Burnt Island . . . .[26]

Thus, even in third person manual *periploi,* first person is likely to intrude.

A rather forthright perpetuation of third person historiographical style appears in the works of Arrian (A.D. 96-ca. 180) who imitated Xenophon in his *Anabasis of Alexander* and Herodotus in his *Indica.*[27] Therefore his account of Nearchus' sea voyage in *Indica* 8.20.1-8.36.9 is recounted in third person, though the reader is told that it is Nearchus' personal account.

> On this Nearchus writes thus: Alexander had a vehement desire to sail the sea which stretches from India to Persia; but he disliked the length of the voyage and feared lest, meeting with some country desert or without roadstands, or not properly provided with the fruits of the earth, his whole fleet might be destroyed (8.20.1f) . . . . And Nearchus says that Alexander discussed with him whom he should select to be admiral of his fleet (8.20.4) . . . . At length Alexander accepted

---

Anabasis, evidently because he was a participant in it. Instead, he claims, in *Hellenica* 3.1.2., that the *Anabasis* was written by Themistogenes of Syracuse.

[23]Walter W. Hyde, *Ancient Greek Mariners,* pp. 19, 116. Text in Karl Müller, *Geographi Graeci Minores,* I, 15-96.

[24]*epaneimi de palin epi tēn epeiron, hothen exetrapomēn* (with slight variation): 7, 13, 29, 34, 48, 53, 58, 67 (twice), 97, 98, 99 (twice), 103. In 21 he refers to *nēsoi hōn echo eipein ta onomata* and in 40 to *hē hodos pros tēn epi hēmōn thalassan.*

[25]Wilfred H. Schoff, *The Periplus of the Erythraean Sea,* pp. 8-9. Text in Müller, *Geographi,* pp. 257-305.

[26]Schoff, *Periplus,* p. 30. Also in 57, first person emerges: *kata ton kairon tōn par' hēmin, etēsiōn en to Indikō pelagei ho lithontos phainetai [hippalos] prosonomazesthai [apo tēs prosēgorias tou protos exeurekotos ton diaploun].*

[27]See Lionel Pearson, *The Lost Histories of Alexander the Great,* p. 112. A similar style is perpetuated by Apollonius of Rhodes in *Argonautica.*

> Nearchus' willing spirit, and appointed him admiral of the entire fleet (8.20.7) . . .
> Now when the trade winds had sunk to rest . . . they put to sea . . . (8.21.1).

Arrian, however, is credited with a *Periplus of the Euxine Sea.* Because the author formulated the account as a letter to Hadrian, he was able to recount the voyage in first person plural.[28]

While Arrian perpetuated the third person historiographical style as employed by Xenophon, Caesar (1st cent. B.C.) allowed first person plural comments within a third person narrative style. Most frequently, in the *Gallic Wars*, first person plural emerges in accounts of battle. But in at least one voyage account the author allows first person plural to intrude.

> When the ships had been beached and the camp thoroughly well entrenched, Ceasar left the same forces as before to guard the ships . . . . Here in mid-channel is an island called Man; . . . some have written that in midwinter, night there lasts for thirty whole days. We could discover nothing about this by inquiries; but by exact measurements, we observed that the nights were shorter than on the continent (5.11).

In Caesar's account, therefore, an autobiographical feature is allowed within historiography, especially in battles and a voyage. Is it too much to suggest that this becomes a characteristic typology for historiography in the 1st century B.C. and A.D., and that the writer of Luke-Acts construes his narrative in relation to this typology?

This survey has been designed to show two things: (a) the genre of sea voyage narrative within Greek literature uses first person plural narration; (b) the standards of historiography brought in a necessity for third person narration, but, in spite of this, first person plural narration emerges in accounts of battles and voyages.

Parallels to the Voyages in Acts

But if the we-passages in Acts are to be understood in relation to these features in narrative literature, are there not more precise parallels? In Acts the narration shifts from third person to first person plural, and the narrator is not the main actor. A precise parallel exists in the *Voyage of Hanno the Carthaginian.*[29] This document exists in Greek and was written down between 350-125 B.C. It reflects the convergence of the historiographical tradition and sea voyage tradition as it appears in Acts. Some interpreters suggest it was translated from Punic into Greek under the influence of the historian Polybius; others suggest the influence of Herodotus.[30] This three page account begins with third person

[28]Text in Müller, *Geographi*, pp. 370-401. On the letter form as a technique for presenting the account as a personal voyage, see Henry Chotard, *Le Périple de la Mer Noire par Arrien*, pp. 3-7.

[29]Text in Müller, *Geographi*, pp. 1-14. At this point I must express my sincere gratitude to Professor Emeritus John L. Heller who called my attention to this document. His conversation with me about the shift from third person to first person plural in this voyage account inspired this entire investigation.

[30]W. Aly, "Die Entdeckung des Westens," *Hermes*, LXII (1927), 317-339, suggests Polybian influence; G. Germain, "Qu'est-ce que le Périple d'Hannon? Document, amplification littéraire ou faux intégral?", *Hesperis*, XLIV (1957), 205-48, suggests that a later writer was influenced by Herodotus' style.

narration and shifts into first person narration in the following manner:

> It pleased the Carthaginians that Hanno should voyage outside the Pillars of Hercules, and found cities of the Libyphoenicians. And he set forth with sixty ships of fifty oars, and a multitude of men and women, to the number of thirty thousand, and with wheat and other provisions. After passing through the Pillars we went on and sailed for two days' journey beyond, where we founded the first city . . . . Having set up an altar to Neptune, we proceeded again, going toward the east for half the day . . . (1-3).[31]

First person plural narration continues to the end of the document, where, on account of the lack of further supplies, they return to Carthage.

Another parallel to the style of narration in Acts is present in a four-column papyrus dated ca. 246 B.C., which is best entitled *Episodes from the Third Syrian War*.[32] I.1-II.11 contains third person narration. In II.12 the narration shifts to first person plural as a sea voyage is recounted:

> . . . Arzibazos, the satrap in Cilicia, intended to send [the captured money] to Ephesus for Laodice's group, but when the people of Soli and the satraps immediately agreed among themselves, and the associates of Pythagoras and Aristocles vigorously helped, and all were good men, it happened that the money was kept and both the city and the citadel became ours. But when Arzibazos escaped and reached the passes of the Tauros and some of the inhabitants cut him off at the entrance, he went back to Antioch. Then we [made ready] the things on the ships, and, when the first watch began, we embarked in as many ships as the harbor of Seleucia (at Orontes) was likely to hold and sailed to a port called Poseidon and we anchored ourselves at the eighth hour. Then, getting away from there in the morning, we went to Seleucia. And the priest and rulers and other citizens and officers and soldiers, crowned with wreaths, met us . . . (2.6-25).[33]

In second and third century Christianity, two documents of the Acts-genre contain first person plural in relation to sea voyages. Undoubtedly the first century *Acts of the Apostles* has influenced these documents. It is informative, however, to observe first person plural narration in the midst of sea voyage material. In the *Antiochene Acts of the Martyrdom of Ignatius*, third person narration shifts unannounced to first person plural as the author gives a summary of the voyage:

> . . . passing through Philippi he [Ignatius] journeyed by land across Macedonia and the part of Epirus which lies by Epidamnus. And here on the sea coast he took ship and sailed across the Hadriatic sea, and thence entering the Tyrrhene and passing by islands and cities, the holy man when he came in view of Puteoli was eager himself to disembark, desiring to tread in the footsteps of the Apostle [Paul]; but forasmuch as a stiff breeze springing up prevented it, the ship being driven by a stern wind, he commended the love of the brethren in that place, and so sailed by. Thus in one single day and night, meeting with favourable winds, we ourselves were carried forward against our will, mourning over the separation which must soon come between ourselves and this righteous man . . . .[34]

---

[31]Wilfred H. Schoff, *The Periplus of Hanno*, p. 3.

[32]The first edition of the text is found in John P. Mahaffy, *The Flinders Petri Papyri, II, III:* XLV (II, pp. 145-9), CXLIV (III, pp. 334-8). The re-edited text is available in L. Mitteis and U. Wilcken, *Grundzüge und Chrestomathie der Papyruskunde*, Vol. I, Part 2, pp. 1-7.

[33]Translation by the author, consulting Mahaffy.

[34]J. B. Lightfoot, *The Apostolic Fathers*, II, 577.

In these three texts and the book of Acts, third person narration is established as the style for recounting the events that occur. However, when a sea voyage begins the narration shifts, without explanation, to first person plural.

Yet another text holds interest for this study, although it does not represent an exact parallel to the narrative style of Acts. In *The Acts of Peter and the Twelve Apostles*, Nag Hammadi codex VI.1, the narrative alternates between first person and third person narration. Unfortunately, the first part of the text has been destroyed, so that it is impossible to know if the document began with first person or third person narrative style. The extant portion begins with a scene in which Peter and the apostles covenant with one another to take a special voyage on the sea. Immediately after this scene, they go down to the sea and begin their venture. First person plural narration governs the composition of these two episodes.

> [. . .] which [. . .] purpose [. . .. after . . .] us [. . .] apostles [. . .]. We sailed [. . .] of the body. [Others] were not anxious in [their hearts]. And in our hearts, we were united. We agreed to fulfill the ministry to which the Lord appointed us. And we made a covenant with each other.
>
> We went down to the sea at an opportune moment, which came to us from the Lord. We found a ship moored at the shore ready to embark, and we spoke with the sailors of the ship about our coming aboard with them. They showed great kindliness toward us as was ordained by the Lord. And after we had embarked, we sailed a day and a night. After that, a wind came up behind the ship and brought us to a small city in the midst of the sea (VI.1.1-29).[35]

The first person plural narrative style shifts to first person singular when the boat arrives at the dock.

> And I, Peter, inquired about the name of this city from residents who were standing on the dock. [A man] among [them] answered, [saying, "The name] of this [city is Habitation, that is], Foundation [. . .] endurance." And the leader [among them . . . holding] the palm branch at the edge of [the dock]. And after we had gone ashore [with the] baggage, I [went] into [the] city, to seek [advice] about the lodging (VI.1.30-2.10).

At this point it appears that the narrative is recounted entirely in first person, with Peter telling the story. A little further on, however, Peter is presented, without comment, through narration by the author in third person style.

> [The men asked Peter] about the hardships. Peter answered [that it was impossible to tell] those things that he had heard about the hardships of [the] way, because [interpreters were] difficult [. . .] in their ministry.
>
> He said to the man who sells this pearl, "I want to know your name and the hardships of the way to your city because we are strangers and servants of God. It is necessary for us to spread the word of God in every city harmoniously." He answered and said, "If you seek my name, Lithargoel is my name, the interpretation of which is, the light, gazelle-like stone" (VI.5.2-19).

---

[35]The quotations from *The Acts of Peter and the Twelve Apostles* are taken from *The Nag Hammadi Library in English*, ed. James M. Robinson, trans. of this document by Douglas M. Parrott and R. McL. Wilson, p. 454-9, and are used by permission of Harper and Row. I am grateful to Professor George W. MacRae, Harvard University, for calling these references to my attention.

As the story continues, the narrative style alternates, without explanation, between first person and third person narration. Sometimes, in other words, Peter is telling the story, and at other times Peter is talked about in third person as a participant in the events. Finally, the document ends with a third person account of "the Lord" with the disciples (VI.10.14-12.22).

For the purposes of this study, it would be informative to know if *The Acts of Peter and the Twelve Aposles* began, as well as concluded, with third person narration. There is a possibility that it began with third person narrative style, adopted first person narrative style in the context of the sea voyage, then returned to third person style at the end of the account. Without further evidence, it is impossible to know. It does seem fair to conclude that this document, probably written during the latter part of the second century,[36] has been influenced both by the sea voyage material in the canonical book of Acts and by first person narrative style in romance literature.[37] Among the apocryphal Acts material, it attracts special interest because of the coincidence of first plural narration with a sea voyage. During the second and third centuries, however, first person narrative style infuenced the apocryphal material beyond the context of sea voyages.[38]

In conclusion, there are three texts, in addition to the book of Acts, where third person narrative style shifts to first person plural when a sea voyage is initiated. In a fourth text, *The Acts of Peter and the Twelve Apostles,* the narration shifts freely among first person plural, first person singular, and third person narration.

It may be well to notice a feature of Luke-Acts that has not yet been mentioned. The author begins his narrative with a first person singular preface to Luke and another at the beginning of Acts. Therefore, the author uses first person narration in the prefaces, third person narration in the basic text, and first person plural narration in the accounts of sea voyages. Luke evidently adapts his style to the content that he presents. The we-passages fit the genre of sea voyage narratives. Such accounts would be expected to contain first person narration, whether or not the author was an actual participant in the voyage. Without first person narration the account would limp. By the first century A.D., a sea voyage recounted in third person narration would be considered out of vogue, especially if a shipwreck or other amazing events were recounted. For this reason an alert writer like Luke would place himself on the journey by using first person plural.

The We-Passages as Sea Voyage Literature

The we-passages in Acts have captivated interpreters from Irenaeus[39] to the present.[40] And, for the most part, Irenaeus' shadow has fallen over the whole

---

[36]*Ibid.,* p. 265.

[37]For a discussion of first person narration in romance literature, see Ben E. Perry, "Appendix III: The Ego-Narrative in Comic Stories," *The Ancient Romances,* pp. 325-9.

[38]See, e.g., *Acts of John* and *Acts of Thomas* 1, in *The Apocryphal New Testament,* trans. M. R. James, pp. 228-70, 365.

[39]*Against Heresies 3.14.1.*

[40]See Ernst Haenchen, *The Acts of the Apostles* and Ward Gasque, *A History of Criticism of the Acts of the Apostles.*

enterprise. For Irenaeus, the we-passages demonstrated that the author of Luke-Acts was a companion of Paul. Many interpreters since Irenaeus have left the impression that an author who used first person plural narration in his account must, by necessity, have been a participant in those events or must have used a diary of a participant.

Internally, however, the we-passages are not a unity. The variation from "we," which includes Paul, to "Paul and us" (16:17; 21:18) exhibits the use of first person plural as a stylistic device by the author himself. Also, the tension between "we" and "they" in Acts 27:1-44 reflects the author's employment of first person plural for sea voyaging even when it is difficult to sustain the personal narration in the context of the events that occur on the voyage.

Eduard Norden was aware that the we-passages in Acts represent the sea voyage genre.[41] Henry J. Cadbury read Norden's work and knew that these sections were a different genre from the other material in Acts.[42] He mentioned that it was a "regular custom for the *periplous,* as the account of a coasting voyage was called, to be written in first person . . .,"[43] but he did not take the next step. He concluded that the abrupt shift from third person narration to "we" was "peculiar and unexplained."[44]

The evidence within contemporary Mediterranean literature suggests that the author of Luke-Acts used "we" narration as a stylistic device. The influence for this lies in the Classical, Hellenistic, and Roman literary milieu.[45] This first plural technique is simply a feature of the sea voyage genre in Mediterranean antiquity. All of the features of this genre arise out of the dynamics of sailing on the sea, landing in unfamiliar places, and hoping to establish an amiable relationship with the people in the area where the landing occurs.[46] During the short stay on land, before resuming the voyage, two kinds of episodes are especially frequent. First, an event often occurs in which some people of the area are friendly toward the voyagers. This event usually leads to an invitation to stay at someone's home.[47]

---

[41]*Ibid.,* pp. 313-27.

[42]Henry J. Cadbury, *The Making of Luke-Acts,* pp. 60-1.

[43]*Ibid.,* p. 144.

[44]*Ibid.,* p. 358.

[45]During this time period, Semitic voyages do not use first person plural narrative style. Neither the biblical accounts of Noah nor Jonah use this technique. The voyage of Jonah raises the most interesting possibilities because of its widespread popularity. Beginning with the end of the third century A.D., Jonah's voyage appears frequently in *sarcophagi.* For this information, see Cornelia C. Coulter, "The 'Great Fish' in Ancient and Medieval Story," *TAPA,* LVII (1926), 32-50; Joseph Engemann, *Untersuchungen zur Sepulkralsymbolik der späteren römischen Kaizerzeit,* pp. 70-4. First person plural narration does appear in the Islamic account of Jonah's voyage: Koran Sure 37;139-141; see Richard Delbrueck, *Probleme der Lipsanothek in Brescia,* pp. 22-3. For a study of the Jonah traditions in the NT, see Richard A. Edwards, *The Sign of Jonah.*

[46]For all kinds of information about ships and sea travel on and around the Mediterranean, including information about Paul's voyages, see the four works by Lionel Casson: *Travel in the Ancient World; Ships and Seamanship in the Ancient World; The Ancient Mariners.* For an account of the search for the remains of ancient ships, and the estimates regarding the number of ships that traveled the Mediterranean and went down in the deep, see Willard Bascom, *Deep Water, Ancient Ships.*

[47]Cf. *Voyage of Hanno* 6; Vergil, *Aeneid* 3.80-83, 306-355; Dio Chrysostom 7.3-5;

The voyagers seldom remain neutral visitors in a locale where they land. Thus, a second event will divide the people of the area over whether or not these voyagers are to be trusted. Usually the leader of the voyage will become involved in a major episode in which his extraordinary abilities are displayed. Often he will speak eloquently and perform some unusual feat.[48] If the voyagers are not driven forcibly from the place where they have landed, an emotional farewell scene occurs in which the people bring provisions and other gifts to the boat.[49]

A sea voyage account often opens with a statement regarding the purpose of the voyage, a comment about preparations for it, and a list of some of the participants in it.[50] When the voyage is under way, there is an account of the places by which the voyagers sail, and frequently short descriptive comments are given about the places. Also, the length of time it takes to sail from one place to another usually is indicated, and frequently the span of time is linked with the direction and force of the wind.[51] Gods are portrayed as determining the fate of the voyage. Visits of the gods, and signs and portents, frequently attend the voyage. In response, prayers are offered, altars are built, and sacred rituals are enacted.[52] At some point, almost every good sea voyage account portrays a storm that threatens or actually ends in a shipwreck.[53]

Virtually all of the features of ancient sea voyage literature are present in the we-passages in Acts. The first we-section, 16:10-17, begins in response to a vision which occurs during the night. In this vision a Macedonian says to Paul, "Come over to Macedonia and help us:" (16:9). The narrator interprets this summons to mean that God is calling them to this area to preach the gospel (16:10). The success of this venture is assured by divine destiny no matter what obstacles threaten to undo it. Especially the sea voyages of Odysseus and Aeneas established visions, signs, and portents as a characteristic feature of this kind of literature. The first we-section emerges in the narrative of Acts with a dynamic that is well-known in Mediterranean sea voyage literature.

As first person plural narration begins and the boat is launched for Macedonia, the narrator recounts the places by which they sail and the time it takes to sail the distance (16:11-12). This is the first instance of a detailed account of a voyage in Acts, and it includes a comment about the prestige and role of Philippi — a typical feature in a sea voyage account. The narration of the voyage ends with the statement: "We remained in this city some days." This is a customary clause at the end of a paragraph in a voyage manual.[54]

Once they land at Philippi, a series of events occur that lead to the

---

Lucian, *A True Story* 1.33; 2.34; Achilles Tatius 2.33; Heliodorus, *Ethiopian Story* 5.18.

[48]Cf. *Odyssey* 9.43-61, 195-470.

[49]Cf. Vergil, *Aeneid* 3.463-505; Lucian, *A True Story* 2.27; Achilles Tatius 2.32.2.

[50]Cf. *Voyage of Hanno* 1; Lucian, *A True Story* 1.5.

[51]Cf. *Voyage of Hanno* 2-6, 8-17; Vergil *Aeneid* 3.124-127, 692-708.

[52]Cf. *Voyage of Hanno* 4; Vergil, *Aeneid* 3.4-5, 19-21, 26-48, 84-120, 147-178, 358-460, 373-376, 528-529; Lucian, *A True Story* 2.47; Achilles Tatius 2.32.2; 3.5.1-4; 3.10.1-6.

[53]Cf. *Odyssey* 9.67-73; Vergil, *Aeneid* 3.192-208; Dio Chrysostom 7.2; Lucian, *A True Story* 2.40; 2.47; Achilles Tatius 3.1.1-3.5.6; Heliodorus, *Ethiopian Story* 5.27.

[54]Cf.*Voyage of Hanno* 6: *par' hois emeinamen achri tinos, philoi genomenoi.*

imprisonment and spectacular release of Paul and Silas. Only the first two events are narrated in first person plural. In the first event (16:13-15) the voyagers meet some women and begin to talk to them. A woman named Lydia "opens her heart" so that she invites them to come to her house and stay. This scene is a typical component of voyage narratives, and it contains first plural narrative style.

The second event (16:16-18) begins with first person plural narration but makes a transition to third person narration in 16:17. This event has a dynamic that is often present in sea voyage accounts. Paul performs an extraordinary act of power, and this act causes a disturbance among the local people. In this instance, Paul drives a spirit of divination out of a slave girl who brings money to her owners by soothsaying. As the episode develops into a detailed event in the city, first plural narration is left behind. With the re-emergence of third person narrative style, the events move from the sea to "the land." The next series of events does not conclude with a return to the boat; Paul and his company travel to Amphipolis, Apollonia, and Thessalonica on foot (17:1).

The transition from first plural to third person narration is achieved through the phrase "Paul and us" (16:10). This phrase is a signal to the reader that the events lead away from the boat to the land and its challenges. The same technique appears at the end of the third we-passage (21:18). At the end of the final we-passage, the transition is made by indicating that Paul was permitted to remain "by himself" with only the soldier guarding him (28:16). In all three instances the transition takes the event away from the sea; third person narration centers on Paul's influential activity on land.

The second we-section, 20:5-15, is the first half of a sea voyage to Jerusalem. First person plural narration emerges at the conclusion of a list of people who accompany Paul on the voyage (20:4). As in the first we-section, the voyage opens with a detailed account of the places to which they sailed and the duration of time. This introduction ends with the comment that they stayed in Troas for seven days (20:5-6). Again, first person plural narration begins as a boat is launched on the sea, and the opening verses are a typical beginning for a sea voyage account.

An event is recounted at Troas before the voyage continues, and it is narrated in first plural style (20:7-12). The episode begins as a farewell scene (20:7), but it ends as a spectacular event performed by Paul. When Paul's speech lasts far into the night, and a young man falls out of a third story window and is dead, Paul embraces him and revives him. This miraculous event is placed on the first day of the week, and Paul appears to "break bread" both before and after he brings the young man back to life. This setting for the event is not interpreted by the narrator, but it creates a context similar to the one created by the vision at the outset of the first voyage. This voyage is in the hands of God. Paul carefully follows the religious rites of the Christian community, and the power of God works through him. The reader knows (19:21) that Paul is headed for Jerusalem, and the reader also knows what happened to Jesus at Jerusalem. As the danger of taking this voyage to Jerusalem becomes prominent in the narrative, the will of God for Paul to go to Rome (19:21) becomes increasingly important. If Paul truly is an apostle through God's will, then he will fulfill the proper religious rites and receive the benefits of God's favor. For a person in the Hellenistic world, this feature is a natural part of a sea voyage account. It was the will of Zeus/Jupiter that both Odysseus and Aeneas complete their voyages without suffering death. All the delays, hardships, and apparent reversals of the decision are overcome by the rituals the voyagers perform and the destiny the supreme gods refuse to alter.

The final part of the second we-section (20:13-16) contains a typical detailed account of sailing from place to place and meeting people to take them on board. It ends by thematizing the purpose of the voyage: Paul "was hastening to be at Jerusalem, if possible, on the day of Pentecost" (20:16). At this point there is an interlude in the voyage. They have sailed as far as Miletus, and Paul summons the elders of the church at Ephesus to come to him there. This event features Paul giving a speech, and third person narration is used to recount Paul's meeting with these church leaders (20:17-38).

The third we-section begins as soon as the Ephesian elders bring Paul back to the ship. The parting scene depicts them kneeling in prayer and bidding Paul farewell with weeping, embracing, and kissing. As the first person plural narration resumes, again there is a detailed account of the voyage that ends with a remark about the length of their stay in the city where they landed (21:1-4). This opening part reiterates the purpose of the voyage as the disciples tell Paul not to go on to Jerusalem.

The next two verses contain another typical parting scene. All the disciples, with their wives and children, accompany the voyagers to the beach, pray with them, and bid them farewell (21:5-6). After this, typical voyage narration occurs until they reach Caesarea (21:7-8). At Caesarea a prophet enacts a scene that foretells Paul's arrest and delivery to the Gentiles when he reached Jerusalem (21:8-14). In the sphere of literature in the Hellenistic world, this scene is like Odysseus' encounter with the prophet Teiresias in *Odyssey* 11.90-137. Both the reader and the protagonist in the story know the dangers that lie ahead and the outcome. For the moment, however, Paul forgets that "he must go to Rome" (19:21). He is ready "not only to be imprisoned but even to die at Jerusalem" (21:13). The destination at Jerusalem is the sole concern of the voyage, and scenes that are typical components of sea voyage literature are used to emphasize the danger that lurks at the end of the voyage.[55]

The final verses of the third we-section describe the trek from Caesarea to Jerusalem (21:15-18). Since the destination of the sea voyage is Jerusalem, first person plural narration continues until Paul goes in to James and the elders (21:18). At this point the events are committed to land, and the narration moves back to third person style. As the first we-section stopped once Paul and his company began the activity which brought them before the leaders of the city (16:17), so the second and third we-sections stop once Paul and his company begin the consultation with James and the elders at Jerusalem. The trials that ensue are Paul's mission on land once he has voyaged to this area.

The fourth we-section, 27:1-28:16, presents the final, climactic sea voyage of Paul and his company. There is a dramatic progression in the length and drama of the we-sections in Acts. The first we-section is brief (16:10-17), and it takes Paul and his associates on a straight sailing course from Troas to Philippi (16:11). The drama of the voyage arises from the vision at the outset, the invitation to stay at Lydia's house, and the encounter with the slave girl who has a spirit of divination. The second and third we-sections are longer (20:5-15; 21:1-18), and

---

[55]Cf. the danger that awaits Odysseus when he returns to Ithaca.

they take Paul and his company on an episodic, tearful voyage that systematically moves to Jerusalem. The drama of the voyage emerges through the farewell speech that develops into a miraculous event when Paul revives a young man (20:7-12), the farewell speech and scene with the Ephesian elders at Miletus (20:17-38), the farewell scene at Tyre (21:5-6), and the prophetic enactment at Caesarea of Paul's imprisonment and delivery to the Gentiles (21:8-14). The fourth we-section is longer yet, and more dramatic.

As Paul is taken to the boat to sail for Rome, first plural narrative again emerges in Acts (27:1). The opening part contains the typical information about sailing from port to port, and passing islands and other places (27:1-8). Beginning with 27:4, the narrator introduces the dynamic that furnishes the drama for this voyage. The wind is against them, and the sailing becomes more and more difficult. The second part of the section thematizes the danger that is increasing and features Paul in conversation with the people in charge about their plight (27:9-12). Paul's advice that the voyage temporarily be aborted is overruled by a majority of the people on the boat. The narration of the increasing danger impels the action to the next part with skill. The wind grows into the fury of a storm, and the detailed portrayal of the inability to control the ship, the necessity of throwing the cargo overboard, and the absence of sun and stars for many days takes the reader to the heart of the sea voyage narratives (21:13-20). Paul knows the divine destiny of the voyage that includes storm and shipwreck, just as Odysseus knows what will happen when the Sirens, Scylla and Charybdis threaten to kill every mortal on board including himself (*Odyssey* 12.35-126). Therefore, Paul tells them they should have listened to him, and he tells them what the outcome of this storm will be (27:21-26). As Paul predicts, the ship runs aground as the crew attempts to beach it, and everyone is forced to abandon ship and escape to the island of Malta (27:27-44). The detailed description of the maneuvering of the ship by the sailors, the sounding for fathoms, the casting of anchors, and the manning of ropes and sails ranks this account among the most exciting depictions of storms and shipwrecks in the sphere of Greek and Roman literature. In the midst of it Paul takes bread, gives thanks to God, breaks it in the presence of all, and begins to eat (27:35). As all the members of the ship eat, the sacred ritual for receiving God's favor is performed. Everyone escapes safely to land, in spite of plans by the crew to abandon the ship (27:30) and intentions by the soldiers to kill the prisoners (27:42). Divine destiny holds the controlling hand when storm and shipwreck dash ships and mortals back and forth upon the sea.

The storm and shipwreck take the voyagers to the island of Malta. The opening scene portrays the islanders as unusually friendly (28:1-6), and the islanders become even more kindly disposed before the voyagers depart. When a viper bites Paul and he does not fall down dead, the islanders perceive Paul as every bit as godlike as Odysseus or Aeneas (28:6). The warm relationship between the islanders and Paul grows even more when Paul heals the father of the chief man of the island. Not only does the chief man receive them and entertain them for three days, but the scene develops into a general healing episode after which the islanders bid them farewell by bringing gifts and provisions to the boat (28:7-10). These events on the island are narrated in typical sea voyage style. All detail is suppressed except the information that highlights the welcome to the island, the spectacular abilities of the protagonist on the voyage, and the farewell scene.

The final part of the voyage contains the customary sailing information as the boat proceeds from Malta to Rome (28:11-16). Details about putting in at ports and staying for a few days are included; the favorable winds and the warm receptions at the harbors also receive attention. As the boat lands, Paul offers the proper prayer to God and takes courage that the voyage has concluded with God's favor still upon him (28:15). The voyage is ended, and third person narration emerges once again as Paul turns toward his new mission on land (28:18).

The final we-section in Acts represents the sea voyage genre *par excellence*. Each time a we-section begins, the drama heightens; movement through space becomes a voyage across the sea. The final voyage takes the gospel to ports and islands far away, and the adventure, danger, and fear bring "Paul and us" to Rome with thanksgiving.

The We-Passages in the Structure of Luke-Acts

If the dynamic of sea voyaging is crucial for understanding the we-sections in Acts, the place of the passages in the arrangement of this two volume work is as important. There are two perspectives from which the arrangement is important for interpretation. First, the we-sections occur in the last half of Acts. Comparison of Luke with Acts indicates that both volumes contain a long travel narrative that leads into the concluding scenes. This feature suggests that the volumes contain some type of parallel structure. Second, the portion of Acts in which the we-sections occur represents the last fourth of this two volume narrative. In this final segment, Paul's travels spread the gospel "to the end of the earth" (1:8; 13:47). It will be important to discover the techniques by which the author has brought the entire narrative to its dramatic conclusion. The first aspect of the arrangement will be discussed here; the second aspect will be discussed in the next section.

The we-sections occur in a portion of Acts that shows significant points of relation with Luke. The journey narrative in Luke 9:51-19:28 is a distinctive feature of the Lukan narrative,[56] and the journeys of Paul in Acts 13:1-28:16 comprise the highpoint of the narrative of Acts. In general terms, Jesus' journey in Luke corresponds to Paul's journey in Acts. The journeys reflect the movement through time and space that is a central feature of Luke-Acts.

Closer observation reveals that specific architectonic parallels exist between the journeys in Luke and Acts.[57] There are three sections in Acts that correspond to three sections in the Lukan travel narrative. Paul's mission to the churches in Asia Minor, Macedonia, and Greece (Acts 13:1-19:20) corresponds to the mission of the seventy (Luke 10:1-24).[58] Paul's journey to Jerusalem (Acts 19:21-21:26) corresponds to Jesus' journey to Jerusalem (Luke 13:22-19:46). Agrippa's handing over of Paul to a centurion to be escorted to Rome (Acts 27:1-28:16) corresponds to Pilate's handing over of Jesus to the chief priests, rulers, and

---

[56]Cf. Hans Conzelmann, *The Theology of St. Luke*, trans. G. Buswell, pp. 60-73.

[57]For an explanation of architectonic structure and the correspondences between Luke and Acts, see Charles H. Talbert, *Literary Patterns, Theological Themes and the Genre of Luke-Acts*, esp. pp. 1-65.

[58]*Ibid.*, p. 20.

people to be crucified (Luke 23:26-49). Because of these correspondences, this study could include detailed analysis of Luke as well as Acts. Our immediate goal, however, is to interpret the role of the we-sections in the overall setting of Paul's journeys. Therefore, having noticed this parallel architectonic structure, we will proceed with analysis in Acts only. In the next section, more features of Luke will come into the discussion.

All three sections of Paul's journeys contain we-passages, and the length of the we-sections increases as the end of the narrative draws near. The first journey section (13:1-19:20) only contains eight verses of first plural narration. (16:10-17). The second journey section (19:21-21:26) contains twenty-nine verses of first plural narrative style, and the third journey section (27:1-28:16) is entirely a we-section (60 verses). Of course, the increasing amount of first plural narration is linked with the increasing amount of sea travel. The increasing length of sea voyage material affects the structure of Acts 13-28.

Perhaps the most striking aspect of the structure in the journey sections is the chiastic arrangement that unifies the first and second sections. The second half of the first section (15:1-19:20) and the second section (19:21-21:26) represent a generally balanced chiastic structure.[59] The perimeters of the chiasmus are the Jerusalem council in 15:1-33 and Paul's return visit to Jerusalem in 21:15-26. The inside of the chiasmus is filled out by three balancing units and a series of episodes at the center. The travel and imprisonment in 15:36-17:15 is balanced by the travel and prophecy of arrest and imprisonment in 21:1-14. The speech at Athens in 17:16-24 is balanced by the speech at Ephesus in 20:17-38. The assembly at Corinth and subsequent travel in 18:1-23 is balanced by the assembly at Ephesus and subsequent travel in 19:21-20:16. The center of the chiastic structure is found in 18:24-19:20. This, therefore, is the chiastic outline:

A 15:1-34 Jerusalem council

B 15:36-17:15 Travel and Imprisonment

C 17:16-24 Speech at Athens

D 18:1-23 Assembly at Corinth and Travel

A' 21:15-26 Report to Jerusalem Leaders

B' 21:1-14 Travel and Scene of Binding

C' 20:17-38 Speech at Ephesus

D' 19:21-20:16 Assembly at Ephesus and Travel

E 18:24-19:20 Spreading the Gospel Throughout Asia from Ephesus

The center of a chiastic structure, in relation to the outside portions, reveals the essential dynamic of the literary arrangement.[60] Events at Ephesus where Paul corrects inadequate or improper understanding of the gospel stand at the center. Paul's encounters with the authoritative leaders at Jerusalem stand on the perimeters of the structure. The literary arrangement presents an interplay between Jerusalem and Ephesus as centers for spreading the gospel. Ephesus is the center for preaching the gospel to all residents of Asia, both Jews and

---

[59]*Ibid.*, pp. 56-8. Our analysis varies some from Talbert's, though agreement with regard to the extent of the chiasmus exists.

[60]For an excellent analysis of chiastic structure see Joanna Dewey, "The Literary Structure of Controversy Stories in Mark 2:1-3:6," *JBL*, XCII (1973), 394-401.

Greeks (19:10). This assertion stands at the heart of the Ephesus events. Jerusalem is the locale from which Paul's mission to Jews and Gentiles is authorized.

The relation of the we-passages to the chiastic arrangement introduces another dimension of this portion of Acts. There are no we-passages in the first half of the initial travel section (13:1-14:28), and this part of the first section is not a segment of the chiasmus. In other words, all of the we-sections except for the final dramatic voyage are included in the material that has been given a chiastic structure. This means that only with the chiasmus is mission "by land" and "by sea" emphasized.

With regard to structure, therefore, the initial travel section (13:1-19:20) has two halves. The Jerusalem council (Acts 15) stands between the first and second half. The first half portrays Paul establishing and nurturing churches in Galatia and Cyprus. This mission is inaugurated by the Holy Spirit who says, "Set apart for me Barnabas and Saul for the work to which I have called them."[61] After the prophets and teachers at Antioch fast and pray, they lay their hands on Barnabas and Saul and send them off (13:2-3). The Barnabas and Saul mission occurs in 13:1-14:28. This mission does not have the blessings of the Jerusalem leaders and it does not take Paul "to the other side of the sea." Travel by boat is included in this first half (13:4, 13; 14:26), and "Saul" becomes "Paul" after he has "sailed" to Cyprus (13:9). Paul and Barnabas travel by boat, but their mission occurs prior to the Jerusalem council and is limited to the easternmost portion of the Mediterranean Sea.

With the Jerusalem council (15:1-35) a new phase enters into Paul's mission activity. He no longer travels with Barnabas, and his mission is not limited to the environs of the eastern portion of the Mediterranean. Beginning with the Jerusalem council, the material is balanced chiastically, and after this council there is an interplay of mission "by land" and "by sea."

Paul's authoritative mission "by land" begins in Acts 15:36. Severing his relation with Barnabas, Paul chooses Silas and establishes a valid mission to the churches in Syria and Cilicia by delivering to them "the decisions which had been reached by the apostles and elders who were at Jerusalem" (16:4). But Paul does not stop with this; his mission by land is on the move in a way it could not be before the Jerusalem council. Paul and Silas travel through Phrygia and Galatia and would appear to have "a clear road ahead." But then the mission by land is temporarily hindered. The Holy Spirit will not allow Paul and Silas to speak the word in Asia, so they are forced to go down to Troas (16:6-7).

The apparent hindrance to Paul's mission by land inaugurates a new phase: mission "by sea." The first we-section introduces this phase (16:10-17). In contrast to the previous sea travel by Paul (13:4, 13; 14:26), now the destination lies "on the other side" of the sea. In a night vision a man of Macedonia says to Paul, "Come over to Macedonia and help us" (16:9). In response, the first true sea voyage is launched, first plural narration emerges, and a new mission area opens to Paul and Silas.

Once Paul and Silas have reached Macedonia, their mission spreads "by

---

[61]For the relation of statements by the Holy Spirit and prophets, see Ernst Haenchen, *The Acts of the Apostles*, p. 395.

land" (16:19-17:13). When Paul goes to another new area, Achaia,[62] again he goes "by sea" (17:14-15). The effort of the author to assert this mode of opening the mission at Athens has created an unusual grammatical construction in 17:14. The verse states that the brethren at Beroea sent Paul out "to go as far as upon the sea" (*poreuesthai heōs epi tēn thalassan*). The peculiarity of *heōs* and *epi* in sequence evidently caused copyists either to omit *heōs* or replace it with *hōs*.[63] The problem evidently arises because Beroea is not a coastal city, and the author wanted to indicate that Paul went to Athens "by sea." The meaning is clear, because the verse is constructed in parallel with 17:15a: *hoi de kathistantes ton Paulon ēgagon heōs Athēnōn* ("those who conducted Paul brought him as far as Athens"). In like manner, the brethren at Beroea sent Paul out to go (by land) as far as "upon the sea." The narrator distinguishes between spreading the gospel "by land" and "by sea." The gospel spreads to new areas, e.g., Macedonia and Achaia, "by sea." Once Paul and his company arrive at a new area, the gospel spreads "by land." Later in the narrative, Paul travels "by land" between Achaia and Macedonia (20:2), but the initial mission is "by sea."

The irony of the chiastic structure is that mission "by sea" to Macedonia is balanced with mission "by sea" to Jerusalem. It would be wrong to think this is accidental. The voyage that takes Paul and Silas to Philippi where they are imprisoned and miraculously released (16:10-40) is balanced by the sea voyage that takes Paul to Caesarea where the prophet Agabus symbolically enacts the binding of Paul and his delivery to the Gentiles (21:1-14). Both voyages are we-sections, and Paul's voyage to Jerusalem is mission "by sea." Prior to this Paul has not had an opportunity to spread the gospel in Jerusalem. This area was closed to him. Now he goes to Jerusalem "ready not only to be imprisoned but even to die at Jerusalem for the name of the Lord Jesus" (21:13). His voyage to Jerusalem opens up an extensive mission "by land" from Jerusalem to Caesarea. Paul spreads the gospel not only to the people in Jerusalem (22:1-21) but also to the Sanhedrin in Jerusalem (23:1-10), the governor Felix in Caesarea (24:10-21), and to King Agrippa (26:1-29). Mission by sea has taken Paul not only to Macedonia and Achaia; it has taken Paul to Jerusalem itself and the political leaders who rule the area. Counterbalanced we-sections open both areas of mission to Paul "by sea."

As Paul's mission by sea to Macedonia provides the base for mission by sea to Jerusalem, so Paul's mission by sea to Jerusalem provides the base for mission by sea to Rome. All three missions are by sea, and all three missions are inaugurated by we-sections. The long, dramatic voyage to Rome (27:1-28:16) stands in notable contrast with the circumscribed beginnings of Paul's mission in the easternmost part of the Mediterranean Sea (13:1-14:28). On the way to Rome Paul even has a mission "upon the sea." When the voyage becomes dangerous, Paul begins conversation with the people in charge (27:10), and when a storm

---

[62]During the first century, Achaia included the areas in which both Athens and Corinth were located, but it did not include the area in which Philippi and Thessalonica were located.

[63]Evidently the reading with *hōs* would mean that they sent Paul away pretending that he would go by sea but actually going by land: "as though to go upon the sea" or "to go as it were upon the sea." See Bruce M. Metzger, *A Textual Commentary on the Greek New Testament*, p. 455.

begins to hurl them mercilessly about on the sea, Paul has the opportunity to tell the people on the ship about the God to whom he belongs and whom he worships (27:21-26). The foreknowledge of events that he received from an angel of his God not only proves to be accurate, but it provides the opportunity for Paul to take bread, give thanks to God in the presence of all, and eat (27:35). And, says the narrator, "they all were encouraged and ate some food themselves" (27:36). This imagery will certainly not be missed by the reader; Paul has "broken bread" with the entire group on the ship. But this still is not enough. Paul's mission on the sea is made complete by miracles that attend his leadership.[64] When he sustains a viper bite, the natives on the island of Malta think he is a god (28:3-7); and when Paul heals the father of the chief man, Publius, all the diseased come to him and are cured (28:7-10). This mission "upon the sea" takes Paul to Rome. The remaining part of Acts presents Paul's mission by land in and around Rome.

The we-sections play a decisive role in the section in Acts that narrates the journeys of Paul. These sections add mission by sea to mission by land. By careful structuring throughtout chapters 13-28, the author includes sections of sea voyage material that open new areas until the gospel spreads "to the end of the earth." By composing the journeys in three sections (13:1-19:20; 19:21-21:26; 27:1-28:16), the author develops a linear schema that portrays the spreading of the gospel from the land east of the Mediterranean to Italy. By a chiastic arrangement of the episodes from the Jerusalem council to Paul's return to Jerusalem (15:1-21:26), the author counterbalances the mission "to Macedonia and Achaia" with the mission "to Jerusalem and its environs." The first person plural sea voyages furnish the dynamic for the movement through space, and the careful structuring of the episodes relates Paul's mission to Jerusalem and Rome.

The Function of the We-Passages in Luke-Acts

Analysis of the structure of Acts 13-28 indicates that the author uses the we-sections to create a special role for mission by sea. In this section of the paper the analysis moves a step further. Three aggregates of information suggest that the entire two volume work is designed to replace the Sea of Galilee, which dominates Mark, with the Mediterranean Sea. The we-passages systematically increase in length to focus all attention on the Great Sea that lies between Jerusalem and Rome. We recall that Paul's journeys in Acts 13:1-28:16 correspond to the long journey of Jesus in Luke 9:51-19:46. This suggests that the travel sections in Acts were designed to bring Lukan themes and actions to a dramatic conclusion. Our interest is to find any relationship between Luke and Acts that illumines the role of the we-passages.

The first items of importance are found in the vocabulary of Luke and Acts. The author never allows Jesus to go alongside or onto a "sea" (*thalassa*) in Luke. This stands in notable contrast to Matthew and Mark where Jesus does both many times.[65] This difference arises, because the Sea of Galilee is never mentioned in Luke; it does not seem to exist in Lukan geography. Instead, there is a place on the eastern edge of Galilee which the author calls "the lake" (*hē*

---

[64]Cf. Acts 19:11-20.

[65]See n. 1.

limnē: Luke 5:1, 2; 8:22, 23, 33). Once this lake is called the Lake of Gennesaret (5:1).

The existence of "the lake" but not "the sea" in Luke appears to relate to the overall purpose of the author. It is designed to limit Jesus' activity in a particular way. Jesus is allowed to go to the lake only twice in Luke. All other occasions when Jesus went to the Sea of Galilee in Mark are omitted. On the first occasion, Jesus goes out in a boat with Simon, and James and John, the sons of Zebedee (5:1-11). The entire episode moves toward the conclusion in which the three fishermen become disciples of Jesus and turn to "catching men" (5:10-11). On the second occasion, Jesus gets in a boat and sails to the other side of the lake (8:22). This setting allows for the inclusion of the accounts of the calming of the storm and the healing of the demoniac in the country of the Gerasenes (8:22-39).

Each of the occasions when Jesus is linked with the lake in Luke has a twofold dimension in Luke-Acts. On the one hand, the occasions set a precedent for later action in the narrative. When Jesus goes onto the lake in 5:1-11, circles around, and comes back, he evokes the image of the disciple as one who travels on water and fishes for men. It appears to be important that he does not go "across" the lake. This eisode set a precedent that corrsponds to the situation in Acts 13:1-14:28. We recall that this section in Acts presents the first instance of sea travel. The Holy Spirit calls Barnabas and Saul to "the work" to which they have been called (13:2), and they sail out from Antioch in a circle to Cyprus, then to Pamphylia, and back to Antioch (13:4, 13; 14:26). When Paul and Barnabas return, they are sent to Jerusalem where they are sanctioned as apostles to the Gentiles (15:23-29). Paul and Barnabas have traveled on the sea; therefore they "have risked their lives for the sake of our Lord Jesus Christ" (15:26). Paul has been called to his work as the disciples are called to their work in Luke 5:1-11. But Paul does not go "across" the sea until after the Jerusalem council.

In Luke 8:22-39 Jesus sets the precedent for "crossing over" the sea that occurs for the first time in the initial we-section (Acts 16:10-17). In the Lukan episode, Jesus gets into the boat and announces, "Let us go across to the other side of the lake" (8:22). This corresponds to the Macedonian's call to Paul, "Come over to Macedonia and help us" (Acts 16:9). With the voyage across the body of water, God's work is spread to a new region. The author of Luke revises Markan vocabulary in the account of the storm on the lake to orient the story toward the climactic voyage and storm in which Paul participates at the end of Acts. Jesus and the disciples "set out from shore" (*anēchthēsan*: Luke 8:22), just as Paul and his company "set out" on a boat many times.[66] As they are "sailing along" (*pleontōn autōn*: Luke 8:23), Jesus falls asleep. References to sailing are frequent in the voyages of Paul.[67] The revision of Markan vocabulary suggests that the author already has the sea voyages of Paul in view as he composes.

The other dimension of these two episodes in Luke has already been mentioned, but it must be recalled as we move to the next reference to "the sea" in episodes with Jesus and the disciples. Only Paul and his company voyage on the sea. In the first episode not only Jesus but Simon Peter is in the boat. But Peter never voyages on the sea in Luke-Acts; he was called to his work by sailing

---

[66]Cf. Acts 13:13; 16:11; 18:21; 20:3, 13; 21:1, 2; 27:2, 4, 12, 21; 28:10, 11.

[67]Cf. Acts 21:3; 27:2, 6, 24.

in a boat on "the lake" (Luke 5:1, 2). Likewise, the author suppresses any reference to "the sea" in the storm episode. Instead of saying the wind and sea obey Jesus (Mark 4:41), the disciples refer to the winds and "the water" (Luke 8:25).

The selection of vocabulary in the first volume suggests that the author is setting precedents during the time of Jesus which become the major challenge during the time of the church. In order to do this, the author presents corresponding episodes in Luke and Acts, and he suppresses certain features in the account in Luke so these features can be more dramatically carried out during the time of the church.[68]

This vocabulary usage grows in importance when other information is added to it. Although the author never depicts Jesus on or alongside a "sea," he betrays special interest in "the sea" in sayings of Jesus. He does not refrain from including the saying about being cast into the sea with a millstone around one's neck (Luke 17:2) and the saying about the sycamine tree that can be rooted up and planted in the sea by faith (Luke 17:6). Luke is the only gospel that refers to the "distress of nations in perplexity at the roaring of the sea and the waves" in the apocalyptic discourse (Luke 21:25). The sea has a special place in his theology even in the gospel of Luke, but the author will not link Jesus directly with it. The sea is linked with Paul's mission to new regions around the Mediterranean. This conception is further indicated by the references to God "who made the heaven and the earth *and the sea*" in Acts 4:24 and 14:15. Also it is probably not accidental that Simon Peter is associated with "Simon a tanner, whose house is by the sea" in the dramatic sequence of episodes in which the Gentile Cornelius is converted and blessed by Simon Peter (10:6, 32). Mission on the sea presupposes mission to Gentiles as well as Jews, and the author systematically builds toward mission by sea in Luke and Acts 1-12.

Perhaps the most important piece of information which indicates that the author is composing toward a dramatic finish that is achieved through sea voyages is "the great omission" in Luke.[69] Luke shows dependence upon Mark as a source for most of the material in Mark 1-6:44. But beginning with Mark 6:45, and continuing through Mark 8:26, Markan material is not recounted in Luke. The proposal in this paper is that the manuscript of Mark that the author of Luke-Acts used contained Mark 6:45-8:26. He omitted this section of Mark because it took the ministry of Jesus too far into the type of mission that he wanted to portray for Paul.

As Luke used the material in Mark 1-6:44, he systematically omitted references to the sea.[70] As we have just previously noticed, Luke places the call of the disciples (Mark 1:16-20), the stilling of the storm (Mark 4:35-41), and the healing of the Gerasene demoniac (Mark 5:1-20) on "the lake." In this way he avoids reference to the sea. But when he gets to Mark 6:45, the mission of Jesus

---

[68]For a well known example of the technique in Luke-Acts, cf. Mark 14:62 with Luke 22:69 and Acts 7:56.

[69]For a summary of discussions of the great omission, see Walter E. Bundy, *Jesus and the First Three Gospels*, pp. 265-7. He concludes that "there is no satisfactory explanation" for this omission (p. 265).

[70]Mark used *thalassa* 12 times in 1:1-6:44.

develops into a mission all around the Sea of Galilee and deep into Gentile territory. Precisely with the episode where Jesus walks on the sea (Mark 6:45-52), the author begins to omit all of the material. After this episode, Jesus and his disciples cross the sea again (Mark 6:53-56), a rationale for Gentile mission is established (Mark 7:1-23), then Jesus travels through Tyre and Sidon (7:24-37). Since the boat and the sea continue to play an important role through 8:21, the author of Luke omits all the episodes in the section from the walking on the sea (Mark 6:45-52) until the confession of Peter in 8:27-33. By omitting this material, the author narrates an uninterrupted ministry of Jesus in Galilee without excursions into Tyre and Sidon and other Gentile territory. Also, the author keeps Jesus out of a boat and off a body of water that may begin to play a major role in his ministry.

In sum, the vocabulary of Luke, the two episodes where Jesus goes onto the lake, and the great omission indicate that the two volume work of Luke-Acts has been designed to replace the Sea of Galilee with the Mediterranean Sea. The role of the we-passages is to orient early Christianity toward the sea that lies between Jerusalem and Rome. The author disapproves of the emphasis upon the Sea of Galilee in Mark. No inland body of water in Palestine should be called "the sea." The sea that explains the history of early Christianity is the Great Sea that extends to the end of the earth.

Conclusion

Why, then, does the author use first plural "we" as he narrates those voyages that move the Christian church "across the sea?" First, it appears that the natural tendency to employ first person plural style within the sea voyage genre was a major factor. The second reason appears in the preface to Luke. As the author, a member of the church, pens his narrative sitting in Rome, the question is how "we" got here when we started out in Jerusalem. This author feels a strong sense of union with the early Christian leaders about whom he writes. He says that all of the things about which he writes have been accomplished "among us" (Luke 1:1). This includes all of the events he recounts in the gospel of Luke as well as the narrative of Acts. For him, the conception and birth of John the Baptist (Luke 1:5-80) is an example of an event that happened "among us." The author participates in these events even when they are transmitted to him by others (Luke 1:2). Therefore, he can say both that these things happened among us and that they were delivered to us. As he sits in Rome, he participates in the events of the Christian church, and explains to "Theophilus" how his community of believers got to be where they are (Luke 1:3-4). A Christian in Rome who knows the events well enough to pen them as this author does becomes a full participant in them. This is true even if he has experienced these events only through oral transmission and the written page. Thus he can say in his preface that the activities of Jesus, the disciples, and the apostles happened "among us." As Paul voyaged across the sea, "we" got here.

If we think it would be impossible for an author who did not participate in the events to compose in this style, we need to entertain one more piece of information. Xenophon, we recall, used third person narration throughout the *Anabasis*, even for scenes in which he depicts himself as a participant. A later copyist of the *Anabasis,* obviously not a participant in the events, wrote a concluding summary which he attached to the narrative. From his pen flowed these words:

> The governors of all the king's territories that we traversed were as follows: Artimas of Lydia, Artacamas of Phrygia, Mithradates of Lycaonia and Cappadocia, Syennesis of Cilicia . . . . The length of the entire journey, upward and downward, was two hundred and fifteen stages, one thousand, one hundred and fifty parasangs, or thirty-four thousand, two hundred and fifty-five stadia; and the length in time, upward and downward, a year and three months (7.8.25-26).[71]

This copyist, and many writers, entered into the narrative as a participant even though later analysts can see that the style of narration does not comply with the rest of the document. Perhaps we should suggest that Luke participated in the sea voyages precisely in this way.

If the author felt such a close relation to all of the events he wrote about, why did he not use first person plural all the way through? Why did he use it only in the we-sections? He did not use first person plural only in the we-sections. He used it in the two settings where it is eminently appropriate if the author construes his work in the genre of historical biography in the Hellenistic milieu toward the end of the first century A.D. These two settings are prefaces and sea voyages.[72]

---

[71]*Archontes de hoide tes basileōs chōras, hosēn epēlthomen. Ludias Artimas, Phrugias Artakamas, Lukaonias kai Kappadokias Mithradatēs, Kilikias Suennesis . . . . arithmos sumpasēs tēs hodou tēs anabaseōs kai katabaseōs stathmoi diakosioi dekapente, parasaggai chilioi hekaton pentēkonta, stadia trismuria tetrakischilia diakosia pentēkonta pente. Chronou plēthos tēs anabaseōs kai katabaseōs eniautos kai treis mēnes.*

[72]I am grateful to the University of Illinois Research Board at the Urbana-Champaign campus for funds that facilitated the final production of this study. See my forthcoming study of the prefaces to Luke and Acts in *SBL 1978 Seminar Papers* (Missoula: Scholars, 1978).

The Defense
Speeches of Paul in Acts

Fred Veltman

There is general agreement among the interpreters of Luke-Acts that the speeches as well as the narrative material of Acts were composed by Luke. With fully one-third of the composition presented in the form of speeches, it is not surprising that much of the literature on Acts has focused on the interpretation of these addresses.

Not all the speeches, however, have received equal treatment. As late as 1960 it could be said that Stephen's speech before the Sanhedrin and Paul's speech on the Areopagus had received more coverage than all the other speeches combined.[1]

Although Norden,[2] Dibelius,[3] and Cadbury[4] paved the way for giving serious attention to Luke as a literary figure and to his speech compositions as the key for unlocking his style, as late as a decade ago W. C. van Unnik[5] could lament that a thorough comparative study of Luke with ancient historians was yet to be found. Happily it appears that this problem is being corrected.[6]

---

[1]John T. Townsend, "The Speeches in Acts," *ATR*, XLII (1969), 153.

[2]Eduard Norden, *Agnostos Theos*, pp. 143-308; 1-30.

[3]Martin Dibelius, *Studies in the Acts of the Apostles,* ed. Heinrich Greeven, trans. Mary Ling, pp. 123-37; 138-85.

[4]Henry J. Cadbury, *The Making of Luke-Acts*, p. 190.

[5]W. C. van Unnik, "Luke-Acts, a Storm Center in Contemporary Scholarship," *Studies in Luke-Acts*, ed. by L. E. Keck and J. L. Martyn, p. 27.

[6]Cf. Charles H. Talbert, *Literary Patterns, Theological Themes and the Genre of Luke-Acts*, and Vernon K. Robbins, "The We-Passages in Acts and Ancient Sea Voyages," *BR*, XX (1975), 5-18.

The present investigation attempts to make a careful analysis of the defense speeches of Paul in Acts and those to be found in ancient literature in the interest of discovering if these Pauline speeches were constructed according to a set genre or *Gattung* of defense speech. If a speech pattern can be isolated we will have taken the first steps toward some understanding as to how these speeches function in the composition as a whole.

The following guidelines have been used to control the comparative study.[7]

1. The comparative materials are not limited to one type of literature, such as history or biography or romance. If the Pauline defense speeches show affinity with any ancient defense speech genre, it will be crucial to note if such a genre was a common speech form or peculiar to a given type of literature.

2. The contemporary literature, i.e., those materials dating roughly within a century of the date of the composition of Acts (c. 80 A. D.), will carry more weight than earlier or later compositions.

3. The defense speeches to be analyzed will be limited to those which appear in the context of some type of historical or romance writing in which one (or more) of the chief characters being treated in the narrative composition is being defended in the immediate context of a trial scene.[8]

4. Since the defense speech does not exist in isolation but is an integral part of a literary sub-unit involving a trial episode, both the speech and its narrative framework will be submitted to analysis.

5. In the interest of discerning literary patterns rather than stylistic features, the study will emphasize the formal elements in the construction and content arrangement of the speech and its narrative framework.[9]

The paper is divided into two major divisions. The first section will treat the ancient defense speeches as they are to be found in various types of ancient narrative sources. This first part will conclude with an attempt to isolate a defense speech form characteristic of this literature or any one of its literary traditions. The second section will cover the analysis of the Pauline defense speeches and how their form compares to that of the typical (?) defense speech in ancient times.

The Defense Speech in Ancient Literature

1. Greek Historiography. The most significant of the Greek historical writers date from the classical period and thus are hardly contemporary with Luke. Even so, they have little to offer our study. Herodotus (c. 450 B. C.) makes only one reference to a trial with a defense (4.82).[10] The charge and reply are both given in

---

[7]For further details on these guidelines and their rationale see Frederick Veltman, *The Defense Speeches of Paul in Acts*, pp. 64-9.

[8]The defense speech as part of a narrative composition is to be distinguished from the defense speech as a literary form existing on its own merit as a literary art form. For information on this development see Werner Jaeger, *Paideia: The Ideals of Greek Culture*, trans. Gilbert Highet, pp. 132, 133.

[9]Cf. Morton Smith, *Tannaitic Parallels to the Gospels*, pp. 78-114, and Peder Johan Borgen, *Bread from Heaven*, pp. 28-98.

[10]All quotations from or references to the classical authors are taken from the Loeb

indirect discourse and there is no mention of an apology (*apologia*). Among the many speeches of Thucydides (c. 440 B. C.) only two concern a defense. These speeches are given at the trial of the Plataeans (3.52.1-58.2). The two speeches are given by more than one person, are not identified as apologies by the speakers, and neither one opens with a *captatio benevolentiae* (introductory remarks aimed at gaining favor). The speeches do not follow any charges or accusations. The introduction deals with the occasion and reason for the speech. In both speeches this introduction is followed by a defense of sorts and counter charges. The final part of the speeches contains an appeal for justice. The trial ends with a guilty verdict based not on the speeches and the charges but on the answer of each Platean to one basic question which was put to the defendants at the opening of the trial. On another occasion Thucydides mentions the defense of Alcibiades (4.29.1) but the speech is not reported. Xenophon (c. 400 B. C.) handles defense speeches in various ways. He may merely mention a defense speech (*Hellenica*, 1.4.20), give the speech in indirect discourse (*Hellenica*, 5.2.35-36; 5.4.22-23), omit the speech (*Anabasis*, 1.6.5-11), or make speeches which have the nature of defense speeches but are not so called and are not given in the context of a trial (*Anabasis*, 5.8.2-26; 7.6.11-38). In one trial account he does include a defense speech (*huperapologesomenos*) in *oratio recta* (direct discourse). The apology opens with an address to the assembly, continues with a list of the accusations, and advises the court on the proper way to conduct a fair trial. The speech then turns to defend the accused and concludes with another address to the court on procedure. The speech is followed by the vote of the assembly. In what survives of the *Histories*, Polybius (c. 150 B. C.) includes thirty-seven speeches and at least eleven references to trials,[11] but there is not one apology.

Dionysius of Halicarnassus (c. 25 B. C.) has left us one defense speech in his *Roman Antiquities*. In this trial of Servillius (9.29-32), the accusation (*kategorese*) appears in indirect speech and is followed by the corroboration of the charges by witnesses. The historian clearly labels the speech as an apology. The apology has three parts to it—an introduction, the main defense, and a short conclusion. The introduction consists of the designation of the speech as an apology, a term of address (*o politai*), the identification of the speech as an apology by the speaker in first person, and an attempt to gain favor with the judge(s), "Well then, citizens, if you are to be my judges and not my enemies, I believe I shall easily convince you that I am guilty of no crime." The body of the speech progresses along clearly defined lines, moving from a general defense to the question of personal guilt and on to the defense of the senate at large. At each juncture the speaker clearly indicates the point in the accusation to which he is addressing his remarks. The speech ends with references to his sincerity. The address is sprinkled throughout with rhetorical questions which call for answers in favor of the defendant. The closing framework nicely balances the opening of the trial episode with its description of the speaker's deportment while addressing the assembly and of the witnesses who spoke on behalf of the accused. The report closes with an account of the result of the trial.

Classical Library editions unless otherwise indicated.

[11] Polybius, *Histories*, 1.52.1-3; 5.16.5-8; 18.54.1-7; 22.4.6-7; 23.1.1ff; 23.14.1-4; 24.7.7-8; 30.7; 31.1.2-5; 33.11.2-6; 38.18.1-4.

The one remaining Greek historian[12] is Appian (c. A. D. 150) who records one defense speech.[13] The spoeech of Lucius Piso[14] in defense of Antony follows the address of Cicero which lists the charges. The historian identifies the speech of Piso as one "from the other side" (*anteipein*). The apology has three well-defined sections—an introduction, body, and conclusion. The introduction includes a term of address and clearly indicates that the nature of the speech is that of an apology. There is no *captatio benevolentiae*. The body of the speech moves from charge to charge, refuting each one in turn, and reinforcing the rebuttal with rhetorical questions. The conclusion of the speech makes a general appeal to the senate on behalf of Antony and, as in the introduction, identifies the speech as one of defense. Though the introduction includes the use of the first person, the majority of the speech is presented in third person since it is given on behalf of the accused who is not present.

2. Roman Historiography. There are three Roman historians who have left us defense speeches in direct speech.[15] In his comprehensive history of Rome Livy (57 B. C.—A. D. 17) records seven defense speeches.[16] Even though the speeches when considered individually exhibit a great degree of variation, when viewed together they appear to have an over-all structure quite similar in arrangement and certain elements of form and content occur often enough (in at least two-thirds of the total number of defense speeches) to suggest a literary form for the defense speech must have been in Livy's mind (regardless of the source) at the time of composition. An analysis of these seven apologies furnishes us with the following details on the divisions of the speeches and their formal elements. Livy's defense speeches are divided into three parts—the introduction, the main defense or body of the speech, and the conclusion. The introduction includes a term of address directed to the judge personally or to the court, such as *patres conscripti*. In addition, this part of the speech stresses the innocence of the accused or the falsity of the charges, usually in first person, and provides the defense speech designation formula, usually formed with some tense of the verb "to speak (*dicere*)" and the noun "cause (*causa*)." The body of the speech opens with a general reference to the charges or calls attention to the first charge to be answered in the defense. The rebuttal includes the frequent use of rhetorical questions from which the innocence of the defendant or the falseness of the charges is to be inferred. In this section of the speech the first-person form of the verbs predominate. The conclusion forms a chiastic or ring

---

[12]For full references on the reporting of speeches in reference to trial episodes in the ancient historical and romance writings of the Greek, Roman, and Jewish literary traditions see Frederick Veltman, *The Defense Speeches of Paul in Acts*.

[13]The speeches of Appian at the trials of Scipio and Epaminondas are too short to permit analysis (*Roman History* 11.40,41).

[14]Appian, *Roman History*, The Civil Wars, 3.52-61.

[15]Cornelius Nepos (*Lives of Eminent Commanders*) and Gaius Suetonius Tranquillus (Suetonius) speak of trials but record no defense speeches. Neither are there defense speeches in the surviving works of C. Sallustius Crispus (Sallust) and C. Velleius Paterculus.

[16]Livy, *Ab urbe condita,* 3.45.6-11; 26.30.11-31.11; 40.9.1-15.16; 42.41-42; 45.22-24; 38.47-49; 39.36.7-37.17. In reference to more than twenty other trials Livy does not record the defense speeches. He does not even give us the "magnificent" speech of Scipio whose speeches on other occasions Livy appears only too anxious to include.

construction for the speech by repeating the more general claims of blamelessness as also found in the introduction. The term of address will also be repeated in the conclusion and once more the first-person form will be used. In the framework of the speech it is most often the practice of Livy to omit any formal designation of a trial or court scene. Neither is it his custom to call the speech a defense or have the presiding officer authorize the accused to begin his defense. What is always present, however, is the verdict of the court following the conclusio apology.

Q. Curtius Rufus (A.D. 41-54)[17] includes two defense speeches among the many addresses to be found in his history of Alexander the Great.[18] In the apology of Philotas[19] the introduction is not clearly defined, there is no term of address used and no *captatio benevolentiae* appears. The opening passage does, however, identify the speech as a defense (*defensio*). The main section of the address consists of four parts, each one treating a specific charge. First-person forms are used and twice the speaker identifies his speech as one of defense (*num hodie dicerem causam—non recuso defendere*). Since the speaker brings his speech to an end rather abruptly after being interrupted in the midst of his rhetorical questions, it cannot be argued with certainty that the speech has a formal conclusion. The opening framework includes the speeches of accusation, the order of the king to the accused to begin his speech, and a description of the emotional state of the defendant. A further delay of the speech takes place due to the discussion over the question of the language to be used and the exit of the king from the assembly. The closing framework is also rather extended by reason of the inclusion of another speech of accusation in indirect discourse. Only at this point is the assembly dismissed and the accused is put to torture. There is no other type of verdict offered at the conclusion to this trial episode. In the trial of Amyntas[20] the framework opens with the accusations presented in descriptive language and the permission for the accused to speak (*facta dicendi potestate*). The body of the speech follows a short introduction involving a term of address and a *captatio benevolentiae*. The main defense opens with a specific reference to the last of the four charges made against him. The speech is clearly divided into sections, each one dealing with a specific charge. As happened in the apology of Philotas, Amyntas is interrupted at the point where his rebuttal to the fourth charge reaches the length of two of the other sections of his main defense (27 lines). There is no conclusion to the speech. The closing framework of this trial scene mentions a few works of the king to the people absolving the defendant (and his brother) of any guilt, some words of counsel to the brothers, and the dismissal of the assembly.

C. Cornelius Tacitus (A. D. 55-120) reports only three brief speeches of

---

[17]For the arguments favoring this particular Q. Curtius Rufus over the other writers by the same name who wrote at other times, see Wikelm Sigimund Teuffel, *History of Roman Literature,* rev. Ludwig Schwabe, trans. George C. W. Warr, pp. 54, 55.

[18]Rufus does include a speech of Alexander defending his leadership. This speech has been excluded because in the context the king is not on trial and there is no mention that the speech is a defense (*History of Alexander,* 8.7.16ff.).

[19]Q. Curtius Rufus, *History of Alexander the Great of Macedon,* 6.10-1-37.

[20]*Ibid.,* 7.1.18-2.11.

defense in the 15 trials he covers in his *Annals*.[21] In the trial of Marcus Terentius[22] the content has more to do with praise to Caesar, who is present at the trial, than with a defense against the charges. The introduction and the conclusion are not easily recognized from their form and no term of address appears at the opening of the speech, though the speaker alternates between the two terms of address as the speech proceeds. Even though the accused admits to defending himself (*meo unius discrimine defendam*), the historian prefers to describe the speech as an "exordium" (*ad hunc modum apud senatum ordiendo*). One rhetorical question appears in the address. In the speech of Agrippina there is no claim to making a defense, there is no specific reference to the charge, and no term of address. As to arrangement of content there is no clearly defined introduction or conclusion and the content which includes only one rhetorical question is concerned with attacking the accusers rather than with defending oneself. The closing framework of the trial episode does, however, include the verdict of the judge.[23] The trial of a girl, Servilia,[24] is included by Tacitus in the trial of her father. When the accusation is levelled at the girl, she is described as being in a fit of weeping and holding to the altar as she begins her speech. There is no command for her to speak. As a defendant she is asked to answer one question. Her opening lines contain two terms of address and her plea of innocence. After a short speech (9 lines) she is interrupted by her father whose remarks are presented in indirect discourse.

The Roman historians have provided us with twelve defense speeches, three of which are too short to permit a comparative analysis. If it is reasonable to construct a defense speech pattern on the basis of a two-thirds majority among the remaining nine speeches, the following structural outline with its formal elements emerges.

As to the defense speech proper, there are three parts—the introduction, the body, and the conclusion. Characteristic of the introduction are the following: a term of address, first-person speech forms, a defense speech designation formula, a *captatio benevolentiae*, and remarks stressing the innocence of the accused or the falseness of the charges. The body of the speech follows the pattern as described above in the analysis of the defense speeches of Livy. The closing part of the speech appears to have a broken pattern among the Roman historians due to the added feature of interruptions which have the effect of curtailing the conclusion or breaking the speech before (evidently) the conclusion is reached. Except for this element of interruption the conclusions also follow the pattern outlined in the discussion of the Livy speeches.

The greatest degree of inconsistency among the Roman writers is to be found in the framework. One cannot at all count on the historian to designate the scene as a trial or court situation, to label the speech as an apology, or to include either command or permission for the defendant to begin speaking. At times there is included the description of the emotional state of the accused. When it comes to

---

[21] It might be expected that Tacitus, having been for years a rhetor in the law courts, would have included a good number of defense speeches in describing the many trials which are mentioned in his writings. This is not the case.

[22] Tacitus, *Annals* 6.8.

[23] *Ibid.*, 13.21.

[24] *Ibid.*, 16.21-35.

the closing framework, however, we can count on the writer to give us the verdict of the court.

3. Jewish Historiography. A survey of the extant writing of Jewish historiographers provides us with only one defense speech.[25] Flavius Josephus (A. D. 37-c. 100) does not label the speech of Alexander as an apology.[26] But it is clear from the content, form, and the claim of the speaker that the remarks are to be taken as a defense. At the beginning of the conclusion the defendant admits that he could have said more in defense of himself and his brother (*pleio men apologeisthai dunametha*). The opening framework describes the scene, the emotional state of Herod's sons, and the attitude of Caesar before whom the charges are made. The introduction opens with a long *captatio benevolentiae* aimed directly at the father who is accusing them and indirectly at Caesar. In this part of the speech there is a term of address and a reference to their innocence. The body of the speech opens with specific reference to the charges and moves on to declare the innocence of the defendants and to challenge the opposition to prove the truth of the allegations. Twelve rhetorical questions are presented in the main section of the address. The conclusion is clearly marked out by the speaker's admission that he will not say more. There follows a final appeal to the father to accept them as blameless, a term of address and a repetition of the closing thoughts of the introduction. The closing framework describes the emotional state of the defendants and the bystanders and the verdict of Caesar. The speech uses first- and second-person verb forms.

A defense speech form cannot be based upon one speech. If we can judge by the speech of Alexander there is no need to construct a model. This speech from the writings of Josephus is in striking agreement with what we have found in the Greek and Roman traditions in respect to form and arrangement.

4. Historical Sources. The limitations of this paper and the fragmentary condition of our sources will permit only a brief notice of other types of materials which would have been available to the ancient historian, whether directly or indirectly, and which might have influenced the development of a defense speech form. For lack of a better term these written items are classified as "historical sources." Of course we must also admit to the influence of the writer's personal knowledge as to how defense speeches were presented in court.[27]

According to Revel A. Coles[28] official and unofficial records of court proceedings included speeches of the presiding officials and the participants. In the fragments which remain in the papyri from Greco-Egypt the protocols are shown to have been prepared in a four-part composition: the introduction with its

---

[25]We have only two very short defense speeches in the historical writings of the Old Testament (1 Samuel 22 and 1 Kings 3). No defense speeches appear in the historical books of the Old Testament Apocrypha nor in the writing of Philo. Josephus will at times present the defense speech in indirect discourse or in both direct and indirect discourse. One speech by a defendant has been omitted because it is not so identified and when it comes time in the trial for the accused to make his defense he declines (*War* 1.617-640).

[26]Josephus, *Antiquities* 16.91-126.

[27]For further reference to the affinity of historiography and oratory in ancient times see Cicero, (*De oratore* 1.5.16-18; *Orator* 34.120; 20.66; 9.31; *Brutus* 11.42); Quintillian, (*Institutes* 12.1.25; 2.4.1,2).

[28]Revel A. Coles, *Reports of Proceedings in Papyri*, pp. 9,19,29-54.

trial date, location, and participants; the trial and its speeches; the decision of the judge; and the conclusion containing the certification of the record and signatures of the court scribes. These items mentioned as being part of the conclusion do not appear in papyri earlier than the second century.[29] The historian's account according to our survey typically reflects similarities with the second and third parts of the protocol form.

The martyrdom literature, whether pagan or Christian, includes defense speeches of those on trial. In the opinion of Herbert Musurillo[30] and E. G. Turner[31] the *acta* exhibit the protocol form. One difference to be noted is that where the protocols have the speech of the official in *oratio recta* and that of the participants in indirect speech, the *acta* have the speeches of the defendants in direct speech. This difference is no doubt to be expected since the *acta* were produced and preserved for the glory of the martyr and the protocols were preserved officially for the fame of the magistrates. The fragmentary state of the pagan *acta* does not admit comparative study. But since they appear to share a common heritage with the later Christian *acta*,[32] the content of which we know more about, it will be assumed in this paper that they are supportive of the general defense speech form we have located elsewhere. This assumption appears justified since where we have adequate sources for comparative study of the speeches in the Christian *acta*, we have found that the introduction uses a term of address, identifies the speech as an apology, and invites those present to listen. The closing framework, where the account in the text is complete, likewise, carries the verdict of the court.[33] The Christian had no desire to plead innocence of the charges and no wish to please Rome, hence we would expect in these speeches such variations from the usual form as the omission of the *captatio benevolentiae* and the claim of innocence.

5. Romance Literature. The romance literature has been included in this survey in an attempt to extend the comparative analysis beyond the one genre of historiography. If the defense speech pattern occurs in various types of ancient literature without significant variation it will mean that great caution should be exercised in establishing a composition's genre from the study of the literary form of its various literary units.

The romance of Chariton, *Chaereas and Callirhoe*,[34] is dated around A. D. 150.[35] The opening framework of the defense speech found in this novel describes the officials present, the reading of the letters which provide a background of the case for the judges, and the adjournment of the trial speeches until the next day. When the trial commences later, the narrator provides only very brief scene

[29]*Ibid.*, p. 52, n. 4.

[30]Herbert A Musurillo, "The Pagan Acts of the Martyrs," *TS* (1949), 556.

[31]E. G. Turner, *Greek Papyri, An Introduction*, p. 128.

[32]Hippolyte Delehaye, *Les Passions des martyrs et les genres litteraires*, pp. 150-73.

[33]For the texts of the *Martyrdom of Apollonius* and the *Martyrdom of Pionius* to which reference is made see E. C. E. Owel, *Some Authentic Acts of the Early Martyrs.*

[34]For the text of Chariton's romance see Chariton, *Chaereas and Callirhoe*, trans. Warren E. Blake. For the Greek text see *Charitonis Aphrodisiensis, de Chaerea et Callirhoe amatoriarum narrationus libri octo*, ed. Warren E. Blake.

[35]Elizabeth Hazelton Haight, *Essays on the Greek Romances*, p. 12.

detail. The first speech is that of the plaintiff. The introduction of the second speech, that of the defendant, contains the term of address, a short *captatio benevolentiae*, and a claim of innocence. As the main section of the speech is entered the speaker admits he is now to make his defense (*nun apologesomai*) and uses a second term of address coupled with a plea for the attention of the king. This section of the speech is brief and specific. There are no rhetorical questions. The final part of the speech is not clearly designated. It follows a final appeal to the plaintiff to drop the charges and then consists of a dramatic appeal to the powers of heaven and hell to produce the one witness necessary to clear the defendant. At this dramatic moment the planned interruption occurs and the narrator centers the reader's attention in the excitement caused by the confrontation. The trial scene closes with the king dismissing the spectators, counseling with his advisors, convening the assembly once more and acquitting the defendant.

The only complete romance in the Latin tradition which contains a defense speech is the *Metamorphoses*, penned by Apuleius of Madaura about A. D. 160.[36] In this trial episode the narrator describes the court scene, the accuser, and introduces the speech of accusation. At this point the defendant is commanded to speak. When he finally manages to control his emotions enough to speak, his address is introduced with the words, "*sic ad illa.*" At the end of his speech the writer takes up the story with the words, "*haec profatus.*" From these expressions the narrator informs the reader that the speech, while in direct-speech form, is actually only the gist of the (supposed) real speech. The address is not clearly defined in terms of its structure. The speech is not identified as being an apology and no obvious *captatio benevolentiae* appears. The opening and closing lines of the speech form a chiasma by their repetition of the ideas that the accused had admirable motives and therefore while not innocent is deserving of mercy. A term of address does appear once in the body of the speech. The framework also exhibits chiastic structure in its reference to the emotional state of the defendant both at the opening and closing of the narrative account. The closing framework also includes the verdict of the assembly, which in this instance was the revelation that the whole trial was meant to be a joke on the accused.

6. The Defense Speech Pattern. The survey of defense speeches in ancient literature which have been presented in the context of a trial episode has revealed a fair degree of variation between the speeches of the different writers as well as between the speeches of any single author who records more than one speech. At the same time it does seem reasonable to conclude on the basis of the similarities which are apparent when reviewing all the speeches, that some general consensus did exist among the writers as to how defense speeches were composed. We may schematically outline the pattern of the framework and the speech with their elements as follows (Elements appearing in half or more of the speeches have been underlined.):[37]

---

[36]The *Satyricon,* an earlier Latin novel credited to Petronius Arbiter, a contemporary of Nero, exists only in fragmentary condition.

[37]For more detailed information on comparison of these speeches see the unpublished dissertation already mentioned under notes 7 and 12 above.

1.   Opening Framework
     <u>Trial scene described</u>
     <u>Charges mentioned</u>
     <u>Defendant described</u>
     <u>Speech identified as an apology</u>
     Defendant ordered or permitted to speak
     <u>Defendant speaks on own initiative</u>

2.   Introduction of the Apology
     <u>Uses term of address</u>
     <u>Speech identified as an apology</u>
     Captatio benevolentiae
     Claims innocence
     Short (comparative length)
     Clearly defined

     3. Body of the Apology
         <u>Opens with mention/refutation of charges</u>
         <u>Clearly treats the charges</u>
         <u>Rhetorical questions</u>
         Uses term of address
         <u>Claims innocence</u>
         Speech identified as an apology
         <u>Clearly defined</u>

2/   Conclusion of the Apology
     <u>Uses term of address</u>
     <u>Claims innocence</u>
     Speech identified as an apology
     Short (comparative length)
     Speech interrupted
     Repeats introduction content
     Indicates speech is ending
     <u>Clearly defined</u>

1/   Closing Framework
     <u>Trial scene described</u>
     Speech identified as an apology
     Verdict revealed

The defense speech pattern appears to have had a loose enough structure to permit individualization by the various writers as they brought their creative talents into play in the accounting of any given defense speech. Evidently they did not feel obliged to report a speech for every such speech which was claimed to have been given in court. The survey has not shown that any appreciable difference existed between the defense speeches of the various cultural traditions or those of the differing genres of ancient literature. The question now to be raised concerns the defense speeches of Paul. Do they reflect this same general pattern?

The Defense Speeches of Paul in Acts

The book of Acts records seven episodes which have been taken as trial scenes by various interpreters: Paul's speech on the Areopagus (Acts 17:19-32); the defense before the Hebrews in the temple court (Acts 21:27-22:29); the hearings before the Sanhedrin (Acts 22:30-23:10), before Felix (Acts 24:1-23), before Felix and Drusilla (Acts 24:24, 25), before Festus (Acts 25:6-12), and before Festus and Herod Agrippa II (Acts 26:1-32). Only four of these accounts include a speech:[38] the temple scene, the appearance before Felix, that before Festus and Agrippa, and the Areopagus meeting. The Areopagus speech has been omitted in this survey because of the absence of a clear reference to a trial. Norden concluded from his form critical study of this address that it was a typical utterance "*zum Zwecke religioser Propaganda.*"[39]

1. Before the Jews in Jerusalem. The confrontation of Paul and the Jewish people in the temple courtyard (21:27-22:29) is obviously intended by Luke to be understood by the reader as a defense by Paul before the people as his judge.[40] The entire scene takes on the coloration of a typical court hearing. The narrative opens with Paul's being seized and accused of crimes against the people, the law, and the temple. The accusation follows the notation that the people had "laid hands on him" (*epebalan ep' auton tas cheiras*), a common expression used by New Testament writers to indicate arrest.[41] The framework concludes with a brief description of the defendant standing before the people and motioning for silence.

The introduction appears to consist of one sentence separated from the body of the speech by a further comment of the narrator. In this short introduction are to be found the terms of address and the admission that the speech is a defense. There is no *captatio benevolentiae.*[42]

The main part of the speech is biographical in content and does not specifically refer to the charges.[43] The speaker, nevertheless, claims his innocence in respect to them. He calls to his support Ananias of Damascus who was "a devout man according to the law." He meets the charge that he was against the people in his argument that Ananias was "well spoken of by all the

---

[38]There is nothing in the account of the appearance before Felix and Drusilla to indicate a trial, especialy in the light of verse 26.

[39]Norden, *Agnostos Theos,* p. 113.

[40]Cf. C. F. Evans, " 'Speeches' in Acts," *Mélanges Bibliques en hommage au R. P. Beda Rigaux,* ed. by Albert Descamps and R. P. André de Halleux, pp. 292, 293 and Ernst Haenchen, *The Acts of the Apostles,* trans. R. McL. Wilson, p. 624.

[41]Cf. Acts 4:3; 5:18: Luke 20:19; 21:12: Mark 14:46.

[42]For contrary viewpoint see Haenchen, *Acts,* p. 109.

[43]The typical Greek term for "charges," *aitian,* occurs only in the closing framework to this speech (22:24).

Jews who lived there (22:12)," and that he was formerly involved in persecuting those who were regarded as enemies of the people (22:4, 5, 19, 20). The final charge that Paul was against the temple is rebutted in his claim that in the past he had come to the temple for prayer (22:17).

The defense is interrupted before it is allowed to reach its conclusion.[44] The closing framework includes the verdict, "Away with such a fellow from the earth! For he ought not to live (22:22)," the description of the reaction of the people, and the involvement of Paul with the tribune. The dialogue between Paul and the tribune over Paul's citizenship unites the closing framework to the opening framework in a ring or chiastic structure.

2. Before Felix in Caesarea. The defense of Paul before Felix has all the earmarks of a typical apology. In the narration of this episode (24:1-23) the writer clearly identifies the participants of the trial and records the speech of accusation. The accuser charges that Paul is "an agitator among all the Jews throughout the world, and a ringleader of the sect of the Nazarenes." At the last position is the charge that Paul "tried to profane the temple" (24:4, 5). The opening framework ends with the governor's giving the signal that Paul is permitted to speak (24:10).

The address of Paul opens with a short introduction containing a brief *captatio benevolentiae* and the identification of the speech as a defense. No term of address appears. The body of the speech takes seriously the changes of Tertullus and offers a refutation to two of them. He denies that he is an agitator or that he had defiled the temple. He does, however, admit that he is a member of the sect of the Nazarenes. Paul uses the reference to being of the Nazarenes to bolster his previous defense against the charges of being against the law and the Jewish people. He reaffirms his claim to being innocent of the charges.

The conclusion to the speech is not well defined. The difficulties have to do with both form and content. The Alexandrian text breaks off at verse 19 to produce an anacoluthon. The Byzantine textual variants appear to be later attempts to smooth over the textual problem created by the abrupt ending. We have no record of the Western textual tradition at this point. In terms of content, we notice a shift in the trend of the argument at this juncture. Where in the verses preceding Paul had been considering the charges of Tertullus, at this point he begins to challenge his accusers to provide the proper witnesses to the charges or to charge him on grounds for which they could provide first-hand evidence. The speech is concluded without the introduction of one rhetorical question in the entire address.

The encounter before Felix is brought to a close by the writer in typical fashion. The governor is described as adjourning the trial and giving orders in respect to the custody of Paul. Since the case is presented by Luke as being undecided at this point in time the usual verdict is naturally missing.

It will be noticed that the first-person verb forms have been predominant in the Pauline defense speeches studied.

---

[44] The claim by Dibelius (*Studies in the Acts of the Apostles,* pp. 160, 161) and Haenchen (*Acts,* p. 628) that the interruption is a "literary device" of Luke's invention has not been verified by this study.

3. Before Festus and Agrippa. The defense speech of Paul before Festus and Agrippa is the longest of the apologies credited by Luke to Paul (25:23-26:32).

Luke sets the stage for the speech by giving a detailed description of the court scene and its participants. There is no specific mention that a trial is taking place, but he does record the words of Festus that a "preliminary hearing" (*amakrisis*) was taking place. And Paul explicitly refers to himself as standing on trial (*hesteka krinomenos*) in the body of the speech (26:6). Though the opening framework does not specifically deal with the charges, it is obvious from the narrative (25:18-20) and the closing lines of the opening remarks of the writer (25:27) that it is in reference to the charges (*aitia*) that the hearing is being held. The author presents Agrippa as giving permission for Paul to speak and identifies Paul's remarks as a defense (*apolgeito*).

The short introduction to the speech includes the use of a term of address which will with some variation occur three more times in the speech, the admission that the speech is an apology (*apologeisthai*), and a brief *captatio benevolentiae.*

The body of the speech is first concerned to speak of Paul's innocence. The accusation of the Jews (21:28), the charges of Tertullus (24:5,6), and the understanding of the problem by Festus (25:17-19) are all in substantial agreement. The issue is a religious one and Luke is consistent in keeping that point at the forefront of the argumentation. The basic question was the orthodoxy of Paul's religion. For this reason the defense of Paul emphasizes his relationship to the Jewish religion, its teachers and its hopes. The Damascus road experience becomes important because it is only since he has seen Jesus that he can speak of the truth of the resurrection, the heart of the hope of which he speaks (24:15,21; 5:19; 26:7,8,23). Paul clearly states that it was a religious issue and not the temple problem that was at the heart of the charges (26:21), even though he also included in his various defense statements the denial of the profanation of the temple (24:18; 25:8).

Once again the conclusion of the Pauline defense speech is difficult to establish. It could be argued that the conclusion begins at verse 22 and the reference to Paul standing before them giving his testimony. In some ways these words remind one of the introduction. On the other hand, the genitive absolute construction of verse 24 suggests that Paul is once more being interrupted. If the writer intends for the reader to see the speech as interrupted, it is more likely that the interruption would take place in the body of the speech than within the conclusion. Since the speech before the Jews was not interrupted at the references implying the resurrection of Jesus, and the defense before Felix was not interrupted at the mentioning of the resurrection (24:15,21), it cannot be argued with certainty that Luke breaks the speech here for purposes of highlighting the resurrection theme.

The closing framework identifies the speech of Paul as one of defense and includes some dialogue between the participants of the trial. The episode ends with the verdict.

4. Conclusion. A comparison of the Lukan speeches of Paul with the defense speech pattern which emerged from our study of the ancient literature reveals the following similarities and differences. Obviously we cannot speak of degrees of affinity when we have only three Pauline speeches to consider and our survey

has shown that each writer varied his form and style while still generally reflecting agreement with the pattern as a whole.

The speeches of Paul are set in a framework very similar to the pattern presented above. All elements found in the opening and closing frameworks of the typical form are found in the Lukan compositions.

The introductions to the Pauline speeches likewise show great affinity with the defense speech model. The opening remarks were clearly defined, identified the speech as an apology, were comparatively short, and generally used a term of address. Some differences in the construction were noted in terms of content. The Pauline speeches did not make a claim of innocence in the introductions if our arrangement of the construction of the speeches is correct.

The bodies of the Lukan speeches also appear to be in general harmony with the pattern. They open with a refutation of the charges and treat the accusations levelled at the defendant. They consist largely of first-person verb forms and use a term of address. They also stress the innocence of the accused. The Pauline speeches differed in that they never used rhetorical questions and never specifically identified the speech as an apology in the body of the address. It must be noted, however, that such variations were also found in the speeches surveyed in this study.

Since in our analysis of the Pauline speeches we were able to locate only one conclusion, and that one only tentatively, no attempt will be made here to compare the Lukan speeches in respect to their conclusions apart from the notation that like a number of the ancient defense speeches, the Pauline speeches were usually interrupted before they were completed.

From the foregoing analysis it would therefore appear reasonable to conclude that the defense speeches of Paul in Acts exhibit the same form, the same arrangement, and the same general elements which are characteristic of defense speeches in other narrative literature from ancient times.

It should also be noted that the defense speech form or *Gattung* does not undergo any noticeable change when used in the differing literary genre, at least insofar as historiography, romance, and the Pauline speeches in Acts are concerned.

Bibliography

Anonymous, ed., *Essays in Modern Theology and Related Subjects: A Testimonial to Charles A. Briggs.* New York: Charles Scribner's, 1911.

Anonymous, ed., *XIV Semana biblica espanola: 21-26 Sept., 1953.* Madrid: Consejo superior de investigaciones cientificas, 1954.

Allmen, J.J. von, ed. *Aux sources de la tradition chrétinne: Mélanges Gougel.* Neuchatel: Delachoux, 1950.

Arndt, W.F. *The Gospel according to St. Luke.* St. Louis: Concordia, 1956.

Arndt, W.F. and Gingrich, F.W., eds., *A Greek-English Lexicon of the New Testament and Other Early Christian Literature.* Chicago: University of Chicago Press, 1957.

Aune, D., ed., *Studies in New Testament and Early Christian Literature: Essays in Honor of A.P. Wikgren.* Leiden: Brill, 1972.

Bacon, S. W. and Marx, A., eds., *Jewish Studies in Honor of A. Kohut.* New York: The Alexander Kohut Memorial Foundation, 1935.

Baelz, P.R. *Prayer and Providence: A Background Study.* New York: Seabury Press, 1968.

Bailey, K., *Poet and Peasant.* Grand Rapids: Eerdmans, 1976.

Baird, W., "Luke," *The Interpreter's One Volume Commentary on the Bible,* ed. C.M. Laymon. New York: Abingdon, 1971.

Banks, R., ed., *Reconciliation and Hope: New Testament Essays on Atonement Eschatology Presented to L.L. Morris on his 60th Birthday.* Grand Rapids: Eerdmans, 1974.

Barker, C.J. *The Acts of the Apostles.* London: Epworth, 1969.

Barth, K. *The Epistle to the Romans,* trans. E.C. Hoskyns. Oxford: Oxford University Press, 1933.

Bascom, W., *Deep Water, Ancient Ships.* Garden City, N.J.: Doubleday, 1976.

Bauer, B. *Die Apostelgeschichte.* Berlin: Hempel, 1850.

Bauer, J.B., ed., *Sacramentum Verbi.* New York: Herder & Herder, 1970.

Bauerfeind, O., *Die Worte der Dämonen im Markusevangelium.* Stuttgart: Kohlhammer, 1927.

Baumer, R. and Dolch, H., eds., *Volk Gottes: Festgabe für Josef Hafer.* Freiburg: Herder, 1967.

Benoit, P. and Boismard, M.E. *Synopse des Quatre Evangiles en Francais.* Paris: Les Editions du Cerf, 1973.

Bernard, J.H., *The Gospel according to St. John,* 2 vols. Edinburgh: T. & T. Clark, 1928.

Betz, H.D. and Schottroff, L. eds., *Neues Testament und Christliche Existenz: Festschrift für Herbert Braun.* Tübingen: Mohr, 1973.

Beyer, K., *Semitische Syntax im Neuen Testament I/1.* Göttingen: Vandenhoeck & Ruprecht, 1962.

Black, M., *An Aramaic Approach to the Gospels and Acts.* 3d ed. Oxford: Clarendon, 1967.

Blass, F. *Philology of the Gospels.* London: Macmillan, 1898.

Blass, F. and Debrunner, A., *A Greek Grammar of the New Testament,* trans. R.W. Funk. Chicago: University of Chicago Press, 1961.

Bligh, J. *Christian Deuteronomy (Luke 9-18).* Langley, Bucks: St. Paul Publications, 1970.

Blinzler, J. *Gesammelte Aufsatze.* Stuttgart: Katholisches Bibelwerk, 1969.

Bogaert, P., *L'Apocalypse syriaque de Baruch.* Paris: Cerf, 1969.

Bolkstein, H., *Wohltätigkeit und Armenpflege im vorchristlichen Altertum: Ein Beitrag zur Problem 'Moral und Gesellschaft.'* Utrecht: A. Oosthoek Verlag, 1939.

Bompaire, J., *Lucien écrivain: imitation et creation.* Paris: E. de Bouard, 1958.

Borgen, P.J., *Bread from Heaven.* Leiden: Brill, 1965.

Bouwman, G., *Das dritte Evangelium.* Dusseldorf: Patmos, 1968.

Braun, F.M., *Jean le Theologien II: Les grandes traditions d'Israel.* Paris: Gabalda, 1964.

Bright, J.,*The Kingdom of God.* New York: Abingdon, 1963.

Brown, R.E., *The Birth of the Messiah.* New York: Doubleday, 1977.

_____., *The Gospel accoding to John,* 2 vols. Garden City: N.Y.: Doubleday, 1966, 1970.

_____., *The Virginal Conception and Bodily Resurrection of Jesus.* New York: Paulist Press, 1973.

Brown, S., *Apostasy and Perserverence in the Theology of Luke.* Rome: Pontifical Biblical Institute, 1969.

Brox, N., *Falsche Verfasserangabem zur Erklarung der frühchristlichen Pseudepigraphie.* Stuttgart: KBW, 1975.

Bruce, F.F., *The Acts of the Apostles: The Greek Text.* Grand Rapids: Eerdmans, 1951.

_____., *Commentary on the Book of Acts.* Grand Rapids: Eerdmans, 1956.

Buecheler, F., ed., *Petronii Sarturae.* Berlin: Weidmann, 1904.

Buffiere, F., *Heraclite: Allegories d'Homere.* Paris: Societe d'edition 'Les Belles Lettres', 1962.

Bundy, W.E., *Jesus and the First Three Gospels.* Cambridge: Harvard University Press, 1955.

Burchard, C., *Der dreizehnte Zeuge: Traditions- und kompositionsgeschichtliche Untersuchungen zu Lukas' Darstellung der Frühzeit des Paulus.* Göttingen: Vandenhoeck & Ruprecht, 1970.

Burney, C.F., *The Aramaic Origin of the Fourth Gospel.* Oxford: Oxford University Press, 1922.

——————., *The Poetry of Our Lord.* Oxford: Oxford University Press, 1945.

Burton, E.D. *Some Principles of Literary Criticism and Their Application to the Synoptic Problem.* Chicago: University of Chicago Press, 1904.

Butler, B.C., *The Originality of St. Matthew.* Cambridge: Cambridge University Press, 1951.

Buttrick, D. G., ed., *Jesus and Man's Hope,* 2 vols. Pittsburgh: Pittsburgh Theological Seminary, 1970.

Buttrick, G.A., ed., *The Interpreter's Dictionary of the Bible.* 4 vols. New York: Abingdon, 1962.

——————., *Prayer.* New York: Abingdon-Cokesbury, 1942.

Cadbury, H.J., *The Making of Luke-Acts.* New York: Macmillan, 1927.

Cadman, W.H., *The Last Journey of Jesus to Jerusalem: Its Purpose in The Light of the Synoptic Gospels.* London: Oxford University Press, 1923.

Cameron, H.D., *Studies on the Seven against Thebes of Aeschylus.* Paris: Mouton, 1971.

Campbell, D.A., *Greek Lyric Poetry.* London: Macmillan, 1967.

Carey, M., ed., *Oxford Classical Dictionary.* Oxford: Clarendon, 1949.

Casson, L., *Illustrated History of Ships and Boats.* Garden City, N.Y.: Doubleday, 1964.

——————. *Ships and Seamanship in the Ancient World.* Princeton: Princeton University Press, 1971.

——————., *Travel in the Ancient World.* Garden City, N.Y.: Doubleday, 1964.

——————., *The Ancient Mariners.* New York: Macmillan, 1959.

Catchpole, D.R., *The Trial of Jesus.* Leiden: Brill, 1971.

Chariton, *Chaeras and Callirhoe,* trans. W.E. Blake. Ann Arbor: University of Michigan Press, 1939.

Charitonis Aphrodisiensis, *de Chaerea et Callirhoe amatoriarum narrationus libri octo,* ed. W.E. Blake. London: Oxford University Press, 1938.

Charlesworth, J. H., *The Pseudepigrapha and Modern Research.* Missoula: Scholars Press, 1976.

Chase, F. H., *The Old Syraic Element in the Text of Codex Bezae.* London: Macmillan, 1893.

Chotard, H., *Le Periple de la Mer Noire par Arrien.* Paris: Remquet, 1860.

Cleator, P. E., *Lost Languages.* New York: John Day, 1961.

Coggan, D., *The Prayers of the New Testament.* London: Hodder & Stoughton, 1967.

Coles, R. A., *Reports of Proceedings in Papyri.* Bruxelles: Fondation Egyptologique Reine Elizabeth, 1966.

Conzelmann, H., *Die Mitte der Zeit.* Tübingen: Mohr, 1953. ET, *The Theology of St. Luke,* trans. G. Buswell. New York: Harpers, 1960.

——————— ., *Die Apostelgeschichte.* Tübingen: Mohr, 1963.

Crenshaw, J. L. and Willis, J. T., eds., *Essays in Old Testament Ethics: J. Philip Hyatt, In Memoriam.* New York: KTAV, 1974.

Cross, F. L., ed., *Studia Evangelica II.* Berlin: Akademie Verlag, 1964.

Cullmann, O., *The Christology of the New Testament,* trans. S. C. Guthrie and C.A. M. Hall. Philadelphia: Westminster, 1959.

——————— ., *Peter,* trans. F. V. Filson. Philadelphia: Westminster, 1962.

Dalman, G., *The Words of Jesus,* trans. D. M. Kay. Edinburgh: T. & T. Clark, 1902.

Degenhardt, H. J., *Lukas, Evangelist der Armen: Besitz und Besitzverzicht in den lukanischen Schriften.* Stuttgart: Verlag Katholische Bibelwerk, 1965.

Deissmann, A., *Bible Stories,* trans. A. Grieve. Edinburgh: T. & T. Clark, 1909.

——————— ., *Light from the Ancient East,* trans. L. R. M. Strachan. Grand Rapids: Baker, 1965.

Delbrueck, R., *Probleme der Lipsanothek in Brescia.* Bonn: P. Hanstein, 1952.

Delehaye, H., *Les Passions des Martyrs et les genres letteraires.* Brussels: Bureaux de la Societe des Bollandistes, 1921.

Descamps, A. and Halleux, A. de, eds., *Mélanges bibliques en hommage au R.P. Béda Rigaux.* Gembloux: Duculot, 1970.

Dibelius, M., *Studies in the Acts of the Apostles,* ed. H. Greeven, trans. M. Ling. New York: Scribners, 1956.

Dietrich, W., *Das Petrusbild der lukanischen Schriften.* Stuttgart: Kohlhammer, 1972.

Dillon, R., "The Acts of the Apostles," *The Jerome Biblical Commentary,* ed. R. E. Brown, J. A. Fitzmyer, R. Murphy. Englewood Cliffs, N. J.: Prentice-Hall, 1968.

Dinkler, E., ed., *Zeit und Geschichte.* Tübingen: Mohr, 1964.

Doty, W., *Letters in Primitive Christianity.* Philadelphia: Fortress, 1973.

Driver, S. R., Cheyne, T. K., Sanday, W., eds., *Studia Biblica et Ecclesiastica II.* Oxford: Clarendon, 1886.

Duckworth, G. E., *Structural Patterns and Proportions in Vergil's Aeneid.* Ann Arbor: University of Michigan Press, 1962.

Dungan, D. L., *The Sayings of Jesus in the Churches of Paul.* Philadelphia: Fortress, 1971.

Dupont, J., *Etudes sur les Actes des Apôtres.* Paris: Cerf, 1967.

——————— ., *Les Béatitudes. Tomes II & III.* Paris Gabalda, 1969, 1973.

——————— ., *Le discours Milet.* Paris: Cerf, 1962.

——————— ., *The Sources of Acts,* trans. K. Pond. London: Darton, Longman, & & Todd, 1964.

Edwards, D. L., *Good News in Acts*. Glasgow: Collins, 1974.

Edwards, R. A., *The Sign of Jonah*. Naperville: Allenson, 1971.

Eissfeldt, O., *The Old Testament: An Introduction,* trans. P. R. Ackroyd. Oxford: Blackwell, 1965.

Elliott, J. K., ed., *Studies in New Testament Language and Text*. Leiden: Brill, 1976.

_____., *The Greek Text of Timothy and Titus*. Salt Lake City: University of Utah, 1968.

Ellis, E. E., *The Gospel of Luke*. London: Nelson, 1966.

Empie, P. and Murphy, T. A., eds., *Lutherans and Catholics in Dialogue*. Washington, D. C.: NCCB, 1970.

Engemann, J., *Untersuchungen zur Sepulkralsymbolik der späteren römischen Kaiserzeit.* Münster: Aschendorff, 1973.

Enslin, M. S., *Reapproaching Paul*. Philadelphia: Westminster, 1972.

Epp, E. J., *The Theological Tendencies of Codex Bezae Catabrigiensis in Acts*. Cambridge: Cambridge University Press, 1966.

Evans, H. H., *St. Paul, the Author of the Acts of the Apostles and of the Third Gospel*. 2 vols.; London: Wyman, 1884-86.

Farmer, W. R. *et al,* eds., *Christian History and Interpretation: Studies Presented to John Knox*. Cambridge: Cambridge University Press, 1967.

_____., *The Synoptic Problem*. New York: Macmillan, 1964; 2d ed.; Dillsboro, N. C.: Western North Carolina Press, 1976.

Farrar, F. W.,*The Gospel according to St. Luke*. Cambridge: Cambridge University Press, 1910.

_____., *The Message of the Books*. New York: E. P. Dutton, 1897.

Feine, P., Behm, J., Kümmel, W. G., *Introduction to the New Testament*. Nashville: Abingdon, 1966.

Fisher, F. L., *Prayer in the New Testament*. Philadelphia: Westminster, 1964.

Fitzmyer, J. A., *The Genesis Apocryphon of Qumran Cave I: A Commentary*. 2d ed.; Rome: Pontifical Biblical Institute, 1971.

Flender, H., *Heil und Geschichte in der Theologie des Lukas*. Munich: Kaiser Verlag, 1965; ET, *St. Luke: Theologian of Redemptive History,* trans. I. and R. H. Fuller. Philadelphia: Fortress, 1967.

Foakes Jackson, F. J. and Lake, K., eds., *The Beginnings of Christianity*. 5 vols. London: Macmillan, 1922-23.

Fortna, R. T., *The Gospel of Signs*. London: Cambridge University Press, 1970.

Fuller, R. H., *The New Testament in Current Study*. New York Scribners, 1962.

Gaboury, A., *La Structure des Evangiles Synoptique*. Leiden: Brill, 1970.

Gamble, H., *The Textual History of the Letter to the Romans*. Grand Rapids: Eerdmans, 1977.

Gasque, W. W., *A History of the Criticism of the Acts of the Apostles.* Tübingen, Mohr, 1975.

Gasque, W. W. and Martin, R., eds., *Apostolic History and the Gospel: Biblical and Historical Essays Presented to F. F. Bruce on his 60th Birthday.* Exeter: Paternoster, 1970.

Geldenhuys, N., *Commentary of the Gospel of Luke.* London: Marshall, Morgan & Scott, 1950.

Gilmour, S. McL., "Luke," *The Interpreter's Bible,* vol. VIII, ed. G. A. Buttrick. New York: Abingdon, 1952.

Girard, L., *L'Evangile des voyages de Jesus: Ou la section 9:51-18:14 de saint Luc.* Paris: Gabalda, 1951.

Glasson, T. F., *Moses in the Fourth Gospel.* London: SCM, 1963.

Goodspeed, E. J., *New Solutions of New Testament Problems.* Chicago: Chicago University Press, 1927.

Goulder, M. D., *Midrash and Lection in Matthew.* London: SPCK, 1974.

——————., *Type and History in Acts.* London: SPCK, 1964.

Grant, R. M., *Historical Introduction to the New Testament.* New York: Harper & Row, 1963.

Green, M., *Evangelism in the Early Church.* Grand Rapids: Eerdmans, 1970.

Grundmann, W., *Das Evangelium nach Lukas.* 7th ed.; Berlin: Evangelische Verlagsanstalt, 1974.

Haenchen, E., *Die Apostelgeschichte.* 5th ed.; Göttingen: Vandenhoeck & Ruprecht, 1965; ET, *The Acts of the Apostles,* trans. R. McL. Wilson *et al.* Philadelphia: Westminster Press, 1971.

Hafer, J. and Rahner, K., eds., *Lexikon für Theologie und Kirche.* 10 vols. Freiburg: Herder, 1957-64.

Haight, E. H., *Essays on the Greek Romances.* Port Washington, N. Y.: Kennikat Press, 1965 (reprint).

Hamann, H., ed., *Theologia Crucis: Studies in Honor of H. Sasse.* Adelaide, Australia: Lutheran Publishing, 1975.

Hamman, A., *La priere.l. Le Nouveau Testament.* Tournai: Desclee, 1959.

Hands, A. R., *Charity and Social Aid in Greece and Rome.* Ithaca: Cornell University Press, 1968.

Harnack, A., *Ist die Rede des Paulus in Athens ein ursprunglicher Bestandteil der Apostelgeschichte?* Leipzig: J. C. Hinrichs, 1913.

——————., *Luke the Physician,* trans. New York: Putnam, 1908.

——————., *The Acts of the Apostles,* trans. J. R. Wilkinson. New York: Putnam, 1909.

——————., *The Date of the Acts and of the Synoptic Gospels,* trans. J. R. Wilkinson. New York: Putnam, 1911.

Harris, O. G., *Prayer in Luke-Acts: A Study in the Theology of Luke.* Nashville: Ph.D. Dissertation, Vanderbilt University, 1966.

Hastings, A., *Prophet and Witness in Jerusalem.* Baltimore: Helicon Press, 1958.

Hastings, J., ed., *A Dictionary of Christ and the Gospels.* 2 vols. New York: Scribners, 1913.

Hauck, F., *Die Stellung des Urchristentums zu Arbeit und Geld.* Gutersloh: C. Bertelsmann, 1921.

Heiler, F., *Prayer: A Study in the History and Psychology of Religion.* London: Oxford University Press, 1932.

Heliodorus, *Ethiopian Story*, trans. W. Lamb. New York: Dutton, 1961.

Hennecke, E., ed., *New Testament Apocrypha,* trans. R. McL. Wilson *et al.* 2 vols. Philadelphia: Westminster, 1963, 1965.

Hill, D., *Greek Words and Hebrew Meanings: Studies in the Semantics of Soteriological Terms.* Cambridge: Cambridge University Press, 1967.

Hillers, D. R., *Lamentations.* New York: Doubleday, 1972.

Hoffmann, P. *et al*, eds., *Orientierung an Jesus: Zur Theologie der Synoptiker. Für Josef Schmid.* Freiburg im B.: Herder, 1973.

Holtzmann, H. J., *Die Synoptischen Evangelien: Ihr Ursprung und Geschichtlichen Charakter.* Leipzig: Wilhelm Engelmann, 1863.

Howard, P. E., *The Book of Acts as a Source for the Life of Paul.* Ann Arbor: University Microfilms, 1959.

Hubbard, B. J., *The Matthean Redaction of a Primitive Apostolic Commissioning: An Exegesis of Matthew 28:16-20.* Missoula: Scholars Press, 1974.

Hull, J., *Hellenistic Magic and the Synoptic Tradition.* London: SCM, 1974.

Hurd, J. C., *The Origin of I Corinthians.* New York: Seabury, 1965.

Hyde, W. W., *Ancient Greek Mariners.* New York: Oxford University Press, 1947.

Jaeger, W., *Paideia: The Ideals of Greek Culture,* trans. G. Highet. New York: Oxford University Press, 1944.

James, M. R., ed. and trans., *The Apocryphal New Testament.* Oxford: Clarendon, 1953.

Jastrow, M., *Dictionary of the Targumim, the Talmud Babli and Yerushalmi, and the Midrashic Literature.* 2 vols. Brooklyn: Shalom Publishing Co., 1967.

Jeremias, J., *New Testament Theology I: The Proclamation of Jesus,* trans. J. Bowden. New York: Scribners, 1971.

——————., *The Central Message of the New Testament.* London: SCM, 1965.

——————., *The Eucharistic Words of Jesus,* trans. N. Perrin. London: SCM, 1966.

——————., *The Lord's Prayer,* trans. J. Reumann. Philadelphia: Fortress, 1965.

——————., *The Prayers of Jesus,* trans. J. Bowden *et al.* Naperville: Allenson, 1967.

Jervell, J., *Luke and the People of God.* Minneapolis: Augsburg, 1972.

Johnson, S. E., "Matthew," *The Interpreter's Bible,* vol. VII, ed. G. A. Buttrick. New York: Abingdon, 1952.

Jülicher, A., *Neue Linien in der Kritik der evangelischen Überlieferung.* Giessen: Topelmann, 1906.

Kahle, P., *The Cairo Geniza.* 2d. ed.; Oxford: Blackwells, 1959.

Käsemann, E., *The Testament of Jesus according to John 17,* trans. G. Krodel. Philadelphia: Fortress, 1968.

Keck, L, E. and Martyn, J. L., eds., *Studies in Luke-Acts.* Nashville: Abingdon, 1966.

Klein, G., *Die Zwölf Apostel.* Göttingen: Vandenhoeck & Ruprecht, 1961.

Knox, J., *Chapters in a Life of Paul.* Nashville: Abingdon, 1950.

————., *Marcion and the New Testament.* Chicago: Chicago University Press, 1942.

Lampe, G., ed., *The Cambridge History of the Bible.* 3 vols. Cambridge: Cambridge University Press, 1969.

Légasse, S., *L'appel du riches (Marc 10:17-31 et paralleles).* Paris: Beauchesne, 1966.

Lightfoot, J. B., *the Apostolic Fathers.* London: Macmillan, 1885-90.

Lindsey, R. L., *A New Approach to the Synoptic Gospels.* Jerusalem: Dugith Publishers, 1971.

————., *Hebrew Translation of the Gospel of Mark.* Jerusalem: Dugith Publishers, 1969.

Lohmeyer, E., *The Lord's Prayer,* trans. J. Bowden. London: Collins, 1965.

Loisy, A., *Les Actes des Apôtres.* Paris: Nourry, 1920.

Longenecker, R. and Tenney, M., eds., *New Dimensions in New Testament Study.* Grand Rapids: Zondervan, 1974.

Lyon, D. G., ed., *Studies in the History of Religions Presented to Crawford Howell Toy.* New York: Macmillan, 1912.

Macdonald, J., *The Theology of the Samaritans.* Philadelphia: Westminster, 1964.

MacGregor, G. H. C., "The Acts of the Apostles," *The Interpreter's Bible,* vol. IX, ed. G. A. Buttrick. New York: Abingdon, 1954.

MacLaurin, E. C. B., ed., *Essays in Honor of G. W. Thatcher.* Sydney: Sydney University Press, 1967.

MacRae, G. W., ed., *Society of Biblical Literature 1974 Seminar Papers.* 2 vols. Missoula: Scholars Press, 1974.

————., *Society of Biblical Literature 1976 Seminar Papers.* Missoula: Scholars Press, 1976.

Mahaffy, J. P., *The Flinders Petrie Papyri, II, III.* Dublin: Academy House, 1893, 1905.

Marshall, I. H., *Luke: Historian and Theologian.* Grand Rapids: Zondervan, 1971.

Martin, R. A., *Syntactical Evidence of Semitic Sources in Greek Documents.* Cambridge: Society of Biblical Literature, 1974.

Marxsen, W., *Mark the Evangelist,* trans. J. Boyce. Nashville: Abingdon, 1969.

Mattill, A. J., Jr., *Luke as a Historian in Criticism since 1840.* Ann Arbor: University Microfilms, 1959.

Mattill, A. J. and M. B., *A Classified Bibliography of Literature on the Acts of the Apostles.* Leiden: Brill, 1966.

McNamara, M., *Targum and Testament.* Grand Rapids: Eerdmans, 1971.

Meeks, W., *The Prophet King.* Leiden: Brill, 1967.

Meeus, X. de, *La composition de Lc 9:51-18:14.* Louvain: Dissertation, 1954.

Metzger, B. M., *A Textual Commentary on the Greek New Testament.* New York: United Bible Societies, 1971.

_____., *Index to Periodical Literature on Christ and the Gospels.* Leiden: Brill, 1966.

Meyer, E., *Ursprung und Anfänge des Christentums.* 3 vols. Berlin: Cota, 1921-23.

Miesner, D. R., *Chiasm and the Composition and Message of Paul's Missionary Sermons.* Chicago: S.T.D. Dissertation, Lutheran School of Theology, 1974.

Milik, J. T., *The Books of Enoch.* Oxford: Clarendon, 1976.

Miller, M. H., *The Character of Miracles in Luke-Acts.* Berkeley: GTU Th.D. Dissertation, 1971.

Mitteis, L. and Wilcken, U., *Grundzüge und Chrestomathie der Papyruskunde, I/2.* Leipzig: Teubner, 1912.

Moore, C. A., *Daniel, Esther and Jeremiah: The Additions.* New York: Doubleday, 1977.

Morgenthaler, R., *Die lukanische Geschichtsschreibung als Zeugnis.* 2 vols. Zürich: Zwingli Verlag, 1949.

_____., *Statistik des neutestamentlichen Wortschatzes.* Zürich: Gotthelf Verlag, 1958.

_____., *Statistische Synopse.* Zürich: Gotthelf, 1971.

Moule, C. F. D., *The Birth of the New Testament.* London: Black, 1962.

Moulton, J. H., Howard, W. F., Turner, N., *A Grammar of New Testament Greek.* 3 vols. Edinburgh: T. & T. Clark, 1908, 1960, 1963.

Moulton, J. and Milligan, G., *The Vocabulary of the Greek Testament.* Grand Rapids: Eerdmans, 1972.

Müller, K., *Geographi Graeci Minores, I.* Paris: Instituti Franciae, 1855.

Munck, J., *The Acts of the Apostles.* Garden City, N.Y.: Doubleday, 1967.

Myres, J. L., *Herodotus: Father of History.* Oxford: Clarendon, 1953.

Navone, J., *Themes of St. Luke.* Rome: Gregorian University Press, 1970.

Neil, W., *The Acts of the Apostles*. London: Oliphants, 1973.

Neirynck, F., *The Minor Agreements of Matthew and Luke against Mark*. Leuven: University Press, 1974.

—————., ed., *L'Evangile de Luc: Problèmes littéraires et théologiques. Memorial Lucien Cerfaux*. Gembloux: Duculot, 1973.

Neusner, J., ed., *Christianity, Judaism, and Other Greco-Roman Cults*. Leiden: Brill, 1975.

Nineham, D. E., ed., *Studies in the Gospels*. Oxford: Blackwell, 1955.

Norden, E., *Agnostos Theos*. Leipzig: Tuebner, 1913.

O'Brien, P. T., *Introductory Thanksgiving in the Letters of Paul*. Leiden: Brill, 1977.

Oertel, J. R., *Paulus in der Apostelgeschichte*. Halle: Schwabe, 1868.

Oppenheim, A. L., *The Interpretation of Dreams in the Ancient Near East*. Philadelphia: American Philosophical Society, 1956.

Orchard, B., *Matthew, Luke and Mark*. Manchester: Koinonia Press, 1976.

Otis, B., *Virgil: A Study in Civilized Poetry*. Oxford: Clarendon, 1963.

Ott, W., *Gebet und Heil: Die Bedeutung der Gebetsparänese in der lukanische Theologie*. Munchen: Kosel Verlag, 1965.

Owel, E. C. E., *Some Authentic Acts of the Early Martyrs*. Oxford: Clarendon, 1927.

Page, D. L., *Sappho and Alcaeus*. Oxford: Clarendon, 1955.

Parker, P. *The Gospel before Mark*. Chicago: Chicago University Press, 1953.

Parkes, J., *Judaism and Christianity*. Chicago: Chicago University Press, 1948.

Pearson, L., *The Lost Histories of Alexander the Great*. London: American Philological Association, 1960.

Peron, J., *Les Images maritimes de Pindare*. Paris: C. Klincksieck, 1974.

Perry, B.E., *The Ancient Romances*. Berkeley: University of California Press, 1967.

Phillips, J.B., *The Gospels in Modern English*. London: Geoffrey Bles, 1952.

Plümacher, E., *Lukas als hellenistischen Schriftsteller: Studien zur Apostelgeschichte*. Göttingen: Vandenhoeck & Ruprecht, 1972.

Plummer, A., *A Critical and Exegetical Commentary on the Gospels according to St. Luke*. 5th ed.; Edinburgh: T. & T. Clark, 1922.

Pritchard, J.B., ed., *Ancient Near Eastern Texts*. Princeton: Princeton University Press, 1955.

Rackham, R. B., *The Acts of the Apostles*. London: Methuen, 1901.

Ramsay, W.M., *St. Paul the Traveller and the Roman Citizen*. London: Hodder & Stoughton, 1895.

Reardon, B.P., *Courants litteraires grecs des IIe et IIIe siécles après J.C.* Paris: Les Belles Lettres, 1971.

Rehkopf, F., *Die lukanische Sonderquelle*. Tübingen: Mohr, 1959.

Rengstorf, K.H., *Das Evangelium nach Lukas*. 9th ed.; Göttingen: Vandenhoeck & Ruprecht, 1962.

Ridderbos, H., *The Coming of the Kingdom*. Philadelphia: Presbyterian and Reformed Publishing Co., 1962.

Ridderbos, H., *The Coming of the Kingdom*. Philadelphia: Presbyterian and Reformed Publishing Co., 1962.

Robert, A. and Feuillet, A., eds., *Introduction to the New Testament*. New York: Desclee, 1965.

Roberts, W.R., *Greek Rhetoric and Literary Criticism*. New York: Longmans, Green, & Co., 1928.

Robinson, J.A.T., *Redating the New Testament*. Philadelphia: Westminster, 1976.

―――――――――――., *Twelve New Testament Studies*. London: SCM, 1962.

Robinson, J. M., ed., *The Nag Hammadi Library*. New York: Harper & Row, 1978.

Robinson, W. C., Jr., *Der Weg des Herrn: Studien zur Geschichte und Eschatologie im Lukas-Evangelium*. Hamburg: H. Reich, 1964.

S. Safrai and M. Stern, eds., *The Jewish People in the First Century, II*. Philadelphia: Fortress, 1976.

Sanday, W., *Studies in the Synoptic Problem*. Oxford: Clarendon, 1911.

Sanders, E.P., *The Tendencies of the Synoptic Tradition*. Cambridge: Cambridge University Press, 1969.

Sandmel, S., *The Genius of Paul*. New York: Schocken, 1970.

Scharlemann, M.H., *Stephen: A Singular Saint*. Rome: Pontifical Biblical Institute, 1968.

Schmid, J. and Vogtle, A., eds., *Synoptische Studien Alfred Wikenhauser zum siebzigsten Geburtstag. . . dargebraucht*. Munich: Zink, 1953.

Schmidt, K.L., *Der Rahmen der Geschichte Jesu*. Berlin: Trowitzsch & Sohn, 1919.

Schneckenburger, M., *Ueber den Zweck der Apostelgeschichte*. Bern: Fisher, 1841.

Schneider, G., *Verleugnung, Verspottung, und Verhör Jesu nach Lukas 22:54-71*. Munchen: Kosel, 1961.

Schoff, W.H., *The Periplus of the Erythraean Sea*. New York: Longmans, Green, 1912.

―――――――――――., *The Periplus of Hanno*. Philadelphia: Commercial Museum, 1913.

Schramm, T., *Der Markus-Stoff bei Lukas: Eine literarkritische und redaktionsgeschichtliche Untersuchung*. Cambridge: Cambridge University Press, 1971.

Schürmann, H., *Das Lukasevangelium: Erster Teil. Kommentar zum Kap. 1:1-9:50*. Freiburg: Herder, 1969.

Scott, E. F., *The Lord's Prayer*. New York: Scribners, 1951.

Selby, D. J., *Introduction to the New Testament*. New York: Macmillan, 1971.

Sherwin-White, A. N., *Roman Society and Roman Law in the New Testament*. Oxford: Clarendon, 1963.

Smith, M., *Tannaitic Parallels to the Gospels*. Philadelphia: Society of Biblical Literature, 1951.

Smity, J. P., *A Compendious Syriac Dictionary*. Oxford: Clarendon, 1903.

Stagg, F., *The Book of Acts*. Nashville: Broadman, 1955.

Stauffer, E., *New Testament Theology,* trans. J. Marsh. London: SCM, 1963.

Strecker, G., ed., *Jesus Christus in Historie und Theologie: Neutestamentliche Festschrift für Hans Conzelmann zum 60. Geburtstag*. Tübingen: Mohr, 1975.

Talbert, C. H., *Literary Patterns, Theological Themes and the Genre of Luke-Acts*. Missoula: Scholars Press, 1974.

—————., *Luke and the Gnostics*. Nashville: Abingdon, 1966.

Taylor, V., *Behind the Third Gospel*. Oxford: Clarendon, 1926.

—————., *New Testament Essays*. Grand Rapids: Eerdmans, 1972.

—————., *The First Draft of St. Luke's Gospel*. London: SPCK, 1927.

—————., *The Gospels: A Short Introduction*. London: Epworth, 1930.

—————., *The Passion Narrative of St. Luke,* ed. O. E. Evans. Cambridge: Cambridge University Press, 1972.

Teuffel, W. S., *History of Roman Literature,* rev. L. Schwabe, trans. G. C. W. Warr. London: George Bell, 1892.

Thielicke, H., *The Prayer that Spans the World,* trans. J. W. Doberstein. London: J. Clarke, 1965.

Tinsley, E. J., *The Gospel according to Luke*. Cambridge: Cambridge University Press, 1965.

Torrey, C. C., *Documents of the Primitive Church*. New York: Harper, 1941.

—————., *Our Translated Gospels*. New York: Harper, 1936.

—————., *The Composition and Date of Acts*. Cambridge: Harvard University Press, 1916.

—————., *The Four Gospels*. 2d ed.; New York: Harper, 1947.

Trites, A. A., *The New Testament Concept of Witness*. Cambridge: Cambridge University Press, 1977.

Trueblood, E., *The Lord's Prayer*. New York: Harper, 1965.

Turner, E. G., *Greek Papyri, An Introduction*. Princeton: Princeton University Press, 1968.

Unnik, W. C. van, ed., *Studies in John, for J. Sevenster*. Leiden: Brill, 1970.

Varronis, M. Terenti, *Saturarum Menippearum,* ed. A. Riese. Leipzig: Teubner, 1865.

Veltman, F., *The Defense Speeches of Paul in Acts.* Berkeley: GTU Th.D. Dissertation, 1975.

Vergil, *The Aeneid,* trans. F. O. Copley. New York: Bobbs-Merril, 1965.

Walker, W. O., Jr., *The Relationship Among the Gospels.* San Antonio: Trinity University Press, 1978.

Ward, M., ed., *Biblical Studies in Contemporary Thought.* Boston: Greene, 1975.

Weinreich, U., *Languages in Contact.* London: Mouton, 1967.

White, J. L., *The Body of the Greek Letter.* Missoula: Scholars Press, 1972.

Wikenhauser, A., *Die Apostelgeschichte und ihr Geschichtswert.* München: Aschendorff, 1921.

_____., and Schmidt, J., *Einleitung in das Neue Testament.* Freiburg: Herder, 1973.

Wilckens, U., *Die Missionsreden der Apostelgeschichte.* 2d ed.; Neukirchen: Neukirchener Verlag, 1963.

Wilcox, M., *The Semitisms of Acts.* Oxford: Clarendon, 1965.

Wilson, S. G., *The Gentiles and the Gentile Mission in Luke-Acts.* Cambridge: Cambridge University Press, 1973.

Wink, W., *John the Baptist in the Gospel Tradition.* Cambridge: Cambridge University Press, 1968.

Winter, P., *On the Trial of Jesus.* Philadelphia: Fortress, 1973.

Woodhouse, W. J., *The Composition of Homer's Odyssey.* Oxford: Clarendon, 1930.

Zehnle, R., *Peter's Pentecost Discourse.* New York: Abingdon, 1971.

Zeller, E., *The Contents and Origin of the Acts of the Apostles,* trans. J. Dare. 2 vols. Edinburgh: Williams & Norgate, 1875-76.

Zerwick, M., *Leben ans Gottes Wort: Erwägungen zum lukanischen Reisebericht.* Zürich: Schweizerische Katholische Bibelwegung, 1959.

Zuntz, G., *Opuscula Selecta.* Manchester: Rowman, 1972.

_____., *The Text of the Epistles.* London: British Acadeny, 1953.